PYRENEAN
HIGH ROUTE

A SKI MOUNTAINEERING
ODYSSEY

PYRENEAN HIGH ROUTE

A SKI MOUNTAINEERING ODYSSEY

John Harding

With best wishes

John Harding

Tiercel *SB*
PUBLISHING

ISBN 0 9532002 1 3

First published November 2000

*Tiercel*SB PUBLISHING 23 High Street Wheathampstead Herts AL4 8BB

Text and Photographs © John Harding
Maps © Gary Haley

A catalogue record for this book is available.

*In memory of Alain and all my companions
on the Pyrenean High Route*

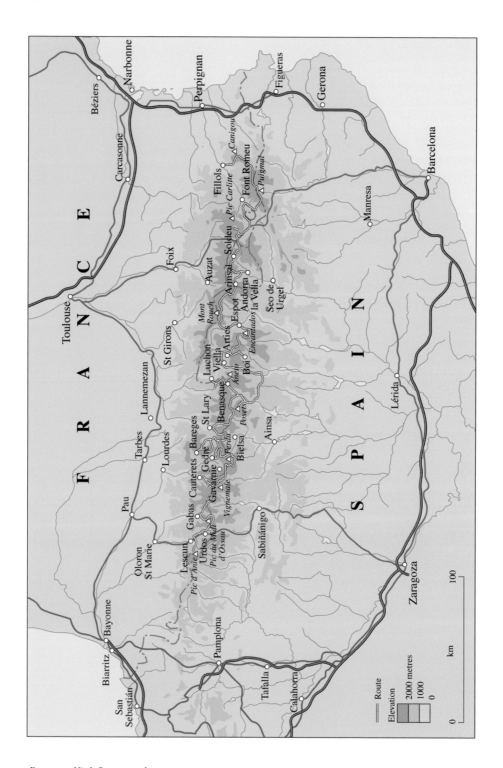

Pyrenean High Route on ski

CONTENTS

FOREWORD

by Sir Chris Bonington

When I skied the High Level Route from Chamonix to Zermatt in 1967 I learned at first hand about the pleasures and pains of ski mountaineering. This is what Sir Arnold Lunn, one of its outstanding pioneer exponents and the Father of downhill racing, once described as "the marriage of two great sports". Exhilarating and demanding, it combines the techniques of skiing with the navigational skills and adventure of mountaineering. Both mountaineering and skiing have become enormously popular British sports in their own right, yet ski mountaineering has a much smaller following. There are complex reasons for this – the season is limited, so much hinges on the weather and the threat of avalanche is always present. Even in Scotland, skiable snow cannot be guaranteed.

There is a paradox here for in the sport's pioneer days the British were up with the best. Today's piste skier tends to forget that ski mountaineering pre-dated downhill skiing and that both the High Level Route and Lunn's first *integrale* crossing of the Bernese Oberland in 1911 were accomplished nineteen years before the first World Downhill Championships. When skiing first caught on in the Alps little more than 100 years ago you had to use skins to get uphill. Few of today's downhill skiers know what a skin looks like whereas for ski mountaineers they remain an essential item of kit.

For today's world of professional mountaineering ski mountaineering is a prerequisite to a guide's qualification. In Britain, the sport's popularity is steadily growing as more and more climbers and skiers explore new horizons. It came of age in the Seventies when British parties first tackled ski traverses of the Alps and Scandinavia. Since then British pioneer parties have broken new ground in more distant ranges where initiative and imagination are key factors.

John Harding's *Pyrenean High Route* is a thrilling and atmospheric adventure memoir of his quest to become the first Briton to complete a ski traverse of the High Pyrenees. This book celebrates the mountains, the power of nature and the author's enthusiasm for the sport. It is also a very human story of courage and determination, exhilaration and despair, tragedy and triumph, engagingly and modestly told. Unlike some mountaineering epics, John recounts frankly and humorously the strains and stresses and often complex relationships that developed between the diverse characters who accompanied him on his journey. Very few books in English have been written about ski mountaineering and this one fills an important gap. With its historical and literary insights it will appeal as much to general travellers as to mountaineers, skiers and walkers. This exciting and inspiring read deserves to become a ski mountaineering classic.

PREFACE

It was the nineteenth century Franco-Irish Pyrenean pioneer Count Henri Russell who wrote that "it is to the Pyrenees that the smiles of the artist and the heart of the poet will always turn". English Romantics such as Wordsworth, Shelley, Byron and Turner might have drawn their inspiration from the Alps but Flaubert, Merimee, Hugo, Zola, Borrow, Tennyson, Kipling, Augustus John and Hilaire Belloc derived theirs from the Pyrenees.

The elusive quality of Europe's second range, successively the natural barrier between Roman Gaul and Hispania, Moorish Spain and Christian Europe, will also appeal to the traveller, walker, skier and mountaineer. Not for nothing do the French call these mountains *la Frontière Sauvage* for they still retain an outlandish fringe and a host of *montagnard* sub-cultures which sedulously preserve arcane mysteries that long pre-date the legends of Charlemagne.

I came to the Pyrenees by chance one summer and, like so many others, fell wittingly under their spell. Within a year of that first visit I returned to see something of the range in winter. Thereafter I was hooked. The seed which germinated became my Pyrenean High Route and that concept became a quest.

This therefore is an account of a series of mountain journeys on skis along the chain of the Pyrenees from west to east. The mountains were its inspiration and provide its backcloth but this is also a celebration of ski mountaineering and, above all, the story of the companionship and courage of those friends who made the journey possible.

Val de Gaube. En route to Baysallance Hut.   (L to R) – Jean-Pierre, Richard, Alain and Susan

A Pyrenean Tragedy

" ohn, have you seen what's behind you?" Richard, still gasping for breath, was bellowing in my ear with his gauntlets cupped. Only moments before he had emerged through the jagged hole I had hacked through the corniced lip of the couloir, his entire body encased in snow, his face red and his mouth contorted after this last scrambling effort.

"Well done Richard," I had shouted out of pure relief when his head had first appeared through the snow hole three metres from where I had anchored myself to pull the rope that attached us taut.

"Well done. Bloody well done."

From that distance he couldn't have heard a word I had said over the wind. It was a biting, vicious wind and it had floored me the moment I had tried to stand up after first breaking through the cornice. It was making normal conversation impossible but none of that mattered. The only thing which seemed to matter was the fact that at last we had reached the Hourquette d'Ossoue. From now on it should be a relatively easy run to the Baysallence Hut. I was more relieved than words could have expressed to have reached the *hourquette* but was beginning to feel very tired. My physical and nervous reserves were almost spent as we had been climbing on skis for most of the past nine hours with scarcely a break. As the day had dragged by, the weather had become worse and worse and for the last two hours we had been climbing blind up an ever steepening snow couloir in zero visibility. It had been impossible to see the lie of the slope so I had had to break the trail by feel alone, making kick turns back into the couloir in knee-deep snow whenever the angle became too steep to continue. As I rammed my skis into the snow up to the bindings well behind the cornice lip to make a safe belay to bring up the others, I had become totally preoccupied with the job in hand. When Richard came up to me and began yelling into my ear, I wondered what on earth he could be on about.

"What is it?" I shouted back at him tersely, glancing round behind me to where he was standing. He had already torn off his rucksack and was kneeling on the ground unfastening a ski. "What are you doing?" His hand was pointing towards a ragged bundle of feathers partly covered in snow and heaving spasmodically.

"It's a young eagle," shouted Richard. "It must have broken a wing. I'm afraid it's a gonna."

Without a moment's hesitation, he grasped the tail end of a ski with both hands and lifting it high above his head, brought it down like an executioner's sword to shatter the bird's neck. It was all over in an instant. Richard's a countryman with an expert knowledge of birds of prey. He knew immediately that this one couldn't be saved and had acted instinctively and compassionately to spare it further suffering but, as I watched the sudden splash of blood discolouring the snow, I felt shocked and uneasy. I was leading a ski tour sponsored by the Eagle Ski Club. As members, we called ourselves Eagles. Now, barely started on this ski mountaineering tour, a young eagle lay dead on the Hourquette d'Ossoue.

*   *   *   *   *

No sight in the Pyrenees is more dramatic than the North East Face of the Vignemale. Its uncompromising height and steepness sets it apart from any other in the range and there are few better places from which to view this sight than the Hourquette d'Ossoue. An *hourquette,* in Pyrenean patois, is a high col and that of the d'Ossoue is one of the highest in the range. For best effect, you should approach it from the south-east up the Ossoue Valley for then, as you breast it, the Vignemale's bleak wall stands full frontal before you – 1,000 metres of leached limestone sheering vertically into the shadows of its dying glacial base.

Five years before, on a brilliant summer's day, I had crossed this same Hourquette d'Ossoue with my friend John Blacker. We had just climbed the Arete de Gaube, the soaring fin of rock which defines the Vignemale's North Ridge and whose juncture with the face gives an airy finale to this classic route. Relieved to be off the glacier and to escape the reflected glare and searing heat of the mid-afternoon sun, we had paused for a breather on the lip of the *hourquette*, stripped down to our shirtsleeves to make the most of the cool breeze that wafted across it. Over the past ten days, the Spanish sun had glazed our faces and forearms nut brown. We were feeling that special sense of physical and mental well-being that only a mountain holiday can give and this last route on the Vignemale had marked the climax of my first Pyrenean season. 500 metres below us, hidden in the dark gulf of the Oulettes du Vignemale overhung by the vertical cliffs of the Vignemale, lay the Oulette Hut. With a good route chalked up, it was delicious to anticipate my wife Georgina and our friend Sarah waiting at the hut for their heroes' return with mugs of hot tea and maybe something to stiffen it. With any luck we might even be down there within the hour. It could never have occurred to me then that the Oulettes de Vignemale would become a place that I would regret for the rest of my life.

*   *   *   *   *

Five years on. Another time, another season. It was winter now and blowing a blizzard. Yesterday's incident of the slain eagle had passed into my subconscious. Barely two days into this ski tour, we were having to retreat from the Baysallence Hut. My body was straining to force my skis forward through the snow against a head-on wind and fighting every foot of the way to reach the Hourquette d'Ossoue – the same col that John Blacker and I had crossed so carelessly on that glorious summer afternoon all those years ago and which had given us so much trouble in crossing only yesterday.

My mind was racing with a series of past images. Once again, we were battling with the weather. Nothing unusual about this in the Pyrenees: it had been unpromising enough when we had arrived in Cauterets three days earlier. However you always live in hope and when it had turned from poor to worse and eventually to the worst and forced us to abandon our planned ascent of the Vignemale and everything so hardly won the day before, I had been bitterly disappointed.

Last night, we had arrived exhausted at the Baysallence Hut in a storm after ten hours on the trot. Squeezed tight between Susan and Alain like sardines along the hut's wooden bunk, trying to eke out some warmth under a mound of mildewed blankets, I had scarcely slept a wink wondering what the weather had in store for us. In the morning, when I had peered through the crack in the door which wouldn't close properly and stared into the maelstrom outside, I had realised that today was about to begin as badly as yesterday had ended.

I blamed myself for making that first day too long. The 1,250 metres climb from the Pont d'Espagne through deep snow with heavy sacs had taken us near our limits. No one had complained but I knew that Richard for one had been having a hard time of it. He's a strong skier and sterling companion – we had served in the Army together and had often climbed as a pair in his native Lake District – but this was his first serious ski tour and yesterday a strenuous introduction. I also felt a particular responsibility towards him as his solicitor for I knew something of his life and the problems and pressures he was facing in preserving his historic house Leighton Hall. I know, too, the dilemmas that confront the desk bound in finding time to get sufficiently fit to undertake a ski tour. I had been worried but now, thank God, Richard seemed none the worse for it. That in itself was one less worry. I couldn't have realised that within an hour, I would owe Richard my life.

As we marched on, I re-lived the decisions of yesterday. Maybe I should have called it a day when we had reached the Oulettes Hut in the afternoon. It was so much lower than the Baysallence and even then the weather wasn't looking good. Instead we had climbed on another 500 metres to the higher hut. Yet, if we hadn't reached the Baysallence, we would have foregone any chance of climbing the Vignemale, the Queen of the Pyrenees and a special prize. On the

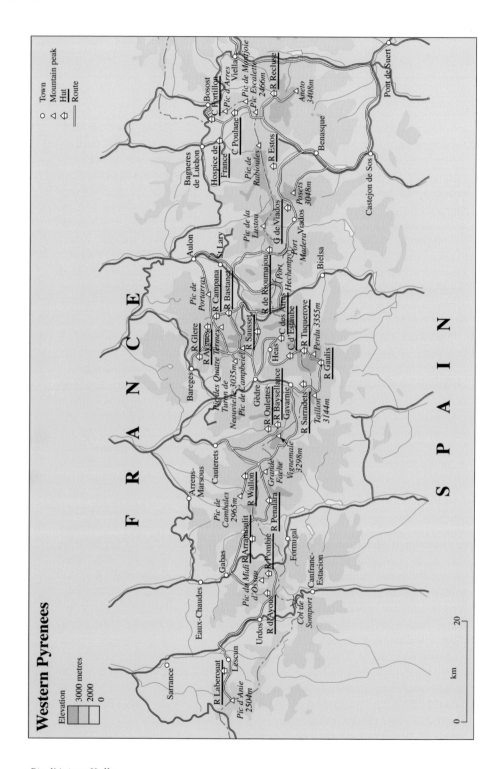

Western Pyrenees

Elevation

- 3000 metres
- 2000
- 0

F R A N C E

S P A I N

○ Town
△ Mountain peak
⬡ Hut
— Route

Bosost
C Portillon
Pic d'Arres
Pic de Montjoie
R Rechuse
C Poulane
Pic Escalette 2466m
Viella
R Estos
Aneto 3408m
Pic de Rabioules
Benasque
Bagneres de Luchon
Hospice de France
Posets 3048m
Castejon de Sos
Aulon
Pic de la Luston
G de Viados
St Lary
Madera Viados
Port Hechempy
Bielsa
Pic de Porturas
R Campana
R Bastane
R de Rioumajou
Port
C des Arres
R Glere
R Aygue
Pic des Quatre Termes
R Sausset
C d'Estaube
R Tuqueroye
Perdu 3355m
Turon de Neouvielle 3035m
Pic de Campbeil
Heas
R Gaulis
Bareges
Gedre
R Oulettes
R Baysellance
Gavarnie
R Sarradets
Taillon 3144m
Cauterets
Grande Fache
Vignemale 3298m
Arrens-Marsous
Pic de Cambales 2965m
R Wallon
R Penafara
Gabas
Eaux-Chaudes
Pic du Midi d'Ossau
R Arramboulit
R Pombie
R Ayous
R d'Ayous
Formigal
Urdos
Col de Somport
Canfranc-Estacion
Sarrance
R Laberouat
Lescun
Pic d'Anie 2504m
Pont de Suert

km

0   20

Pic d'Anie to Viella

tight schedule I had devised back in London, there would be only one possible day to attempt it – today. Anyway, when we had reached the Oulettes Hut, the spacious main hut that I well remembered from two previous visits had been locked and bolted with only the mean and dirty winter room left open. There was no contest between spending the night there or at the much better-appointed Baysallence Hut which I knew to be open. I couldn't have known that a predecessor had failed to close the door properly and that, as a result, the ground floor would be two foot deep in snow.

It had also concerned me that yesterday's hut flog had fazed even my new French friend Jean-Pierre, a 6 foot 4 inch Pau hotelier whom I had first met the previous year in the course of another Pyrenean epic. Jean-Pierre was immensely strong, an excellent skier, with bags of bonhomie. The Pyrenees were also his backyard and he knew their foibles. Yet, when we had staggered into the Baysallence Hut last night, the strain of the day had shown even on Jean-Pierre. He had simply kicked off his skis at the hut door and left them in the snow without bothering to strip off the wet skins. By morning, skin and ski had welded into a block of ice and, as a result, Jean-Pierre was now having to foot slog while the rest of us were on skis. Not that it made that much difference. The wind had stripped the snow off the ground leaving a treacherous icy undersurface across which it was easier to walk than ski. Jean-Pierre plodded along steadily besides the rest of us while we slipped and slithered uncontrollably in the gusts of wind.

We had taken the decision to quit the Baysallence Hut over a muted breakfast. Ever since I had tried unsuccessfully to hack away at a stubborn accumulation of black ice at the threshold to shut the hut's massive iron door and stem the snow flood, I had been wondering whether we were making the right decision to be leaving. Stick or twist? It was a familiar ski mountaineering dilemma. Maybe we should have stayed put. Abandoning the Vignemale ascent was inevitable given the weather but that was only one bit of a complicated itinerary which had necessitated dumping our main food supply back at the Oulettes Hut. A tight itinerary imposes its own logistics and food, or the lack of it, always weighs heavily in the decision making process. We could easily have lasted another couple of days but to have done so would have thrown the entire programme.

Well, we had made our decision to retreat and now we would have to live with it. All five of us – Jean-Pierre Leire, Richard Reynolds, Susan Baldock, Alain Bevan-John and me – marched along together roughly abreast, immersed in our own thoughts but barely a ski length away from each other for fear of losing contact. With a constant stream of spindrift racing across the snow, yesterday's tracks had long been obliterated. My goggles were encrusted in ice and the brim of my anorak hood kept cracking like a bull whip. The spindrift peppered my face like pin pricks and the roar of the wind made conversation impossible.

On a fine summer's day, you would never have given a thought about reaching the Hourquette d'Ossoue from the Baysallence. It is barely 600 metres away from the hut and, even with a heavy load, you scarcely raise sweat to climb the slight incline. But in a winter storm, where snow and sky merge in a white blur and no landmark is visible, the business of hitting off the Hourquette on a compass bearing became a serious exercise where you couldn't afford to chalk up a miss. As we marched on, I was becoming more and more preoccupied with the recurring thought of how much new snow had fallen overnight. This was a critical factor in determining the avalanche risk to which we would be exposed when descending the Oulettes Couloir. Cocooned within the solid pine clad walls of the Baysallence last night, with the wind reduced to a muffled sigh, there had been no way of answering this question. Safety in mountains is not an exact science – merely an assessment of risk. I had weighed one factor against another in making the decision to retreat but that which concerned me most was the one I had least control over – the avalanche threat. It was to this that my mind kept returning.

We seemed to have been on the move for hours but when I forced back my frozen anorak sleeve to glance at my watch, I was surprised to see that we had only left the hut some twenty minutes earlier. Had the watch stopped? Surely, we should have reached the Hourquette by now? The trouble was that, in this visibility, you wouldn't necessarily know whether you were on or above it ... not until you had walked through a cornice and become airborne.

Ah, huh ... It was then that I sensed a subtle change in the feel and consistency of the snow. Suddenly, the ground ahead felt blank. I felt that I was standing on the crest of a rolling wave about to break. Sniffing the air like some animal sensing danger, I realised that I must be standing on the very edge of a cornice. These overhanging shelves of snow form on the leeward side of cols and ridges and can be notoriously unstable.

STOP! I said to myself. *Reverse the way you've just come ... very, very slowly.*

Some sixth sense had warned me. If I hadn't been wearing skis I would certainly have fallen through for a long drop into deep space. This near miss was a bonus, for a cornice here could only mark the lip of the Hourquette d'Ossoue where we had come up yesterday. I turned round to the others and yelled into the wind – "We've arrived ... We're at the Hourquette!"

No one could have heard me but when I waved my ski sticks above my head they got the message. We closed ranks and took stock. In theory, it should have been easy to decide what to do next but when you can't see what's below and can't hear what anyone else is saying, thought processes are slowed. Two very different pictures of this same place suddenly swam from memory. One was that glorious summer view I had had of the Vignemale's stupendous face years before with John Blacker; the other was yesterday's still vivid incident of the dying eagle.

We might have reached the Hourquette but the real test was yet to come – the 600 metres descent of the Oulettes Couloir back to the Oulettes Hut. Yesterday, we had had our work cut out to climb the couloir. Today, we would have to ski it blind. It was critical to find the right place to start from.

Not a trace remained of the waist deep trench I had excavated through the cornice yesterday, and was it my imagination or had those cornices really grown so much bigger? Sprouting outwards into space they looked like grotesque fungi. I walked slowly around the Hourquette's snowy arc, peering through the murk trying to see a way down and always prodding at the snow with my ski pole while keeping a respectful distance from the corniced lip. If that lot came away, it would take me and several thousand tons of snow with it. I couldn't see further than a few metres in any direction but we couldn't afford to hang around debating the issue.

I rejoined the others who were clustered together in a frozen huddle. Craning our heads inches from each other's I bellowed out: "Can't see a thing but I think it should go here. I'll make a start. Keep an eye on me."

"You watch how you go," cautioned Susan. "Those cornices look enormous."

Sometimes, you don't want to think too much about consequences or allow imagination free rein. As I steeled myself to take off, it felt as if I was about to ski off a cliff without being able to see the bottom. At least, I comforted myself, it should be a soft landing – provided I didn't start a snow slide. *Snow slide* sounded innocuous. I didn't dare use the word *avalanche*.

Here goes then ... I flexed my knees, leaned into my boots and, trying hard to relax, started to ski down what seemed the least baleful section of the lip.

Whoosh ... scarcely started, the whole thing collapsed from under me with a dull *CRUMP.* As I fell free through the air I thought to myself – now for the long ride ... but it was all over in a moment. I had come to a dead stop still upright on my skis with the snow up to my knees. Down here out of the wind, it was so much quieter. Peaceful even.

Looking up to where I had just come from, I could just about pick out the blurred silhouettes of the others peering anxiously over the rim.

"John – are you okay?" Susan's voice wafted down through the swirling snow.

"Yes thanks," I shouted back, "I'm fine. Follow my track one by one but watch it all the way."

I didn't have to say any of this. They all knew the form but there wasn't a proper track to follow, just a hole through the cornice and a very steep slope below. I thought I had cleared a secure path but as Susan, Richard, Alain and Jean-Pierre followed down in quick succession, each of them started a fresh snow slide.

That wasn't so good. Clearly, since yesterday, either a lot more snow had fallen or old snow had been blown over the col and been dumped on this leeward side. In either case that could spell danger and once again I asked myself: were we doing the right thing? Was it still too late to retreat to the Baysallence? Even then, I rehearsed in my mind the old arguments that we had thrashed out in the hut, weighing up the pros and cons.

Better get on with it and stop messing about. At least we were now safely across the Hourquette and poised to start the homeward run. From here on, route finding should be straightforward and it was downhill all the way. Although I couldn't actually see anything, in a snapshot of memory I could envisage the scene. We were perched on the edge of a colossal amphitheatre, backed on its western side by the line of 1,000 metre cliffs that culminated in the Vignemale's north-east face. 500 metres below us, on a patch of level ground at the bottom of the couloir, lay the Oulettes Hut, safety and food.

Yesterday, we had had to take our skis off to tackle the steep top section of the couloir. You can usually ski down whatever snow you've climbed up but it suddenly came back to me that just about here John Blacker had slipped on the ice and only managed to check his fall by rolling onto his side and forcing the pick of his ice axe into the snow. The friction of the fall had taken all the skin off his right forearm. This was a place to watch.

Suddenly I felt that sixth sense again. The wind had dropped but you couldn't see anything but snow. Susan felt uneasy too.

"John, it's just too dangerous to ski this slope," she urged. "We should walk down in single file."

"Good idea," I replied, "Let's do just that."

I turned to the others leaving Alain to do a quick translation for Jean-Pierre.

"We'll take our skis off here and walk this steep bit as Susan suggests. Loosen your rucksack straps and bindings. Space out well but don't lose contact."

These were standard avalanche measures and soon the five of us were stretched out vertically along the back of the couloir like flies on a wall. Stamping our heels into the slope to get purchase and daggering in a ski pole with one arm and an ice axe with the other, we made slow going through the

Vignemale and Petit Vignemale – North Face

heavy, knee deep snow but, gradually, I began to feel the pressure lifting and stopped to take another quick look at the map.

The blue line which marked the ski route and the general lie of the slope indicated that we would soon have to swing over to the left towards the Petit Vignemale before swinging out again into the main couloir. Just below the summit of this peak, the map showed there was a small hanging glacier. I didn't like the look of it but there was no alternative but to traverse under it.

Quite perceptibly, the ground was beginning to flatten and then, as if to encourage us, the clouds parted momentarily for the first time that day. Through shifting veils of mist, enormous slabs of grey rock thrust upwards into the denser clouds above. We were now directly beneath the face of the Petit Vignemale. Its proximity was unnerving and I sensed its menace.

"John, John": Jean-Pierre was at my shoulder. *"C'est possible que nous pouvons skier ici – les skis sont meilleurs."*

Yes indeed, this was easier ground so it seemed only sensible to start skiing again. We would certainly get down that much quicker and in the mountains speed is safety.

Jean-Pierre was our strongest skier and I motioned to him to take the lead.

"D'accord Jean-Pierre ..." I said to him. *"En avant – vous êtes le moniteur."*

Then turning to the others I said: "Jean-Pierre will take us down this last stretch: we can't be that far away from the hut now."

Sacs off, take off skis, peel off skins, pack them away, put on skis, re-adjust bindings, put sacs on ... However fast you do it, the routine motions of ski mountaineering always take time. Time that is infinitely precious. The doctrine of the wasted minute was born with mountaineering when minutes, seconds even, can spell the difference between safety and disaster. What I couldn't have known then was that the course of our lives would have been so different had we only left the Baysallence Hut that much earlier or that much later.

The snow was heavy and difficult but Jean-Pierre set off stylishly in a series of sweeping turns. He came to an elegant halt a little way below me just visible through the cloud.

"I'll go next," I said. "Susan, you bring up the rear."

Then, as I set off after Jean-Pierre with the others following just behind, I had an awful premonition. Surely, we're straying too far over to the left ... we're getting too close to those cliffs ... we should be heading further over to the right of the couloir ... We *must* change course.

I cut short my turns and took the fall line straight to Jean-Pierre stopping dead besides him in a flurry of snow with the others closing up behind. I tried to speak to him quickly and urgently but at this critical moment, my French came haltingly.

"Jean-Pierre – cette route est mal ..."

I never finished what I had to say. In an endless second there came from above a tremendous roar like an explosion. I couldn't see anything but that terrible noise told me everything.

I tensed like a cat and shouted at the top of my voice:

"A V A L A N C H E – SKI FOR YOUR LIVES!"

All the elemental instincts of fear, self-preservation and flight burst to the surface in a flash flood of adrenalin. We could see nothing but each had heard the bell's toll. Blindly, like a flight of terrified birds, we took off down the mountain in a race for survival. Yet scarcely started, I felt an ice cold rush of wind pass over me like the kiss of death.

I never saw the all-enveloping wall of snow which hit me from behind. Like a dam burst it smashed into me, picked me up, buried me beneath it and carried me with it like so much flotsam under its tide.

I had been caught in avalanches before but nothing had felt like this one. The first impact completely winded and turned me upside down. The strength of the thing was maniacal and there was nothing I could do to resist it. My world became a tumbling, black void controlled by elemental forces. Three times, maybe four, vice-like pressures built up in ever tightening crescendos to crush my body. I shouted impulsively and fought for breath and for very life.

The shadow of death is never far away in the mountains. When previously I had been involved in falls and accidents, brilliant images of my past life had flashed by in split seconds of memory. Now, in a fragment of time between life and oblivion, all I could think of was survival. Somehow I *must* stay alive.

Bizarrely, I now remembered the advice of a famous Swiss guide, Martin Epp, who had likened an avalanche's flow to that of a river.

"You must get yourself out of the main stream," he had advised. "Roll vigorously sideways so as to get into the shallows."

That might have worked for Martin but I might as well have tried rolling out of the Niagara Falls in a barrel. The brute force of this avalanche was irresistible. Besides, I hadn't got shot of my rucksack and my ski bindings stubbornly refused to break.

I well knew that somehow I must keep near the surface of the flood and swim as I had never swum before. Too long under and I would be crushed and suffocated. Snow is much less forgiving than water. With my skis flailing about like giant flippers, I kept up a frantic breast-stroke motion alternately thrashing and kicking with my legs. Most avalanche deaths are caused by inhaling snow and the asphyxiation that follows, yet my first instinct was to shout: a mixture of primal scream and the noise that weight-lifters make before they lift and jerk; a compound of fear, *banzai* and defiance.

I wasn't so much frightened as angry and shocked at what was happening to me. Appalled by the thought that my life was about to be snuffed out, I vowed to fight it all the way.

The snow tide flowed, flooded and ebbed in successive waves, but, all of a sudden, after one last almost unbearable paroxysm of pressure, it stopped dead. Not a movement. Not so much as a tremor. Just silence.

Silence … not the still silence of calm but rather a cold, eerie quiet as if every living thing had been cowed and hushed. After the shrieking wind on the col; after the noise and tumult of the avalanche; after the helpless tumbling and tossing in its black void; after that frantic fight for life, this silence was uncanny and unnerving.

Yet – and this I could scarcely believe – I was alive.

Alive! Somehow, I had managed to come through this one. Emerged from the end of the darkest tunnel I had been through in my life and survived. I was overwhelmed by feelings of joy, relief and thanksgiving.

Stuck fast in the snow, I rested and took stock of the situation. The fight for life seemed to have lasted a small lifetime but, in fact, the whole episode could not have spanned more than minutes. Seconds even. What to do now?

I was buried up to and just beyond my neck. The mean depth of most avalanche victims' burial is a metre but by surfing the tide, I had managed to fetch up only with my head just below the surface and my body more or less vertical.

In those last traumatic seconds before the pressures stopped, I didn't know whether I was upside or down but instinctively I had reached out with one arm which, providentially, had emerged skywards. That same arm was still upheld, still grasping a ski pole which stuck out through the snow like some incongruous marker.

After clearing the loose snow around my head and neck, I could breathe and move my head quite freely. When I had first been engulfed I had yelled like a lunatic but at the end had instinctively clamped my free hand over my mouth. That last movement had stopped me inhaling the snow and had probably saved my life.

Was anything broken? I couldn't feel any pain but when I tried to move my legs and lower arm, nothing budged so much as an inch. After so much relief, a tiny worry. Following an avalanche, wet snow sets rock hard. Incredibly, my ski bindings hadn't broken as they should have done and as a result, my skis were still firmly attached to my boots. I could wiggle my toes but I couldn't move my feet. I might as well have been dumped in the Hudson River with my feet set in a barrel of concrete.

After an initial, instinctive burst of frantic movement to free myself, measured consideration took over. On the way down, I had refused to countenance death. I had been determined to live for myself and my family. I gave another silent, simple prayer of thanks but then shifted my thoughts to the others. Where were Susan, Richard, Jean-Pierre and Alain? Had they survived and were they perhaps, like me, buried up to their necks but still kicking. Or were they dead and buried under a thousand tons of avalanche debris?

I switched to another gear. I must get out of this hole and find them – fast. With my one free arm I slashed away at the snow with the ski pole, gradually clearing away a bigger space around my head and shoulders. The limits of my visible world still remained the small circle of snow rubble just above eye level and beyond that all I could see was a veil of mist and low cloud shrouding the flanks of the valley.

After much wriggling and kicking, one leg began to feel less rigid than the other. Kick and jab ... kick and jab. I kept battering the snow repeatedly with my left boot and excavating with the ski pole. Eventually, something shifted below. I had managed to unset one of the bindings and kicked my boot free. Small beginnings and a great morale booster yet, struggle as I would, the other foot stuck solid to its ski.

My back too remained pinioned: cemented into the snow by the rucksack which clung to me like the Old Man of the Sea. I fought the snow in explosive bursts like a wild thing but then realised that I was only exhausting myself. It was immensely frustrating and I began to feel as helpless as an upturned turtle.

"This is bloody ridiculous!" I shouted aloud to vent my frustration.

After those first glorious moments of pure elation now this. I was having to face up to the darker realities. Stop reacting: start thinking, I told myself. I looked at my watch for the first time and made some rough calculations. We had left the Baysallence Hut at 11 am. and must have reached the Hourquette some 25 minutes later. It was now 12.30. At first, I couldn't believe it. It had seemed that I had only been stuck here for a matter of minutes but, if my watch was right, I had been here for over an hour.

What had happened to the others? This thought now became a refrain. Perhaps they were already searching but couldn't find me as nothing was visible above the surface. I had better start shouting for help. Better still, use my whistle – the whistle that was attached to my rucksack. I tried to reach it but my back was still pinioned and, try as I would, I couldn't get near it. Never mind, I'll shout anyway.

"Jean–Pierre…Alain…Richard…Susan…"

I shouted out their names repeatedly but even in that silence, the sound was muffled. Soon I grew hoarse and gave up.

Then it suddenly occurred to me that they were all equipped with avalanche search devices. How stupid of me to forget. Each one of us carried a Swiss Barryvox Autophon, specifically hired for the purpose from the Alpine Ski Club, including one I had brought out for Jean-Pierre. On that first day at Cauterets we had thoroughly practised our search and seek techniques. The principle of such electronic rescue transceivers is simple. Set on *Transmit*, they send out *bleeping* signals for the rescuers to pick up on their own sets by switching to *Receive*. With a range of 60 metres, it's then a matter of the searchers locating the victim's position by quartering and honing in guided by the strength of the *bleep*.

Then the more obvious explanation struck me. If anyone else had survived they should have picked up my position by now. For the first time, I felt very cold and stopped struggling. I strained my ears. Not a sound anywhere. Just silence. Now I did feel really worried with the dawning possibility that they were all dead.

I had been so close to death myself and so lucky to survive. The line had been a very fine one. It didn't bear thinking about. These were not only mountaineering comrades but old friends and Alain was my cousin. Susan had for years been a mainstay of the Eagle Ski Club as its seamlessly efficient Touring Secretary. A skilled and experienced ski mountaineer with a blameless temperament, she had only recently married another mountaineering friend, David Baldock. Jean-Pierre and I had met in the closing stages of last year's Pyrenean ski tour when we had survived an avalanche bombardment while retreating down the Val de Gaube. That friendship had been cemented on a family camping holiday the previous summer when my wife and our three daughters had got to know his wife Martine and teenage daughter Veronique.

Richard I had known since National Service days. We had worked so hard together for some years to save his historic estate. Richard dead? The consequences for his family and their heritage appalled me. Alain, the youngest member of our party and my cousin, was an architect and only recently we had been working together professionally. Blood is thicker than water. When he was a boy, we had shared summer holidays together – surfing, climbing cliffs and exploring the caves of my native Gower Peninsula. Through his French mother Paulette, Alain was bi-lingual and it was from her that he had learned his love for the mountains. She too had been a mountaineer and a skier in her youth and had drilled into each of her four children that you can only properly enjoy a ski descent when you have climbed up on skins carrying your own rucksack. Alain had been the link between Jean-Pierre and the rest of us. Surely, I thought, Alain, so young, so strong, so vital, must have survived if I had. He must be stuck in the snow like me. It was just a matter of time before we would all be out of this mess and then have a jolly good laugh about it.

Elation had passed and another chapter in survival begun. Somehow I must get out unaided and help the others. I had been extraordinarily lucky to have survived unscathed and, insulated by the snow, I wasn't really that cold. It might take hours to get myself free but I was determined that eventually I had do it.

Keep digging and don't panic, I told myself. Pray that it doesn't start snowing any harder. The weather hadn't improved much but this was going to be a long game of patience.

Then I heard it. Faint at first but unmistakably the *bleep, bleep* of an Autophon. Before the invention of these electronic aids, your best hope of being found after an avalanche was from clues left by red avalanche cords let out behind you to indicate your burial location. The chances of trailing your chords at the right time or your rescuers ever seeing them were less than evens.

Those *bleeps* were definitely coming in my direction and getting louder every second. I started shouting excitedly, "Over here, over here."

Then like the Angel Gabriel, Richard's flushed face was peering down at me from the lip of my snow hole. He wouldn't have thanked me for it but I could have embraced him. For a second time that day, my heart was suffused with joy. Seldom had I been happier to see anyone and I blurted out: "Richard – thank God you're alive! How did you survive? How did you find me here?"

I wanted to ask him a string of questions but Richard's not one for small talk and this was the last time for chat.

"I got buried too but somehow missed the worst of it and managed to dig myself out. It's chaotic out there. The avalanche was monstrous. It's been the very devil to find you. Are you all right?"

"Yes, I'm fine," I replied, "but stuck fast. What about the others?"

"I've found Susan. She's okay and quite close by but stuck solid like you. There's no sign of Jean-Pierre or Alain."

I felt myself stiffening. Time is scarcest in the mountains when you most need it. If you're buried by an avalanche, your chances of survival are 80 percent if you're still alive when it comes to rest; 40 percent after an hour and ten percent after three. We were already beyond limits.

"Dig Susan out," I said quickly, "then come back for me ... We'll all search together for the other two."

"Susan's just said the same thing," he replied, "but I'll get her out first and then come back for you."

He vanished and I began another frantic round of scraping and scrabbling at the snow with the ski pole. Every minute lost now could be critical for the lives of the missing two but even with this renewed explosion of energy I didn't make much progress. Richard was back soon enough, furiously digging the snow away with his snow shovel. I thought he would have me out in minutes but it took at least ten and made me wonder whether I would ever have got myself out.

I climbed out of my coffin shaking out the snow which had permeated every article of clothing. Then I stared around me and took stock. The cloud had lifted slightly and I could see at a glance why it had taken Richard so long to find me. The place was like a battlefield. A scene of total devastation.

The avalanche had carried me at least 200 metres down the couloir and had filled it from one side to the other with debris, transforming yesterday's pristine white into an ugly mess of discoloured heaps of congealed snow interspersed with chunks of ice. Like some monstrous snow plough, it had carved a succession of deep channels in whose wake spoil was now heaped in parallel ridges that snaked down to the bottom of the Oulettes de Gaube.

The sheer scale of the thing was awesome. 150 metres across certainly – but how long? I could see where it ended from the rubble heaped up like a glacial snout at a point where the slope flattened out some 200 metres below but where had it started? Somewhere far above us, out of sight and lost in the mist.

Richard had already raced away down the slope to finish the job of digging out Susan who, like me, had been buried up to her neck. Susan had just emerged from the snow and the two of them were now standing together some way across the couloir but not far below. Looking around at this terrible scene of chaos, I wondered how any of us could have survived. I waved and shouted at them and Susan waved back.

But what of Alain and Jean-Pierre? I glanced at my watch. Time had again slipped by imperceptibly. It was now at least two hours since the avalanche had hit us. Every moment was precious. I ran across the slope to join the others.

"Richard – you search this intermediate slope. Susan – you do the lower. Spread out and follow the main flow. I'll search the upper slopes. For God's sake move fast."

We had assiduously practised our avalanche search and rescue techniques at Cauterets but that had been on level ground in good visibility with the simple task of locating just one buried Autophon. The real thing was entirely different. Our Autophons had a maximum range of 60 metres in optimum conditions but how do you begin to search an avalanche field at least a quarter of a mile long and over 150 metres wide?

They had already fanned and started to begin their search even before I had switched my own Autophon from *Transmit* to *Receive*.

I pounded uphill with my heart thumping, half stumbling, half running in a loping series of zigzags to quarter the main avalanche flow. Now that every second mattered, time seemed to have stopped. I wasn't getting a glimmer of a signal and when I looked back down the hill, I had almost lost sight of the others. This couldn't be the right place. I then heard Richard shouting at me through the mist.

"John, John ... Come down quickly ... Susan's found Jean-Pierre."

I charged downhill again through the debris-strewn slope, falling and plunging through the snow to where Richard and Susan were digging away frantically into a huge bank of frozen snow.

Then I saw Jean-Pierre. His body was completely buried two metres down but his head and one arm were just protruding through the compacted snow. He wasn't moving and his eyes were glazed. He hadn't spoken a word since they had found him. Buried under tons of snow, I thought he must be dead but he was still breathing. Then his eyelids flickered. I used my skis as a crude lever to relieve the pressure that was slowly crushing the life out of him. To get him out, Richard cut his pack free and severed his safety straps. We were only just in time. He was a strong man but he couldn't have lasted much longer and when we dragged him out, he was shaking uncontrollably.

I took him round the arm and led him away:

"Doucement, Jean-Pierre, doucement ... Restez ici."

He didn't respond. He just sat passively on the snow with his head in his hands and his massive shoulders heaving.

Richard and Susan had left us to continue the search for Alain, methodically working their way down the mountainside, walking parallel some fifty metres apart. I ran down to join them with a bemused Jean-Pierre not far behind. He was badly shocked but had dug into his deepest reserves to help.

"I'm getting signals," shouted Richard.

"Me too," said Susan.

As our paths converged, I also started to pick up strengthening *bleeps* on my own Autophon. In an avalanche search with transceivers, this is the most critical stage and the most confusing. Speed is everything but having once picked up signals, only one searcher should be left to establish the victim's location. He or she must then systematically quarter the ground, gradually switching down the sound volume to pin point the exact spot.

"Richard, Susan – switch off your sets. We only need one Autophon now."

When it's not for real it's like playing some game. Even then, some people never get the hang of it. Alain's life might now depend as much on my instinct as technique. The *bleeps* were reaching a crescendo. The dirty snow rubble at my feet looked much the same as any other on that fatal slope but somewhere beneath it was Alain.

I shouted, "He *must* be here just below us – for Christ's sake dig ..."

But I had gone cold inside and asked myself – How can anyone still be alive under this? All four of us were now digging with controlled frenzy, using everything to hand – shovel, skis, bare hands.

It was Jean-Pierre who first made contact with a ski probe. Then I saw a blue rucksack. I knew it well. It was the one I had lent Alain for this trip.

He was buried face down, lying horizontally about one metre below the surface. We scraped and scooped away the snow from his face firmly but gently. When it was uncovered, he looked serene. So peaceful: so youthful as if he were asleep. Each of us in turn administered the kiss of life but from the moment I saw his face, I knew we had lost him. His body was already quite cold. He must have died instantly from traumatic asphyxiation.

Dead! My dear cousin Alain. Dead.

A wave of horror and despair overtook me. I sat down in the snow and wept. It was 3.30 pm. and the snow was thickening. Jean-Pierre's watch had stopped at 11.45 am. Avalanches *do* strike twice. Four out of five of us were still alive and had a duty to remain so.

I had recovered myself by now and said to the others:

"We can't hang around here. It's too dangerous. We must get down to the Oulettes Hut as fast as possible."

We placed a light covering of snow over Alain's face; planted a ski pole to mark where he lay and started to walk downhill towards the hut. No question of skiing now. Susan had lost both her poles as well as her rucksack with everything in it and both her skis had laminated. Jean-Pierre had lost one ski and Richard one ski and a pole. We marched together in silence through flurries of softly falling snow.

The dank winter room of the Oulettes Hut had nothing for our comfort but comfort no longer mattered. We brewed up some soup as if in a trance. It was bitterly cold but we didn't attempt to light a fire. We didn't talk much either for there was nothing to be said. Jean-Pierre, still stunned, had retreated within himself. Richard was cool and business-like. Susan calm and compassionate.

That night, the wind never stopped howling but nothing could have lulled me to sleep. A hundred times over, I re-lived the events of the past twenty-four hours, turning over and over in my mind everything that had happened and every decision I had made. Mountains are inherently dangerous. Risk is an integral part of the game. Post-mortems pose more questions than answers. Yet I couldn't help asking myself a string of them.

Should we have set off up the Val de Gaube in indifferent weather in the first place?

Should we have continued on to the Baysallence?

Should we have left the Baysallence when we did?

Should we have skied that last bit?

Had I failed to communicate my fears fast and clearly enough to Jean-Pierre?

Would any of this have made any difference?

In several respects the answer to the last question had to be, Yes. We had been in the wrong place at the wrong time. Just a little earlier or later, everything might have been different. Some decisions in life seem so obviously flawed in retrospect but in any mountaineering venture there is always an element of risk. Once the decision to leave Cauterets had been taken, the die was cast and events had taken their own course.

Yet, however much one rationalises and attempts to justify one's decisions, the finality of death puts everything into a different perspective. When a young life – any life for that matter – is lost, remorse is never extirpated.

Next morning, the cloud still hung low over the valley but it had stopped snowing. I walked outside the hut and took stock. It was much colder now and the snow had frozen. Another decision to be taken. Should we play safe and stay put a while longer or make a break for it down the Val de Gaube to Cauterets? It wasn't that clear cut. The Val de Gaube is an avalanche trap. Retreating down it the previous year, I had almost lost my life. I felt in two minds and took Richard and Susan aside.

"I don't fancy chancing the Val de Gaube unless the snow's really settled. On the other hand, it would be intolerable to stay here unless we really have to. What do you both think?"

"The snow's certainly much firmer than it was yesterday," said Susan. "I think it has consolidated."

"I'm all for getting out now," said Richard. "I don't like the thought of leaving Alain's body up there on the mountain."

Jean-Pierre was still in a state of shock but I felt that I must put the same question to him.

"Jean-Pierre – qu'est-ce que tu penses?"

He answered me quite calmly.

"Je voudrais partir immédiatement. C'est mieux. La neige est solide maintenant."

After the avalanche. Retreat down the Val de Gaube

We hung around no longer and for the next five hours marched down that doleful valley strung out in file, always watchful of the slopes above. Not that there was much to see. The Val de Gaube looked as grey and sullen as the day we had come up it.

How impossibly long ago all that seemed now. If only I could have put the clock back. Then, thinking of happier times, my mind raced back to that matchless summer's day five years ago when I had first walked up this valley with my wife Georgina, John and Sarah. An Arcadian scene had greeted us when first we had emerged from the forest at the lakeside. Cows were safely grazing on the green sward and fishermen casting for trout on the strand with four metre long rods. The meadows were carpeted with wild flowers and the slopes on either side of the lake garnered with banks of pink azalea which intermingled with clumps of gentians and orchids. A succession of spurs receding up the valley were covered with blue-green pines, interspersed with dazzling white screes of white limestone which rose up to a skyline of crenallated *cretes*.

It was a classic tableau and a favourite with painters of the sublime. Yet the sight which had really gripped me and seized my imagination had been the gaunt, grey rock face framed at the valley's head which I knew from photographs could only be the north-east face of the Vignemale. Nothing of that view was visible now and I reflected bitterly that the same mountain which had once been such an inspiration had just destroyed one life and blighted four others. The Val de Gaube had become as much a place of ghosts for me as it had been for Tennyson. His poem *In the Valley of Cauteretz* commemorates the premature death of Hallam, the boon companion of his youth with whom, as an idealistic revolutionary, he had marched amongst these mountains with Spanish irredentists.

As we dropped down to the Lac de Gaube, a faint patch of blue sky appeared in the north. Momentarily it relieved the monochrome uniformity of snow and rock which was all we had seen of the mountains since we arrived. Then it disappeared. Like Alain's life, a light extinguished.

At the Pont d'Espagne we reached the end of a journey which no longer had meaning. A bad tempered inspector of the local Gendarmerie took our statements with ill grace, brusquely cross-examined Jean-Pierre and drove us to the headquarters of the Mountain Gendarmerie at Pierrefitte. The young commandant was kinder, brisk and to the point. He explained that we had been hit by the full force of a 400 metre avalanche which had come off the seracs of the Petit Vignemale and were extraordinarily lucky to have survived. Alain's body had already been flown out by helicopter to Lourdes. The pilot had been so concerned about the conditions at the Oulettes de Gaube that he had only been prepared to land on the roof of the Oulettes Hut to pick up the rescue party.

At the public hospital at Lourdes, a sympathetic staff and the routine business of filling in forms and sorting the administrative detail temporarily blunted my mind to the enormity of what had happened. Having identified Alain's body in the mortuary, I braced myself to make the telephone call to his parents that I had been so dreading.

We spent that last night in France at a pilgrim hotel in Lourdes. Next morning, Jean-Pierre and his wife Martine insisted on driving the three of us all the way to Bordeaux where the British Consul would issue Susan with a new passport. As we sped along the *autoroute*, the sun shone down from a cloudless sky for the first time in six days. Away to the south, the snow-capped wall of the Pyrenees filled the horizon with an array of peaks, crests and curves. It was a view that Alain had never seen but its brilliance mirrored the qualities by which I shall always remember him.

Outside our house on Putney Heath, my wife and I planted an Australian eucalyptus in Alain's memory. It is a symbol of that young, vigorous country that he too knew well and it grows like no other in our garden. I see it every day and remember his mother Paulette's comforting words: *"He is no longer where we are, he is now wherever we are."*

Pleta de Llosas under the Maladetta. Georgina

2

THE FIRST TOUR

Pic d'Anie to Gabas

Flying back to London from Bordeaux, four days after the avalanche disaster under the Petit Vignemale, I had had all the time in the world to mourn Alain's death and recall every detail of what had happened over the past few days. As I did so, I pondered about the future and whether I would ever want to return to the Pyrenees after this dreadful accident. How had I got so caught up with these mountains? It wasn't as if I had come to them unprepared. This had been my fourth visit and I was fully aware of the dangers of ski mountaineering in the capricious Pyrenean winter. So why had I come back for more?

On that bitter return journey to England I tried to remember everything that might be relevant about the past so as to put the present into perspective. Five years ago I had first come to the Pyrenees with Georgina and our friends John and Sarah. If there had been one defining moment which cast the Pyrenean spell, it had been the day we had camped in the meadow of the Pleta de Llosas. Forestalling the shepherds to that highest pasture of the Vallibiera, we had set our makeshift campsite in a tuck of a glaciated valley under the southern flanks of the Cresta de Tempestados, the saw toothed ridge that forms the backbone to Aneto, the apex of the Pyrenees.

The meadow ran to the edge of the tree line abutting a wilderness of boulders and scree where solitary, misshapen dwarf pines fought to survive and left their dead as whitened, barkless skeletons clean polished by the wind. Now, at the onset of summer, the place was coming back to life. Clusters of violet crocuses were pushing their way up through the remnants of last winter's snows. A granite obelisk tall as a man had become our campsite landmark where we swam and washed our clothes in the icy waters of the infant River Llosas river. The place was touched by the wand of enchantment.

That was why I had come back to the Pyrenees in winter barely a year later – to satisfy my own curiosity and gratify the mountains' compulsion. My Pyrenean affair might have begun with that first summer holiday but the knot had been tied on my first ski tour. That story had begun, where so many end, in a bar – the bar of the Hotel de Paris, Pau, where I had first met Michael de Pret Roose and Martin Epp. I could remember that scene as if it were yesterday.

*   *   *   *   *

"Have a glass of this stuff," he smiled "I think you'll like it – it's really rather good."

Michael de Pret Roose poured out a glass of *Madiran*, the muscular wine of the Pyrenees Atlantiques, and propelled it across the polished oak dining-room table in my direction. He was a tall man, slightly stooped, with an enigmatic smile and the bleached blue eyes of a sailor. I had met him for the first time that morning when I had wandered into the bar of the Hotel de Paris still recovering from nine hours in a stuffy SNCF couchette and soaking wet from the thunderstorm that had drenched me as I had walked there from the railway station.

Michael was the leader of what the Eagle Ski Club Yearbook's Golden Jubilee edition had advertised as a ski tour for "a small, strong party of experienced ski mountaineers". Founded in 1925 at the once fashionable but now forgotten Swiss ski resort of Maloja, the Club's object was to encourage ski mountaineering. I had joined the Club over a decade before but in the intervening years had almost become a lapsed member. British ski mountaineering tours to the Pyrenees were then a rarity. The Eagles' only previous visit to the range had been in 1966 so when I heard that a tour was being led by de Pret Roose and the renowned Swiss guide Martin Epp, I jumped at the chance of joining it. The object was to traverse a 65 kilometre stretch of the French Pyrenees from Arette Pierre St Martin to Cauterets on ski. It sounded an exciting and unusual project and a refreshing change from the usual Alpine ski tour.

Another man was sitting beside de Pret Roose. Lithe and restless, I guessed it must be Epp.

"And this is Martin Epp," Michael drawled. "You probably know him."

Actually, I had never met either de Pret Roose or Epp but I had heard a lot about them. Michael de Pret Roose, already a legend in British ski mountaineering circles, had become the driving force behind the Club's ski touring programme. Epp had a big mountaineering reputation for difficult Alpine routes and had also made a speciality of guiding British ski mountaineering parties.

For all this, I was a touch apprehensive. One of my climbing friends who had toured with Epp had described him as "cocky, competitive and aggressive". Certainly, he was the antithesis of the patrician de Pret Roose – a small, bearded man with a leprechaun-like grin and quicksilver movements. He positively radiated energy.

I made the first move: "How d'you do, Herr Epp – I'm John Harding."

Quick off the mark, he jumped to his feet to greet me with a friendly grin.

"Call me Martin," he said and grasped my hand.

"Ouch!"

That hurt! His grip was vice-like. Was he trying to prove something?

"So – vee climb zee high Pyrenees together!" he said with a grin – *"Bergheil!"*

This friendly welcome lifted a small cloud. As I had squelched through the rain in search of the elusive Hotel de Paris, staggering under the weight of an overladen rucksack and feeling thoroughly self-conscious with my over-long, old fashioned skis slung over my shoulder, I had wondered whether this whole enterprise might not have been a colossal mistake. The close friend I had hoped would accompany me had cried off at the last moment. With the rain thudding down, I could scarcely recognise the dank streets of Pau in March as those of the same joyous city that we had chosen as our final port of call at the end of that first Pyrenean summer holiday only nine months before.

As I trudged past the dripping, leafless plane trees lining the square in the lea of Gaston Febus's great castle, it suddenly came back to me that at this very spot last summer, the four of us had eaten that gourmet picnic to celebrate our discovery of the Pyrenees. We had drunk and eaten too much but, after a siesta, had managed to totter all of fifty metres to the end of the square to bear witness to the view from the Boulevard des Pyrenees that Napoleon himself had commissioned to give the citizens of Pau the *Palois,* a belvedere worthy of this grandest of Pyrenean panoramas.

There, beyond the rolling green foothills of Jurançon whose wine had been smeared on the infant lips of Pau's most famous son Henri IV, the Pyrenees rose before us in a glittering arc of snow-white peaks stuck to a sheet of navy blue like cardboard cut-outs.

This time I had seen nothing but clouds but in that cheery bar, lighter by a bottle of *Madiran*, my dark mood had lifted. Relaxing by the minute, I took a closer look at the two men who would be guiding our party of seven over the fortnight. They were an unusual combination, ostensibly a throw back to the Golden Age of Mountaineering. De Pret Roose, the Old Etonian cavalryman and Ocean Racer with a Belgian title, had a chalet in Andermatt and a château in Brittany – the quintessential amateur yet a man with a mission. Epp, by comparison, looked the archetypal Swiss guide but with a twinkle in his eye.

Emboldened, I opened up the conversation.

"You must know the Pyrenees very well Michael," I began, "What's the ski touring like?"

"Actually, this is our first visit," he replied offhandedly. "However, we made a thorough recce of the route last autumn and we've just been checking it out again over the past few days."

This candid confidence took me slightly aback.

"What's the weather been like?" I enquired mildly.

"Pretty awful I'm afraid," replied Michael. "It's been raining like this for days on end."

"Ah yes," I said, the steam still rising from the sopping woollen *vorlages* I had bought aeons ago at a Lillywhites' sale.

"What about the longer term forecast?"

"Not so good," said Michael shortly. "Bad in fact. Typically Pyrenean."

"That's strange," I said. "We had marvellous weather when I was climbing here last year. Sunny for days on end. Almost boring actually."

Both men were now looking at me closely.

"That must have been in the summer," Michael said. "Pyrenean winter weather's quite different – and totally unpredictable."

It was Martin who came in quickly now: "So you climb ze mountains?"

"I've done a bit," I said and, taking this as an opening, gave them a resumé of the routes that John Blacker and I had done last summer.

Neither looked in the least impressed. I had played a weak hand too early so I thought I might as well double while I still had their attention and hint at my climbing credentials.

"I'm sure the weather will improve," I said brightly. "Oddly enough, I've always been lucky with the weather – even in the Ruwenzori and the New Zealand Alps …"

Both these ranges were renowned for appalling weather but even as I uttered this irrelevant brag, I knew it was misplaced and tailed off in mid-sentence.

Michael's pale blue eyes were now looking at me levelly but he said nothing. Martin grinned as if he was enjoying himself.

"Ha!" he exclaimed, "John ze mountaineer and weather expert. We will remember that."

Before joining this tour, I had had some explaining to do with Michael in an exchange of letters as to why I could only manage the first week owing to work commitments and he must have wondered whether I was a genuinely serious participant. After my silly puffs, conversation spluttered. Michael remained entirely affable but he had become somewhat distant. I couldn't blame him. Any guide is rightly suspicious of a braggard. It is one thing to bang on with friends but quite another to burden professionals with fatuous climbing anecdotes.

As the rest of the Eagles party rolled up, Michael and Martin greeted each of the new arrivals with an easy familiarity. It's a guide's job to get to know everybody and this gave me the excuse to take my leave. I too was anxious to get to know my companions. Congeniality makes or mars a tour and we would be landed with each other for at least the next week. I had wondered how we would all gell for only once before had I toured with people I had not previously climbed with.

This time round, the only member of the party I knew slightly was Robin Day, a distinguished designer whose work adorned the Royal Festival Hall, Shakespeare Memorial Theatre and airports round the world. I had been surprised to learn that de Pret Roose was pushing 50 but when Robin confided that he was nearer 60 I didn't believe him. When I joined the others at the bar, I discovered that two of them had come on the same train as myself – Mike Williamson, a City stockbroker, and David Dorrell, a West Country doctor. Both were in their mid-20s which was young by the standards of a party consisting mainly of climbers turned skiers approaching the cusp of middle age. They turned out to be classier skiers than the rest of us and probably thought us rather square. Another pair who obviously knew each other well were Hamish Brown, a Scottish schoolmaster poet who later achieved literary fame for his travels through the Scottish Highlands and Atlas Mountains, and his chartered surveyor friend Charles Knowles.

Brown and Knowles tended to be exclusive in their conversation and confidences but I reckoned that Patrick Fagan, a professional soldier who had just returned from the Antarctic after an extended Inter-Services expedition to South Georgia, shared some common strands and would be good for a laugh. At a stage when we were all feeling our way and sizing each other up, my concern was whether I was properly qualified to join this group of *"experienced ski mountaineers"*.

It wasn't that I was new to ski mountaineering but I had become rusty. I had been climbing since National Service days but had come to skiing late in life. Longing to take up the sport since boyhood, my imagination had been caught by my mother's tales of glamorous skiing parties in the 1920s at then fashionable resorts but, when I was at school, my father had considered quite properly that the cost of skiing holidays at St Moritz with an enthusiastic schoolmaster in the austere 1950s was an extravagance. At university I scuppered my first real chance to ski when I broke my wrist during an inter-college Cuppers Rugby match and when my next opportunity came I was close on thirty.

Like much else in life, you'll never be a really good skier unless you start young. However, as an enthusiastic re-tread, I had developed a serviceable survival technique which by my second season enabled me to make the conversion to ski mountaineering. Skiing is a great sport in itself but from the outset I had wanted to escape the bustle, queues and razzmatazz of *pistes* and over-crowded ski resorts so when I spotted an advert for the Eagle Ski Club's High Alpine Meet at Grindelwald run by a charismatic Old Etonian Neil Hogg, I promptly signed on.

British ski mountaineering owes much to Neil Hogg for it was he who revived its near moribund corpse in the early 1960s. It was also his enthusiasm and encouragement that got me hooked but, after that inspirational introduction, I did most of my ski mountaineering guideless with climbing friends and drifted away from the Eagles. Active participation in the sport subsequently declined when my career with the Colonial Service in South Arabia and its wondrously generous leaves came to an abrupt end. Thereafter, the combination of marriage, children, emigration to Australia on the "£10 Pom's Ticket" and a succession of career changes meant that for six years, I had had neither opportunity, time nor money for ski mountaineering.

By the time de Pret Roose's Pyrenean tour came up, the locust years were behind me. I had landed a job in the City and, thus established, was anxious to re-join the fray. However, as the moment of truth arrived, I was plagued by misgivings. I had a dicky hip, was less than fully fit and sported a rag-bag of antiquated equipment. I also had somewhat mixed memories of my last serious ski tour with Richard Brooke. We had been attempting a west to east High Level Route from Chamonix to Zermatt, the sort of thing Richard took lightly ever since a friend of his had gone the full distance on kick turns. In the event, we had had to cry off halfway through as a result of my tearing off a chunk of calf muscle in a fall and Richard losing both his skis in an avalanche.

Michael's first formal briefing about the tour took place that evening. His innate charm and laid back manner were deceptive and after some self-deprecating preliminaries, his military provenance was evident.

"Martin and I extend a very warm welcome to you all," he began. "We've been out here for the past few days on our second recce. The good news is that we've already dumped a couple of food caches along the route to save weight. The bad news is that virtually no snow has fallen in the Pyrenees since last October."

He hadn't mentioned anything about this absence of snow to me in the bar. I had employed special pleading with both my wife and my employers to take this week off. It was hugely disappointing to hear that the whole thing might now be hanging in the balance. Michael sensed that this opener had cast gloom and carried on cheerfully.

"However," he went on with a quick glance in my direction, "as it's been raining like this for days, masses of snow should have been dumped higher up."

"What's the forecast like?" interrupted Hamish Brown.

"Not too good," Michael replied. "However, in the Pyrenees nothing is for certain. The weather's totally capricious and can change from day to day – even from hour to hour. We'll have to take it as it comes."

Mike Williamson Le Skier now piped up: "Any chances of powder snow up above?"

Michael gave him a quizzical look.

"I can't guarantee that but I rather doubt it. The weather here is not like the

Pic d'Anie

Alps. It's Atlantic rather than Continental. The snow's more like the sort you find in Scotland – wet and heavy. You'll probably find Pyrenean touring very different to what you've been used to."

I glanced round to gauge the group's general reaction. Only Hamish Brown, reared on skiing Scottish heather, looked happy. It was he who asked the next question.

"Can you tell us what the huts are like?"

"Most are pretty primitive," Michael replied, "and some of the better ones are shut at this time of year."

This was bad news for me. I had experienced the austerity of Pyrenean huts in summer but had gambled that my twenty-year old Black's Icelandic sleeping bag might just last one more season.

"But don't worry," he added, with a flicker of a smile. "We've arranged for some key huts to be opened up specially for our party."

Patrick Fagan had evidently been busy making his own military appreciation:

"Assuming there's still enough snow, Michael, are we sticking to the original programme?"

The original plan had been to start with an easy introductory leg from Arette Pierre St Martin to Lescun with the unstated object of seeing how everyone was going to shake down. It wasn't unheard of for weaker Eagles to be sent home after the first couple of days. Thereafter, the programme would follow a classic ski mountaineering route along the axis of the main range.

"No, not quite," Michael replied coolly.

"We'll aim to keep to the basic plan of climbing as many peaks as possible as per the itinerary you've all received. But there may be some hiccups. We've just learned that the road to Pierre St Martin is blocked by snow so we'll have to scrap that first stage anyway. Instead, we'll be taking the bus direct to Lescun tomorrow morning, ski up to the Laberouat Hut for that night and climb the Pic d'Anie the next day ... Has anyone any more questions?"

He didn't give the impression that he expected any and I certainly wasn't going to expose myself a second time. By its very nature, this was bound to be a tour of Chiefs and Injuns but the flavour of Michael's briefing revived my misgivings. Only once before had I toured with guides and then during my first ski mountaineering season in 1964. The climax had been the Zermatt/Chamonix High Level Route which was then a rarity for British parties. The Swiss guide had been a humourless and bad tempered chap and I had sworn not to repeat the experience. At first blush, the Michael/Martin duo seemed to be in an altogether different category but it was early days. I asked myself again whether a guided tour was going to be my style.

When the professionals retired, the amateurs repaired to the bar and opened the forecasting game to all. The optimists reckoned that rain in the plain meant powder snow higher up. The pessimists predicted that it would be wet, unconsolidated stuff just ripe for avalanche. Patrick Fagan told me that he expected a strenuous fortnight ahead given that Michael's itinerary listed no less than seven peaks to be climbed. I went to bed early anticipating that this would be my last comfortable night for a while and gazed up at the ornate ceiling with its *fin de siècle* decor. I wasn't worried about the mountaineering side of things but ski touring through heavy deep snow was another matter. With this unsettling thought I dozed off to sleep.

It seemed only minutes later when Epp's noisy wakey wakey roused me next morning well before dawn. Still half asleep, I dunked my tired croissant into a tepid bowl of *café au lait* while Epp bustled around the dining-room exhorting us to get a move on. It was still raining outside as we bundled ourselves, our rucksacks and skis into the waiting bus. I felt a pang to be leaving the fusty 19th century traces of the Hotel de Paris as the lights of Pau winked then finally vanished behind us as we headed due South up the Aspe Valley into the mountains.

At first, there was none of the usual chatter of anticipation that you usually get with a group of friends for each of us seemed to be preoccupied with private thoughts. However, when the driver changed down through his entire gear range to negotiate a ninety degree right hand bend that swung us off the main road to begin a spiralling climb up the Lescun valley, the party suddenly came to life.

We were now travelling in the wake of an enormous snow plough which was shifting from its path huge mounds of fresh snow which had drifted to hedge height. Nine necks craned upwards to catch a glimpse of the amphitheatre of Dolomitic type mountains that an old black and white photograph in the Hotel de Paris's dining-room showed as closing the end of the valley. We couldn't see a thing: the cloud was so low that not even the sides of the valley were visible.

Before they built this motor road up the valley, the village of Lescun was so inaccessible that the dead had had to be carried down the mountainside to the Aspe Valley cemetry strapped on mule. Modern Lescun is a popular tourist and climbing base and the old inn at the edge of the cobbled square looked just the sort of place to offer refreshment and a warm reception.

"Hope we'll be stopping here for coffee," I threw across to Michael as the bus came to a halt.

He glanced up at me with a thin smile and shook his head.

"No John," he replied. "No time for that. We've got to keep moving and get to the hut straight away."

Within minutes the bus had been cleared of both party and kit as if Martin had set off an air raid siren. As last man out, I found everyone else already engrossed in the business of fastening skins to skis, testing ski bindings, tuning their Autophon avalanche transceivers, adjusting rucksacks and generally preparing themselves for the off.

"All ready?" shouted Martin.

I was still in the process of tightening my ski boot laces but this was no time to display unpreparedness so I let them be and fell in behind the pack with a heave of my rucksack. We sidled off in file through the village with Michael and Martin in the van and the rest of us following behind. The show was on the road.

Although there are tens of thousands of British downhill skiers and mountaineers, British ski mountaineers are rare birds. In Europe, America and New Zealand ski mountaineering skills are considered an essential part of the all-round mountaineer's portfolio. In Britain they are still regarded as optional extras. This reveals a curious paradox for, when skiing was introduced to the Alps from Norway, barely a hundred years ago, the British were at the forefront of this new sport. Sir Arthur Conan Doyle made one of the earliest ski mountaineering traverses when he crossed the Mayenfelder Furka from Davos to Arosa on March 23 1894 and Sir Arnold Lunn was one of ski mountaineering's leading exponents during its Golden Age in the first quarter of the 20th century. Lunn went on to invent the Slalom as a downhill event, organised skiing's first world championship, was principally responsible for skiing's inclusion as an Olympic sport in 1936 and, for fifty years, he was the moving spirit of British downhill skiing. For all this, his first love remained ski mountaineering which he envisaged would bring together both climbers and skiers.

Yet, after this promising start, ski mountaineering never really caught on with the British. The reasons for this are complex but stem in part from a bizarre conflict in the 1930s between Lunn and the Alpine Club's old guard who regarded Lunn as a cocky *arriviste* promoting a new fangled sport. The Alpine Club first blackballed Lunn but relented in later years to make the Grand Old Man an Honorary Member of the Club.

A more serious effect of this preposterous controversy was to discourage the coalescence of mountaineering and skiing at the level where it mattered most. British ski mountaineering reached its nadir after the Second World War but since then has gradually staged a recovery and is now gaining popularity with skiers who want to lift their game beyond the piste and climbers seeking new horizons.

A fundamental difference between the two sports is the way you get uphill. Downhill skiers rely on lifts, tows, T bars, bubbles, funiculars, trains and helicopters to get ski borne. Ski mountaineers rely on skins as did the Nordic hunter gatherers, Nansen and Amundsen and all the old-timers before them. Originally, skiing skins were made of the real stuff – reindeer or seal hide – but today synthetics have taken over. Apart from boots, poles and ski, skins are your most vital piece of equipment. Approximately the length and breadth of a ski, you attach them to the ski's tip, end and base. When you move the ski forward, the skin's angled grain slides easily along the snow but when you pull backwards, the grain digs into the snow and prevents the ski from slipping back. Using skins is not like boarding the Number 14 bus but with practice you can climb at almost as steep an angle as you can walk.

A hut march of 550 vertical metres is usually no problem but on the first day of any ski tour you re-discover a host of obscure muscles. Our trek to the Laberouat Hut only took two and a half hours but unfamiliarity made it seem much longer. Touring equipment improves every year and is almost unrecognisable from the crude, heavy gear used by the pioneers. But weight is, was, and always will be the ski mountaineer's bugbear and, as you grind upwards, sweat stinging your eyes and rucksack straps biting into your shoulders, you will curse yourself for not chucking out that spare shirt, extra jersey or slim paperback slipped in at the last moment for sitting out bad weather in a frigid hut.

For Alpine hut-to-hut tours you can get away with standard ski touring equipment – ice-axe, crampons, snow shovel, *harscheisen* (a ski crampon), slings, karabiners, water bottle, gaiters, anorak, under- and over-trousers, spare shirt and jerseys, balaclava, over- and under-mittens and gloves, goggles, sun glasses, sun cream, torches, spare batteries and avalanche transceiver.

However, for this Pyrenean tour Michael had told us to bring along a range of additional kit including sleeping bags, sleeping mats, cooking stoves, pots, pans and candles. I didn't demur for I had already learned that some Pyrenean huts offer few comforts. Yet, as I had painstakingly repacked this extra kit in my hotel room, I wondered what had happened to those guarded huts Michael had promised us.

In the event, I needn't have worried about the Laberouat Hut which turned out to be a cross between bedlam and a two star hotel. Bedlam took the form of ninety French school children raging around out of control whereas the hut/hotel itself offered many civilised comforts including an *à la carte* menu, hot showers and a bar. As we sat round a crackling log fire, doe-eyed Gascon barmaids enticed us with steaming *vin chaud* served in earthenware mugs and dangled before us the day's luncheon menu of soup, trout, chips and cheese.

"So this is Pyrenean touring?" I murmured to Patrick. "I think I'm going to enjoy this."

"Nice hut," he replied, appraising a barmaid's curvature. "D'you think Michael will be calling it a day here?"

If he seriously thought that, he hadn't got the measure of the régime. Barely had we put back our hot drinks than Sergeant Major Epp was back on parade.

"Tomorrow vee climb ze Pic d'Anie," he barked out in his staccato English, "So ... today vee must inspect the route."

"What about lunch, Martin?" Patrick ventured. Epp looked at him pityingly.

"No time for lunch, Patrick. Vee must go now. *Schnell!*"

So that was it. Stale croissants for breakfast and not even a smell of lunch but time spent on reconnaissance and all that, I muttered to myself. Anyway, they had to test the troops. At this stage, we were all on spec.

We dumped our heavy kit, trooped outside and for the second time that day fell into line behind our leaders. They were moving faster now, forcing the pace up the valley through a dense forest of conifer and beech. Esquimaux can recognise at least fifteen different types of snow but that afternoon's selection was of a uniform variety – fresh, wet and heavy with the boughs of the pine trees near to breaking point under the weight of it.

Any self-respecting Alpine mountain path climbs steadily upwards in a series of modulated bends. This one undulated like a yo-yo, up and down, up and down. Soon enough, my equipment was showing its age. Modern touring bindings – the bits which attach the boot to the ski – allow your heel to lift free and high when climbing so as to give your legs maximum stretch and your skis maximum slide. I was still using my original cable bindings which had the advantage of lightness but only allowed my skis to make forward progress in short shuffles. Although frustrating, that in itself was tolerable but, for reasons beyond me, my bindings kept breaking at a touch. No one else's did this and no amount of improvised re-adjustment on the trot made a jot of difference. I knew that I was committing the cardinal ski touring sin of repeatedly holding up the party and felt very embarrassed. Every time my binding broke, the whole column ground to a halt while I made an ineffectual show of fiddling around knowing full well that there was nothing I could do about it. Something altogether more radical was needed to cure this defect – like a new pair of bindings.

The air was muggy and the going sticky but after two hours, we reached a tiny *cabane.*

"We've reached our high point," announced Michael.

Thank God for that, I muttered to myself. I was longing to have a short break if only to fix these confounded bindings but evidently this wasn't going to be the place. Someone had failed to shut the hut door properly and spindrift filled it to roof height.

Not that we were going to stop here anyway.

"We won't hang around here," pronounced Michael. "We'll call it a day now and ski back to the hut. Leave your skins on your ski. It'll save time."

This unexceptionable advice was intended to save us the fag of repeatedly having to take skins off and on again as we retraced our way down and up the long, undulating path that we had just slogged up.

It wasn't that I thought I knew better than Michael but this useful technique was then outside my repertoire. Further, I had been having a lot of trouble with my skins which, being of the old strap-on type, had allowed a wadge of snow to build up between the skins and skis. The weight was now such that I was bound to take them off to get rid of the accumulated snow. But more importantly, I hadn't actually skied for years and for this reason alone, I was desperately anxious to put in a bit of downhill practice on easy ground before we tackled the serious stuff. Memories of a particularly humiliating first day on my very first ski tour in the Bernese Oberland had never left me. We had just emerged from the Jungfraujoch tunnel after a day and night of storm to find that the snow outside was waist deep. I was the last to go but one and as I ineptly negotiated a series of knee wrenching turns, the heels of both my boots snapped off. This technique and equipment lapse put me twenty-four hours behind the rest of the party and years to live down. Anticipating a similar trick, I was spurred to do my own thing but, as I began to unbuckle my skins, Michael walked over to me.

"Not leaving your skins on John?" he asked sharply.

"No thanks, Michael, I don't think so – if you don't mind. I would like to give myself a bit of a work out on the way down. My skiing's a bit rusty."

He stared at me briefly.

"Of course not. Do as you like."

As Epp glided away down the narrow path without perceptible effort, I deftly manoeuvred myself into pole position. I had already calculated that to stay in this game, I must stick to his tail.

"Let's go, everyone!" he shouted back over his shoulder.

With both poles flailing I made a clumsy but effective racing start which tucked me tight in behind him before anyone else rumbled. Yet, barely started, I realised why de Pret Roose had advocated skins. They acted as a brake and, without them, the business of following Epp down a track polished to an icy glaze by nine pairs of skis was like attempting the Cresta Run without brakes. Thirty metres on and I was desperately trying to slow down to avoid running up Epp's taut backside. By now I could see that in no way was I going to be able to avoid him.

"*Achtung* Martin! Watch Out!" I yelled despairingly.

He glanced round momentarily, "Vot you doing John? You trying to race me or something?"

"Sorry Martin, I just can't stop."

I overtook him on the outside and for a few seconds led the field by maintaining a teetering line along the lip of a steep bank. It could only be a matter of time before I lost it completely and when I did over-shoot the edge with a mini ski jump, I flew into the air, dropped several metres to the ground and disappeared into a snow bank. As I landed face down, skis extended behind me, both bindings snapped simultaneously under the impact and an icy douche of snow shot down the back of my neck.

It took several minutes to get myself upright and recover my goggles by which time all dignity and composure had vanished. From someway up above, Michael's voice floated down to me.

"John – are you all right? Nothing broken I hope."

"Yes thanks … No," I grunted, feeling a complete Wally.

The rest of the party, gathered above on the lip of the path, now looked on while I shook myself and brushed off the snow. I wasn't hurt but my pride was punctured and try as I might, I simply couldn't find my skis. Desperately, I started thrashing wildly around at the snow using my sticks like sabres.

From the ringside, Epp took over.

"John, John, pleez, pleez – you must do this right. Vatch me!"

Up to my waist in snow four metres below him, in no way could I see his demonstration of the authorized Swiss method of locating skis in deep snow nor had I any inclination to do so. I muttered some obscenity under my breath and carried on regardless.

By the time I had found the skis, got myself together and clambered back up the slope, wet and cold, everyone had disappeared save for Michael who was waiting impassively above.

"Bad luck old boy," he drawled. "Better stay behind me this time. It'll soon be getting dark."

Some shred of *amour propre* had to be salved but I was too fazed to stop and think and do the sensible thing which was simply to put on my skins.

"I'm right behind you Michael," I muttered. "Please carry on."

"As you like," he replied.

It was not a happy return journey. I had over-estimated my ability to climb without skins and under-estimated how much of that downward path went uphill. Re-discovering in the process how exhausting herring-boning can be, I reached the Laberouat Hut an easy last in a muck sweat to find Martin was waiting for me outside the hut door.

Eagle Ski Club Team.   (L to R) – Martin Epp, Michael de Pret Roose, Hamish Brown, David Dorrell, Patrick Fagan, Charles Knowles, Mike Williamson and Robin Day

"John, John – where haf you been?" he grinned. "Und zat is zee easiest day!"

It hadn't been my day and that evening I felt a touch isolated. I knew I was short of skiing practice but today even the most basic technique seemed to have deserted me. Mountaineering simpliciter demands many skills and qualities but ski mountaineering, which Arnold Lunn once described as "the marriage of two great sports, mountaineering and skiing", puts an emphasis on skiing ability and demands a longer apprenticeship.

It is not simply a matter of climbing up mountains and skiing down the other side when the sky is blue and the sun is shining. In its purest form ski mountaineering is a winter voyage when you explore new country and climb new peaks through weather good and bad. To reach this state of the art, you must possess the full range of skiing and climbing techniques and know something of snowcraft, avalanche evaluation, navigation and weather forecasting. Above all, be blessed with a mountaineer's temperament.

In the sport's premier league, the superstars are those who excel both as skiers and mountaineers. The ski mountaineer who can ski the fall line with a heavy pack through any type or condition of snow is a rare bird indeed. Most British players are hybrids – skiers turned mountaineers or mountaineers turned skiers. An old adage, which I had once heard from the peerless Swiss guide Herman Steuri, was that to undertake a serious ski tour, you must either climb without exhaustion or ski with proficiency. That's fair advice but most guides prefer good skiers to fit climbers.

If I fell into any category it was not the former. Mountaineers tend to over-estimate their ability to compete with genuinely good skiers and I had under-estimated what Pyrenean ski touring involved. Speed and reliability on skis is as essential to mountain safety as it is on foot.

As I lay ruminating on my bunk trying to restore my battered self-confidence with the thought that the Pic d'Anie was bound to involve some climbing at which I might make a better showing, I muttered to myself, maybe it will all come right tomorrow.

At a mere 2,504 metres, the Pic d'Anie falls far short of a Pyrenean Three Thousander yet it has the character of a big mountain; marks the boundary between the Basque Country and Gascony and also delimits the most westerly end of the High Pyrenees. For these reasons, it is the peak from which any traverse of the range should begin or end.

At 5.30 next morning Epp was buzzing around like an angry wasp pitching everyone out of bed. Early starts are the bane of mountaineering though at the end of the day you never regret them. Yet, from the moment I opened the front door and stared out into the black of night, I could see that this one was a start too soon. Outside, the wind was howling and the snow billowing. We breakfasted all the same and then sat around the table apprehensively while Martin and Michael conferred in a corner poring over the map and guidebook. By 7 am it was light but when the weather showed no intention of improving, Martin suddenly announced:

"Now ve go anyhow. The mountains don't vait for anyvon."

For the next five hours, we climbed steadily upwards in file sticking faithfully to the line of Epp's tracks while the snow stuck to our clothing like glue. The visibility was never more than thirty metres but through country that was entirely new to him, he steered an unerring course in, out and around every bump and hollow, up and along every slope and ridge that came our way as if he had known every feature of this unseen and unfamiliar landscape all his life.

The only indication to me that we might have come face to face with the mountain proper was when the gradient suddenly steepened and we seemed to be skiing into a wall of snow. The column halted while Michael and Martin went into a huddle to pore over their maps and altimeters. From now on, this was to become a familiar sight.

"Leave your skis here," said Michael. "You'll need ice axes for this last bit."

Strung out like threaded beads in our leaders' steps, we climbed in unison, onwards and upwards through the cloud until we reached a heap of ice encrusted rocks. Nothing was now visible beyond five metres but Martin was waving his arms: "And zeez is ze summit," he announced gleefully, grasping my hand in that deathly grip.

"Bergheil!"

"Bergheil," indeed and good timing too. My watch showed that it was exactly 12 noon. I hadn't seen a damn thing of the Pic d'Anie but I didn't awfully care. The wind was so cold that no one in their right mind was going to hang around on the off chance of getting a view.

"So now vee go down," announced Martin gleefully as the last man reached the summit cairn, "Keep close together."

As we began to retrace our way through the deep snow furrow stamped out by nine pairs of ski boots only minutes before, Martin turned round to me with a twisted smile.

"John," he grinned, "You're zee mountaineer. You take ze lead."

"Me?" I said.

"Yes, you John. Pleez show us ze vay down!"

Some Swiss joke perhaps or maybe this was his way of giving the tyro a chance to redeem himself after yesterday's fiasco. "Okay, why not?" I heard myself saying.

I peered below me. Already, the track was fast disappearing under a blanket of fresh snow. I set off tentatively trying to follow it but after 50 metres it completely vanished. I cast around trying to pick up the tracks but without map or compass to hand felt completely disorientated. I was bushed but Martin had been shadowing me and now popped up at my shoulder, grinning.

"Sorry Martin," I said. "I've completely lost the track. I can't see a damned thing."

I knew that I had blown it but to have blundered on would have been even more humiliating.

"No matter," said Martin still grinning. "Now you follow me."

Almost immediately, he re-located a faint imprint and, soon enough, we were back at the comforting cluster of skis that we had left at the bottom of the final slope. His route finding appeared to be entirely instinctive and when, back in the hut that evening, I asked him the secret, he answered Delphically – "You must learn to recognise snow shape identification."

With the Pic d'Anie conquered, the hard part of the day should have been behind us. Now, at least in theory, we would have all the fun of skiing back to the hut and then skiing down to Lescun. Yesterday I had made a horlicks of the skiing. Today I had missed my chance of redemption by messing up a minuscule piece of route finding. No matter, I was determined to make up for all that with a fall free descent. I would follow Michael's instructions to the letter but, this time round, Michael had other ideas about the use of skins.

"We'll take our skins off for this first bit," he advised laconically. "It should give us a good, fast run."

The icy path that had given me so much trouble yesterday now had a fresh overlay of snow. At the start, we all set off more or less together but for me any semblance of an orderly descent didn't last long. Having learned one lesson yesterday, I deliberately stuck to the rear to be out of harm's way, but while my companions appeared to be taking in their stride what to me seemed diabolically awkward snow, my technique simply disintegrated and yesterday repeated itself. A series of binding breaks precipitated another cycle of falls and delays. Flustered, white faced and snow encrusted, I reached the Laberouat Hut at the end of an extended line to find both Martin and Michael waiting outside.

"Please hurry up, John," said Michael with an edge to his voice. "We've got to ski down to Lescun to catch the last bus and we haven't got much time. Please get yourself ready immediately."

This was not the time to seek comforting words or get Martin's technical advice on what I should be doing about my bindings. I cursed myself for not having sorted all that out last night so I cranked my bindings up to their tightest setting and mustered outside the hut to find Martin marshalling his troops for a massed start in the style of an old-fashioned downhill race.

"Now vee must go fast," cried Martin – *"Schnell!"*

He was already gliding away half turning, shouting and gesticulating with his sticks for the rest of us to follow him and so we did – in a rush. Then, all of a sudden I felt a new pulse of excitement.

Come on, I said to myself, this is supposed to be fun. You've just climbed your first Pyrenean peak on ski and what do falls and lousy bindings matter? Relax ... try to enjoy yourself.

Skiing's a curious thing. Just when you're about to despair, it all comes together again: it did for me on this helter-skelter descent as we cut across fields, barged through hedges, disappeared into ditches and tangled with barbed wire fences half hidden under the snow. The whole thing became a marvellous romp with all the tensions of the day releasing themselves like an uncoiling spring. The bus was revving up impatiently as we swept noisily into the village square, pink cheeked, laughing and elated.

Dusk had fallen but our day wasn't ended. Michael had booked us in for that night some 15 kilometres away up the Aspe Valley at the Hotel des Voyageurs in the village of Urdos. The ancient bus was now grinding its way up into the heart of the Western Pyrenees by the most typical and spectacular of all Pyrenean *"gaves"* – the Val d'Aspe. I was to come this way again another time but now it was too late to see anything of our surroundings.

Urdos itself, the last village in France before the Spanish frontier, lies just below that most famous of all Pyrenean passes – the Somport, the Romans' *Summus Portus* or Highest Pass. Across it, the Phoenicians came in search of tin; Hasdrubal's Carthaginians marched in an attempt to rescue the beleaguered Hannibal from Italy and Moorish raiding parties rode their Arab steeds to lay waste the fields of France.

Although it was Napoleon's idea to build the modern road he was merely following the example of the Romans who, 2000 years before him, had built this great road across the High Pyrenees. They called this the Antonine Way, the highway to Saragossa, the City of Caesar Augustus. This was the highway that brought to Spain 400 years of peace, prosperity and civilisation. Spain, in turn, repaid the Roman debt by providing four of its Emperors – Trajan, Hadrian, Marcus Aurelius and Theodosius – and three of Latin's greatest writers – Seneca, Martial and Lucan.

Urdos had been a key Roman military station along the way and takes its name from the Latin for bear – *ursus*. Bears were once so common that they became the symbol of Pyrenean life, folklore and ritual but have long since been hunted to virtual extinction. Happily there is still wildlife in these mountains. In the Hotel des Voyageurs' cosy bar-cum-dining-room, stuffed wild boar, wild cat, polecat and deer were on display in every alcove.

Michael, always first to buy a couple of bottles of wine, was dispensing his customary hospitality. His modest, quiet manner contrasted sharply with the bellicosity of another amateur of wine who had stayed at this same inn at the turn of the century. I had been brought up on Hilaire Belloc's *Cautionary Tales* but only learned much later of Belloc's prodigious walking feats. He had long held the record for walking to London from Oxford; had trekked across the breadth of America to woo his wife and had quartered the hills and valleys of the Pyrenees, recording his experiences in prose and poetry. His book, *The Pyrenees,* remains the most comprehensive English monograph on the range's history and topography. Belloc, the son of a French barrister, was a gourmet. Our dinner of soup, *lotte à l'armoricain,* beefsteak, haricot beans and ice-cream confirmed his verdict that there was no inn *"pleasanter in Urdos".*

According to Michael's original itinerary, tomorrow would see us all the way to the Pombie Hut. He had described this as a *long day* but, over dinner, I overheard him and Martin discussing our programme in the light of the weather forecast. This had given them some second thoughts for, after coffee, Michael made his ritual evening pronouncement: "Slight change of plan for tomorrow chaps, I'm afraid," he began. "We've got problems with the weather again. The outlook's none too good so Martin and I have decided to make it a shorter day tomorrow and settle for the Ayous Hut."

"Where exactly is the Ayous Hut, Michael?"

Patrick, always in his element at briefings, sounded a touch disappointed.

"I'll show you on the map later, Patrick," Michael replied. "However, in these conditions, the Ayous will be quite far enough for one day. It's 1,400 metres up the Larry Valley to the Ayous Col and, although the hut's just down the other side, the descent could be quite tricky. We will also make arrangements to get the main Ayous Hut opened for us."

I was much relieved at this news for I had taken a surreptitious look at Michael's 1:25,000 IGN skiers map and concluded that the Pombie Hut looked as if it might be days away. There were no more questions from the floor and, after dinner, three days worth of food was divided up between the nine of us. My share included a mega chunk of Swiss cheese which I had difficulty squeezing into my over-stretched rucksack.

I was earliest to bed that night and, as I hauled myself up the banisters hand over hand to my bedroom, feeling my bruises anew, pondered on the events of the past two days. Michael's assessment of Pyrenean weather and snow had been spot on. This dank, murky world of impenetrable cloud was light years away from the weather we had enjoyed last summer and bore no resemblance to those crisp, clear mornings and intoxicating air of the sunlit Alps in winter.

As for this heavy, wet snow ... Where were those orderly Swiss snow crystals which, by some wondrous process of osmosis – overnight freeze followed by morning thaw – became the stuff of skiers' dreams – *Firn* or Spring Snow? *Firn's* thin coating of newly melted snow overlaying a hard base gives a consistency and certainty that allows even the most inadequate performers to ski with style. If you get your timing right in the Alps, *Firn* can be your due. So far in the Pyrenees we had had nothing but ice, crust or mush.

I had to admit that my performance on ski over the past two days had been abysmal and, though I might sometimes have used old equipment as an excuse, I well knew where the true explanation lay. For all that, I would have given good money to discover why only *my* skis seemed to have a penchant for nose-diving into the snow while others floated the surface and why my cable bindings should either release at a touch or remain so rigid as to threaten the severance of femur from knee joint. Another matter which bugged me were my skins. Save for Michael and Martin with their "stick-ons", everyone picked up a bit of snow between their skin and ski as a matter of course but no one began to rival the fat wadges that mine managed to build up. As the days had worn on I had been cataloguing mentally all the stuff that I would be chucking out at the end of this tour if I ever reached the end of it. For starters, that frameless climbing rucksack that was never designed to carry skis; the 1950s style woollen trousers that had never been dry since that first morning and the water-saturated leather boots which were already as soft as cardboard.

At this early stage I hadn't identified a victim upon whom I could unburden my numbing equipment grumbles. Ski mountaineering equipment is an excruciatingly boring subject of conversation for the uninitiated but provides a sure source of conversation and common currency for ski mountaineering bores. Mindless hours are spent discussing the relative "wicking" qualities of cotton, wool, nylon or fleece; the advantages or disadvantages of various types of inner, outer or under clothing; the comparative performances and technical attributes of stoves, be these petrol, paraffin, Gaz, solid fuel, pot bellied or Primus.

All this laddish stuff had so far been denied me for we hadn't had that much time to get to know each and our luxurious hotel style accommodation had not encouraged the commonplace intimacies that are shared when you're cooped up together in a hut for days on end riding out a storm. It usually takes something akin to crisis for some mountaineers to express their feelings. The obsessive nature of the game appeals as much to introverts as extroverts.

It wasn't as if I hadn't made an attempt to probe deeper into this equipment puzzle. Just before dinner, I sidled up to Michael to pick his brains on the subject and cut a bit more ice.

"Michael," I began tentatively, "I'm intrigued by the skins you and Martin are using. They don't have buckles or straps and seem to be glued to your skis."

He looked at me indulgently.

"Yes, John, that's precisely it. They're Coll-tex stick-ons. A great improvement on the old type. I strongly recommend you buy yourself a pair."

This was quite a positive start so I probed further.

"And where d'you get your ski boots? Mine have gone soft as wet cardboard."

"Why, Bohren of Grindelwald, of course!" he replied.

When I had vulgarly asked him how much they cost, I swallowed hard. I might as well have had them made by Lobb in St James's. I didn't pursue the matter further.

The Eagles' flight hit the road at 8 am precisely on the following day. We weren't exactly singing as we marched away up the road in strict file, with skis and sticks riding high at the vertical above our sacs and baguettes sprouting out at a variety of angles but we were launched on a key passage.

No ski touring day is exactly like another but there's a common pattern to most. Sometimes you are on skis for the entire day from the moment you step out of your hut or tent until you reach the next one. On others, you may have to walk a very long way to the snowline and have another long walk out at the other end. Paradoxically, the most confusing part of route finding is sometimes at the very start of the day – making sure that you are on the right track heading up the right valley. With Michael and Martin in command, there was no question of their making such elementary route finding mistakes particularly as they had already recce'ed this route. Nonetheless, I was heartened to have spotted for myself a little way up the road a small signpost pointing to *"rue de Larry"* and made a mental note for future reference.

"This is the start of it," announced Michael. "We'll be climbing for most of the day from now on."

We swung sharply to the east up a steep, cobbled mule track hedged in by thirty foot high box trees. These soon gave way to a forest of beech trees along whose boughs the snow was heaped in symmetrical drifts like miniature foresails.

If it can be arranged, it is good for morale that some ridiculous incident – for instance, a spectacular but non-injurious fall – enliven the day so that everyone can have a belly laugh about it in the evening. When we came to a stream which could only be crossed by stepping stones sheeted with ice, I sensed a photo-opportunity.

Bound for the Ayous Hut

"Vatch out for this one," shouted Martin, "or haf a cold bath."

The stones were incredibly slippery and it was the Devil's job to stay in balance. Robin Day slipped and fell in. He recovered himself immediately but came out with wet feet. Had it had been anyone else, we would have found the incident screamingly funny but Robin carried with him an air of sanctity.

At the snowline, Michael and Martin stopped to put on their skins – a manoeuvre which both completed in seconds. My strap ons always took me minutes to fix and as we had already been going for well over an hour, I assumed that we had be having a short stop.

"Time for a breather and a quick bite, Michael?" I ventured.

"Sorry, John, we can't stop now," he replied. "Martin and I don't like the look of this weather. We must press on."

Lescun all over again, I thought, thinking of the succulent ham sandwich at the top of my sac. But I could see what they meant. The weather had looked promising enough earlier in the morning but, true to Martin's forecast, the clouds which had been hovering about the mountain tops when we left the inn were now closing in like a dark fog which was thickening all the time.

Summer or winter, you never lightly confront bad weather in the mountains and never before had I wittingly walked straight into it. However, both Martin and Michael were professionals and, with them up front alternating the lead, I felt a sense of security as the nine of us climbed rhythmically together into the gathering cloud. Following my two leaders with none of the cares of leadership, my mind drifted to other things – like hunger and thirst. Why the hell hadn't I re-filled my water bottle back at the stream or pulled out that sandwich?

As morning merged into afternoon, the composition of the snowflakes changed from fluffy down to grit which came at us in stinging waves. The higher we climbed, the stronger the wind blew. There was nothing to be seen of the country about us save for the occasional rock that loomed up grey from out of a monochrome snowscape. A darker tone to the snow indicated that the ground was rising but in that flat light, perspective vanished and we seemed to be travelling into an opaque vacuum. Epp and de Pret Roose's navigation stops – earnest huddles over maps with compasses and altimeters – became more frequent and protracted. The contour lines of their French IGN maps were difficult enough to decipher in bright daylight but in driving snow, map reading became a Chinese puzzle.

It took us nearly eight hours to reach the Col d'Ayous and here it really was blowing a blizzard with visibility down to five metres. The day was also drawing to a close and I couldn't decide whether the darkness was due to the cloud or the onset of night.

"Close in around us all of you!"

We might have been an infantry platoon though it was out of character for Michael to shout. We huddled round him in a circle with our heads bowed and our necks craned but it was still difficult to catch a word of what he was saying.

"We've reached the Ayous Col," he bellowed, "The Ayous Hut's not far from here but it's right at the bottom of the cirque below us."

He was gesticulating with his arms but it wasn't clear in which direction because we were in a whiteout and a blizzard. The place had a sense of drama and, although I couldn't see anything that remotely resembled a cirque, I had studied its topography on the map back at the inn and could envisage in my mind's eye what it must look like – a gigantic cauldron surrounded by peaks and ringed with vertical cliffs.

It followed that if this was the col, we must now be standing at the very edge of those cliffs … Crikey! I stepped back involuntarily. Then, through a momentary lightening in the cloud, I spotted at our feet an indented line of grey cornices reaching out into space like monstrous barn eaves.

This was exactly the sort of col you would hope and pray that you would only have to cross on a bright, sunny day with the snow set solid. Michael's original plan to reach the Pombie Hut tonight came back to me. The Pombie Hut! Bloody Hell, in these conditions, I would settle for the Ayous Hut on any terms.

Michael hadn't finished with us yet.

"There's only one way down through the cliffs," he yelled. "It's tricky to find so Martin and I are going to look for it. You'll have to hang around here for a bit. Try to keep warm … We've got to get this one right."

I believed him.

For the next 50 minutes he and Martin walked up and down the lip of the cirque like a couple of cats, comparing altitude readings, checking and re-checking their map and prodding and probing the cornices to find the right way down. The rest of us stood around banging our gloves together, beating our arms across our chests and jumping up and down. I felt completely spare but knew that I could add nothing to the proceedings. It was now so dark that it was becoming difficult to differentiate between the two of them until Martin began waving his sticks above his head.

"Kom – we haf found ze vay," he yelled triumphantly as we all closed in on him. "Follow me."

Martin's way down wasn't that far from the place where we had first arrived and looked no different from anywhere else. The demarcation line between the edge of a cornice and space was virtually impossible to define but ours was not to reason why. Ours was to follow Martin like blind mice down through the trench he was excavating through a cornice with his ice axe flailing.

Any moment now, I thought, we'll all be falling fast and free through thin air. But once below the lip of the col, we were leeward of the wind and in this pocket of calm, keeping close to one another, could at last hear each other speak. We closed up together in another huddle.

Michael the anchorman came down last to join us. The ground sheered away into a blank white void and the light was now so bad that I couldn't begin to gauge its angle.

"Ski this section very carefully," Michael warned. "Ski as if you're on eggs. Keep your distance but don't lose touch."

No fear of that. As we ploughed on downwards through waist deep snow, each shadowy form stuck to the next man in line like a limpet. The same thought must have been going through all our minds – was this lot going to avalanche and take us with it?

Then, uncharacteristically, Michael lost his balance and took a heavy fall. It left him buried so deep in snow that, weighted down with his enormously heavy rucksack, he was finding it impossible to get enough purchase to lever himself up with his sticks.

I happened to be right behind him and immediately closed up. "Michael, can I give you a hand?" I asked hesitantly.

He glanced up at me and then, with one muscle-bursting effort, heaved himself to his feet. Then, without a word, he skied over to join Martin to check map, compass and altimeter for the umpteenth time that day.

Even in the Pyrenees, you sometimes get a break. This time, we really needed one. For a few seconds, the clouds lifted and there, miraculously, at the bottom of an immense snow bowl, there appeared the unmistakable triangular outline of a building which could only be the Ayous Hut. The clouds closed in again but we couldn't miss it now. By the time we got there it was dark but a battery of head torches soon located the entrance and we quickly cleared the door of snow which had drifted roof high.

"Damned door's bolted," muttered Michael. "Where the hell's the guardian got to?"

As we weighed the logistics of squeezing nine into winter quarters designed for four, three bobbing lights could be seen moving up towards us from the valley below. The hut guardian and his two assistants had made a special journey from Gabas to open up the main hut.

Even Michael admitted that it had been a tough day. For him and Martin, there had never been any let up. Although they had recce'ed this same route the previous autumn, I reckoned that they had taken a chance to push it through such a storm. Getting up and over the Col d'Ayous had taken two hours and I wondered if that would have been prudent had it been anyone else. However, at the end of the day we had made our objective safe and sound. Nothing else mattered.

The jolly guardian had the hut's wood burning stove going within minutes of arrival and now, relaxing over a Swiss gruyère and spaghetti dish concocted by Martin, I took another look at the two men who had shepherded us thus far. Throughout the day they had been working together as a seamless double act with the one always seeming to know what the other was thinking. They had never inspired anything but confidence and yet they looked an unlikely pair, the tall and the short of it. At first sight you might have said Gentleman and Player or Amateur and Guide but it wasn't remotely like that. It was a thoroughly modern arrangement which defied traditional analysis.

Martin could be prickly and combative but Michael, on the face of it the more conventional and easy going, was altogether less approachable and enigmatic. After supper, I thought I would try to get closer to him. I had already done some homework before the tour and discovered that he was one of the Ski Club of Great Britain's chief instructors and racing organisers; that he had led innumerable ski mountaineering tours and been joint leader of Alan Blackshaw's 1972 British Ski Traverse of the Alps. What made the man tick? Why had this former 12th Lancer given up his previous existence of training race horses, playing cricket and racing yachts across the Atlantic for the precarious life of a quasi-professional ski mountaineer living in Andermatt helping Martin Epp run his Alpine Sports School?

"I gather you've led quite a variegated sort of life, Michael," I began. "What made you decide to leave England and live in Andermatt?"

Even as I asked him the question, I realised that I had trespassed onto private ground and immediately regretted it.

He didn't so much as look up at me but said quite simply: "The Mountains."

Next morning, it was still snowing as it had done throughout the night. Our intended route to the Pombie Hut – an "easier day" according to Michael – was going to involve a descent to the Gave de Bious, a climb up the other side of the valley followed by a rising circular traverse around the south eastern outliers of the Pic du Midi d'Ossau before descending to the hut. It looked like another day of lousy weather ahead when we left the hut to course gently round the lake side and then down into the trough of the valley through a metre of fresh snow. The hut guardian's party was hard on our heels. Ski touring parties at this time of the year were a rarity. With our departure, the Ayous Hut would now be closed until the spring.

Thanks to Martin re-adjusting my bindings last night, I reached the floor of the Gave without incident. From here, we climbed a steep, rock-walled gully in a circular staircase of short zigzags, kicking outward turns at every bend. Contouring is the essence of uphill progress on ski. With an experienced leader, you will save time and energy by staying exactly in his tracks for he will take the best, which means the easiest, line. I marvelled at the way Epp and de Pret Roose seemed to slide upwards with an effortless gliding movement as if on rollers. With the rest of us following in their slipstream, it was unfair to compare their stylish progess with that of the man immediately in front of me. As any ski mountaineer will tell you, if you follow in someone else's wake for hour after hour, the least offensive idiosyncracies begin to irritate and annoy. This chap was doing his best but his clumsy kick turns stopped everyone in their tracks and upset the team's collective rhythm. It reminded me how tiresome my repetitive binding breaks must have been to everyone else.

At the top of the gully, stopping to rest on a mound of snow, I plunged in my ski pole and hit something hard. It was the roof of the abandoned Cabane de Peygeret, now completely buried in snow. This apart, the scene about us was much the same as it had been four days ago – another grey blur of mist and cloud. It was depressing to see nothing of the mountains and, while we took a quick bite, my mind again wandered to the sunlit snowfields and blue skies of the Alps.

Then, without warning, through a rent in the cloud there appeared ahead and above us an overwhelming mountain tableau of plunging walls, soaring ridges and teetering towers plastered in snow and ice. We stood transfixed for we had come face to face with one of the grandest mountains in the range – the double summited Pic du Midi d'Ossau, the Matterhorn of the Pyrenees.

The silhouette of the Pic du Midi resembles a giant tooth and from afar is best seen from Pau's Boulevard des Pyrenees. Although its ascent is technically more difficult than that of any of the three highest Pyrenean peaks – Aneto, Posets and Perdu – it was climbed before any of them and then by an Englishman. Excepting the claims of a 16th century bishop, a 17th century alchemist and an 18th century shepherd, the French historian Pierre de Gorsse in his book *Les Anglais aux Pyrenees* un-chauvenistically credits Henry Swinburne to have been the first summiteer in 1776.

The sight of this tremendous mountain emerging through veils of mist set my pulse racing. I had seen and read about it before Michael had included it on our climbing list. Even before I had managed to cock the shutter of my old fashioned bellows camera to get a picture, the clouds closed in again and the vision vanished. Its reddish igneous rock and uncompromising verticality reminded me of Mount Kenya. However, on the evidence of this sighting I doubted that we would be emulating Swinburne's ascent.

The Pombie Hut, set in a hollow besides its own lake, was half buried in snow. There was no guardian here to greet us and none had been booked to come. Martin was excitedly sniffing around like a dog.

"And now vee find zee door!" he announced, brandishing his snow shovel like an offensive weapon. With that he set to work on a snow drift like a mini-JCB. Inside, the place was a shambles. Snow had blown in from everywhere and was now banked up against the table, chairs, windows and walls in pure white drifts.

"So ve get varm digging," Martin exclaimed. "Ve move this snow outside – *Schnell!*"

Snow was Martin's element. Digging out the hut was warm work while it lasted but once we had finished, the place felt like a refrigerator and the sweat froze to my shirt like cold tin foil.

"No problem," said Martin, "We haf a stove!"

He had located this squat object after excavation and from the hut's remoter recesses also unearthed a four foot long, four inch thick pine plank.

"Firewood," he exclaimed triumphantly. "To me, it didn't figure. The plank looked inviolable."

"Won't you need a saw and axe for that, Martin?" I asked ingenuously.

"And vot is a Sviss Army knife for?" he snorted.

What indeed? – though it had never occurred to me that a two inch long saw, no different from the one on my own penknife, could inflict such damage. With his right arm working like a piston, Epp set about the plank like a chain-saw maniac. Soon enough, he had cut it up into chunks which he then split with the adze of his ice axe, reducing premium pine to a neat pile of Swiss-style logettes.

A measure of comfort and joy had returned to the Pombie Hut and by the time we had chomped our way through Martin's heavily mustarded mega-steaks, we were back to the old routine of he and Michael retiring to a corner for their traditional huddle. The outlook wasn't encouraging. For the past five days, it had never stopped snowing and with every passing day the avalanche risk was increasing. I wasn't the only one to have noticed the house-sized snow slabs which had sheared off the Pic du Midi d'Ossau to build up a glacis of avalanche debris at its base.

Over cold custard cream, Michael delivered the management's final verdict on tomorrow's programme: "I'm afraid we'll have to skip the Pic du Midi d'Ossau," he began. "It's too dangerous to attempt in these conditions."

I felt relieved. The Pic looked lethal under its sheath of snow and ice but, looking round, I could see some disappointed faces.

"What's the new plan, Michael?" Patrick asked.

"We'll just have to get down to Gabas tomorrow and re-assess the situation from there," Michael replied. "That's still subject to the weather. If it doesn't improve, we'll have our work cut out just doing that."

"What's the problem then?" broke in Hamish Brown's less pliant voice.

Michael continued evenly: "There are two problems. One's the increasing danger of our being avalanched. The other's the business of getting across the Col Suzon. It's high and very steep on the north side. If we don't make the break tomorrow and the bad weather continues, we could be stuck up here for days."

No one argued this and with matters thus decided Michael seemed to relax. In other company this might have been the time for a silly card game but Martin now took the stage. Untypically for a Swiss guide, his outlook was international. Having established his own Alpine Sports School in Andermatt, he had gone on to set up a string of Survival Schools from Lapland to Wyoming. With a captive audience, he now expounded on philosophy, religion and politics, leavening this diet with some practical tips on the manufacture and storage of Swiss cheese. After a while, my concentration began to waver and when the subject switched to mountaineering reminiscence, I was overcome by over-exposure and sloped off to bed.

That night the barometer plumbed new depths and by morning the wind was doing its best to detach the Pombie Hut from the steel hawsers that secured it to a concrete base. The temper of this weather looked worse than anything we had experienced to date. Over breakfast Michael confirmed his earlier decision.

"We must get down to Gabas as soon as we can," he announced. "Please get yourselves packed up immediately."

At last a chance to dump my two kilo chunk of Swiss cheese. I dropped it in a corner and then joined the others mustering by the door where Michael was dispensing last minute survival tips.

"Get your goggles on, make sure all your zips are done up and fasten your gauntlets *before* you get outside."

Outside the hut, the snow was eddying and backing in whirligigs but only when we had climbed out of the hollow of drift which had formed a protective shield around it did the storm's full force hit us like a flanker's head high tackle.

Martin was in the van with Michael bringing up the rear. Both were shouting the same message: "Stick together, keep moving – don't lose contact!"

We were now ploughing our way through another full scale blizzard in a whiteout. Once again, Epp displayed his uncanny navigational skills, seemingly feeling the lie of the land in the same way as others might see it. It was a virtuoso performance and, as before, the expertise of both Epp and de Pret

Roose inspired my admiration. Yet, for all that, I had still not got used to the pair taking every decision, big or small, on this tour. With no personal responsibility, I felt divorced from their achievement. It had nothing to do with my limited skills or lack of them. Mountaineers prefer to do their own thing however badly. Although you may never match a guide's expertise, you prefer to stand or fall by your own decisions. When a guide takes these for you, your bread's without salt.

Even so, this time round it was no hardship not to be navigating. We were moving as fast as we could to generate heat and avoid frostbite but as we climbed upwards towards the Col Suzon, the wind was slicing through my woollen trousers as if they were mesh. To get a frost nipped face was one thing but at crotch level I was experiencing intimations of emasculation and could no longer feel the tip of my penis. Holding one gloved hand in front of my manhood to shield it from the cruel blast, I rubbed my frozen part frantically with the other to restore feeling. Windproof ski trousers rather than boots or skins had shot to the top of my new equipment list.

The Col Suzon didn't disappoint Michael's billing. The last ten metres reared up angrily in a near vertical ice sheet into which neither my *harscheisen* nor ice-axe made the slightest impression. Out of the corner of one eye, I could see trouble below as two of my companions began slithering and sliding backwards out of control. Disaster was checked by Michael but the north side of the col was even more challenging and here, without the guidance of our good shepherds, there would have been real trouble. Once we had reached the valley's trough, the wind dropped and our passage to Gabas through the dark, silent forest of Bious Artigues was like sailing from storm to calm waters.

That evening, in the cosy bar of Gabas's Hotel Biscau, Michael made what for me was to be his last pronouncement.

"Sorry chaps," he began, looking almost contrite, "I'm afraid we're going to have to scrap the rest of the traverse to Cauterets. The route from here on is too dangerous to risk after all this snow. Even if we have a spell of good weather, it will take a couple of days to settle. We'll all take a break tomorrow and ski the piste at Artouste. If the weather clears, we can bus round to Cauterets and bag some peaks from the Wallon and Oulettes Huts."

For me, that was it – the end of the road. My leave had only two more days to run.

If we had only had a couple of days' decent weather, I thought to myself, we could surely have made Cauterets. However, you can't beat the weather and the brash forecast I had made to Michael that first morning in Pau now came back to haunt me.

Two days later, at the car park of the Pont d'Espagne, I said goodbye to the others before they set off in column up the Marcadau Valley for the Wallon Hut. For the first time in eight days the sky was cloudless. High above, ranks of snow clad peaks were glistening in the sunshine as if on parade.

As my train headed north for Paris late that afternoon, I took a last look at the Pyrenees. Stretched out in an arc across the southern horizon, they rose from the plain like a ghostly wall suffused in gold by the sun's dying rays. They looked so peaceful and I envied the others who would be up at the hut, having a jolly supper, cracking jokes and making their plans for tomorrow.

It soon became dark but as the train thundered on, all the images of the past few days came crowding back to me – the appalling weather, the difficult snow and the steepness of the terrain. This range was quite unlike the Alps and, apart from that last day, we had never even seen the mountains let alone made a decent ski descent. I totted up the balance sheet and found that on the face of it, I didn't have that much in credit. The tour had been too short to have achieved anything significant or to have made close friends. I had liked both Michael and Martin and been greatly impressed by their ski mountaineering skills but the experience had confirmed that guided tours were not for me.

Yet, despite the frustrations and disappointments, the genius of the place had caught my imagination as much in winter as it had the previous year in summer. When I came in from the corridor window to face a torrid night in my couchette, the Pyrenees had long since vanished from sight but I promised myself that one day I would come back to discover for myself something more of this range and the wild country that lay beyond Gabas.

Party on Col Pallas

3

GUIDELESS TO CAUTERETS

Three years had elapsed since that first Pyrenean ski tour with Michael de Pret Roose's Eagles party, yet, when I got his letter, it all came back to me as if it were yesterday.

"The weather pattern is Atlantic rather than Alpine," he had written, "... the huts are usually nothing but bare and rather dirty winter rooms ... the maps are the usual French sort with pretty unreliable contours and the refuges marked in lettering that covers about a square kilometre ..."

Thanks Michael! I had not forgotten any of it but it was good of him to write by return. Typical of the man.

In the intervening years, I had totally lost touch with my fellow Eagles of that trip, save for Robin Day and Patrick Fagan who became a good friend with whom I later shared several adventures. For Michael, that Pyrenean ski tour had merely been an incident in his tightly programmed ski mountaineering life and, like most of the others, he never returned to the Pyrenees. For me it was different. The weather might have been dreadful and the snow unpredictable but these mountains had caught my imagination and had left me with a fringe of unsatisfied curiosity. I had also promised myself that when I did come back it would be with my own party without the crutch of professional guides.

Since that first Pyrenean ski tour, much had changed in my professional and private life. Now in my mid-forties, I had settled for the humdrum. I had become a partner in a City law firm; had moved the family from deepest Wales to London and got back into the swing of the mountaineering round with a regular diet of rock climbing weekends, family skiing holidays, Alpine summer seasons and winter ski tours. Life was busy and generally fulfilling but time and again I found myself thinking back to the Pyrenees and of returning there to complete unfinished business.

Yet, as the years slipped by, I realised that something was holding me back and, when I was honest with myself, it wasn't that difficult to identify. With only one week's winter apprenticeship in those storm swept mountains to my credit, I simply didn't think that I was competent enough to lead a Pyrenean ski tour with an amateur party. So I had written to Michael for his advice. It wasn't just to get his confirmatory information about weather, huts and maps. I was really looking for reassurance.

There's an element of danger in every type of mountaineering with Himalayan climbing topping the list. Without it, the sport wouldn't exist. Ski mountaineering comes lower down the scale but this too can be a risky game – more so than the run of Alpine summer climbing. Where you do it also makes a difference. The Alps may be higher but the Pyrenees are steeper and the weather is altogether more capricious. Whether climbing or ski mountaineering, you should avoid bad weather whenever you can but, as I had learned from Michael's tour, exposure to bad weather in the Pyrenees is inevitable. For this reason above all, you must know something of navigation and snowcraft and, most particularly, about avalanches.

There's a world of difference between a professionally guided tour and one you organise yourself with friends. A guide will usually make the administrative arrangements, take all the mountaineering decisions and also the flak if things go wrong, but if you arrange it yourself, everything becomes your baby – from the composition of the party, the itinerary, the food, transport and logistics. In picking your team, you will want people with some mountaineering experience who can ski steadily and safely in all conditions and have the right temperament. Once launched, you will have to make your own decisions about the route, the weather and snow conditions; whether to advance or retreat; whether to climb on or come down. This is the stuff of every mountaineering venture but ski mountaineering in the Pyrenees seemed to me to have an extra dimension. Hence my correspondence with Michael. He was as generous with his advice as he had been with his hospitality.

His letter went on: "All ski routes shown on French ski maps should be treated with caution as should the avalanche slopes which are marked in profusion by blue arrows and, apparently, flow not only down but also along and, in some cases, up the slopes!"

He also explained how to get hold of the French IGN 1:25,000 Parc National des Pyrenées ski maps and the *Federation Française de la Montagne's* ski touring guidebooks which I had so often seen him studying intently with Martin but which were unobtainable in London. Apparently, the source was one Raymond Ollivier of Pau – "a nice little man who wrote most of the guide books himself." I wrote immediately for the set.

First time round with my own Pyrenean ski tour, I was going to play it dead safe. The itinerary I planned would be broadly the same as Michael's original but would finish with a flourish. We would leave out the Pic d'Anie section and, starting from Urdos, would traverse the main range all the way to Gavarnie, climbing as many peaks as we could en route.

That part was settled easily enough but it was going to be a lot more difficult to find the right team. A good guide can cope with misfits, incompetents and almost anyone else but with friends, no one is paying for the pleasure of your company so you should choose those you really like from the start. A sense of humour makes the difference between good fun and a bad experience.

However, when it really mattered, none of my old ski mountaineering buddies were available. I then remembered the article written by Patrick Fagan about Michael's tour in the Eagle Ski Club Yearbook and went public by advertising my own tour in the same publication. Michael had received an avalanche of applicants but when the only two respondents to show any interest cried off after I had taken them through the programme, I asked the Club's Touring Secretary Susan Baldock where I was going wrong.

As she delicately put it: "... its always a bit tricky for a leader who is not well known in the club. Undoubtedly, some will have been put off by the emphasis on mountaineering experience."

This emphasis was the one aspect I thought I had pitched right for I needed some security about the type I would be taking on. But I took the point on Susan's other comment. Although I had been a Club member for over ten years, I hadn't been a good clubman and was virtually unknown within the Club. I thought back to Michael's tour. Maybe the committee had devised some subtle system of reporting back on individual performance and I hadn't come up to the mark? I got part of the message on how Susan's mind might be working from her letter which contained a freehand drawing of how to rig up a rescue sledge. She also advised that we should certainly take a snow shovel – though "two would be excessive". A year on, we would both have cause to remember that advice.

When it became clear that no other Eagles would be flighting, I cast my mind back to the previous year when I had met someone who seemed to share my own ski mountaineering philosophy. During a Climbers Club meet in North Wales on a particularly vile January day, Alan Wedgwood and I had found ourselves scrambling up the Parson's Nose on Snowdon's Crib y Ddisgyl. The cloud was low, the wind was howling, the rocks were plastered in snow and Alan was in his element. Later that year, I joined Alan's ski touring party in central Switzerland and, for several years thereafter, our families were to spend a succession of summer and winter holidays together.

Alan was an outstanding personality and mountaineer, a former President of the Oxford University Mountaineering Club and a member of the Alpine Climbing Group which had been founded after the Second World War as British mountaineering's ginger group. A scion of Josiah Wedgwood, his professional career had mainly been spent at Harwell as a research physicist and engineer. He looked several sizes larger than his actual height of six foot two inches but, in all that formidable physique, it was his hands which fascinated. They were not only enormous but, as I later discovered, capable of making anything whether it was welding a ski binding, knocking up a dozen refectory tables for a party or building a steamboat engine. Alan was lucid, imaginative, practical and unflustered in any crisis but not a man to cross. His personality had an edge to it and the cast of his face had something of the beardless young Lenin.

Once Alan had agreed to come, everything else started to fit into place and, after various entrances and exits, the final team shook down as Alan, his younger brother Nick, Richard Morgan and me. Nick was even taller than Alan and an airline pilot. He wasn't a climber as such but he knew a lot about weather and as a *moniteur* of the peripatetic *Weekend Ski Club* was obviously a strong skier. Richard was an aspiring captain of industry whom I had known from way back. Like Alan, he was a serious mountaineer with extensive Alpine experience and had notched up some impressive routes including the North Faces of the Cime Grande de Lavaredo and Triglav. Nick apart, we were typical mountaineers turned skiers though for a trip of this kind none the worse for that. On a wild March night, the four of us caught the overnight ferry from Southampton to Le Havre, drove all day across France and reached Pau's Hotel de Paris that same evening.

Now on my fourth visit to Pau, I was getting a proprietorial feel for the place and instinctively made for Le Printemps Brasserie. The dining-room/bar was full to bursting as the television showed a replay of that afternoon's Wales *vs* France Rugby match. As a Welshman in this stronghold of French Rugby, I felt a wary *cameraderie* with the local fans. My father, who had captained Cambridge and Wales in the 1920s, had held the robust teams of south-west France in great respect and had reminisced about Gascon hospitality.

Pau's British connection goes back a lot further than the *Belle Epoque* when the English introduced the game of Rugby Football to these parts. In 1151 Eleanor of Aquitaine married the future king of England Henry II and for the next three centuries until the triumph of Joan of Arc, Gascony was an English dominion. The provincial capital of Pau has retained a fondness for the British ever since its peaceful occupation by Wellington's soldiers at the end of the Peninsula War when many veterans settled in this elegant city with its equable climate. By the mid-19th century, the fast set of Pau's 2000-strong English community were given over to steeplechasing, foxhunting and golf but the new railway from Paris ended the town's exclusivity and when, in 1889, Queen Victoria began to holiday regularly in Biarritz, the smarter English *Palois* deserted the city of their adoption for the chic of the coast.

I had always liked the place and when next morning dawned clear and sunny, I wanted to show the others Pau's famous view of the Pyrenees from its eponymous Boulevard. In summer I had been enchanted by the panorama of vineyards and woodlands, backed by an unbroken arc of snow mountains beyond but in the winter sunshine it looked even more impressive. This was the view that had moved the French poet Lamartine to write *"Pau est la plus belle vue de terre, comme Naples est la plus belle vue de mer"*. It was a tableau that I hoped would also inspire my companions and set the scene for our trip.

"Great view," commented Richard.

"But where does our route go?" asked Alan.

"Very broadly, we'll be following the line of the frontier ridge you can see along the southern skyline. That should take us as far as Gabas. After that, we'll be heading south into Spain making a series of overnight stops at huts before fetching up at Gavarnie."

I had already circulated a detailed itinerary of the route but was never sure how much of this Alan bothered to read. He preferred to take things as they came.

"Fine," he said, "but what peaks will we be climbing, John?" I had already listed nine of these in the itinerary starting with the Pic du Midi d'Ossau and ending with Perdu. It was a preposterously over-ambitious list but I thought it might appeal to both Alan and Richard. Anyway, I didn't want to be out-gunned by what Michael had planned for the Eagles so I went through it again. Alan looked dubious.

"That's quite a tall order," he quipped. "Aren't you being a bit ambitious?"

"Maybe," I retorted, "but it's little different from what de Pret Roose was proposing for the Eagles. Take a look at the Pic du Midi d'Ossau."

Of the many splendoured peaks that sparkled in the sunlight, the Pic du Midi d'Ossau outshone all others – a giant's tooth plastered in snow and ice.

"Yeah, that's quite a peak," admitted Alan. "Looks quite difficult from here. Have you climbed it?"

"No," I replied, "When I was here with the Eagles, we had to give it a miss."

"Ah!" exclaimed Alan, "in that case, we must certainly climb it."

Later that morning, we drove up the trench-like Ossau valley to dump a food cache at the Hotel Biscau, Gabas. I was following another de Pret Roose precedent and, over coffee, asked Madame if she remembered a party of *Anglais* from three years back.

Yes indeed she did – there had been none before or since. No, she didn't remember me but she did remember the tall, blond man – *"Michel, très distingué."* Then, pointing to her gnarled index finger to complete the physiographic picture, she winked at me – *"mais sec."*

For the rest of that day we skied the piste at Artouste to warm up and shake down but, by mid-afternoon, visibility was deteriorating fast with dark, baggy clouds moving in from the Atlantic. The weather was taking a turn for the worse.

That night I had a bad dream. The story line was simple and had everything to do with our forthcoming ski tour. In a nutshell, we were going to be dogged by appalling weather from start to finish. I didn't tell the others but it worried me. I had been clinging to the hope that the weather on that first Pyrenean ski tour had been an aberration but what if we had to contend with the same mixture of blizzard and whiteout? It was one thing to be setting off with the likes of Michael and Martin who had both spent their lifetimes ranging through mountains in storm and stress. Epp could read an altimeter and compass as fast as others might tell the time but were we, I wondered, competent enough to cope with such conditions?

By next morning my nightmare had become reality. The sky was a violet black and the rain was teeming down just as it had three years before. We joined a couple of dispiriting commercial travellers noisily slurping their coffee in the dining-room and ate stale croissants in silence. No one broached the subject of the weather but this one was clearly in my court. Were we going to stay in Pau waiting for it to clear or should we make a start? This was just Day One and as only I had been to the Pyrenees before, the others expected me to know some-thing about these mountains.

"This weather's quite appalling," I began tensely.

"Yes, we can all see that," came in Alan, grimly, "but what are we going to do about it?"

At that particular moment, I hadn't the slightest clue except to play it both ways lawyer fashion.

"We may have to delay our start as it may clear later," I replied Delphically but then, with more conviction, "In any event, we'll have to wait until the shops open to buy Nick some new ski poles."

That was my let out. Nick had broken both his poles yesterday on the piste and in no way could he start the tour without new ones.

"Certainly Nick's got to have new poles," said Alan, "but maybe he can borrow some. If we miss the first train up the valley we won't get the bus connection to Urdos and that'll mean that we could miss a whole day."

All this was true but there was nothing I could do about it. When you're geared up to go, it's always bad for morale to have to hang around at the start. This time fate took a hand for the ski poles dilemma was solved by the hotel proprietor who produced a pair of his own and insisted on driving us to the railway station just in time to catch the 7.47 am train to Etsaut. Willy nilly we were on our way.

The Aspe Valley railway was built in 1928 and, until the Spanish Civil War, went all the way into Spain. Now it stops half way up the valley at Etsaut. This should have been one of life's most unforgettably scenic train journeys had not the cloud been impenetrable. At Etsaut, we boarded a bus which ground its way up a twisting road awash with water that was cascading down the hillside. Through a break in the cloud, I spotted a Transylvanian-style castle perched on a crag like a bird of prey. The map identified this as the Fort de Portalet which was once guarded by the poet Alfred de Vigny, then a dashing young Captain in the Royal Guards. His romantic poems recall the valley's grave, gloomy scenery. It was here, too, that in 1940 Petain imprisoned the ministers of France's Third Republic only to find himself as its prisoner five years later awaiting his trial for treason.

We de-bussed at Urdos in a steady stream of sleet and took refuge in the Hotel des Voyageurs' cosy bar. I had forgotten what a very congenial place this was and, after a carafe or two of *vin ordinaire*, found less to complain about the weather.

"We could do a lot worse than be stuck here for tonight," I ventured. "This weather looks set in and we haven't a hope in hell of reaching the Ayous Hut today. In fact, we had be hard pushed to reach that hut in one day even in good weather."

"You could be right there, John," said Alan, "Maybe we could use this place as a base for day tours. A spell here would give us time to find our feet."

When Richard and Nick agreed with him, I immediately regretted that I had ever suggested staying at Urdos whatever the weather. I didn't like the sound of "day tours". I had come to do a ski traverse to Gavarnie. A couple of day tours would completely throw my carefully thought out plans. However, I reasoned, we had at least made a start and there wasn't much else we could be doing.

"Right then," I said. "I'll tell Madame that we'll be staying tonight," and, glancing out of the window and noticing that the rain was easing up slightly, suggested, "Why don't we have a quick walk before lunch to work up an appetite?"

Madame showed us to our communal room where we dumped our kit and, with no more ado, pushed on up the road for the pre-prandial stroll. I wondered whether I would still remember that critical turnoff to *rue de Larry* but needn't have worried. The signpost was still there plain to see.

It was at this point that something unusual happened. All of a sudden the rain tailed off, the clouds began to lift and the sun came out. For the past hour or so, I had been thinking about The Voyageurs' *table d'hôte* and the lunch we had promised ourselves but, when I looked at my companions and they looked back at me, I realised that we were about to forego our last decent meal for days.

"Well that's it then," I said as to a man we turned tail and hot-footed it back to the hotel. Madame took our cancellations in good part but, as we marched up the road for the second time that day with skis at the vertical and rucksacks a-saggin', I glanced over my shoulder to see her still standing in the hotel doorway with her arms akimbo and a quizzical look on her face.

The same signpost said, *"Larry 3h: Col d'Ayous 4h"* but these were summer walking times and I distinctly remembered that it had taken the Eagles eight hours to reach the Col d'Ayous from here. It was already midday and I thought to myself: we can't possibly make the Ayous Hut tonight: we're starting ridiculously late but maybe we can stay at the Larry Hut.

We reached the snow line and transferred to skis. There was much more snow about this year and the icy stepping stones above the Pont de Coustey, which had dunked some Eagles' feathers, were now buried in it a metre deep. Better still, the higher we climbed the bluer the sky, and the air had become almost balmy.

We had never stopped at the Larry Hut with the Eagles and I barely recognised this Hanzel and Gretel cottage, roofed and walled with pine shingles so conveniently sited at the treeline. We had made good time and, peering inside, I was surprised to see that the previous occupants had left the place immaculately clean and had even taken the trouble to stack a neat pile of logs beside the pot-bellied stove. Alan was busy testing the taps on a jumbo-sized Gaz cooker. "Hey," he shouted, "this thing actually works – and look up here on this shelf, – there's crockery and a canteen of cutlery plus a bottle of wine and a bottle of rum, both unopened!"

Richard had also been nosing around: "Would you believe it," he exclaimed, "there's even a stack of clean blankets on the top of this bunk."

That clinched it.

"What d'you think we stay here tonight?" I suggested, "the weather may be improving but we had be very pushed to make the Ayous Hut tonight. We've barely got two hours of daylight left."

"I agree," said Alan. "This is quite far enough for a first day and we can put what's left of it to good use with some Autophon practice."

Everyone seemed happy enough to pack it in. Avalanche search and rescue practice may be a bit of a bore but it is essential and should always be done before a tour has got under way and before you forget about it. This was Alan's department. While he buried his Autophon in the snow, the rest of us shut our eyes and, in turns, set about trying to locate it within a given time. I felt relieved that we had got this essential chore out of the way.

Just before going to bed, we all stood outside the hut in the snow, sipping Alan's hot rum punch and marvelling at the brightness of the stars. It was a clear and frosty night. Everything looked set fair for an early start tomorrow.

Pic du Midi d'Ossau.   (L to R) – Nick Wedgwood, Richard Morgan and Alan Wedgwood

Alan was first awake next morning at 6.30 am and lost no time unburdening himself upon me from within his sleeping bag.

"John, I want you to know about this terrible nightmare I had last night."

"Oh yes," I said with a sinking feeling. "Something dreadful to do with the weather I suppose."

"Oh no," he replied cheerfully, "nothing like that. It was all to do with that wretched Eagle Ski Club of yours with all their funny badges. If you can believe it, they wanted me to pass a French oral examination before qualifying for membership." I didn't feel up to humouring Alan at this hour of the morning. For reasons best known to himself, he had taken against the Eagles. Maybe he thought them a touch precious or it was something that I had told him about Epp and de Pret Roose that had aroused his competitive instincts.

"Rubbish Alan," I replied, "you know there's nothing quite as silly as that. Why don't you join the Club – you might even enjoy it."

"No, no," he replied, "no chance of that. I failed the Eagles' French test – *ergo* I won't have to join that Club and I can't tell you how relieved I am."

My own dreams had once again been about the weather. Round about midnight, I had heard the rain pattering down on the shingle roof. By early morning, the rain had turned to snow and now it was blowing a blizzard with the Larry Hut at its epicentre. For the next two hours, the wind tugged and shook it like a dog while we lay doggo in our sleeping bags, hoping it would go away. When it didn't, Richard the eager beaver got up to brew a cup of tea and, once he was up and about, everyone else felt honour bound to follow suit.

We sat around spinning out an exiguous breakfast of tea and porridge cake. To pass the time, we tried firing each other up with improbable recollections of National Service escapades. Three hours later, there had been no let-up in the weather and conversation had completely dried up. With nothing to read, we mooched about peering out from time to time through the frosted windows at the snow devils spiralling around in a merry dance outside.

When the weather's good, you just get up and go but when it's bad, you start having second thoughts about the route, your timing, snow conditions, whether there's enough food and just about everything else. This weather looked very bad. But how long would it last? Should we stick or twist?

At midday there was still no change and our bullish breakfast mood had long since evaporated. I wasn't quite sure how to play this game or, indeed, whether anyone else really wanted to join in but I kept thinking to myself: surely we can't just shy at this first fence? We must do *something*.

"Can't see any point in hanging around here much longer," I said brightly, trying to break the lethargy that had set in. "Time's getting on. I'm all for making a start for the Ayous Hut."

"But this weather's diabolical," Alan shot back. "I can't see a damn thing outside."

"We can always take a bearing on the Col d'Ayous and get there on a compass march," I continued. "The col's pretty well due east of here. We can just keep going until we hit it. Once we're there, the hut's down in the cirque on the other side."

"How far away is the col anyway?" asked Richard.

"Can't be more than two kilometres from here and about 500 metres higher," I replied.

"That's all very well," said Alan, "but if this weather gets worse or we don't hit off the col, we could be in real trouble."

"Agreed," I replied, "but if we haven't reached the col within a couple of hours, we've still got time to turn about and come back to this hut."

Dead simple when it was put like that but I was thinking back to the problems that Epp and de Pret Roose had experienced in just reaching the Col d'Ayous, let alone finding a way off it down the other side. I was feeling far from confident but, before spilling the beans about what I really thought about our chances of reaching the hut, Alan broke in and said; "Okay, John, I'm willing to give it a go if everyone else is."

"Right," I replied, "if everyone else is on for this let's pack up and get going."

The weather had looked bad from inside the hut but only when we got outside did I realise quite what we were letting ourselves in for. Visibility was down to 15 metres, with a bitterly cold north-east wind blowing straight into our faces. I reckoned that the only possible justification for setting off in such conditions was that our line of march was clear cut – 90 degrees due east. Richard was posted ahead to act as front marker for the navigator and, shuffling into line, we skinned off into the blizzard.

I had never really had to think about route finding the last time I had come this way but was disconcerted when I had no recollection of the couloir walled in by rocky bluffs which we found ourselves climbing at an increasingly steep angle. We were still dead on our bearing but maybe Epp had chosen an altogether better line. Richard is a canny sort of chap with a nose for trouble. At the bottom of the couloir, he alone had taken the precaution of putting on his *harscheisen* – a ski crampon that fits between boot and binding to give your skis bite on icy ground when the skins alone can no longer grip. The rest of us had simply pressed on regardless but higher up, where the wind had swept the upper slopes clean of snow to an icy undersurface, Richard was still climbing securely and steadily whereas Alan, Nick and I were all over the place, slipping and sliding backwards in our tracks.

Even on a level playing field, the business of putting on *harscheisen* is fiddly enough – but try doing this half way up a 40 degree ice slope. You go through an elaborate balancing act standing on one ski at exactly the right point of balance while taking off the other and then, teetering on one foot, fixing one *harscheisen* between boot sole and binding. You then repeat the process praying that you don't drop your *harscheisen* or fall off the mountain.

Richard had got it right. After some heart thumping manoeuvres, which wasted much time, Alan, Nick and I gave the *harscheisen* game away, took off our skis, strapped them to our sacs and kicked steps all the way to the top of the couloir.

Cols are invariably the coldest, windiest and most inconvenient places to do all the things that are unavoidably necessary when you reach them – like taking off and packing away skins and *harscheisen,* adjusting boots, bindings and clothing and checking that you are still on route. Breasting this one was like going over the top and being hit by a hail of ice pellets. The ground felt unfamiliar but when I saw that the other side was uncorniced and fell away at an angle rather than vertically, I took it that we had reached an intermediate col and not the dreaded Col d'Ayous whose crossing had been exercising my mind since early morning.

Richard was waiting for us at the top like some marble statue – impassive, patient and chilled to the marrow. He, more than any of us, was desperately anxious to get off this miserable place as quickly as possible before hypothermia set in. Now he had to endure another wait while we laggards put on skis and *harscheisen.* To do this I had to take off my over-mittens but, as they had become frozen solid, I had to ask Alan to yank them off for me. When I touched the aluminium *harscheisen*, my bare fingers stuck fast to the metal.

Richard was now looking so miserable that I shouted in his ear: "For God's sake don't hang around here – it's too effing cold. Go on ahead and wait for us at the bottom."

"I'll see you down there," he shouted back.

We can't have been more than minutes behind him but by the time we reached the bottom, he was nowhere to be seen. Visibility was down to five metres so all we could do was to bellow, "Richard, Richard". We could have shouted ourselves hoarse for nothing was going to carry in that wind and I thought to myself: how the Devil are we going to find him? He's completely vanished. Instinctively, we closed in on each other and, spreading out to arm's length, slowly moved forward in line to sweep the ground. In that whiteout and driving snow which caked our goggles in ice, we could have passed within metres of Richard yet completely failed to have seen him. Minutes passed like hours. We went into a huddle but intelligible conversation was impossible. My imagination was racing and jumping to all sorts of conclusions. Richard was an experienced mountaineer but anyone could get totally disorientated in this whiteout and wander off course. The Col d'Ayous couldn't be that far away and he might easily have blundered on, reached the Col d'Ayous and walked over a cornice.

Mountain lore is a catalogue of natural and unnatural phenomenon. Mountaineers will tell you strange tales of broken spectres, invisible companions, Yeti, Old Grey Men and the like but, for me, nothing was ever more miraculous than the sight of Richard's snow-encrusted figure looming out the blizzard. It was if he had been delivered to us from the grave. We pummelled his back to prove his reality and went into yet another huddle, inter-twining our arms around each other's shoulders out of sheer relief.

"The Col must be very close now," I yelled hoarsely, "Let's press on but if we can't find it soon, we must turn back."

This was just a re-run of what we had agreed over breakfast. In that shrieking wind nobody heard me but we all knew that we had to keep moving or freeze in our tracks so we broke the magic circle and shuffled on abreast through the storm.

My eyes had been so fixed on my compass that I almost walked into the signpost. It suddenly appeared in front of me as the cloud momentarily lifted, looking like a weathercock that had sprouted horizontal icicles. I waved my ski sticks above my head and yelled at the top of my voice, "We've made it. We've made the Col!"

I couldn't believe it but we had hit the Col d'Ayous spot on. The signpost could only mark the top of the summer path where it emerges from its zig-zagging ascent from the bottom of the cirque.

Their faces were expressionless behind their goggled masks but Alan, ever pragmatic, cupped his hands and shouted back: "I'll take a belay here to get you through the cornice."

The cloud closed in again but I knew exactly where we were and it took eight minutes precisely for Alan and me to sink two pairs of skis up to their bindings into the snow for a belay; fix a rope sling around them and thread through the climbing rope. In securing the knot to tie myself on, I had had to take off my overmitts and, by the time I had finished, my fingers had gone white and numb. Alan saw what was happening and quickly beat some feeling back into them. Belayed by Alan, I launched myself backwards over the edge of the cornice, slashing at it with my ice axe and kicking inwards to carve a passage through it. Almost immediately, I was under the cornice eaves sheltered from the wind and took a quick compass bearing on where the map showed the Ayous Hut to be. The others soon joined me and we inched our way downwards through thigh-deep snow as great chunks of it broke away from under our skis to disappear noiselessly to invisible depths.

There were no more miraculous cloud clearings after that. We could have passed within ten metres of the Ayous Hut without even noticing it but when its triangular profile reared up before me like a ship's prow cutting through sea fog, I shouted out triumphantly – "Thar she blows."

We had made it! I felt a huge surge of relief. For one blissful moment, nothing else in life seemed to matter.

Our hut-coming was a very different affair from that of the Eagles. There would be no hut guardian haring up from Gabas to open up the main hut which was now secured impregnable behind a quarter inch steel door. But what did that matter? The winter room was an iron box equipped with nothing except four steel framed sleeping berths. It might have fitted the needs of a smaller party exactly but when the six foot two inch Alan and six foot four inch Nick tried their bunks for size they both overshot by several inches. Yet we didn't give a damn. As we made seats of our sacs, swigging tea and treating ourselves to a double ration of porridge cakes, we just felt inordinately pleased with ourselves. We had cracked a key passage guideless and, in making the crossing from the Larry Hut in three hours through a blizzard, had easily outflown the Eagles.

Next morning, I was again woken by Alan. His mood was very different from what it had been the day before.

"Take a look at this," he shouted back at us from outside the hut, "It's bloody *FANTASTIC!*"

The sun had not yet reached us and the inside of the hut's steel walls were coated in rime. Alan was framed in the doorway, standing barefoot in the snow in nothing but his longjohns. When he spoke, his breath came out in frozen puffs.

I leapt out of my sleeping bag to join him. We both stared to the east to where two black tusks were silhouetted against the dawning sky.

"The twin summits of the Pic du Midi d'Ossau," I gasped.

It was the first sunlit morning I had ever experienced in the Pyrenees in winter. All that any of us wanted now was to be up and away from this cramped ice box, out into the sunlight, free to ski the powder. Yesterday, we had seemed to be moving in slow motion. Today, our tempo changed to *prestissimo*. We swigged down some tea, half digested a lump of porridge cake and made ready for the off. Emerging from the hut for the second time, I recoiled from the glare. Only minutes ago, the valley had been in shadow but now it had become an incandescent bowl of dazzling white. Yesterday our world had been all noise and commotion. Today there was silence. The blizzard had left a pristine landscape in which each individual snow crystal had been preserved in its perfect symmetry. The wind had sculpted the snow on the frozen lake at our feet into a pattern of whorled ripples. Beyond the lake's lip the ground fell away in a motionless swell of white whalebacks. Huge snow mountains, previously invisible to us, rose up from the base of the cirque. Away to the north the steely ridges of a distant range lit luminous in the sun were etched against the sky. Never before had I seen the Pyrenees look as beautiful as this. Never again did they look quite the same.

Nick had somehow climbed up onto the roof of the hut on ski, and now bestrode its ridge like a colossus. Poised like a bird, he then let out a triumphal yodel before launching himself off and sped off down the valley with the rest of us following behind like a wolf pack. The snow was perfect. All three of us stuck fast to the heels of our moniteur – curving, carving and roller-coastering in his wake; sheering and chancing our way past the chasmic *gouffres* – bottomless limestone potholes – that lie in wait for the unwary. It was the first decent ski run I had ever had in the Pyrenees and as we powered on down the valley in rhythmic harmony it exorcised a great chunk of uncertainty.

That run to the bottom of the valley not only lifted our spirits but released our energies. This was just as well because from now on it would mostly be uphill for the rest of the day. I well remembered the steep, rock walled gully that three years ago had seemed such a tedious flog through heavy snow but we had struck a high note at the start and the hard packed and wind polished surface now became a challenge. We reached the top without stopping, criss-crossing the couloir with a flourish of zigzag traverses.

I looked back across the three kilometre gulf that separated us from the cirque of cliffs above the hut. It was scarcely visible now. Just a black dot in the snow below an enormous wall of snow and ice. I could scarcely believe that we had threaded a way down that wall through that blizzard.

Eastwards was a still more dramatic sight. The fairy tale Pic du Midi d'Ossau rose barely two kilometres away from where we were standing, its western face black in shadow and its crenellated summit crowned with snow. As I stared at those *verglassed* walls and ridges, I reckoned that, once again, this would be a mountain too far for us.

It took an hour to dig out the door of the Pombie Hut. It had been over-whelmed by snow and the inside was filled to table top level. When we reached floor level there was nothing but accumulated filth. The place had been neglected and the pot-bellied stove had vanished. It was cold and damp inside but outside, the sun was too fierce to sit around in comfort. To conserve our own fuel, we shovelled heaps of snow onto the hot tin roof. It quickly melted and ran down the corrugations from where we filled pots and pans and water bottles.

Halfway through the afternoon, three young Spaniards fetched up with food for a month and a quiver full of foot-long ice pitons. They were the first winter mountaineers I had ever come across in the Pyrenees and, having got used to having the huts to ourselves, selfishly resented their presence.

Usually, there's *bonhomie* between men in mountains even when neither side speaks the other's language but these three were totally preoccupied with their climbing plans and made no effort to communicate. We got their drift when they kept pointing to an ugly looking *dièdre* backed by a dribble of ice running up the length of the Pic's west face. They spent the rest of the day poring over a battered French guidebook laboriously translating its route description and then copying it out in Spanish with a pencil stub onto the back of an empty cheese carton while we played interminable rounds of Oh Hell. Yet they knew how to look after themselves better than we did. I would have swopped their *tapas* and *paella* for our packet soup and porridge cake any day. When the cold became unendurable, all seven of us trooped upstairs and huddled up together on the communal bunk. They reeked of garlic but our collective body temperatures were raised by several degrees and gave the bed bugs a feast.

The brave Spaniards never started their climb for by early morning it was blowing another blizzard. I felt I had been here before and, as we sat around morosely sipping sweet tea, thought back to the composed efficiency of Michael's Orders Groups. We would have to sort this one out for ourselves and make our own choice whether to stick or twist.

"I don't fancy sitting around in this freezing hut for the next couple of days," I began warily. "I'm for making the break for Gabas while we still can."

"But what about the Pic du Midi," demanded Alan. "I thought you wanted to knock it off?"

"Maybe in decent conditions," I replied, "but I can't see how we can climb anything in this weather. It looks completely set in. What does anyone else think?"

"Agreed that we'll probably have to forget about the pic for today," continued Alan, "but this storm looks appalling. The pressure's still falling and I don't fancy another Col d'Ayous epic. Why can't we stay here until the weather improves? We can surely stick it out here for a couple more days and then climb the pic."

"For one thing we're practically out of food." I replied. "Our main cache is waiting for us at Gabas. Another is that we're not here just to climb peaks but to traverse to Gavarnie."

"Is that so?" said Alan as if I had issued a challenge.

The Val d'Ayous. Morning after the storm

"Yes," I replied, "we don't want to get bogged down by the weather. That's just what happened to the Eagles."

That was neither true nor fair but I knew that the comparison would rile him and he didn't reply.

"What's this route like down to Gabas?" asked Richard mollifyingly.

This question had also been exercising my mind ever since I had poked my head out of the hut door that morning and slammed it quickly behind me. It was one thing to hit off the Col d'Ayous on a relatively simple compass bearing but the route to the Col Suzon was a touch more complicated and the col itself, icy and steep both ways, had clipped several Eagle wings.

"The Col Suzon's steep," I replied guardedly, "but it's fine once we're over it and down the other side."

"Okay," said Alan suddenly, "let's give it a go but let's get moving."

The Spaniards were still sitting silently around the table as we slipped the hut during a short lull in the weather. They didn't even say a*dios* but some way down the valley, a faint whisper on the wind seemed to be following us: *"Altimetro, altimetro …"*

"Listen. I can hear something," said Alan, wheeling round in his ski tracks. "I think it's those bloody Spaniards. What the hell are they shouting about."

"Where's your altimeter, Al?" broke in Nick as if he were clairvoyant.

Alan owned the expedition's only altimeter, a simplistic Japanese model which he had ingeniously calibrated in feet by super-imposing over the altimeter's metric scale his own milled version. It was quite indispensable.

"Bloody hell!" said Alan searching through his pockets, "I must have left the damned thing behind in the hut on the table."

"I'll nip back and get it," volunteered Nick and, like all dutiful younger brothers, slogged all the way back to the hut to pick it up. Never again did we speak ill of Spanish climbers.

The blizzard really closed in upon us after that lucky break and, as we climbed higher and higher on a compass bearing through near zero visibility, the wind got stronger and stronger. When its pitch crescendoed to a scream and the aluminium edges of my *harscheisen* started to grate on ice, I knew we must be near to Col Suzon. We were back to the business of bawling into each other's ears.

"John, have you the slightest idea where we are?" Alan yelled.

"We're almost at the col," I yelled back. "Let's check our height with your altimeter."

He struggled to fish it out of his trouser pocket while I yanked at my anorak pocket for the plastic envelope protecting my map. We put our heads together.

"Something wrong here," he bellowed jabbing his finger at the altimeter scale, "this altimeter's registering 25 metres higher than your map's spot height. Either we've climbed too high or there's been a big fall in barometric pressure since we started."

In a 90-kilometre wind, very unusual qualities are required to conduct a rational discussion about relative spot and barometric pressures. It flashed through my mind that we might have landed up in completely the wrong place.

"Could be something wrong with your Jap altimeter," I yelled back though I didn't really believe it.

It might have been possible to protract this debate a fraction longer but, before he had time to reply, I saw something out of the corner of my eye dropping like a stone.

A moment ago, Nick had been closing in right behind us. Now you see him, now you don't.

"Christ, Alan, where's Nick gone!" I bawled out.

We both kick turned our skis simultaneously and peered down the slope. For a second or two I couldn't see a thing but then I spotted a blurred shape in the scud below moving very slowly.

Please, I thought, let it be Nick. But if he's bust a leg here we're in real trouble.

We had already started to climb down when the shape below took on a recognisably human form and began waving its ski sticks. Nick came up to join us very carefully.

"Sorry about that one," he grinned ruefully. "Hit a patch of gravel on the way down and it stopped me short."

He had fallen on his luck. Without that gravel patch he could never have stopped himself on the ice and would have gone all the way to the bottom.

When all four of us were together again I took a few more steps to the north and realised that the ground was beginning to fall away.

"This has to be the Col Suzon," I yelled back, "we've made it."

We closed up again and Alan shouted, "Okay – but where do we go from here?"

The cloud was so thick that I couldn't work out whether we were near the middle of the col or, as seemed quite possible from Alan's altimeter reading, nearer one of the edges which overlooked steep rock bluffs. Dead ahead, left or right? It was anyone's guess but following my instinct I pointed one stick forward and confidently shouted "straight ahead" as we launched ourselves off the corniced lip like men blindfolded.

I had forgotten quite how steep it was – and icy too. Like stepping onto a wall.

To keep some semblance of control, we were still wearing skins and *harscheisen* but didn't use the rope, for a slip here would have been impossible to check. Hunched and crab-like, punching in each step with the ski's full length with all my weight over it, I didn't dare look about me to see what the others were making of it. Each of us was wrapped up in his own individual battle for survival.

Forty minutes on, the angle began to ease and the tension fell away. We reached a fold of the valley where the wind lost its bite and then, as the cloud began to lift, I recognised familiar ground. Once across the Col Long de Magnabait, kick turns saw us safely through the metre-deep, leg-breaking snow of the Bious-Artigues forest and so on down to Gabas.

Save for ourselves, the dining-room of the Hotel de Biscau was deserted. One of the greatest miracles of French culture is that even in the darkest recesses of the close season, the chef of this tiny hotel could produce a slap up lunch of soup, *saucissons variés et crudités*, beefsteak and chips and Pyrenean pudding. For days, we had dreamed of meals like this and now we gorged ourselves, spinning it out to within two hours of dinner. After a short tea break, I had reckoned I could still go the full dinner distance with the chef's *menu complet,* but when it came to it, our stomachs had shrunk and even Nick stagged on the second course.

Not that it mattered. Not that anything much mattered. Propping up the Biscau's bar surrounded by an array of empty beer bottles we were worlds away from cols, blizzards and huts. We were also feeling inordinately smug. In crossing from Urdos to Gabas, we had flown faster than the guided Eagles and done the distance in equally bad weather. Nothing could stop us now. Gavarnie – here we come!

The morning we reached Gabas in time for lunch had been one of life's high points. The flush of success and the delights of the table had left our cups overfull. It was therefore all the harder to understand why, within a mere twenty-four hours, morale should have plunged to its nadir. Walking into dinner last night, I had wondered why Richard had been walking askew. By breakfast, he was listing heavily to port and his face looked strained.

"Anything the matter, Richard?" I asked him anxiously, "You don't look too good."

"I'm afraid I've fixed my back," he replied apologetically. "It's an old complaint but when we made that nasty descent from the Col Suzon, I felt something go. When I woke this morning, it had gone quite rigid."

"That sounds bad. D'you think you can carry on? The weather's none too good. We could always rest up here for a day."

"Sorry, John, but I don't think so. At best I would slow you down, at worst we could have an epic. It's altogether too risky to continue. I'm afraid I'll have to get home."

It took a moment or two for this to sink in. I had had to abandon my first Pyrenean ski tour at exactly this point and knew exactly how Richard must be feeling. We had counted our chickens too early last night and been altogether too pleased with ourselves. After hubris, nemesis.

To lose Richard – so steady, so dependable – was a blow for him but also a serious setback for the rest of us. The safety angle had always worried me about this tour. Small parties may be faster but as a rule of thumb, the bigger the party, the wider your safety margin to cope with an avalanche or rescue. The standard French Mountain Gendarmerie mountain rescue team comprises eight to ten specially trained mountaineers. Four was the minimum number I had been prepared to go down to for the simple reason that, in case of accident, two can go for help, leaving one to stay behind with the casualty. A party of only three leaves itself very exposed.

We sat around the empty bar. Last night, this had been the scene of our celebrations. Now, with the snow coming down outside like a grey blind, it had begun to look like a seedy dive. It had never entered my calculations that we would be losing anyone at this or any other stage of the tour. I was now at a complete loss to know what to suggest. I desperately wanted to carry on but with Richard injured that seemed neither right nor sensible. Anyway, this sort of decision had to be made jointly. Effectively, it now rested with Alan, for if he was in favour of continuing, Nick would follow suit.

"What d'you reckon Alan?" I began tentatively, "With Richard having to go home, I'm not sure where we go from here."

"It's bloody bad luck," he replied, "but just now, I don't know what we can do. This weather looks terrible and, unless it clears, we can't do anything today. It would also be stretching things to carry on with only three of us. Overall, I would be in favour of sticking around here, day touring and climbing a peak or two."

"But don't you want to go on with the traverse?" I pressed. "We must at least get to the Wallon Hut."

"Ask Nick what he feels about it," he replied non-committally.

"What do you want to do, Nick?" I asked, well knowing his answer in advance.

"I'm happy to go along with Al," he replied.

Things seemed to be slipping away from us and I felt powerless to do anything about it. Our mood swing might be temporary and merely reflect this dreadful weather but I couldn't allow things to grind to a halt. I then glimpsed the obvious.

"Let's ask Monsieur Morrell for a weather forecast before we take a final decision," I suggested brightly.

Monsieur Morrell, the Biscau's proprietor, was sitting behind his reception desk twiddling his thumbs and looking thoroughly bored. Apart from us, he had no other guests and was obviously dying for a chat.

"Bonjour Monsieur. S'il vous plaît, comment la météo aujourd'hui?" I ventured, hoping that he might speak English. *"Très mauvais,"* he said with relish *"C'est normal pour la saison. Mais oui – il pourrait continuer indéfiniment!"*

"However," he continued, getting the drift of my accent and grammatical construction, "I myself am not a mountaineer nor a meteorologist. You should consult Monsieur Dodu."

"Who is he?" I gasped with relief.

"Monsieur Dodu is the doyen of our local guides," he replied with pride. "He is the guardian of the *Club Alpin Français* refuge at the end of the village. It is not far from here. Monsieur Dodu can surely help you."

As we wandered up the road through a fine, persistent sleet, I wondered why neither the guidebook nor map had made any reference to this distinguished personage or his establishment. We might even have saved ourselves a few bob staying there.

The man who answered the refuge's door bell was squat and weathered. He might have been of any age.

I had rehearsed my introduction on the way up and now delivered it quite fluently.

"Bonjour Monsieur. Nous sommes une équipe anglais – randonneurs de ski," I began confidently.

"Mais oui," he replied laconically.

"Nous espérons faire une route à Gavarnie," I continued, *"mais première-ment, nous voudrions grimper le Pic du Midi d'Ossau – par la voie normale,"* I added quickly.

Monsieur Dodu looked at us quizzically and when he spoke, it was as if he were conducting some kind of kindergarten lesson. *"Mais en hiver, ce n'est pas prudent – cette voie normale est la plus dangéreuse du Pic!"*

Not such a good start but I had written off the Pic du Midi anyway. I would now try another tack and ask him about the route that I had planned to take us to the Penalara Hut in Spain via the formidable Brèche Latour. This way we might even bag the biggest local mountain, the Balaitous, on the way.

"Monsieur – qu'est-ce que c'est le BALAITOUS? C'est un pic formidable n'est-ce pas? Peut être vous pouvez nous recommender faire une petite escalade à Balaitous? Enfin, après ça, il nous sera possible de déscendre au Refuge Penalara en Espagne?"

It wasn't simply my French that was losing us credibility. Monsieur Dodu had begun to look at us warily.

"Non, Monsieur. Absolument NON. Maintenant, le Balaitous est très dangéreux: c'est impossible," he said, slowly shaking his head.

I wasn't getting anywhere and patently Monsieur Dodu wasn't taking us seriously. Somehow, I had to get it across to him that this was an *équipe* of serious ski mountaineers. I would spell it out that we knew what we were doing and were going to get to the Penalara Hut across the Brèche Latour, which happened to be the only route mentioned in the guidebook. Now we would show him our credentials. According to the guidebook, the Brèche Latour was a real challenge – *"du domaine de l'alpinisme classique."*

"Alors," I raised my voice a fraction, *"Qu'est-ce que c'est la Brèche Latour? C'est formidable n'est pas? Nous proposons la Brèche Latour. Vous nous recommendez la Breche Latour?"*

Suddenly, Monsieur Dodu lost his composure as if I had uttered some indescribably foul oath or insulted his mother's parentage.

"La Brèche Latour? La Brèche Latour!" he exploded jumping to his feet. Then, spitting out an unfamiliar expletive, he pointed both index fingers towards his ears and began describing simultaneous corkscrew movements with both his arms at right angles.

"Non, non Monsieur. C'est FOU, FOU, FOU … C'est imbécile," he intoned, his voice rising, *"c'est une idée idiote!"*

I had blown it. The conference was ended but, as he showed us the door, he softened a little.

"Revenez ici ce soir, Monsieur," he said kindly. *"Je vais vous reporter la toute dernière prévision de la météo. Aussi, peut être que je pourrai vous proposer une route alternative à la Penalara en Espagne."*

No one had much to say as we walked back to the Biscau through a morass of discoloured slush. After Richard's taxi for Pau had come and gone, the three of us settled down in the bar for our usual fix of Oh Hell but the spark had left us and, after a couple of rounds, we sat around in silence, thumbing through last season's dog-eared French magazines. It was snowing seriously now with mounds of the stuff piling up against the window sills. Yesterday, the Biscau had seemed like a haven. Now it felt like a prison. Yesterday's lunch had seemed ambrosial but today's commonplace with the wine tasting like old leather.

For want of anything better to do, we made an afternoon recce up the valley. By the time we reached the Artouste dam the snow had turned to sleet and we came back soaked through. Walking through the hotel door, Alan turned to me and said, "Looks to me as if a proper thaw's setting in. I don't think much of all this. Why don't we drive to Chamonix and do some proper ski touring?"

I was about to make some flip reply but, when I looked at him, I realised that he was only half in jest.

That evening, after a short nap, we pulled ourselves together and walked back up the road to Monsieur Dodu's establishment. This time, he welcomed us in with a smile and was altogether more forthcoming. Apparently, more snow had fallen down here in the valley than higher up. Tomorrow's forecast wasn't all that bad and with luck we should reach the Arremoulit Hut.

"*Et après ça?*" I asked eagerly.

"*C'est un jeu de hasard!*" he joked, "*Bonne chance. Mais la Brèche de Latour, Monsieur? ... Non, Non, Non!*"

"*Mais Monsieur,*" I pressed, remembering that he had promised to tell us about his alternative route into Spain, "*Comment va la route alternative au Refuge Penalara?*"

He seemed to have forgotten this bit and became pensive.

"*Mais oui Monsieur. Il y a une route exceptionelle et très belle.*"

He then launched out on a route description. Apparently, from the Arremoulit Hut we must climb to the Col Palas and from there make a four kilometres descent due south down the Arriel Valley to the Paso de la Pena from which the Penalara Hut was only another four kilometres due east. To illustrate his route, he scrawled a squiggle on my map with a pencil stub and added that, if we were really fast, we might even reach the Wallon Hut that same night.

"*Mais chers Messieurs,*" he grinned with a slight shake of the head, "*C'est une course très longue.*" Then, as if it were an after-thought, "*Mais prenez garde au-dessous du Pic d'Arriel.*"

He stood up abruptly to indicate that the audience was over. We shook his horny hand one by one, blurting out our thanks before filing out into the night.

"*Merci Monsieur Dodu ... Merci infiniment.*"

Back at the hotel, I took another look at Ollivier's guide book to see if anything tallied. Ollivier recommended only two ski routes to the Wallon Hut from the Arremoulit. The easier one went eastwards via the Port du Lavedan and Larribet Hut and the other, via the Penalara, crossed the Brèche Latour. There was no mention of the Arriel Valley or of any route down it and once beyond the frontier into Spain, the detailed contouring on my French IGN map disappeared.

Next morning, it looked as if Monsieur Dodu could be right about the weather. Although the sky was still overcast, it had at least stopped snowing. We loaded our sacs with enough lightweight food that, in theory, should see us through the next seven days with the emphasis on accelerated freeze-dried (AFD) stews, soup, dried fruit, tea, sugar and kilos of porridge cake. One week's food represented our maximum range and was made possible by Madame's son kindly agreeing to dump fifteen pounds of surplus kit at Pau. He then saved us another two hours by driving us eight kilometres up the Brousset Valley until his Citroen was stopped by the discoloured snout of an enormous avalanche, which had completely severed the road and climbed 50 metres up the other side of the valley.

For the first time, I was on entirely new ground.

Just beyond the deserted hamlet of Socques, a signpost pointed the way – *"Arremoulit Refuge: 4h."*

"Only four hours worth!" exclaimed Nick, "can't be that bad."

It sounded like an easy day but summer walking times are misleading and I remembered that a similar four-hour signpost time to the Col d'Ayous had taken the Eagles eight hours.

"Don't bank on it Nick," I replied, "we've got over 1,100 metres to climb to the Arremoulit Hut. This could be quite a long haul."

Beneath its carpet of snow, the summer path left a faint impression as it threaded through the beechwoods to a crude log bridge spanning the frozen Arrious River. As we emerged from the forest, a powerfully built animal with cat-like tread and long legs purposefully crossed the open ground just below us. I stopped in my tracks but, before I could pull out my camera, it caught our scent and made off up the hill in a series of bounds before vanishing into the trees. We had just seen a lynx – an animal as rare in the Pyrenees as the near-extinct brown bear.

Higher up the Arrious Valley, tatters of blue sky emerged through the clouds and, for the first time in days, the mountain tops became visible through retreating wreaths of mist. A long way above us, two tiny figures were moving down the hillside carving synchronised turns in unison.

"Must be Frenchmen," muttered Alan. "Frog ski randonneurs. Bit flashy."

They certainly looked good, these French ski mountaineers – the first of their kind I had actually met in the Pyrenees.

They stopped just below us in a billow of snow and gave a friendly greeting. Apparently, they had been holed up at the Arremoulit Hut for the past three days in the bad weather and were now making their escape.

"Comment est le refuge Arremoulit?" I asked solicitously.

"Le refuge? Le refuge, c'est très froid," one of them grinned, *"Bonne chance Messieurs!"*

They vanished down the valley before we had had a chance to chat further but we too wanted to push on. We took a break at the Cabane Arrious, a hut I had once earmarked as an intermediate stop-over if the weather had turned bad on us. Just as well it hadn't. Nothing remained of the cabane but a snow-filled shell. An avalanche had completely demolished it.

Earlier in the day, I had imagined we were going quite strongly but, by the time we reached the 2,463 metre col from which the Arremoulit Hut's black oblong shape first came into view, we had fallen hours behind the advertised signpost time. The day had slipped us by and the long climb had sapped our strength. That last undulating stretch to the hut, up and down a succession of soft snow humps which had looked so easy from the col, took over an hour. It was already dusk when Alan and I began to hack a hole through the ice of the snow-covered lake to draw water with the hut's heavy pickaxe. A metre down, it seeped through the mush like seawater filling a sand hole. I felt drained of energy and no warmer for the exercise. Even Alan, who never seemed to tire, was looking wan.

Although built of reinforced concrete and uncompromisingly utilitarian, the Arremoulit Hut's arched roof retained an incongruous hint of Gothic. An afterglow of burning gold touched the rim of snow peaks surrounding the hut but once inside the cold was deathly. No ready cut pile of logs to await us here but neither was there a stove or cooking pots and pans. Inadvertently, Richard must have taken our complete set home with him. In our one remaining billy, I boiled up a packet of AFD stew tasting of nothing but monosodium glutamate. We ate in silence before curling up in our sleeping bags to face the night.

Could this, I wondered, really be Easter Sunday, the most holy day of the Christian calendar? I had just woken from a ghastly nightmare involving domestic crisis, death and probate and felt as if I had been through purgatory. Or perhaps I was still in passage? I couldn't understand why my watch should be showing 7.30 am when it was still as black as night. Then I rumbled. The snow had drifted over the hut's windows and blocked out all light. I eased myself out of my sleeping bag and tiptoed to the door across a floor that was now patterned with traceries of spindrift blown in through cracks between the door jambs and the leaky window frames.

"What's it like outside?" grunted Alan.

I took a quick look through a crack in the door and then smartly slammed it shut.

"It's blowing an effing blizzard," I groaned.

Pic du Midi d'Ossau

"Thank God for that," said Alan, burrowing deep into his sleeping bag, "I won't have to budge an inch until it stops."

That set the scene. In a decent tent you can usually build up a fug whatever the outside temperature but, in a concrete box, you just get colder and colder. The temperature never rose above zero for the snow on our boots never melted.

It was a pity that we couldn't be bothered to get up even to make breakfast. Although I took little pleasure chomping through my regulation chunk of porridge cake, it would have got the circulation going and filled in a small part of the day. Without a stove it was too cold to sit around so I also lay in my sleeping bag and gleaned from the tattered hut book that only two British parties had passed this way in three years. For the rest, I spun out the time by re-reading the guidebook, writing up my diary and, then, overcome with guilt for not spending this Easter with my family, composed a poem to my wife.

Alan and Nick slept on and off wrapped in their own private worlds. At the start of the tour, we had cheerfully played cards for hours even though the result was invariably the same. Whatever Oh Hell variant was chosen, Alan always seemed to make the right bids but the Arremoulit was too cold for cards even when lying in our sleeping bags. Good humour was also in short supply and desultory conversation deteriorated into a series of unconnected anecdotes.

I was on the fringes of sleep when I heard Alan and Nick quietly discussing short-cuts and opt-outs. I switched on again with a jolt but didn't join the conversation. It made me feel isolated and wary. Surely, I thought to myself, having got this far, we can't possibly disengage now just because we've hit another patch of bad weather?

An uneasy silence had fallen between us. Patently, we couldn't go anywhere in a blizzard but there was no point in simply lying around in a comatose stupor getting colder and more depressed. Someone had to break the mood set and when Nick got up to make a brew I suggested to them both – "Let's get outside and dig away the snow from the windows. We might even see some light."

"What's the point in doing that, John?" Alan grunted from his pit. "If this blizzard continues the snow will simply cover them up again."

"Might at least warm us up a bit," I persisted, "What about you, Nick?"

"Fine by me," he replied cheerfully, "Let's have a go."

We put on all our clothes and walked outside armed with a couple of massive snow shovels. Snow was blowing in horizontally from the north west and had completely buried the leeward side of the hut. As Alan had predicted, as fast as we cleared the snow, the blizzard built up again.

"Nick," I grunted after half an hour's hard work, "this is a no win situation. Let's pack it in."

As we began walking back to the door, three figures loomed up through the murk, plastered from head to foot in snow and rime and marched purposefully towards the hut. A patrol of Mountain Gendarmerie on a rescue mission perhaps? Who else would be crazy enough to come up in this weather?

They flung open the door and walked straight in as if they owned the place. As they brushed themselves down, the leader introduced the other two.

"Bonjour Messieurs – Comment ça va! Je suis Maurice ... ma femme, Michelle, et mon ami Patrick."

Alan rolled out of his sleeping bag unkempt and unshaven. All three of us must have looked dreadful and somewhat grudgingly took turns to introduce ourselves.

"Ah, so you're English," said Maurice with only the hint of an accent.

"We're from Toulouse. We've just come up from Gabas. Welcome to the Arremoulit!"

Maurice, Michelle and Patrick extended their hands towards us, smiling enthusiastically, willing us to be friends.

"How on earth did you manage to get here through this terrific storm?" I asked Maurice.

"We're locals," he replied with a grin as he unzipped his over-trousers, "I'm a dentist by profession but we know these mountains like our backyard. We make *ski randonnées* most weekends."

With a proprietorial air, he went quickly to the back of the hut and with Patrick's help prised up a couple of floorboards. Like some magician performing a trick, he pulled out a heavy wooden box.

"Oup la!" he exclaimed. "Have a bottle of beer. It's icy cold. Go on, help yourselves."

The box was stuffed with tinned foods, bottles of wine and a twelve pack of Stella Artois.

For the best part of that day, we had barely bumped along the bottom. From the moment they arrived, this French trio lightened our darkness like the sun bursting through the clouds and transformed the soured atmosphere. Food is the one subject you never stop thinking about. To keep down weight our staple diet for breakfast, lunch and supper had been porridge cake – a glutinous mixture of oats, honey, syrup and raisins lovingly concocted by Alan's wife Janet. It was so concentrated and nutritious that a couple of bars contained enough calories to keep most systems working for an entire day. However, it never made my gastric juices flow and when I saw the Toulousiennes wolfing down *soupe à l'homard, boeuf en daube, Bresse Bleu* and biscuits with a couple of bottles of Bordeaux, I developed a porridge cake allergy. As they tucked into dinner chatting away, laughing, joking and so obviously enjoying themselves, I felt a twinge of envy.

Maurice must have noticed it for he turned to me in his chair and said sympathetically.

"John, my friend, we must always enjoy the mountains. Let's all drink a toast. *Brava la vie montagne!*"

There was no question as to which of us had the right attitude. We had more to learn from these Frenchmen than mere beer and the pot of Pyrenean honey they donated towards our breakast. Gallic verve and bonhomie had dispelled a bad bout of British bile.

"What are your plans for tomorrow?" I asked Maurice after supper.

"Naturally, it all depends on the weather," he replied. "However, if it's fine, we'll be heading for the Larribet Hut for one night and after that the Wallon before we go home. We're only here for *Pâques*. What about you?"

I explained our plans and we compared routes. Theirs, clearly marked and numbered on the IGN ski map, went north eastwards. Ours, or rather Monsieur Dodu's, went due south into Spain.

"I've never heard of that one," said Maurice dubiously, "but it sounds interesting. At least we'll all be together as far as the Col Palas."

I took another careful look at the map and wondered afresh what we were letting ourselves in for.

We woke to the first fine clear day we had enjoyed since leaving the Ayous Hut. The sun was shining, the air was like ice and the sky indigo blue. Both parties set off together in a friendly race for the sunlit Col de Palas. The French were disciplined, rhythmic and climbing as a team: the British trio strung out in a ragged line. Yet every heart was singing and when we closed up at the col we were genuinely sorry to say goodbye to our new found friends.

"Au revoir, Maurice, Michelle, Patrick ... Bonne chance ... A bientôt!"

Vigorous hand shakes, back slapping, a quick kiss for the petite Michelle and a final obligatory round of group photographs. Reluctant to be parted, we hung around the Col de Palas as we watched them traversing gingerly along the lip of the enormous snow bowl banked up against the headwall of the Pic Palas's south face. Onward bound for the Col de Lavedon, their three retreating figures were dwarfed by the scale of the landscape yet, as old Pyrenean hands, they knew exactly what they were doing and where they were heading. By contrast, we had only the vaguest idea. As they drew away into the distance, it occurred to me that we might have done better to be following them.

Due south, the ground below us fell away like the trough of a rolling wave. I peered beyond its convex plunge and could just about trace a line of descent to where the upper valley flattened out into the cup of a snow-covered lake.

Lake and valley then merged as one into a narrow neck of rock which disappeared into a dark gorge. It looked a most improbable route but when I re-checked the map for the umpteenth time I could see that this was the only way down.

Spain lay at our feet. No time to re-hash plans now but wasn't this exactly what we had come for? You can do a thousand runs down the piste yet never remember one of them. A virgin ski descent is like a new mountaineering route. You can't tell how it will go until you've tried it but once done you'll never forget it.

I went through the old familiar routine – packing away my skins and *harscheisen* into my rucksack; re-adjusting my bindings to the downhill position; tightening my boots and zipping up all my pockets. When I looked expectantly across to Alan and Nick, they were already poised to go. I jumped up and down a few times to loosen up; leaned into my boots and took a deep breath. Right then. This was it.

"Everyone ready," I shouted across to them. "Okay, let's go, go, go …"

I shot forward faster than I had expected. The snow felt iron hard and the speed I immediately picked up took me by surprise.

Take it easy, I muttered to myself. Don't rush it … Watch that first turn.

You never know how the snow's going to run until you're on it but I didn't have to worry this time. Once off the lip of the col the sun had melted the top centimetre, leaving the base hard and solid. This was true *firn* – the stuff of skiers' dreams.

On the col, the sun had been burning my face but once launched on our way the icy air caught my breath. Already, all three of us were flashing down an immense snow slope in long sweeping turns. It felt like going over a frozen waterfall whose bottom was still invisible.

Watch out for that convex section beneath the cliffs and keep clear of those rocks, I muttered to myself.

Within seconds we had dropped 300 metres and were running parallel to a frozen lake – the Lac Arriel. From here there was only one way down – straight across it. Our skis hit the ice with a clatter and the impact and sudden acceleration threw my weight back. For a moment I thought I had lost balance and would crash.

For God's sake get your weight forward or you'll really damage yourself.

My thighs were screaming but we couldn't stop. Barely in control we hurtled on towards the gorge whose rocky gates came rushing up to meet us. If you misjudged your distance here you would finish up a splat on the rock. Racing along that ribbon of ice, the sudden transition from sunshine to shadow made everything go black as if we had entered a tunnel without lights but we just kept charging on. As we shot past clumps of dwarf pine trees sticking out incongruously from crevices in the rock, I kept thinking to myself: what lies beyond this awesome place?

Then – Open Sesame! Suddenly, we were out of the gloom and back into the dazzling sunshine yet still careering across the lower lake. In seconds this too had fallen behind us as we shot from ice to snow and began to wheel and weave our way down an enclosed, winding valley past clutches of smaller snow-covered lakes.

Down, down, down … forever losing height. We had flighted like startled birds off the col but now we had become skiing supermen showering the snow off the heels of our skis as we carved deep turns. We had embarked on some fantastic giant slalom and, although I had lost all feeling in my thighs, I hoped this run would never end. When it did, it was like a long drum roll closed by a thunderclap.

Bursting out of the Arriel Valley's last defile I forced my skis to a juddering halt. My chest was heaving but it was sheer fright that had stopped me. Barring the way before us, daring us to cross, was a skyscraping wall of discoloured snow and ice. It faced directly into the sun and was pitted from top to bottom with the debris of a hundred avalanches. It was as if we had just emerged from the Eigergletscher Station and were now peering sideways across the Eiger Face. Alan was at my shoulder.

"How the hell have we managed to land up here, John?" he gasped indignantly. "Surely, this can't be right."

I was as nonplussed as he and automatically pulled out the map.

"This is the way Dodu marked it, Alan," I replied sharply, "there's no other way down."

"We had better get down quickly then," he said. "Just take a look at those avalanche tracks. They've come straight off that bloody great face above us. When the sun starts to melt that lot we could be in real trouble."

He didn't have to spell it out. We had fetched up at a point half way down the Pic d'Arriel's south face with another 500 metres to go before we hit bottom. Somewhere down there was the Paso del Pino, the place we were heading for. But we couldn't see it for it lay beneath a fall line which dropped away like the Big Dipper's last dive. Surely, the *Brèche Latour* could have nothing on this. No wonder Monsieur Dodu had issued his health warning about the Pic Arriel.

"At least we've got here early," I said defensively. "The snow's still firm so let's get it over." And please, I thought to myself, no falls here whatever happens.

The three of us started down again gingerly. No grand gestures or risky turns this time. Just stop and kick turn whenever necessary, I kept repeating to myself.

Hold your traversing position ... lean outwards ... weight on the lower ski ...

All the old stuff you learn at ski school except here it really mattered. Alan had a slip early on but he is immensely strong and quickly recovered himself by breaking the fall with his ski poles. As we got lower and lower the tension eased and when we had almost reached the valley bottom I took a high traversing line to cut off the corner of a steep spur to save time.

Cautiously nosing my way round it, I was suddenly confronted by a wall of ice. I couldn't stop and I couldn't turn back. As my skis started an uncontrollable slide, I knew that I couldn't hold this position for long and, when they went from under me, I snatched wildly at a dwarf pine tree sticking out of the snow. It slipped from my grasp like soap, leaving my gloved hand full of pine needles. Within split seconds I was gathering speed, totally out of control, lunging desperately at trees, branches, roots or anything else that came to hand. As I somersaulted into space, I thought to myself – If I break a leg now ...

Sixty metres lower down I came to rest head first in a heap of snow with one forearm scraped bare through my anorak. Both my safety bindings had snapped but my skis were still secured by their leather safety straps. I quickly put out of my mind the consequences of having a serious accident in so remote a place.

At the Paso del Pino, a summer pasture set in the middle of the Campo Plano's U-shaped valley, I threw off my rucksack, sat down in the snow and stared back to where we had just come from. The Col de Palas, a kilometre above, was now out of sight but the peaks of the frontier ridge, half as high again and resembling a line of battlements on the skyline, looked impossibly far away. Buttressing those peaks rose the enormous wall of striated and discoloured snow we had just descended.

"Did we really ski down that bastard?" I said, turning to Alan and Nick.

"Yup," replied Nick, "we did just that – but I don't believe it."

Beginning to relax, I said, "We must be in Spain."

With the drama of the descent behind us it felt that we had reached another country. Surrounded by *picos* and *puntas* with unfamiliar names this sunny, silent valley seemed a world away from the leaden skies of the French Pyrenees and already the heat was oppressive. For the past two days we had never been warm. Now we yearned to be cold again. There wasn't a breath of wind and the sun was already pressing the backs of our shirts like a hot iron.

We stripped to our vests, put on skins and skied for four kilometres up the valley when I spotted a squat building on the far side of the Ibon del Respomoso lake. We were now pouring sweat and beginning to feel dehydrated.

"Must be the Penalara Hut," I croaked, "but it's still a helluva long way to reach it along the lakeside."

Reunion at the Wallon Hut.   (L to R) – Michelle, Patrick, John, Nick and Alan

"Let's save time and ski straight across the lake," suggested Alan.

We slithered gingerly onto the ice and, as we slid across it, our hearts leaped at every crack and creak. I kept wondering how long I would last if the ice broke.

It was dirty but deliciously cool inside the Penalara Hut. I had never been to this place before yet the scene was familiar with its miniature pine trees and tiny lakes. Those spiky granite peaks whose crests broke the south-eastern horizon were called the *Picos del Infierno* and had something of that same mysterious quality as the *Maladetta*, those other Peaks of the Damned, where my Pyrenean spell had first been cast.

We evidently had the Penalara to ourselves but I didn't want to hang around.

"Let's have a quick bite here and then keep going," I suggested. "We've made good time. It's only 1 pm. Dodu said we could make the Wallon in a day."

Alan was sitting on the floor stripped to the waist with his long legs outstretched. He had already unpacked half his sac.

"Why d'you want to do that, John," he said, "Why kill ourselves climbing in this heat? We've got this nice little hut to ourselves so I vote we stay put."

"The weather may be fine now," I countered, "but within a few hours it could easily turn."

"Maybe," he retorted, "but it looks set fair to me."

"We've only been going for four and a half hours Alan," I remonstrated. "If we carry on now, we'll have a guaranteed clear run to the Wallon with six hours of daylight in hand."

"Point taken," he countered, "but before we decide, let's have another look at the map."

The three of us pored over it.

"The Col de Fache's only 560 metres higher than we are from here," I pointed out. "It's that V-neck at the head of the valley. It's not that steep and after that it's downhill all the way."

"That's true," replied Alan, "but it's also a good eight kilometres from here to the Wallon and the flog up to that col in this heat would be murder. We could be fried alive now but if we wait until tomorrow morning, we could cross it while the day is still cool and bag the Grande Fache en route."

All this made good sense but I wasn't convinced. I didn't trust Pyrenean weather and so far on this tour good days had alternated with bad.

"I'd just like to take another look at what the weather might be doing before I'm convinced," I said and walked outside the hut. It was then that I spotted them.

"Take a look at this," I called back. "We're about to have company."

They came to the door in stockinged feet.

"Grief," exclaimed Nick, "there must be dozens of them. They'll swamp this hut."

Making its way up the valley, strung out in line, was an extended caravan of *ski randonneurs*. I counted 20 but there might have been more for the distance between the the the van and the rear was at least 800 metres. Except for the leaders, they were moving as if in the dreamtime.

"They can't all possibly fit into this hut," protested Alan. "We had better go down to the lake and see what they're up to."

We wandered down to the water hole we had already cut in the ice. The leading group were clustered round it like camels at a well pouring water down their throats and sloshing it over their heads and shoulders. One man looked seriously dehydrated.

"We started at dawn this morning from the Col de Portalet," the young guide explained. "We go to Cauterets this evening."

"That's one helluva long way," said Alan.

"Maybe," replied the guide. "But these people must be back a work tomorrow morning."

As we wandered back to the hut I said to Alan, "I reckon you're right. No point in going on today. Let's stay here the night."

For the rest of the day we just sat about in the cool of the hut, monitoring from time to time the ant-like progress of the French. The sun was remorseless and, when at last its orange orb sank behind the jagged mountains in the west, all heat and colour drained from the valley. As it grew dark a cluster of black dots was still faintly visible below the Col de Fache. We learned later that only half the party reached Cauterets before midnight.

The wind of morning sowthed up the valley. At dawn a flawless sky and the squeak of hard frozen snow under our boots proclaimed our second successive day of good weather. Alan had got it right. We took barely two hours to reach the same Col de Fache that had taken the Frenchmen most of the previous day and from here a forty-five minute scramble up a rocky ridge saw us on the Grande Fache's summit.

"Bergheil!" We clapped each other on the back and marvelled at the sea of snowy summits that stretched away to the eastern and western horizons. It was our first 3,000 metre Pyrenean winter ascent and, to celebrate, we drained Nick's precious flask of Cointreau.

After those early setbacks everything now seemed to be going our way. Six and a half hours after leaving the Penalara, we were relaxing on the sunlit terrace of the Wallon Hut sinking iced lagers and admiring the view. We had almost forgotten about the three Toulousiennes but when they marched in later on that afternoon, we might have been the oldest of friends and embraced each other with Gallic hugs.

"Chers amis Maurice, Michelle et Patrick!" We will always remember that evening with its toasts to *La Vie Montagne, Les Pyrenees, Les Randonneurs, Les Trois Anglais, Les Trois Toulousiennes* and all the rest. But not much else. We owed you that crate of Stella Artois and maybe those half dozen bottles of the *Patron's Réserve Special*. But why did you have to spoil it all by insisting on those *Ricard* and *Armagnac* nightcaps? My head felt nailed to the bunk next morning and I've never touched a drop of *Ricard* since.

Feeling quite dreadful, we were easily last away from the Wallon next day and if my head had had its way we would never have left it. The Toulousiennes would have reached the Pont d'Espagne by the time we had pulled ourselves together. Even the boorish party of 24 Swiss, who had done their best to ruin last night for everyone else with their interminable Fribourg *karaoke*, had left for the Oulettes Hut an hour and a half ahead of us.

That same Oulettes Hut was also our destination but for the first two hours I never thought I would make it. The 700 metre climb to the 2,528 metre Col d'Aratille felt as it must on the South Col without oxygen. As my head began to clear and the landscape swam into focus, I could see from the gathering clouds that this was not going to be another day of good weather. Muggy and overcast when we left the hut, it was snowing heavily by the time we began the two kilometre circular traverse of the high cirque that lies beneath the Pic Né and the Aiguilles du Chabarrou. The map dignified this place with a hail of blue avalanche arrows but we could only guess at the dangers for nothing ahead, above or below, was now visible except the faint imprint of the Swiss party's ski tracks.

At the Col de Mulets, I marked my card with our fifth blizzard of the tour. It was blowing in from the Atlantic but from here on our route went downhill all the way to the hut via the 450 metre Mulets Couloir. Even this descent through billowing sheets of snow had a sting in its tail. One side of the couloir was thick porridge, the other sheet ice.

The main Oulettes Hut had been opened up specially for the Swiss. Even so, they had managed to put the guardian's back up with a graceless argument about the cost of lighting the stove and more tuneless rounds of Fribourg *Singspiele*. To help cope with this influx, the guardian – a saturnine Gascon called Bernard Dorche – had helicoptered in his pretty young wife Anne-Marie, two elderly retainers and a dog.

The atmosphere in the hut began to reflect our collective unease as the storm gathered intensity. A party of three Frenchmen were still overdue. Last night we had befriended one of them – a tall, elegant Pau hotelier called Jean-Pierre Leire. Earlier in the day, just below the Col d'Aratille, we had overtaken him and the two middle-aged Parisian doctors who were with him but that was three hours ago. Even as we began discussing the logistics of mounting a rescue party, this ill-assorted trio staggered into the hut like drunken snowmen and the two Parisians collapsed over a table.

I walked across to Jean-Pierre and shook his hand.

"Bravo Jean-Pierre. Qu'est-ce que c'est le problème?"

His explanation gave him our unanimous Man of the Day award. Before last night, he had never set eyes on the two doctors but seeing that they were on their own he had offered to accompany them to the Oulettes. Scarcely had they left the Wallon when he realised that both were inexperienced and unfit. On the Col de Mulets, their skiing and nerves had disintegrated. Without Jean-Pierre to shepherd them all the way down the steep Mulets Couloir on foot, Paris would never have seen them again.

We bought them a bottle of wine and initiated Jean-Pierre into the rites of Liar Dice. He, in turn, made the ultimate French sacrifice of swapping Anne-Marie's delicious dinner in the main hut for our accelerated freeze-dried liver and onion stew which Alan perversely insisted that we cook and eat in the hut's squalid winter room. For company we had another trio of wild eyed Spanish climbers who had been living here in filth for the past week. The stink of the blocked sink piled high with unwashed pots and pans put Alan into combative mood but Jean-Pierre's diplomatic intervention resolved a potentially ugly situation. When I reminded Alan of the Pombie Hut altimeter episode, he calmed down and forgave them everything.

Coming down from the *dortoire* next morning, I found the hut pulsating with the collective flap of 24 over-excited Swiss. Their *Bergfuhrer* was shouting orders in German like a *Wehrmacht Feldwebel* while his clients scurried around like disturbed ants.

"What's happening?" I asked Anne-Marie bemused. "What's all the fuss about?"

"Look outside and see for yourself," she replied curtly. "That's why the Swiss are evacuating the hut."

I peered through a window but could see only a white blur so pushed open the hut's massive iron door a fraction. Outside was a Dantesque maelstrom of writhing snow.

Returning to Anne-Marie who was now rushing around the kitchen locking up all the cupboards, I asked ingenuously, "What's happened to Bernard?"

"Bernard's already left for Cauterets," she snapped back. "The weather forecast is terrible and he's just left me to pack up the main hut. Tell your friends that we must all get out of here as soon as possible. The Val de Gaube's a very dangerous avalanche trap and no helicopters will operate in these conditions."

I couldn't believe that the guardian Bernard Dorche had simply pushed off leaving his wife and elderly aides to cope. The Swiss had got his message early for they were now marshalled and sized off ready to follow their B*ergfuhrer* and the guardian's example.

Only then did I face up to the fact that our own tour was virtually at an end. Maybe we would have to get out of here too. Gavarnie and those peaks I had listed on my original itinerary – Vignemale, Cylindre, Marbore, Perdu – we would never get near them in these conditions.

After the Swiss had marched off in column, a dozen of us were still in the hut – Jean-Pierre and his two Parisians, the three Spaniards, the three of us, Anne-Marie, her two elderly aides and their dog. The Spanish *montañeros* made it clear that they would be staying with their food mountain so that left nine of us plus dog. Anne-Marie was a true maid of the mountains but her two aides were long past pensionable age and had no skis.

I explained what was happening to Alan and Nick with the map spread out before us.

"Bloody hell," I whistled through my teeth, "take a look at this. The entire Val de Gaube's showered with blue arrows. It's just one enormous avalanche trap."

"That's just what Anne-Marie's told you," said Alan. "I agree with her. We must get out of here damned quick and take these people with us."

I went over to Anne-Marie and said, "We're coming too. We'll all go out as a single party to the Pont d'Espagne. It's safer that way."

But we hadn't reckoned on the two Parisian doctors. Numbed by yesterday's trauma, they had gone into a decline and were incapable of deciding whether to stay on or get out. We couldn't hang around for them. As every minute passed, more and more snow was building up along the length of the Val de Gaube. I tried reasoning with the one who spoke good English but I couldn't get the message through.

Turning to Alan in exasperation I said to him loudly, "If they can't make up their minds, they'll have to stay here with the Spaniards."

Jean-Pierre standing beside us now spoke sharply to them.

"Messieurs, il est INDISPENSABLE que nous quitterons le refuge immédi-atement – IMMEDIATEMENT. La route dans la vallée est très dangéreux"

"We are leaving now anyway with or without you," I said.

As we moved towards the door they shuffled into line with ill grace.

Eventually, we left the hut at 10 am – three precious hours after Bernard Dorche had done his bunk. Standing under the eaves of the hut, menaced by a line of two metre long Damoclean icicles while waiting for the two doctors to get their skis on, I had last minute doubts about leaving. Visibility was almost down to zero. The wind was shrieking and the snow, whipped to a frenzy, was racing round in spirals. Pushing with our shoulders against the wind, it took Alan, Nick, Jean-Pierre and me all our strength to slam shut the iron door that partitioned the main hut from the winter room where the three Spaniards were sitting silent and impassive.

Four years before, I had walked down this same valley in high summer. The hillside had been ablaze with red azalea. Now, everything was uniform white. The snow not only covered the ground but filled the air and permeated everything from our nostrils to our under clothing.

The agreed order of march was Jean-Pierre, myself, Nick, Alan, Anne-Marie, her two aides – who had dug out some snow shoes – and dog. At their own insistence the Parisians brought up the rear. The tracks of the Swiss had almost been obliterated and, when I looked round ten minutes after starting, the Parisians had already fallen far back.

Alan and I shouted back at them: "Keep together … keep together! You must close up. Don't lose contact." Jean-Pierre joined in with a French bellow: *"Ensemble, Ensemble!"*

Next time I turned round they had disappeared from sight so Alan went back to round them up and command the rear. My admiration for Jean-Pierre's shepherding these two single-handed yesterday went up another notch.

The wind was dead on the nose and coated our goggles with rime so that we were virtually unsighted. But above its roar there rose a more sinister noise which sounded like an artillery barrage. Thunder perhaps? Then I tumbled. This was the sound of avalanches reverberating up and down the valley.

A kilometre below the hut, just above the Cascade de Darre Splumouse, Jean-Pierre stopped in his tracks. In summer the river tumbles over its rock lip in a graceful waterfall. Now it had become a near vertical snow bank coated in ice.

Jean-Pierre turned to me. I couldn't see his eyes through his goggles but I sensed that he was unhappy.

"John – je vois rien, rien … vas y, en avant!"

I couldn't see a damned thing either but he had been breaking the trail for quite long enough. It was time for someone else to take over so I edged past him and then, side slipping cautiously to the bottom of the snow bank, arrived at a rocky bay overlooking a 15-metre deep ravine that dropped plumb to the valley bed.

Glancing back towards the others, it was heartening to see that the two pensioners were taking everything in their stride but Alan was having problems with the Parisians. One was spread-eagled helpless across the steep snow slope with Alan supporting his skis from underneath with one hand and hacking out steps with his ice axe with the other.

Great photo-opportunity, I thought to myself. So, to get a better view, I skied on for another 20 metres along the edge of the ravine away from the protection of the rock bay. Only as I began to focus my camera, did I notice Jean-Pierre and Nick waving at me frantically with hands cupped to their mouths. In that wind I couldn't hear a thing. What on earth were they on about?

Glancing upwards behind me, I got the message.

At first, it looked as if the entire mountainside was exploding with spray. Then I saw the gigantic snow wave tumbling and foaming down towards me. It was moving faster than any wave I had ever seen and was followed by a terrible roaring noise.

A succession of *MOST URGENT* messages raced through my mind. Get rid of your rucksack – release your safety bindings – kick turn *NOW* – get back to that rock bay but, above all, move ... move!

I was trying desperately to do everything at one and the same time, faster than I had ever done anything before but I felt that I could only move in slow motion and that my limbs wer paralysed. The blast of wind which hit me it brought with it an icy chill and a cloud of spindrift which buried me up to the neck like fine sand.

So this is it, I thought. Another avalanche fatality. What a damned silly way to go.

I felt quite calm, even detached, and braced myself fatalistically for the next wave that would surely dump me at the bottom of the ravine under a thousand tons of snow.

It never came. The monster had spent its strength higher up the mountainside and this had been its last gasp.

Alan told me later that from his grandstand view above the frozen waterfall Jean Pierre had been muttering – *"Mon Dieu, il est perdu, il est perdu."*

I had been lucky. All I had lost were my ski pole baskets and a dollop of hubris.

The others were quick to join me. The avalanche even galvanised the Parisians. We couldn't retreat and we couldn't hang around so we raced on down the Val de Gaube putting as much distance as we could between each other without losing contact. Fresh avalanches kept booming down on either side of us. We couldn't see them but we could hear their explosive bursts before, above and behind us like the sighting shells of artillerymen bracketing their target. Any one of them might have had our number on it.

Just before the Lac de Gaube I picked up the Swiss tracks as they crossed the length of the lake. Four and a half hours after leaving the Oulettes, our little party foregathered under the Tourist Information Board at the Pont d'Espagne, tired, sodden but safe. That same evening, Jean-Pierre organised a *grande bouffe* at a chic restaurant in Moneim to which all nine escapees were invited plus a wholly un-contrite Bernard Dorche who, with various others, brought numbers up to thirteen. But this was not to be an unlucky number. Our opera had had a happy ending and, at its finale, encouraged by innumerable champagne toasts and the best *Béarnaise canard confit*, we swore eternal friendship in celebration of *La Vie Montagne,* heroes and heroines all.

Taillon. En route to the Sarradets Hut

4

CIRQUES AND CANYONS

A t the Pont d'Espagne the sky was still as overcast as it had been when we had first arrived at Cauterets and the snow was still falling, light but insistent, as it had done since dawn. Twelve months on from the ski traverse from Urdos to the Pont d'Espagne with the Wedgwood brothers, I was back again in the Pyrenees about to begin a new adventure at the same place where last year's had ended – the Val de Gaube down which our party of nine French and Brits plus dog had made its *Sturm und Drang* exit. This time there were only five of us and as we shouldered our heavy rucksacks and began to climb the familiar rocky path that twisted upwards through the pine trees, I reflected that little seemed to have changed within the past year. I couldn't possibly have foreseen then that twenty-four hours on, our lives would have been turned upside down. For years later, my mind would flash back to the long, slow hut march up the valley on that sullen winter's day and then the nightmarish retreat in the aftermath of the avalanche with Alain's body left behind us in the snow.

Ill fortune seldom comes alone. When Richard, Susan and I had flown back to London from Bordeaux two days after the accident, I had once again telephoned my wife Georgina in Switzerland where she and our three daughters had been spending a family skiing holiday to talk through what had happened. After I had unburdened myself for the second time, Georgina quietly told me that that same afternoon, our eldest daughter Emma, aged 12, had broken her leg ski racing.

The morning after I got back to London, I took the train to see Alain's parents, my cousins Bill and Paulette, to tell them how their beloved son had met his death. It was our second such conversation. Bill was icily matter of fact and, as I explained what had happened, I kept on thinking: this can't be real. It didn't really happen. Any moment now, Alain will be back and just walk through the front door smiling and laughing as I remembered him.

That same night I stayed with Susan and David Baldock and learned for the first time that Susan had been carrying a baby throughout our tour. Typically, she had never let on. The baby was to become their adored son Robert. Next day, Easter Sunday, she and I took communion at her local church. For her, new life was about to be created but for his parents Alain could never come back. On Easter Monday, I flew out to Geneva to bring my Emma home with her leg in plaster. The joy of Spring had faded.

For months afterwards, I tried to excise the Pyrenees and its bitter memories from my mind. Our games in the mountains now seemed such trivial things. The Urdos to Cauterets traverse might have proved that an amateur party could force a route through the Pyrenees in bad weather without the baggage of guides – but so what? Alain's death had changed my mindset and knocked my self-confidence.

Ours hadn't been the only avalanche disaster that season close to home. Some three months earlier on New Year's Day, Michael de Pret Roose, his wife Karin, his stepson Nicholas and his guide, Ernst Renner, had all been killed in an avalanche near Andermatt. Michael's death had marked the end of an era for British ski mountaineering but, for his many friends, it was his exceptional kindness and generosity that will longest be remembered. Only the previous autumn, he and Karin had treated my wife and me to a sumptuous champagne and lobster luncheon at the petit-château he had built at the head of an inlet on the coast of south Brittany. That night at a Quimper restaurant, I had intended to repay their hospitality with a *grande bouffe* but, in typical style, Michael out-manoeuvred me by settling the bill in advance.

Michael was the most experienced British ski mountaineer in the business but he never toured without a guide. Ernst Renner was one of the best, Andermatt was their backyard and every member of that party had been equipped with avalanche transceivers. That an avalanche could have wiped out such a powerful team was deeply disturbing.

I kept wondering what this quest for adventure was all about. It's a question older than Jason's Quest for the Golden Fleece and one which, at some time or other, every mountaineer, sailor, explorer or whoever will ask themselves. Most will dredge up some self-fulfilling answer to justify their obsession and then come back for more. No sport is worth another person's life but I knew that I couldn't just quit and, that having once been thrown, I had better remount quickly or never again.

I persuaded myself that the key was to embark upon a graduated mountaineering programme to get myself back into the frame. The Alpine Club's Family Meet in Cornwall provided a starter with its relaxed mixture of swimming off the rocks and climbing and re-climbing Commando Ridge with three Wedgwood and three Harding children on a very long rope. A more realistic litmus test was likely to be the Alpine Club's Summer Meet at Courmayeur, an old tradition I had helped revive the previous year at Chamonix.

I had driven out from England with Steve Town and the redoubtable Brian Chase who was rarin' to re-establish his reputation as the Wild Man of the 1960s. Chase had insisted on driving his battered wreck of a car solo for 24 hours non-stop and then, on the same afternoon as we arrived, the three of us raced up to the Estelette Bivouac on the southern flank of the Aiguille-Tré-la Tête in preparation for our first climb. A mindlessly competitive mood to get me there first brought on an embarrassing attack of altitude sickness and vertigo which, in turn, precipitated my humiliating retreat to the meet's campsite next morning while the others did their climb. To compound my disgrace, I managed to lose Chase's car keys which meant that he was only able to retrieve his ironmongery from the boot after dismantling the car's rear offside wing.

However, it wasn't Chase's righteous *froideur* that blighted the Meet for me. Courmayeur, when I had first visited it twenty years before, had seemed the grandest and most romantic climbing centre in all the Alps – the quintessential climbers' Mecca. In those days Turner himself would still have recognised it as the same village he had painted in 1802 but in the intervening years, the skiing explosion and the opening of the Mont Blanc Tunnel had made Courmayeur a mountaineering Clapham Junction.

I had begun to wonder where, if anywhere, I fitted into the contemporary climbing scene. Up at the Torino Hut, after climbing the Dôme de Rochfort with Steve, I had seen a Professor of Science from Aberdeen University brewing up his AFD Spaghetti Bolognaise over a Gaz stove in a dark corner of the hut while a jolly gang of Italian construction workers tucked into the real thing in the comfort of the hut's modest *ristorante* sloshing down their *Chianti con brio*. The professor's meal looked as joyless as the dinner I later shared in the dingy respectability of Courmayeur's *Ristorante Venezia* with plus-foured and triconi nailed members of the Association of British Members of the Swiss Alpine Club as they re-lived pre-war hut marches. I didn't feel comfortable in either world and when bad weather was forecast for the next few days, I left Courmayeur with the sad thought that the Alps were an old affair and that new love was in the Pyrenees.

It so happened that in the autumn of that same year, the Alpine, Alpine Ski and Eagle Ski Clubs and Ski Club of Great Britain organised a one day symposium, Snow Avalanche. With anguished memories still fresh, I thought that this would be the last thing with which I would want to be involved but, when I heard that my old mentor Martin Epp would be one of the speakers, I signed up as a participant.

Distinguished British and Continental experts delivered learned treatises on avalanche theory and evaluation, snow formations, location devices and much else. Yet, at the end of the day, I wondered if I was any the wiser.

There is an Avalanche ABC which prescribes certain ground rules which every ski mountaineer should learn by heart:

That avalanche risk is greatest early in the season; in the latter part of the day and, most importantly, during and within 24 hours of heavy snow fall.

That weather forecasts should be studied before and after arrival.

That avalanche evaluation should be undertaken with reference to slope angles, snow profiles, wind and weather.

That everyone *must* know how to use their electronic avalanche transceivers, have practised rescue techniques and always carry the right equipment.

Tomes have been written on this subject and much can be learned from theory and practice. Yet, at the end of the day, an element of risk can not be eliminated. Avalanche victims have included some of ski mountaineering's most eminent exponents and, in his closing address, Andre Roch, an outstanding Swiss mountaineer and avalanche scientist, put the avalanche enigma in a nutshell:

"If you want to avoid involvement in avalanches, there is only one way – don't go into the mountains."

There's the rub, especially for those with limited time and holidays. After months of planning and trying to put a party together, what do you do if the weather's bad or the snow's not in perfect condition when you start your tour? Do you carry on or meekly abandon it? Most likely, you will compromise. Hang about and take your chance when the weather improves. Yet, the mountaineer's instinct is to push the route and, for the ski mountaineer too, the successful passage of difficult ground in bad conditions gives something of the same satisfaction as it does for a sailor navigating the correct course in stormy weather. There are no easy answers: only a balance of uncertainties. You don't court risk in the mountains but without it, the dish has no flavour.

One of the key speakers at the Avalanche Symposium was a Swiss scientist called Walter Good, Deputy Director of the Swiss Avalanche Research Institute at Davos. Walter had stayed with us as our guest and, over breakfast the morning after the symposium, he and I discussed our Pyrenean avalanche disaster.

"You were lucky not all to have been killed in that one, John," said Walter reassuringly. "Believe me, that accident could have happened to anyone. However much you think you know about avalanches, you can never be certain."

A seed had been germinating from the moment I had met Walter. We had struck up an instant rapport and, though I hadn't yet admitted it to my wife, the idea of returning to the Pyrenees had never been far from my mind. Why not ask Walter to join *my* party? Not only was he a scientist specialising in avalanche research but also an expert ski mountaineer. If anyone could help banish my Pyrenean phobias this was the man. When I put it to him and he agreed in principle to come, we really started talking.

"How do you keep fit living in London?" Walter asked me. "You have no mountains here."

"True," I replied. "But we've got quite a few further north – especially in Scotland where there's good ski touring. But for fitness generally, I have to rely on my bicycle. Most days, I ride to the City and back. It's eight miles each way and faster than public transport and almost as dangerous as climbing. What about you?"

"I'm a commuter too," he replied with a smug smile, "but I'm better off than you. My office is on the Weissflujoch. Most days in winter, my journey home involves a 1,100 metre ski descent."

Walter looked lean and fit. I wondered whether I had promoted myself into the wrong league and was only faintly reassured when he admitted to being a family man.

With Walter on board, Alan Wedgwood automatically selected himself but none of my other friends showed keen.

"What about Jean-Pierre Leire?" I asked Alan. "You and he seemed to get on very well together."

"Fine by me," said Alan.

Then I wondered whether Jean-Pierre would still be game. Of all last year's survivors, his burial had been the most traumatic. However, when I wrote, his reply came back by return. The English might have been idiosyncratic but the sentiment was pure Jean-Pierre for, as he put it, "the call of the mountains was stronger than our grief".

I closed the team at four and, with that settled, the itinerary wrote itself – a straight repeat of what I had planned for last year – Cauterets to Gavarnie and thence to Barèges via the three great cirques of Gavarnie, Estaube and Troumousse and the Néouvielle Reserve.

To give us more than a sporting chance with the weather and reduce avalanche risk, I had put our start date back to April 26 which was fully six weeks later than that first Eagles tour. We might be taking a chance with the snow but at least it should have settled. This time round I was determined to play safe.

From my own experience I could now respectfully confirm Michael de Pret Roose's verdict that ski mountaineering in the Pyrenees was very different from the Alps. Pyrenean icefields might be tiny and Pyrenean peaks smaller than their Alpine counterparts but quality is not determined simply by height or size. The unpredictability of the weather, the steep terrain, the lack of decent huts and the inadequacy of the maps made Pyrenean ski mountaineering an altogether more serious proposition. From the outset, it was obvious that Jean-Pierre was going to take this tour seriously. As our man on the spot, he sent me a stream of weather *bulletins* and, even before we had started, he had put in a couple of ski tours including a successful crossing of the Brèche Latour which he described as "sheer ice". Overall, the news was good for, as he put it: "the snow is completely processed and therefore the mountains right now are extremely safe." Best of all, he promised to look after all hotel and hut bookings and what we would be having to eat.

Comprising two Brits, a Frenchman and a Swiss, this genuinely *Equipe Internationale* nonetheless managed to get off to a bad start. Our agreed joint rendezvous at Pau's railway station never materialised, partly because Alan and I missed our connection at Dax and partly because Walter overslept and ended up at Hendaye on the Spanish border. I calculated that the time Jean-Pierre had spent retrieving, ferrying and collecting the team together had squandered twenty percent of the good weather which on previous tours had been par for a fortnight.

However, he never complained and hours later, re-united at his father's Hotel Ronceveaux in Pau, we made our grovelling apologies over a luncheon consisting of *pâté de foie gras* and *canard Béarnaise* accompanied by two bottles of a fragrant Sauternes which he insisted should be on the house.

Jean-Pierre seemed in no way discountenanced by this early blip and made a signal cultural sacrifice by speaking to us in English. Embarrassed by his lavish hospitality and *politesse,* I didn't have the gall to question the variations to my original plan that he now proposed over lunch.

"Martine will now be organising all our food," he began, "and will also be joining us at Gavarnie."

Splendide, I thought to myself. I knew Martine to be *sportive et très athlétique* in a shapely French way. She would be an asset on any team and, I presumed, would do all the cooking too.

"But we *must* reach the Marcadau Hut this evening," Jean-Pierre continued. "A start this afternoon is *indispensable* but Martine must first go shopping. Let us rendezvous at the Pont d'Espagne at 1700 hours."

He must have rehearsed some of this in advance for I couldn't recall such fluency in English before. After lunch, I suggested to Alan and Walter that it didn't seem right that *en France*, a Frenchman should have to speak a foreign language so we agreed that, henceforth, French should be our *lingua franca* – whatever longueurs that might cause.

Nevertheless Jean-Pierre's flying start was an unwelcome departure from my original programme. Alan didn't like it either.

"Why on earth does Jean-Pierre want to reach the Wallon Hut today?" he grumbled. "We're both office worn and I haven't yet fully recovered from that wretched train journey. I thought you said that we would be having an easy first day stretching our legs on the piste."

"I thought so too, Alan," I replied. "I wouldn't have minded spending a night in Pau myself and was even hoping that Jean-Pierre might have suggested his

Summit of Pic de Cambales. Jean-Pierre Leire

Hotel Ronceveaux. However, after all his ferrying and hospitality, I think it would be churlish to argue the toss."

I hadn't understood either why Jean-Pierre had asked us to make our own way to the Pont d'Espagne car park until I saw the two jumbo-sized supermarket carriers that Martine was dividing up into four neat piles on the grass verge. The five of us and those food carriers couldn't possibly have fitted into Jean-Pierre's car.

"Ça suffit, n'est-ce pas, pour la première étape?" she beamed, *"Pour les trois jours jusqu'à Gavarnie!"*

Three days worth! On our last tour, the weight of this pillaging of Mammouth's food hall, translated into its porridge cake equivalent, would have lasted us three months. Moreover, the bulk of it was tinned – pâtés, ham, sardines, *boeuf en daube* – and therefore represented entirely surplus weight. Martine had also bought out her local *quincaillerie's* entire stock of Gaz cylinders. Even if we had brewed up every six hours for a month, we couldn't possibly have got through that lot.

The route I had planned to Gavarnie would avoid both the Val de Gaube and the equally treacherous Barranco d'Ossoue altogether. From the Pont d'Espagne roadhead, we would spend our first night at the Wallon Hut, cross the Col d'Aratille next day and, that same morning, descend the Rio Ara into Spain. At some point in the valley, we would swing round eastwards to cross the Col de Pla d'Aube to bring us a little way down the lower Ossoue Valley where we would spend our second night at the Refuge Lourdes. From there it would be an easy day to Gavarnie. Quite why Jean-Pierre had bought so much food was beyond me.

"But we mustn't complain," I whispered to Alan, "they've obviously gone to immense trouble to get all this food together."

When I tried to shoulder my sac, I needed him to help me lift it off the ground.

The Pont d'Espagne, lying at the confluence of the Gaube and Marcadau Valleys, is something of a misnomer. Although it is the start point for the high passes of Ossoue and Aratille, which cross the frontier ridge into Spain, both lie the best part of a day away.

Our route to the Wallon Hut followed a path through a meadow by the side of a meandering river on whose far bank the forest came down to the water's edge. It was a lovely, tranquil evening with gauzy clouds softening the valley's granite scarps. The snow had long since melted in this lower valley but there was still plenty higher up and, as we began our walk, the sun's last rays flushed pink on the snowy mountain tops.

From the start, I knew that this hut march was going to be a trial. My rucksack felt as if it had been filled with bricks and the knock-on effects of last night's couchette, too much wine at lunch and the altitude made me feel light headed and queasy. More worrying were my boots. By now, both Alan and I had graduated from leather to plastic but I had not walked in these for any length of time and never with so much weight on my back. Their rub and pinch were already getting to me. What had possessed me not to bring my trainers?

I reached the hut well behind the others but Jean-Pierre, sensitive to such situations, had the key for restoring morale: *"Je vous propose pour la première nuit que nous trouverons bien le service complet de la Refuge Wallon – c'est indispensable!"*

How thoughtful of Jean-Pierre. I hadn't forgotten this excellent hotel refuge after that binge we had had two years back with the Toulousiennes. I wasn't going to complain about getting the full treatment.

"I think Jean-Pierre's got a very good idea," I said beaming at Alan.

"Maybe," replied Alan looking less enthusiastic. "But what the hell are we going to do about all the food we've just humped up here I wonder."

I had been wondering about that too but once inside the hut there was no turning back. A group of Béarnais was belting out local ballads. The din was awesome but Jean-Pierre was in his element, yattering away to complete strangers as if he had known them all his life. Neither Alan nor I were feeling that sociable, for fractured French required an effort beyond our concentration that evening.

"At least we'll get a decent meal here and won't have to do our own cooking," I murmured to Alan. "Remember that terrifc meal with the Toulousiennes."

The guardian strode across the room and, with a broad grin and welcoming *"Voilà, Messieurs"*, banged down on the table two bottles of the Marcadau's *Réserve du Patron*. From his anorak pocket Walter whipped out a hunk of something black and hard.

"Viande Sèche de Grisons," he pronounced with relish, shaving off wafer-thin slices with his Swiss Army knife.

"Have some," he said offering it round. "It's delicious – Switzerland's answer to *biltong*."

I've never taken to *biltong* and find dessicated chamois rank and unchewable. I surreptitiously transferred my ration to my trouser pocket with a view to dumping it at an opportune moment. Why bust my jaw with so much better things in prospect.

"Messieurs. Diner est servi!"

Madame, a squat and powerfully muscled woman, sweeps in from her kitchen and, holding high with bare uplifted arms an enormous steaming platter, makes straight for our table.

"Clunk!" … heavy metal makes contact with solid wooden table and the great dish is now set squarely between the four of us.

"Bon appetit, Messieurs," she exclaims with relish.

When the steam clears, I stare down at a grey, gelatinous mass wobbling with Quartermass-like protruberances.

Horreur! Jean-Pierre confirms my worst fears.

"Ce sont les tripes béarnaises," he grins. *"C'est une spécialité de la région. Très délicieuses."*

Now, as every gastronome knows, tripe comes from the paunch and reticulum of a ruminant's stomach. It goes down a treat in Istanbul; was once a favourite dish with onions in Pudsey pre-BSE and is still lovingly eaten like spaghetti in Bearn. However, I had positively loathed the stuff ever since I had been forced to eat it as a child during the War. All the way up the valley I had assumed that we would be making serious in-roads into Martine's tinned *pâté* and *boeuf en daube.* Once here, when we had agreed to Jean-Pierre's civilised suggestion that we enjoy the hut's *service complet,* I had lifted my sights still higher. But *tripes béarnaises!* Surely, there was something else on the menu? I looked despairingly around the room at other people's plates but could recognise no variations. Everyone was tucking into their tripe like trenchermen. With the hellish Hieronymus Bosch dish trembling before me, I was overcome by nausea. I knew that unless these Frenchmen were going to see something of my own stomach lining I would have to reach that door fast. Outside in the snow I shot my rainbow.

Returning white faced to our table Jean-Pierre leaned across to commiserate:

"John, je suis vraiment désolé à propos votre diner. Malhereusement, moi j'adore les tripes béarnaises."

Later on in the trip, he confessed that he had humped up to the hut a two kilo tin of tripe "to give us a treat" but when he had seen my reaction had fed it to the guardian's dog.

Walter's alarm went off before dawn with relentless Swiss precision but last night's hiccup was quickly forgotten when I looked outside to a clear starlit sky. Over breakfast, Jean-Pierre explained why he had been so keen to get up here last night.

"C'est la météo," he said with a knowing grin. *"Aujordhui, c'est bon, mais demain peut être il sera mauvais."*

"Fair enough," I muttered to Alan. "I just wish that he had given us this forecast earlier."

"Et voilà," he continued, *"je vous propose une belle expédition – l'ascension du Pic de Cambales. C'est très populaire. C'est 'très classique'."*

As initiator and organiser of this tour, I had assumed that we would be following the itinerary I had so carefully planned and circulated weeks before. I felt a bit miffed that Jean-Pierre should be changing the touring programme. The Pic de Cambales had never been on my list but when Walter agreed that this was a good idea, Jean-Pierre had achieved another *fait accompli.*

"We needed a work out anyway," I remarked to Alan as we re-packed our sacs and then added as a spur: "It's a good peak. The Eagles climbed it with de Pret Roose and Epp."

A couple of hours later, my chest was heaving and my breath coming out in rasps after the effort of climbing a boss that mimicked the more famous Aiguille de Chardonnet's. By now, I had changed my mind about the Pic de Cambales being a good idea. I also recognised that I was extremely unfit. With an effort, I closed up on Walter who had stopped to wait for me.

"John, you don't look too good," he chuckled as if he had made some sort of joke. "Anything wrong?"

"Nothing that getting up and down this damned mountain won't cure," I spat back. "I've just got a splitting headache and I'm feeling sick."

"Ah!" he said, "You've just got a touch of altitude sickness. You'll soon get over it. Happily, I never get it because I'm totally acclimatised. My office on the Weissflujoch is higher than we are now. It's got marvellous views too. You must come round and see it some time."

At that moment, I couldn't have cared where Walter's office might be or what it looked like or what it looked at but it worried me that while I was panting like a dog, he was breathing as normally as he would have been in his beastly office analysing snow profiles.

"Thanks, Walter," I grimaced, "let's just say that you're damned fit."

"Yes," he replied smugly, "I suppose I am. It's just a matter of lifestyle."

At the top of the Pic de Cambales I collapsed in a heap on the snow to recover. Away to the south, thrusting its four turreted summit through a translucent layer of cloud, rose the fatal mountain that had filled our horizon all day – the Vignemale.

Walter was beginning to fidget.

"I think we should be going," he said. "This snow's perfect just now. What about a bit of fun?"

"What sort of fun Walter?" I asked suspiciously. "What d'you have in mind?"

"That couloir coming off the col we passed on the way up. It would make a great ski descent and get us down to the glacier really fast."

My mind went blank. The only feature I could recall that might conceivably be described as a couloir was the snow-filled crack at the head of the glacier that ran up the length of the Pic's headwall. It was about 150 metres high and pitched at the angle of a lift shaft.

"Walter," I replied looking at him levelly, "there's only one couloir coming off the col and it looks quite desperate. Surely you don't mean that."

"Yes," he said with a broad grin. "You've spotted it. A bit steep at the top but the snow should be excellent. It'll make an exciting run. Are you coming?"

I felt my stomach tighten. This was *Ski Extrème*. In no way would I be coming.

"No thanks, Walter. I'll give this one a miss. I'm taking it easy this first day."

Alan had been listening to this exchange. I looked at him vacantly and he gave me a curt nod.

"I'll be coming with you John," he said. "The same way as we came up."

We left Walter and Jean-Pierre at the col and made our way down to the Aragon Glacier at our own speed. Last night's *chanteurs* had left the hut some time after us and were now gathered in a knot half way up the glacier staring at the top of the couloir where two black dots seemed to be stuck like flies on a wall. We stopped besides them to await the action which was some time coming. Eventually, one of the dots appeared to ski a little way down the couloir only to climb up again.

"Must be testing the snow," I said to Alan.

"More likely they're having second thoughts," he replied.

The tension was mounting but suddenly both started to move together and at first I feared they might be falling. I caught my breath but they went faster and faster, accelerating down the couloir until – *"Pop"*, like corks from a bottle, they burst out from the bottom and sped down the glacier towards us side by side in a flurry of immaculate turns. The *chanteurs* started clapping and we all began chatting together like old friends.

"What delayed you at the top," I asked Walter.

"Nothing serious," he replied, "Jean-Pierre got cramp at the *moment critique*."

Walter digs couloirs. After lunch, to give Alan and me some practice, he led us down another. It was as well that it wasn't as steep as the one off the Cambales for I took most of it head first.

"Why did we come down this way?" I asked Walter.

"To get us down the mountain quicker than those noisy Béarnaises," he replied. "They've taken the easy way."

As we neared the Wallon Hut, Walter stopped suddenly.

"We'll take a short break here," he announced. "Good time for some rescue sledge practice."

"We haven't got one with us, Walter," I replied puzzled. "Too darn heavy to lug around but we can always rig something up if we have to."

Inside my breast pocket I always carried a cellophane-covered diagram of the Ski Club of Great Britain's authorised model – a cats' cradle of skis, sticks and ropes. I had implicit faith in Alan's ability to put something similar together if it ever came to the test.

"Mine's here in my rucksack," said Walter. "Now watch this one carefully."

Like a conjurer, he produced from his toothpaste tube of a rucksack three thin metal bars and a canvas strip which he started to piece together accompanied by a running commentary.

"These metal cross-bars torsion the ski. I then insert my snow shovel into this canvas strip to make a seat – and there's your rescue sledge. I can sleep on it too."

"That's very ingenious Walter," I said genuinelly impressed, but I made a mental note to avoid having an accident. Walter's stretcher looked excruciatingly uncomfortable.

For Walter, the descent of the Pic de Cambales couloir had indeed been good clean fun but it had left me feeling underwhelmingly inferior. As skiers, it was clear that both Walter and Jean-Pierre were in a different league from Alan and me. I tried to comfort myself with the thought that when we were both fitter and it became a matter of survival ski mountaineering, things would even themselves out.

Back in London I had planned that this first leg of our traverse from the Wallon Hut to Gavarnie would set the tone for the rest of the trip. On the second day we were due to cover a distance of over 15 kilometres climbing and descending an aggregate of 1,300 metres before spending that night at the Refuge de Lourdes. Our French IGN maps covered most of the ground except the six kilometres descent down the Ara Valley into Spain from which we would have to climb back into France across the Port de Pla d'Aube.

The clouds lay low when we first left the Wallon Hut but, as we climbed higher up the Aratille Valley, the sun burned the mist away and lit up the snow peaks on either side like beacons. Three and a half hours later at the Col d'Aratille, the lower valleys of France were still covered by a cloud sea but to the south lay Spain and the Ara Valley shone white. The light on this side of the range had a translucent quality but the air felt unsettled and the dark cloud bank topped by billowing cumulus welling up in the south west made me think that Jean-Pierre's original weather forecast might be right.

Col des Tantes. Cirque du Gavernie.   (L to R) – Alan, Veronique, Jean-Pierre, Martine and Walter

From this lonely col the 1,000 metre north-west face of the Vignemale dominated all else. It wasn't as stark or sheer as the north-east face which had buried us with its avalanche but it seemed altogether wilder and more remote. Before yesterday, I had never seen this obverse side of the Vignemale but from wherever you view the mountain, it brings you up short.

The Vignemale is arguably the most dramatic peak in the Pyrenees and a favourite with climbers. For the eccentric Franco-Irish Count Henri Russell it exercised an almost sexual attraction. Returning to his native France after years of adventurous world travel, Russell's passion for this mountain became his life's obsession. He courted the Vignemale like a suitor and, not content with climbing it thirty-three times, he consummated the union by hacking out of the living rock a series of grottoes where he would spend weekends; celebrate mass and entertain friends to dinner in full evening dress. The burghers of Barèges, who owned the Vignemale, indulged Russell's proclivities by granting him a 99-year flying leasehold over its four summits at an annual rent of one franc. Title assured, Russell celebrated the Silver Wedding of his first ascent in one of the lower grottoes. Ten years later, to celebrate his seventieth birthday, he spent a solitary week at his highest grotto Le Paradis, oblivious to the intense cold as he gazed out into the great unknown, wrestling with the riddles of the universe.

Russell and his bosum chum, the Leicestershire squire Charles Packe, were central figures in 19th century Pyrenean exploration. Misleadingly, they are virtually the only British *Pyrénéistes* to feature in the standard histories of British mountaineering yet, Swinburne's 1776 ascent of the Pic du Midi d'Ossou apart, the unsung British pioneer of the Pyrenees was a remarkable Yorkshire lass, Miss Anne Lister, the chatelaine of Sibden Hall, Halifax.

In 1827, Miss Lister narrowly failed to become the first woman to climb Mont Blanc – a prize which only fell to Henriette d'Angeville eleven years later. On her first visit to the Pyrenees in 1830, Anne made the first British ascent of Mont Perdu. Returning to the range eight years later, she learned that the Prince of Moscow, son of Napoleon's Marshall Ney, was planning to climb the Vignemale. With memories of Waterloo still fresh, Anne decided to forestall the Prince and engaged as her guide one Henri Cazaux of Gèdre. Cazaux with another guide had already made the first ascent of the Vignemale the previous year, shattering its myth of inaccessibility but almost at the cost of his life when he fell down a crevasse on the Ossoue Glacier.

Wary of repeating that experience, Cazaux prevailed on Anne to attack the mountain by an entirely different route from the south. Leaving their Gavarnie hotel at 2.45 am on August 11th 1838 on horseback, the party rode up the Ossoue Valley, crossed the Port du Pla d'Aube on foot and, from the upper Ara, climbed the Vignemale by a long rock and snow couloir. Despite altitude sickness, Anne reached the summit at 1 pm and was safely back in Gavarnie early the following morning after a round trip of twenty-two hours.

The climb which should rightly bear Anne Lister's name is still known as the Prince of Moscow's for the duplicitous Prince, having made the second amateur ascent a few days later with Cazaux and a posse of guides, spuriously claimed the route as his own. Happily, the modern French guidebook acknowledges Anne's priority and still rates her climb *"assez difficile"*. Anne Lister's Vignemale ascent remains an unrecognised landmark in British climbing history. It pre-dates Russell and Packe's explorations by twenty years and precedes by four the first British pioneer ascent of *any* Alpine peak – Professor James Forbes's 1842 ascent of the Stockhorn. The full facts of her achievement were only discovered in the Halifax Corporation's archives 120 years after the event.

Gazing up at the Vignemale from that sunlit col, I reckoned it a nice coincidence that we should be re-tracing this British heroine's route back to Gavarnie.

Walter's "Come along John, what are you dreaming about" roused me from my reverie and we saddled up for the descent of the mysterious upper Ara Valley. Our route was like following a broad white motorway. With the angle of Walter's and Jean-Pierre's bodies swinging this way and that and the heels of their skis spurting snow, the run was nothing but pleasure. This time neither Alan nor I were far behind and in minutes France seemed worlds away. We had entered altogether wilder and more remote country and for one magical hour skied deeper and deeper into Spain on perfect snow. Then, quite suddenly, the snow gave out as if a line had been drawn leaving below us yellowed grass and grey limestone.

We stopped within sight of a grubby *cabane* littered around with rusting tins and empty Gaz cannisters. Man had defiled but the only sounds were the gurgling of the infant Ara, the call of ibex and the occasional rumble of a rock fall. Stripped to shirtsleeves as we ate *pâté* and *jambon béarnaise*, Jean-Pierre now revealed that he had been here before and began to reminisce about a Spanish inn further down the Ara valley hidden amongst the pines.

"Vraiment, John," he confessed with a sly smile. *"C'est une belle hostelerie espagnole. Un petit endroit de vin, de chanteuses et danseures. Belles femmes, vous savez?"*

"Pres des remparts de Seville?" I quipped. *"Una taberna Lillas Pastia? Peut-être vous avez une Carmen, Jean-Pierre?"*

"Mais non," he grinned. *"Absolument non. En tous cas, Martine arrivera a Gavarnie demain."*

Those brooding clouds we had seen from the Col d'Aratille had begun to steal up the valley.

"We had better be going," I urged this time. "It's still a long way to the Refuge Lourdes with a long steep climb to the Port de Pla d'Aube."

If the first half of the day had been pure pleasure, the second half was nothing but pain. A fortnight earlier, we should have been able to ski all the way to Gavarnie but at this fag-end of April the snow was melting fast and the 600 metre climb to the Port de Pla up steep, shaley slopes dotted with pin-cushion hummocks of spiny grass was hard graft all the way.

My plastic boots were working like a pressure cooker broiling my feet and bubbling the blisters and I was hugely relieved to reach the Port and change over to skis. By now, the purple-shadowed lower Ara had been submerged in grey cloud and snow had begun to fall. We were back in Northern Europe. Walter chose another steep couloir to brush up our technique and set off from the col taking a flight of small avalanches with him. When we had closed up I joked nervously, "You certainly got a few slides going then Walter. No messing with snow profiles."

He looked at me blankly. "Of course not. No time for that rubbish in a place like that. You've just got to move fast."

"Ah well," I said. "Not so far to go now. I can just see the Refuge over there on that promontory."

"Over where?" queried Walter following my gaze. "You don't mean that hut beyond the cliffs? I don't like the look of that route, John. We would have to traverse underneath some very steep ground. That snow could be dangerous. I don't think we should risk it."

I didn't follow this logic. Walter had just brought us down a very steep couloir taking much of its snow with him. Yet now he seemed to baulk at a relatively simple traverse to a safe haven. More to the point, my feet were killing me. I badly wanted to reach that hut before they suffered serious damage.

However, you don't lightly gainsay a Swiss snow scientist on his subject, and so, not wanting to appear a wimp, I persuaded myself that I didn't like the look of that snow either.

"Okay Walter," I replied, "let's give the Lourdes Hut a miss. There's still the Hount Viscos *cabane* down the valley. We can always stay there."

He probably hadn't even heard me as he shot away across the head of the upper valley towards a sloping shoulder that led to easier ground. As we coursed gently downwards, I glanced longingly across the darkening gulf to the solidly built Refuge de Lourdes standing out like a figurehead on a clipper's bow. Seconds later it had vanished in the clouds.

For the second time that day, we had run out of snow. It was 6 pm, and the rain was coming down as a thin, persistent drizzle. We took off our skis, strapped them onto our sacs and started to walk down the Ossoue Valley. Through a veil of mist and low cloud reminiscent of a bad weekend in North Wales, I picked out a small, box-shaped building standing in a green meadow besides the river. My feet felt as if the soles had been stretched on an air-bed of blisters.

"Thank God for that," I muttered to Alan. "That must be the Cabane de Hount Viscos."

He shrugged his shoulders but said nothing.

"Jean-Pierre," I said catching his arm. *"Voyez-vous la cabane la-bas?"*

"Oui. Bien sur," he replied. *"Pourquoi?"*

"C'est la Cabane de Hount Viscos. C'est un refuge idéal pour nous rester la nuit."

He turned to me and then to the others with a puzzled look.

"Peut-être. Mais je ne le crois pas. C'est une cabane très petite et sâle. Gavarnie est seulement six kilometres de distance – pas loin d'ici. La route est très facile et très simple. L'Hôtel Taillon est excellent. J'ai réservé pour nous deux chambres très agréables. L'hôtel est très confortable et la cuisine est superbe."

Swapping a night at a dirty *cabane* for one in a comfortable hotel would normally have been no contest but in this case there was pain, practicality and principle – in that order – at stake. My feet were killing me. We had never intended to reach Gavarnie in a single day; we had got off the mountain safely; we were in no particular hurry and were still humping around enough of Martine's food mountain to last us for weeks. There within minutes stood a hut in which to stay and eat to bust. Despite all this, Jean-Pierre had taken it upon himself to book us into a hotel at Gavarnie a day early.

Sensing my level of enthusiasm but not my discomfort, he now turned to me appealingly with hands upheld.

"John, mon cher, cette passage intégrale du Refuge Wallon à Gavarnie – c'est très classique. Il faut que nous finissions cette Grande Course."

When Jean-Pierre invoked the magic words *"très classique"*, he was putting his soul on the line. Was I going to deny Jean-Pierre his *Grande Course*?

"Come along John," urged Alan. "What's the problem? It's not that far to Gavarnie. Let's get on with it."

Amour propre was at stake but I would have to forget about mine. When we reached a track a wizened shepherd marshalling a few bedraggled sheep spotted us and rushed over to greet us.

"D'où êtes vous arrivés?" he demanded in an incomprehensible accent. *"Où allez vous?"*

Jean-Pierre told him our story and he burst out laughing. *"Incroyable,"* he cackled, and then, pointing to the snow with two fingers, *"Mais c'est fou. La neige est pourri, pourri, pourri!"*

I charitably assumed that Jean-Pierre had misinterpreted my slow progress as boredom when he suddenly became solicitous and explained that he wanted to enliven our descent to Gavarnie.

"John, je sais que cette chemin est ennuyeux. Je vous propose une route alternative. Raide certainment mais il y a une panorama splendide."

By now, it was raining heavily. Burst blisters had left my heels rare with the soles charring nicely. In no way was I going to follow Jean-Pierre's nature trail. If I was going to get to Gavarnie, it would be by the shortest possible way – preferably by car though any other form of assisted passage would do.

"Non Jean-Pierre, absolument NON," I snapped back, *"Mes pieds sont totalement blessés."*

Nothing more was said after that but as I limped down the track in my stockinged feet, Gavarnie began to assume grail-like status. Maybe it was like this for the early pioneers, maybe it still is for busloads of summer tourists, but when we reached this Mecca of the Pyrenees, it was like a ghost town. It had long since been dark as we shuffled along unlit streets behind the inexaustible Jean-Pierre. I looked in vain for the throbbing bars and crowded restaurants of my imagination. Here there was never a murmur and not even a light. Everything was shut for winter – everything except the Hotel Taillon where he had booked us in. How wrong I had been to think that he had been playing us along the way.

Yesterday's fourteen hour marathon might have concertinaed two stages into one but had almost brought my tour to a premature end. Next morning my feet were a swollen bloody mess and I was quite incapable of walking. Fortunately, Jean-Pierre's weather forecast was correct. It was now raining so hard that we couldn't have carried on even if we had wanted to, so while I spent the day bare footed in the bar willing my blisters to heal, the others wandered up for a walk in the clouds that filled the Cirque de Gavarnie.

Late that evening, Jean-Pierre's wife Martine arrived, bringing with her another food trolley and her fourteen-going-on-twenty-one-year-old daughter Véronique.

"Tomorrow evening," announced Véronique, "my boyfriend Serge will join the party."

"What does Serge do?" I enquired mildly. "Is he a *skieur*?"

"Serge is an *aspirant* for the National Ski Team of France," she replied triumphantly.

Ever since I had first met Jean-Pierre, I had recognised a man of surprises. For a start, he didn't fit the conventional Gallic image. Standing six foot four inches, this fair haired Norman spoke one to one French in the style of Charles de Gaulle – slow, clear and measured. His Rousseauesque approach to mountains was endearing and, although a feckless trait in his personality could effortlessly turn the most well ordered plans on their head, his most disconcerting characteristic was a proclivity to invite anyone who took his fancy – family, friends, lame ducks or mad dogs – to join the party. I had already spent some time with Martine on holiday and had been greatly looking forward to her joining us. But the addition of both Véronique and Serge was a complete surprise.

"What the hell's going on?" snorted Alan when we had found a moment to ourselves. "You never told me that we would be taking on two extra people."

"I had no idea about it either, Alan," I replied. "I'm equally thrown though we always knew that Martine would be joining us."

"Martine's all very well," he retorted, "but we don't really know anything about Véronique or Serge, for all this French ski team guff. It sounds to me like another Jean-Pierre *fait accompli*."

"Let's see how things pan out," I suggested mollifyingly.

"We at least have an agreed plan for tomorrow. We're all going to go up to the Sarradets Hut for the night before pushing on to Spain. Let's take things from there."

Long before the first wave of donkey borne tourists had arrived at Gavarnie, Jean-Pierre had ferried the six of us up to the top of the Vallée des Espécières in his car. The morning was full of promise and from the Col des Tantes, we stopped to marvel at the Cirque de Gavarnie. I had seen many photographs of this 1,600 metres high semi-circular wall which stretches unbroken for ten kilometres from the Grand Astazou to the Pic Taillon. You can't mistake the alternate layers of rock and ice vertically veined with waterfalls. The reality lived up to expectation. Deservedly, it is the most famous spectacle in the Pyrenees and justifying Victor Hugo's description *"a Coliseum of Nature. Perfection – great beyond expression, serene even to sublimity."* Yet, despite its dazzling stage light effect produced by the early morning sun, the great precipice wore a brooding, sullen look as if it needed summer and the release of its frozen waterfalls to bring it to back to life.

Up at the Sarradets Hut, it was Véronique rather than Martine who took over. With my feet still recovering, I had found the hut march an ordeal whereas this nubile 14-year-old thought it a breeze. She made up our beds and single handedly cooked supper as if it were the most natural thing in life. When Serge, a likely lad, joined us later that evening I began to re-think our plans. Patently Véronique was an expert skier and tough with it. Maybe we could persuade both her and Serge to join the team and enliven our passage to Barèges?

However, next morning before I had had a chance to discuss this proposition with anyone, Jean-Pierre had cooked up another plan which he, Martine, Véronique and Serge discussed over breakfast at incomprehensible speed. Walter's face remained expressionless and neither Alan nor I had the slightest idea of what they were talking about as no attempt was made to include us in the conversation. I was fast losing control of the situation and from the grim look on Alan's face I knew that he realised it.

At the close of the Leire family's planning session, I was really none the wiser though I assumed from Jean-Pierre that we would all be going to the Refuge Ubeda in Spain and that Martine would accompany us to Barèges. In essence this was back to square one though we were still carrying enough food for all seven of us to go the whole way. One upshot of all the chat was to delay our start by two hours to 9 am. At the time, I didn't think the delay would matter for it looked such a magnificent day.

As our crocodile made its way up the slope behind the hut towards the Brèche de Roland, the Cirque de Gavarnie below us had become a cauldron of cumulus cloud while the Brèche above was lit crimson by the sun.

This famous notch in the frontier ridge is also the culminating feature of the Cirque. It measures 40 metres high and 100 wide and has been a tourist magnet ever since the Duchess of Berry was carried to see it to best advantage in a porter-borne litter in 1828. However, as every French schoolboy knows, the Brèche's most famous association is with the national hero Roland who, with a single blow from his sword Durendal, cleaved the gash through the mountain wall.

Roland, of course, is the hero of the most famous tale of the romantic canon which tells how he and the flower of French chivalry were ambushed and slain by the treacherous Moors when retreating from Spain. As commander of Charlemagne's rearguard, Roland's stubborn refusal to blow his horn until all was lost has given France a corpus of prose and poetry rivalled only by the Arthurian Legends.

Alfred de Vigny's visit to Gavarnie in 1824 prompted his lyrical poem *La Corne* but like others before him, he had picked the wrong place. The ambush of Charlemagne's army was not here but at Roncevalles, the Pass of Thorns, some 70 miles west. Roland, if he ever existed, was an obscure Breton prefect and it was the Basques, then as now keen to settle old scores, rather than the Moors, who ambushed the Franks. Charlemagne himself, a German by race, language and taste, never forced a military issue with the Moors. Christendom's real hero was his grandfather Charles Martel whose famous victory at Poitiers in 732 stemmed the advance of Islam into Europe.

We crossed the Brèche like pygmies at the threshold of a giant's keep. To the south, a succession of snow peaks and ridges hid numberless valleys stretching away into the purple-tinted mystery of Spain. Immediately below us the folds of the upper Arazas Valley fell away to a dark cleft at the bottom of which lay our destination, the Ubeda Hut, but my eyes were focused beyond the valley towards the hulking massif that closed the eastern skyline. I was looking at the Three Sisters of Marbore, Cylindre and, most particularly, Mont Perdu – the third summit of the Pyrenees. Floating like a white cloud above the grey recesses of the valley some ten kilometres away, we had promised ourselves its summit as tomorrow's prize.

"What d'you think of that," I said turning to Alan. "A fine sight."

"Looks a helluva long way from here," he replied dubiously. "I can pick out Perdu okay but how do we get down the other side?"

"According to the map we have to cross the Col du Cylindre. Must be that slight depression just north of Perdu. Looks damn high to me," I replied. "Anyway, tomorrow's another day."

At 3,100 metres it certainly was high and remote too. Even as I tried to trace a route across the col a collar of cloud closed over it. But all that lay in the future.

Martine and Véronique now announced that they were going to stop at the Brèche to sunbathe. This display of feminine vulnerability fell short of the Amazonian profiles I had constructed but, as we still had eight kilometres and a 1,000 metres of descent to go to the Ubeda Refuge, I reckoned they might need a short rest. The five men nipped up the Taillon for a panoramic view but, when we rejoined the ladies, found they had laid out a magnificent picnic in the snow, Cartier Bresson style. I hadn't taken on board the significance of May Day in France but patently the *Famille Jean-Pierre* were bent on making this lunch a near immoveable feast.

Les Etrangers weren't exactly excluded but it became very much a family affair and, as the laughter got louder and louder, Alan took me aside looking less than happy.

"What the hell's going on, John?" he snorted. "We should have finished lunch ages ago but the French have only just started theirs. We can't stay around here. The weather's deteriorating fast and we should be getting down to the hut."

He was dead right. Even as we had been descending the Taillon, ominous clouds had been stealing up the valley and The Three Sisters had now completely vanished from sight.

"I'll try to get some sense out of Jean-Pierre," I replied and walked across to where he was sitting on his rucksack about to open another bottle of wine. Martine was beside him snoozing elegantly in the snow.

"Jean-Pierre," I began, slipping inadvertently into English, "I think we must get going if we're going to reach that Spanish hut. Has Martine got everything she needs to get to Barèges?"

He looked up from his lunch bemused.

"Absolument NON. Martine, Véronique et Serge retourneront à Gavarnie. Ils sont en vacances."

This was topsy-turvey land. In Pau, he had told me that Martine would be coming with us to Gavarnie. In Gavarnie that she would be coming on to Barèges. Now, apparently, she wasn't going anywhere. My patience was wearing thin but perhaps I had got the wrong end of the stick from the start. Perhaps he had decided to go with them?

"Jean-Pierre," I said, *"Il est tard. Je n'aime pas ce genre de temps. C'est nécessaire que nous avançons au refuge."*

"Ah, oui," he replied carelessly. *"Je comprends. Et maintenant, je vous propose la bonne route par l'arrête de la frontière. C'est très classique."*

Here we go again. We had discussed this route before – the classic route to the Refuge Ubeda that followed a spectacular sloping gangway that ran between the topmost cliff tier of the frontier ridge and its lower rampart before swooping down into the trough of the valley. I had originally written it into the Sportplan. Earlier in the day, with good visibility and firm snow, it would have made a perfectly feasible descent route but things had moved on, the weather had turned and it was now mid-afternoon.

Alan had been listening in to all this and took me aside.

"That's a crazy idea, John," he said impatiently. "It's far too late to attempt that route. The sun's been on it too long and we can't even see it now. We should ski straight down the valley and get to that hut with no more messing about."

"And I entirely agree with Alan," chipped in Walter. "We should leave immediately."

When I told Jean-Pierre what the three of us had decided, he simply shrugged his shoulders and said *"Comme vous voulez."*

When we made our *"au revoirs"* to Martine, Véronique and Serge they behaved as if nothing unusual had happened.

Jean-Pierre's *Route Classique* had long vanished in the clouds when the four of us began our descent down the upper Arazas Valley through heavy snow. I now found myself worrying whether we would find the Refuge Ubeda open. Six years before in summer we had found it comprehensively closed. Ollivier's guidebook had issued a similar warning but Jean-Pierre airily dismissed this with a *"pas de problème"*.

The descent took much longer than expected but, as we approached the hut, it was obvious that we were not going to be alone. A stream of climbers were coming up from Spain and inside the hut was bedlam. A mob of hirsute Spaniards were heaving and shoving to catch the attention of a pretty young guardienne who was allocating bunk spaces with cool authority. Guardiennes are a Pyrenean speciality but this one hailed from Dublin.

"Why's this place so full?" I asked her.

"It's May Day," she replied. "The hut was only opened this morning. You're just in time to book your bunk spaces."

Since our last exchange at the Brèche, Jean-Pierre had gone quiet but, as we fought our way into the dining-room, he came back to life. He had seen someone he knew.

"Bernard, Bernard!" he yelled out across the seething room – *"Nous sommes arrivés."*

It was difficult to pick out individual players in that scrum. However, we simply followed in Jean-Pierre's wake as he barged his way through the maul towards a morose looking man with a baleful stare lodged in a corner with another man. They were defending their table against all comers.

Didn't I know that face? And then it came back to me. Bernard Dorche! The guardian of the Oulettes Hut. The man who had abandoned his wife to make her own way down the Val de Gaube. Bernard was not my favourite man but it had been obvious from their first encounter at the Oulettes Hut that he and Jean-Pierre had a close rapport. Maybe they were old friends? It then occurred to me that Jean-Pierre might have known that Bernard would be here all along. Whether we liked it or not, Bernard and his friend Jean-Luc would be dining with us tonight. Nonetheless, *toujours la politesse.*

"Comment ça va, Bernard," I enquired solicitously, *"Mais où est votre femme, Anne-Marie?"*

Bernard scowled, *"Anne-Marie!"* – he almost spat out the words. *"Je ne sais pas Monsieur. Le mariage est tout à fait fini."*

Inwardly congratulating the delicious Anne-Marie for getting shot of this awkward brute, I stiffened when Jean-Pierre announced that *"heureusement"* Bernard and Jean-Luc would be joining us tomorrow to climb Mont Perdu. Gallic solidarity was one thing but Bernard's proven track record of looking after *Nombre Un* might land us in every sort of trouble, and was it just a matter of climbing Mont Perdu? Now that Martine had fallen out of the frame, perhaps Jean-Pierre had asked these two to come along with us to Barèges.

Walter might be taking this in his stride but I could imagine what was going through Alan's mind.

He tackled me about it soon enough.

"What on earth's the score now, John," he asked me angrily.

"Of course I recognised that clown Dorche from the start. He's no good. I wouldn't trust him on a mountain. God knows what he might get up to."

"I don't think we'll have too much trouble climbing Perdu with him," I replied defensively. "I've done this route once before in summer with Georgina."

"That's all very well," Alan retorted. "It's what happens after that worries me. Tomorrow's going to be a very long day. Climbing Mont Perdu's one thing but we've somehow got to reach the Refuge Tuqueroye."

"I'm quite aware of that Alan," I replied mildly though, in fact, I was as unsure as he was of precisely how we were going to do this. It wasn't a route that featured anywhere in the guidebook although the ski map marked a passage over the col and then down the face with two kilometres worth of dotted lines signifying *"passage difficile ou dangéreux."*

"Have you seen this postcard I picked up at Gavarnie?" demanded Alan. "It clearly shows the north-east face of Perdu that you're proposing to descend. I simply don't believe you can ski down it."

He shoved a crumpled postcard under my nose. It showed a picture of Mont Perdu taken from a frozen lake. The face was covered in ice and looked horrendous.

"I'll speak to Jean-Pierre about his two friends," I said somewhat shaken. "We certainly don't want any misunderstandings."

When I tackled Jean-Pierre about Bernard's and Jean-Luc's plans after Mont Perdu, he simply shrugged his shoulders.

"Bernard . . . Jean-Luc?" he replied, *"Peut-être qu'ils vont continuer. Mais je ne sais pas."*

"You know," I said, returning to Alan, "having Bernard on board needn't necessarily be bad news. After all, he is a hut guardian so he should know these mountains like the back of his hand. He should also be able to tell us whether or not the Tuqueroye Hut is still open."

This was another matter that had long been bugging me. The Tuqueroye Refuge, scheduled as our next stop, was a vital link in the chain and there was no other hut along the way. But a serious question mark hung over it. Ollivier's guidebook had described it as being *"en pitieux état"* and that it was likely to be knocked down and re-built. Perhaps it no longer existed?

When I had first put this matter to Jean-Pierre, he had dismissed it as a *bagatelle*. But as we couldn't afford to get this one wrong, Alan and I decided to have a quiet word with Bernard.

Despite his unprepossessing appearance and uncouth ways, Bernard proved to be as pedantic as any French Academician in matters of pronounciation. In the ensuing *Singspiel* Alan took on the role of a British Belmonte and Bernard a Gascon Osmin.

Alan: *"Bernard, est il ouvert, Le Tuqroi, s'il vous plait?"*

Bernard, blankly as if deaf: *"Eh?"*

Alan, slowly and purposefully: *"Est-ce qu'il est ouvert, Le Refuge Tuqroi, s'il vous plait?"*

Bernard, as if feigning total incomprehension: *"Le Quoi?"*

Alan, voice now rising with an edge to it: *"Le Tuqroi … LE REFUGE TUQROI."*

Bernard, as if perplexed: *"Tuqroi … Tuqroye? – Ah, je comprends – Le Tuqueroye … LE T-U-Q-U-E-R-O-Y-E!"*

Alan, glowering: *"Oui, d'accord. Le T-U-Q-U-E-R-O-Y-E!"*

Bernard, triumphantly: *"Oui, bien sur, c'est ouvert."*

Exit Bernard, grinning malevolently.

The Refugio Ubeda's *dortoire* was hotter than that of any hut I had ever slept in and smelt like a sardine factory. Once wedged into the communal bunk, it was impossible to turn over. I was sandwiched between Alan snoring like an ox and another man whose breath came across like a garlic laden *Sirocco*. Finding it impossible to sleep, I kept thinking about Mont Perdu, the mountain we were planning to climb tomorrow.

Perdu had a special place in my memory as my first Pyrenean peak and my wife Georgina's first big mountain. It also figures prominently in Pyrenean mountaineering history. Why, for example, is it called the Lost Mountain? Although from the Spanish side it is easily seen, from the French side it is almost invisible. Part of the explanation lies in the lawlessness and brigandage that was rife throughout the Spanish Pyrenees during the 18th and 19th centuries. Few ventured into the Spanish mountains and until the Frenchmen Vidal and Reboul's first Pyrenean cartographical survey in 1787, Mont Perdu's exact whereabouts were a geographical mystery though it was then believed to be the culmination of the range.

Coincidentally, when the two young surveyors were taking their bearings from the Pic du Midi de Bigorre, they were joined on the summit by another itinerant Frenchman, Raymond de Carbonnieres. Raymond, having been a bit player in the *scandale extraordinaire* of Marie Antoinette's diamond necklace, had just fled revolutionary Paris to avoid execution. Hoping to make a new life for himself in the country, Raymond had taken to wandering the hills and, when Vidal pointed out Mont Perdu, he determined that he would be the first to climb it. The story of his quest for the Lost Mountain, a mere incident in a life as fantastic as that of any Dumas hero, marks the beginning of Pyrenean mountain exploration and literature.

My fitful sleep was ended at 5 am by Jean-Pierre flashing his torch in my face and trumpeting that the hut lacked *papier de toilette.* It was then that I recognised my other sleeping companion as Bernard. Silent and numb with cold, our strange sextet reached the frozen Etang Glacé as dawn was breaking with a sinister, green tinge. Here Bernard sat down on a rock with a nose bleed and announced that he and Jean-Luc would go no further. The four of us dumped our skis and set off for the summit by the same snow couloir that I had once climbed with my wife on a brilliant summer's day. This time there were no colours but black and grey and the mountain's upper reaches were lost in cloud. Half way up the couloir, teetering on the minute steps hacked out with Walter's ice axe, I bitterly regretted that I had followed his advice to leave my crampons behind at Cauterets.

"I never take them ski touring," he had advised. "It saves weight."

Approaching the summit, we were hit by a vicious wind which precipitated a quick turn about and, as we re-traced our steps, passed on the way down a procession of Spanish climbers strung out along the length of the couloir.

Bernard and Jean-Luc were still perched as stolidy on their rock by the Frozen Lake as when we had left them. They looked like a couple of old crows but Bernard's climbing cop-out had put him in an altogether chirpier mood and, as he sunk his discoloured teeth into the last of Martine's *baguettes avec jambon,* he warmed to a new vision of mountain *cameraderie et amitié.*

"Ah yes," he proclaimed, "when we all get back to Pau I'll throw a party and slaughter a sheep. We'll feast like Gascons and drink like Musketeers."

When he and Jean-Luc said they had to be leaving us for Gavarnie, I almost warmed to him. Perhaps he wasn't such a bad chap after all. We all shook hands, slapped each other on the back and expressed protestations of everlasting friendship but we never saw Bernard or Jean-Luc again and, much later, I learned from Jean-Pierre that they had taken eleven hours to get themselves back to Gavarnie.

I didn't realise it then but our day had barely started. The weather was deteriorating and our first real work was the climb up to the Col du Cylindre. It wasn't that far but trying to keep contact with Walter up icy rocks overlaid with snow, carrying my skis over my shoulder, made me wonder why we couldn't have settled for a second night at the Ubeda Hut sinking a Guinness or two with that comely colleen.

As the angle eased to indicate that we had reached the 3,100 metre col, a bedraggleld bunch of French climbers, plastered in snow and dragging their ropes behind them, emerged from out of the gloom.

"Où allez vous?" I asked the first man conversationally, knowing that there could only be one answer.

"Le Refuge Ubeda," he replied testily looking utterly washed out.

"Eh bien," I persisted, *"Le Refuge Tuqueroye – est-il ouvert?"*

"Oui, c'est ouvert," he shot back, *"mais il est sâle et très petit."*

"Merci bien Monsieur. Et la route en descente – Comment ça va?"

He glanced at our skis, made a grimace and gave a Gallic shrug.

"Elle va, peut-être Monsieur ... peut-être ..." and with that disappeared down the mountain the way we had just come up.

Although in the shifting cloud it was impossible to see exactly what lay below us, I knew from my altimeter, map and Alan's postcard that we must be standing near the edge of the biggest ice face in the Pyrenees. Raymond de Carbonniere, who first saw and recorded the now famous view of Mont Perdu from the Brèche de Tuqueroye, described this face as "the most imposing and frightful scene in the Pyrenees". Ollivier's climbing guidebook prefers the more lyrical *"l'un des spectacles les plus beaux et les plus célèbres des Pyrenees"* but whatever one's perceptions of mountain scenery, the practical problem for us was how to get down it.

I had already discussed tentatively with Alan how we were going to tackle without crampons what had been described as an *"itineraire d'alpinisme hivernal impracticable à ski"*.

"I don't really see any problem," said Alan. "We've got a perfectly good rope and can always *abseil* the tricky bits."

As we edged closer to the lip in the footsteps of the French climbers, the clouds suddenly momentarily parted and I found myself gazing into space. The ground at our feet sheered away into a white abyss. I couldn't see the bottom but I had worked out that it must be 700 metres below. Another two kilometres away across the void I spotted an indistinct nick in the crest of the mountain wall opposite.

"Bloody Hell," I gasped, "We're immediately above the face. And that must be the Brèche de Tuqueroye in the distance."

As the clouds closed in again the only comfort I could derive was from the map's legend – *"impracticable à ski"*. At least there would be no *Ski Extrème* heroics here.

As I threw off my sac, fished out the rope with a couple of karabiners and began buckling my skis onto my sac, Walter walked across to me.

"John, John what are you doing?" he asked anxiously.

"I'm just getting the rope out Walter. We'll need it for the *abseil*."

"What *abseil?*" he replied perplexed. "We don't want to *abseil*. We don't need to *abseil*. We're going to ski this and we won't need your rope to do that."

I felt what had become a familiar tightening of the stomach.

"Walter," I began evenly, "We can't possibly ski down this bloody great face. It would be suicide. We're on a graded ice climb. We can't even see the way down."

"But those Frenchmen have just come up it," he persisted. "If they can climb it, we can ski it. On steep ground, it's always safer to ski."

I was in totally unfamiliar territory and dismayed to see that both Walter and Jean-Pierre had already put on their skis. I looked round wildly towards Alan for support but he was now kneeling on the ground fastening his bindings. I couldn't duck out of it. Another case of *amour propre*.

"Okay, Walter," I said resignedly, "you'd better lead us down – but keep in touch or you may not see me again."

The French tracks soon vanished and from then on it was all edging and side slipping and always in Walter's wake. It's the one ski survival technique I had almost mastered but never until now did it matter so much.

Until the start of the twentieth century, a hanging glacier stretched unbroken from the top to the bottom of Mont Perdu's north-east face – then the most famous ice climb in the Pyrenees – but glacial recession has exposed a section of near vertical rock which now splits the icefall. This was the crux of our route. I still have a vision of Walter's slim figure inching across a near vertical wall with just enough snow to overlay the slick of ice for his skis to get purchase. Somehow, we all managed to follow him down this critical passage without peeling off and for once bad visibility was good for the nerves. When I joined Walter at the bottom of the final runout his bearded face was creased into a broad grin.

"Well done, John," he exclaimed seizing my shoulder. "You've just skied down Mont Perdu's north-east face."

My knees and thighs were just coming back to life when for a second or two the clouds again broke and thinned. I glanced behind me and had to crane my neck upwards to try to fix in my mind the stupendous sweep of snow and ice that soared upwards and then abruptly disappeared into the mist.

"Thanks, Walter," I muttered as I pumped his hand, "that was a fantastic lead. But I'll never believe I really skied down it."

The Cabane des Aires. (L to R) – Walter, Jean-Pierre and Alan

On the far side of the Pineta Cirque, a party of French climbers were camped in the snow at the edge of the frozen Lago Helado. A bitter wind had got up and from the moment we stopped moving I felt cold. I wondered what had induced them to camp in such a miserable spot when the Refuge Tuqueroye was just above us at the top of a snow couloir leading to the Brèche.

"Est-il ouvert, le Refuge Tuqueroye?" I asked.

"Oui, certainement," one of them replied. *"Mais le refuge est un bivouac très simple et il est plein d'ordures!"*

I had never taken into account this confounded May Day weekend when planning this trip but now it seemed to be dogging us at every turn. When we got up to the Brèche itself there was barely standing room for four. Just above it, on a shelf tucked into the rock, were two bivouac shelters shaped like mini-Nissen huts. Their bowed entrances barely a metre high were guarded by Neanderthal look-alikes, growling like dogs defending their patch. The place smelled like a badger set.

"Est-il ouvert ..." I began ...

"For Chrissake John," interrupted Alan. "Spare us that one. Of course the place is open, it's just bloody well full up."

"Okay Alan, – *'y a-t-il de place?'*" I persisted.

"Non," growled the boss cavemen. *"Absolument NON. C'est complet. C'est tout complet."*

I wouldn't have wanted to stay in your filthy hole anyway, I muttered under my breath but suddenly I felt very tired.

What to do now? Patently, all four of us couldn't possibly fit into Alan's two man bivouac tent. For a moment my mind went blank. My original plan had been to spend the night here before descending to Gavarnie across the Hourquette de Pailla. But Gavarnie was a full day away and we had already been on the trot for eight hours non-stop.

"The only alternative is to carry straight on," I suggested guardedly. "We can by-pass Gavarnie altogether, get down into the Cirque d'Estaube and make for Héas."

"That's all very well," snapped Alan looking at his map, "but Héas is bloody miles from here. It's at least another half day's worth."

"Okay," I replied wearily, taking another look at my own map.

"D'you see this cabane that's marked in the Cirque d'Estaube below us. That can't be more than four kilometres away. We can stay there."

"Maybe," said Alan, "but we've got to get down this couloir first. Come and take at look at it. It's horrendous."

When we had first arrived at the Brèche Alan had done a quick recce while I had been parlaying with the cavemen. From this uncompromising col, the 260 metre Couloir Tuqueroye pitched at an angle of 45 degrees seemed the only practicable way into the Cirque d'Estaube. This couloir had a history as the key to the early attempts on Mont Perdu. On Raymond de Carbonnieres second attempt to climb the mountain in September 1797 it had given his guides two hours of continuous step cutting and remains a graded climb with an *"itineraire d'alpinisme hivernal"* tag. It was the last place I wanted to tangle with at the end of a hard day.

I walked over to the corniced edge with Walter. All I could see was a snow chute that dropped plumb before disappearing down a rock funnel. Far below, down in the depths of the cirque, the suspicion of a run-out was marked by parallel furrows of discoloured snow.

"Phew," I whistled through my teeth. "What a bugger."

Turning to Walter I said, "We've got a proper climb on our hands here but at least the snow's soft. Should be no problem kicking steps down this top bit but let's just hope it doesn't avalanche."

Walter shot me one of his incredulous looks.

"Nonsense John," he replied breezily. "If you've skied the Perdu face you can easily ski this one. The angle's steep at the top but it's nothing like as long or as serious."

Jean-Pierre had moved up to my shoulder and, like Lucifer, whispered in my ear.

"C'est très classique," he intoned. *"Le couloir est très classique."*

Walter already had his skis on; Jean-Pierre was crouched down adjusting his bindings and Alan was about to do the same.

Okay then, I thought, we'll all ski this bloody thing together and hang the consequences.

"Ready to go everybody?" Walter was poised at the lip of the couloir testing the snow with his skis.

"Okay Walter," I shouted. "Off you go, we're right behind you."

With that he vanished, with me following him like a leech. I had switched to automatic pilot with my eyes rigidly fixed to the back of his skis. Confound the man! Even in this lift shaft of a couloir, his skiing was as fluid and stylish as it had been at the start of the day. Mine was another exercise in survival but this time I had made up my mind that I would either bomb this bloody gully or die in the attempt. Like a man facing his maker, I locked my jaw and just went for it.

Had the snow been frozen any slip would have spelt disaster but at this time of the day it had turned to mush so it was simply a matter of checking and turning, checking and turning just at the right time. The alternative was self destruct against the rock walls on either side. I skied to the bottom of that couloir like a kamikase pilot, even overtaking Walter in the process.

At the base I could see that we were over the worst but had only reached the second tier of a vast amphitheatre. The main auditorium still lay beneath us but the clouds were thinning and revealed the outlines of snow streaked ridges rising up from the depths of the Cirque. At the very bottom the silver thread of a stream flashed in the late afternoon light.

The angle of the slope had eased but the mental and physical effort of getting down the couloir in one piece had spent my batteries. The snow assumed the consistency of liquid cement and my knees and thighs locked rigid were no longer capable of executing the down/up movement that commands every turn. My sole preoccupation now was to reach the Cabane d'Estaube without breaking a leg.

When we got to the *cabane* it didn't look as if anyone had used it since the French Army built it in 1947 to control the cross border smuggling that became endemic during the War. There was nothing inside except the remnants of an inter-locking steel-framed set of Army beds.

"Cabane de luxe," quipped Walter as he set about making a cat's cradle with what was left of the rusting wire mesh. He torsioned this with a length of nylon cord and announced proudly, "and here's my bedstead."

Alan had been rummaging around a heap of rubbish and now brandished a half filled plastic bottle.

"Village Margnat!" he pronounced. "Looks good to me so here's our nightcap."

As it grew dark, we sat outside on the hut's stone doorstep in our sleeping bags, taking alternate sips of Alan's brew. Warmed up and fortified with a spoonful of sugar it might have been *Chateau Margaux*. The sky had cleared and the sun's afterglow lit the circle of peaks that ringed the back of the Cirque. The Couloir Tuqueroye which had so recently held our lives on a thread glimmered faintly like a pink ribbon.

Alan and I spent that night camped on the grass outside the hut in his bivi-bag and woke in the morning to the sound of a merry brook. The wind had swung round to the south west bringing a fresh, damp feel to it. Jean-Pierre predicted rain and as we marched down the Estaube's wild, bleak valley, more Scottish than Pyrenean in character, the clouds closed, cleared and closed again. For the past four days, we had seen nothing but snow, rock and ice but now we sauntered through green meadows splashed with wild flowers. In a limpid pool, deep set in white limestone, Alan, Walter and Jean-Pierre took an icy dip.

Ollivier's guidebook had said nothing about Héas but it was in this tiny hamlet that Anne Lister's guide Cazaux and the Brothers Passet were born. The Passets put the first climbing route up the Cirque de Gavarnie's great face and so impressed Edward Whymper that he asked them to accompany him on his expedition to the Andes in 1880.

We had come expecting nothing but the lunch Madame provided at *La Chaumiere* – *pâté, omelette, jambon, crêpes, fromage et les vins de la region Corbières et Jurançon* – was even up to Jean-Pierre's exacting standards. I had begun to flag physically before tucking into this feast but three hours later everything again seemed possible and I took stock of what we had achieved since we left Gavarnie – the Cirque de Gavarnie, the Brèche de Roland, Mont Perdu with its formidable north-east face and now the Cirque d'Estaube. Of my original list of cirques only Troumousse remained. We were now at its very threshold.

"So what's the plan now?" asked Alan. "Must say, I wouldn't mind staying here the night. I reckon we deserve it."

"Better press on into the Troumousse Cirque," I replied unenthusiastically. "The Pic Munia's well within our grasp. According to the map there's a nearby *cabane* which we should easily reach this afternoon."

I had scarcely noticed the rain when we left *La Chaumiere*. During the first hour, shod in the suede shoes Martine had brought to Gavarnie, I positively roared up the path into the cirque, oblivious to blisters, but the flame lit by *le bon vin* began to splutter and finally died when the rain turned to sleet and then to snow. By the time we reached the *cabane* I was soaked through and shivering. In wet weather my old Ventile anorak might have been made of blotting paper. I envied Jean-Pierre his brand new Gortex jacket.

The Cirque de Troumousse, a two kilometres high treeless plateau surrounded by a ring of mountains ten kilometres in circumference, was as wild and forbidding a place as I had seen in the Pyrenees and the Cabane des Aires the least attractive hut.

"What's this then, John?" demanded Alan as we stopped outside it. "Looks a real dump."

"It's the Cabane des Aires," I replied testily. "It says so."

The squat, pre-cast concrete box that confronted us had only two embellishments – its name and a patois rune inscribed on the lintel above the iron doorway:

"U toy nou cragn que dieu: ets périclés..."

"Jean-Pierre," I asked him, *"Qu'est-ce que cela signifie?"*

"Je ne sais pas," he replied. *"C'est très bizarre. C'est la provenance des Pyrenees Mystérieuses."*

"What d'you think Walter?"

"Probably Romance," he replied knowingly. "I would translate it as *'Fear God – Danger here abides whatever'*."

The description *cabane* flattered the place. By comparison the *Cabane d'Estaube* had been a palace. It was barely seven foot square with nothing inside it save for a few fencing posts and some boulders sticking out from the three inch deep melt water lake which covered the concrete floor.

I was feeling dog tired and could only think of how I was going to find anywhere to sleep. Walter had already constructed a bed out of his rescue sledge by locking together his skis with metal cross pieces and backing the whole with his shovel and the canvas seat. This time, Alan went one better.

"I'll rig a hammock," said the ex-submariner as he lashed four skis together, suspended them from the two horizontal iron bars that supported the walls and then hoicked this contraption to within six inches of the ceiling. His hammock was suspended two metres off the ground and the business of getting himself and his sleeping bag into it involved the only gymnastic climb of the tour.

Jean-Pierre and I shared out the fencing posts and boulders between us to make a crude duck board. This fakir's bed kept some parts of my body above water but while Jean-Pierre had a foam mattress and full length sleeping bag as a cushion, my half length *pied d'éléphant* was wholly inadequate. On my bed of pain, teeth chattering uncontrollably, I passed the night listening to the snores of strong men vying with the wind, always preoccupied with the consequences of Alan's fifteen and a half stone breaking their moorings.

Next morning, standing outside the cabane in the snow sipping our tea, we compared notes as to who had had the worst night. My feet were a bloody mess and my ankles so swollen that I couldn't squeeze them into my boots. When an armada of ragged clouds began creeping across the lip of the plateau Walter echoed the general feeling.

"I think we should forget about the Pic Munia. Almost a metre of snow fell last night and I don't like the look of this weather."

"Maybe we should give it a chance to clear," I suggested half-heartedly. "We might still be able to see something of the cirque if we ski across to the Cabane Aquila. We can take stock there and maybe stay the night before pushing on to Barèges."

My original plan had been to use the Cabane Aquila as a springboard from which to cross the Crête de Campbieil into the Campbieil Valley. Once there, we would be poised to complete the last leg of the traverse to Barèges. But weather disposes and, as black clouds filled the great cirque and I studied the map yet again, I realised that I had been hopelessly over-ambitious.

It took us two hours to reach the Cabane d'Aquila on a compass bearing through wet, heavy snow. We didn't see anything more of the Cirque de Troumousse and the cabane's water supply took the form of a torrent pouring in through the roof and out through the door.

All of a sudden, I felt terribly tired. My feet were about to disintegrate. I had run out of steam. As we had flogged all the way round this endless cirque I had been wondering what to do and now came out with it straight.

"I think we all need a break before we go any further. Barèges is still days away from here. I really must have a decent night's sleep before pushing on."

"I entirely agree," replied Walter. "And I don't like this weather. The snow's unstable and we should get a proper forecast before we go any further."

"We could get that in Héas," suggested Alan. "It's just at the bottom of this side valley. Can't be more than 500 metres descent."

"Et alors, Jean-Pierre. Qu'en pensez-vous?"

He had understood the drift of our conversation but I reproached myself for breaking into English.

"Je vous propose," he began, *"une autre route, un projet alternatif très, très simple."*

Jean-Pierre sketched out a new plan. According to him we had come to the wrong hut. The Aquila was not the one he would have chosen. There was another hut, higher up an adjacent valley, from which we could reach the Campbieil and then the Aure Valley. From there it would be an easy step to Barèges.

The last thing I could face was another Jean-Pierre change of plan but we had to hear him out so I produced my tattered map and asked him to take us through his route. With his finger he traced a line which climbed steeply for 300 metres up the deep cut Aguillous Valley to a dot marked *Cne*. It was here that he was proposing we stay the night. The following day, we could cross the 2,608 metre Hourquette de Héas into the Campbieil Valley.

"I'm definitely not on for this," growled Alan. "That *cabane's* probably a complete ruin. Anyway, where the hell do we go from there. The map marks that route across the Hourquette de Héas as a *passage dangéreux*. It would be desperate in these conditions."

I looked at Jean-Pierre closely as if for the first time. His eyes had a misty "seek beyond the ranges" look. Visions of Austerlitz perhaps? – more likely Waterloo.

"Sorry, Jean-Pierre," I said brusquely. *"Ce n'est pas possible. C'est trop dangéreux, très longue, c'est mauvais temps et il y a danger d'avalanche."*

"Peut-être," he replied unconcernedly with a shrug. *"Mais c'est une route très classique."*

Walter and Alan had already packed their sacs and were waiting outside the door, skis on and ready for the descent to Héas. There's another inn in the village which is older than *La Chaumiere*. I didn't notice its name but it's a place for *montagnards* run by an elderly couple, relics of a more heroic age. Here perhaps Anne Lister had her famous confrontation with Henri Cazaux when she made him sign the *Declaration,* drawn by a lawyer in Lourdes, confirming that she had beaten the Prince of Moscow to the summit of the Vignemale. Cazaux hugely admired this *"superbe femme"* and they made up their spat over a bottle of wine with handshakes all round. We cracked several while Walter ate a whole kilogram of cheese.

When our kindly hosts confirmed that the weather was going to be bad for days ahead, Walter turned to me and said: "I think I'll be making my way home now, John. Even if the weather clears, this snow's going to take time to settle."

I glanced across the table at Alan. "I think Walter's right," he said, "I'm all for heading home too."

When our taxi arrived from Gèdre, we wrung the gnarled hands of our friends and said goodbye before setting off down the valley. Taking the hairpin bends as if he were racing a slalom, the driver turned to me and said: *"Vous avez eu beau temps et bonnes vacances, Monsieur?"*

Funny, I had never thought of this as a holiday until I had sat back in my seat and let our driver take the strain. As we plunged on down toward the plains, the fields began to fill with yellow jonquils and the grass had turned an emerald hue. The snows of the Pyrenees seemed worlds away. The weather never cleared. It was still raining the following evening when we stole away by train from Pau – Walter to Switzerland, Alan and I to London. We were never to see the mountains again together as a team but I shall never forget our *équipe cordiale*.

Inside the Cabane des Aires

Summit of Turon de Néouvielle. Jean-Pierre and dog

5

In so far as these things matter, I counted our exploration of the French Cirques and Spanish Canyons a success. We might not have completed the full course but we had had some epic days and had been a happy team. Above all, the traverse of this demanding section of the Central Pyrenees had renewed my confidence in a scheme which had been quietly gestating ever since we had completed that first guideless traverse from Urdos to Cauterets. Quite simply, my plan was to do a west to east ski traverse of the range. The Pic d'Anie would serve as my furthest west start point and I would finish on Mount Canigou, the last great mountain of the Pyrenees. The avalanche disaster under the Vignemale had almost killed the concept but the success of the traverse from the Pont d'Espagne to Héas had revived it.

Foot traverses of the Pyrenees from the Atlantic to the Mediterranean have become old hat. However, the first of these, as with all pioneer journeys, was a remarkable achievement which was accomplished in 1817 by one of mountaineering's unsung heroes, the German scientist explorer Friedrich von Parrot. Earlier that year the 26-year-old Parrot had narrowly missed becoming the first man to climb Monte Rosa. Twelve years later he made the first ascent of Mount Ararat, the legendary site of Noah's Ark. His Pyrenean traverse was a solo scientific effort. Assisted by his own invention, the pocket sundial, Parrot meticulously measured snow levels and bagged the odd peak en route including the Maladetta. Nearly 80 years were to elapse before two members of the Alpine Club, Spender and Llewellyn Smith, made a purely mountaineering traverse of the Central Pyrenees from the Col de Puymorens to Gabas in three weeks between 1896 and 1897 accompanied by guides, porters, horses, mules and donkeys to hump their 230 pounds of baggage.

In 1967 a *Grande Randonée* Pyrenean route, the GR10, was inaugurated and a High Level summer walking route does the Atlantic to the Mediterranean in forty-five to fifty stages. But when I first conceived my plan, I had never heard of the complete ski traverse and the only reference to anything resembling it was in Ollivier's four volume ski mountaineering guide, *Pyrénées Itinéraires Skieurs,* which made a passing reference to *"la haute route pyrénéen"* from Fabian to Luchon. From this same guidebook I pieced together an itinerary for the next phase which conveniently dovetailed with what we had already done. By starting at Gèdre, where we had made our final exit last year, I planned to reach Fabian in two days and from there push eastwards across that remote area of the Pyrenees historically known as the Sobrarbe. En route I intended to climb the two highest peaks in the Pyrenées – Posets and Aneto.

Having settled the general plan, the next step was to get a party together. I hoped that I would be able to keep last year's *equipe internationale* en bloc. Alan Wedgwood was a self selection but Walter Good, now aged fifty, had to refuse because my proposed dates clashed with the final month of his Swiss military service. The joker in last year's quartet had been Jean-Pierre but when Alan made no objection to my inviting him again, I wrote to Jean-Pierre with three questions. First, whether he was interested in doing another tour; second, whether he could make a food cache en route and, third, whether he knew anything about Ollivier's *Haute Route Pyrénéen*.

He replied enthusiastically by return of post.

"Trés cher ami ... trés heureux je te lire surtout quand tu me parles d'aventures nouvelles dans mes Pyrénées ..." He made no reference to *Haute Route Pyrénéen* but confirmed that he would be delighted to come, approved the dates and was generally happy with the detail of the proposed itinerary, save to suggest an alternative route into Spain to avoid the avalanche prone Rioumajou Valley. In one important respect he had a counter proposal. As he put it with Rousseauesque sensibility, *"Je regrette que tu ignores la facile et magnifique région du Néouvielle qui permettrait de nous mettre au jambes avant d'affronter les difficultés ulterieures."*

The Néouvielle! I had always intended to cross this *Région des Lacs* as the final phase of last year's tour before we had decided to pull out for it comprises a unique nature reserve within the Parc National des Pyrenées. Because the predominant rock is granite rather than limestone and because it forms an enclave sheltered by the Pic du Midi du Bigorre from the worst of the Atlantic weather, its climate and scenery are closer to that of the Spanish Pyrenees than the French. Its combination of spiky peaks and indented ridges, solitary dwarf pines and a mulitiplicity of lakes merits Ollivier's guidebook description of *"un ensemble granitique de toute beauté ... un monde merveilleux ... en hiver d'un isolement parfait ... ce pays aux itinéraires multiples."*

I took Jean-Pierre's reference to its being *facile* and his warning of *"difficultés ulterieures"* to mean that the Néouvielle would give us an easy ride before we tackled the more serious Sobrarbe crossing. Jean-Pierre's views on matters Pyrenean might sometimes be idiosyncratic but they were also persuasive for we were playing on his home ground. Accordingly, I agreed to revise my original itinerary to start the tour at Barèges rather than Gèdre to make a journey through the Néouvielle, an area I had always wanted to visit in any event.

This minor change of plan triggered a curious reaction in Jean-Pierre. He and I were soon exchanging letters like visiting cards to fine tune the itinerary. At the end of it, I assumed that we had achieved an unusual Anglo/French compromise for both versions appeared to be identical. Yet, with everything apparently settled, I was puzzled by the final sentence of his last letter: *"Que penses-tu de cette proposition?"*

I wondered what nuance I might have missed in translation but owing to work pressures had neither the time nor inclination to prolong negotiations. On the face of it we appeared to be entirely d'accord and it was encouraging that Jean-Pierre was taking the bit between his teeth. Instead of making the single food cache I had originally suggested, he informed me that he would now be making three – one at the Lac d'Orédon, a second at the Hospice Rioumajou and a third at the Portillon d'Oo refuge. Such an exercise was bound to involve considerable time and effort and he subsequently added a fourth by arranging a complicated helicopter drop at the Refuge Sausset in the upper Campbieil Valley. He told me later that he had devoted six Sundays making these elaborate arrangements.

This was immensely gratifying but when I studied the map to see where all this was taking us, I was concerned about the scale and logic behind this gastronomic treasure hunt and into what unchartered financial waters he was taking us. According to my itinerary, we should reach the first cache at the Lac d'Orédon on our second day and the helicopter drop at Le Sausset only a day after that. By the following day we should reach St Lary with its plethora of shops, restaurants and hotels. Compared with the heroic age of porridge cake, it looked as if we would be having a re-run of last year's *embarrass d'alimentation.*

At this stage, I hadn't completed the team so was delighted when Jean-Pierre intimated that Martine would be joining us. This encouraged me to canvass another lady member. Who better qualified than Alan's wife Janet, herself an experienced climber and ski mountaineer? Ideally, I wanted a party of six but had drawn a blank until Susan Baldock, who couldn't come herself, suggested Colin Chapman, a forty-five year old Irish solicitor from County Waterford. Susan told me that Colin had done twenty years of off-piste skiing and, as her personal recommendation, I took his ski mountaineering experience as read. I was also impressed by the attitude of a man who said that he sailed most of the summer and hunted most of the winter so I closed the list.

As the start date approached, the only missing piece in the jigsaw was where and when precisely we were to meet with Jean-Pierre and Martine. The British contingent was scheduled to come out by train but I couldn't pin down Jean-Pierre as to whether our rendezvous would be at Pau or Lourdes railway stations or the bus station at Barèges. Alan, Janet and I agreed to meet Colin Chapman, travelling from Ireland, at the Gare Austerlitz in Paris from where we would catch the sleeper to Lourdes. However, when the three of us foregathered at the ticket barrier there was no sign of Colin.

"What's happened to your new chum, John?" snorted Alan. "Didn't he agree to meet us here?"

"I've never met this chap before," I replied. "but that was certainly the arrangement. If he's missed his plane from Dublin we could have no end of complications. I've still no idea where Jean-Pierre's going to meet us."

Next morning as our train drew into Pau station, Alan and I craned our necks out of the window to see if there was any sign of Jean-Pierre waiting for us on the platform.

"Can't see him anywhere," growled Alan. "Typical."

"He's probably waiting for us at Lourdes station," I ventured. "That's when we've got to get off this train anyway."

Just as the guard blew his whistle for the train to leave, I spotted Jean-Pierre and Martine emerging from the station bar.

"Jean-Pierre, Martine!" I yelled leaning out of the window and waving both arms at them. Jean-Pierre cocked a glance in our direction and then, turning round to give Martine an insouciant wave, clambered onto the train with his skis and an enormous rucksack, closely followed by two young men also with skis and sacs. Martine waved carelessly, turned her back on the train and vanished through the exit doors.

I pushed my way down the crowded corridor to find Jean-Pierre leaning against a window casually puffing at a Gauloise.

"Bonjour, bonjour Jean-Pierre! Comment ca va, comment allez vous – mais pourquoi Martine reste a Lourdes?"

The switch into French was painful and I struggled to find the right words.

"Allo John!" he replied casually, extending his hand. *"Très bien merci mais malhereusement il faut que Martine retourne à Pau. C'est dommage."*

He didn't seem surprised to see me and offered no further explanation as to why Martine had dropped out. Then, gesturing towards the two young men standing besides him in the corridor he said, *"S'il vous plait, faites la connaissance de mes amis Jacques et Jean-Claude."*

Both stepped forward to shake hands. Both looked fit and bronzed. Jacques sported a mop of jet black hair arranged dreadlock style.

"Ils vont unir leurs forces formidables en notre équipe," Jean-Pierre declaimed, looking unusually serious.

Apparently, Jacques was a guide from Toulouse and warden of both the Lac d'Orédon and Espingo Huts. Jean-Claude was a friend from Pau with whom Jean-Pierre had just been touring in the Vanoise.

"Ils sont très bons skieurs!" he confided with a knowing smile.

Burdened with bulging rucksacks, there was no way in which this trio would be able to follow me up the crowded corridor to our compartment further up the train to meet Alan and Janet so I returned on my own.

"What's all this about, John?" said Alan suspiciously. "Who are these two jokers with Jean-Pierre and what's happened to Martine?"

I recounted what Jean-Pierre had told me.

"That's all very well," he snorted, "but what do we know about them? They could turn out complete duds like Jean-Pierre's other friends – that awful Bernard and his useless chum."

"I don't know how long they'll be with us," I countered defensively. "However, there could be several advantages in having Jacques on board. He's a professional guide and also the guardian of two huts that we'll be staying at *en route*."

"I must say, John," Janet broke in. "It's a great disappointment for me that Martine's not coming. I would really prefer not to be the only woman on a tour like this. I really can't understand why Martine should have pushed off without so much as saying 'Hullo – Goodbye' to us."

"I'm very sorry indeed, Janet," I replied. "I'm as surprised as you are at this turn of events. I can only assume that with Martine dropping out, Jean-Pierre had decided to enlist some local support to even up numbers."

"If your friend Colin doesn't show up, we'll soon be outnumbered," growled Alan.

Colin's whereabouts were bothering me too but when we disembarked at Lourdes station to catch the bus to Barèges, I spotted a figure dressed in the unmistakable clothing of a British skier huddled up in a corner of the waiting room. I walked across to him and said, "You must be Colin Chapman."

"That's right," he replied. "I was waiting for you."

"But what happened to you in Paris?" I countered. "I thought we had agreed to meet up at the Gare Austerlitz."

"Oh that," he replied unconcernedly. "Sorry if I caused you any trouble but I decided to fly direct from Dublin to Paris and caught an earlier sleeper."

Back in the seventeenth century, the thermal springs of Barèges were popularised for the French nobility by the Marquise de Montespan, mistress and favourite of Louis XIV, the Sun King. In the eighteenth century the English caught the habit after the example of Arabella Churchill, sister of the Duke of Marlborough. Barèges subsequently lost its premier rating as a spa when its water supply failed to meet demand but in the twentieth century became a popular ski resort. There was no shortage of water now for it was raining steadily but at the end of the season most of the snow seemed to have disappeared except for a dirty avalanche slide which had spilled over the municipal car park. What little we could see of the surrounding mountains was obscured by murky cloud though the predominant impression of the immediate landscape was of shalely slopes coated with a black alluvium.

During our bus journey to Barèges Jean-Pierre had pronounced on the weather past and future. Apparently, there had been an exceptionally heavy snow fall in January which had given excellent early season touring. Since then very little snow had fallen and the outlook was unpromising.

I could see from Janet's expression that she wasn't particularly enjoying this trip so far. However, we all perked up when Jean-Pierre announced that we would be having lunch on him at Barèges' Hotel de Parc conveniently situated opposite the bus stop. Jean-Pierre had ordered the set lunch in advance. Just as I was finishing a jaw challenging hunk of beefsteak, he announced that as Jacques and Jean-Claude would only be with us for the weekend "to help us reach Fabian" it was "imperative" that we get to our first refuge that same night. We should be leaving in half an hour.

Alan turned on me with a black look. "What the hell's Jean-Pierre playing at now, John? We're not remotely ready to start this caper. We've been travelling non-stop for the past thirty hours. The sensible thing would be to ski the Barèges piste this afternoon, spend the night here and make an early start tomorrow morning."

Alan was right. The British contingent needed a rest but when I took a quick look at the itinerary, it seemed that Jean-Pierre and I had agreed to spend tonight at Hotel/Refuge de la Glère.

"I'm very sorry Alan," I replied. "This is my fault. I should probably have organised things differently but Jean-Pierre's only following what was agreed on the programme. Anyway, we should have a comfortable enough night at the Hotel Glère."

Alan muttered something about "damn the programme" but nonetheless, within 25 minutes flat in the busy corridor linking the hotel bar with the gents lavatory, we managed to change, pack and re-pack food and equipment in preparation for the next fourteen days.

There was another surprise at the top of the chairlift which had taken us to the Lienz ski station, for there, clearly awaiting our arrival, were Jean-Pierre's daughter Véronique and her boyfriend Serge.

"'Allo, 'allo," I began, wondering whether another French duo would be joining us for the weekend, "what are you two doing here?"

"We're both *moniteurs* at the Barèges Ski School," enthused the gorgeous Véronique.

"Are you coming with us?" I asked nervously.

"No, no John," she flashed back. "Don't worry."

As we fastened our skins to our skis, Jean-Pierre whispered to me that neither he nor Martine approved of this teenage liaison. I wondered afterwards why he had been so keen to make Barèges our starting point.

By 4 pm that afternoon, an elongated caravan was threading its way up the avalanche scoured Glère Valley. Jacques and Jean-Claude were firmly in the van, Jean-Pierre somewhere in between with a discomposed Anglo-Celtic rump bringing up the rear. Despite this catapult-like start, I took comfort in the thought that the Hotel Glère would at least give us one decent night's sleep and that over a civilised dinner I could discuss the detailed programme with Jean-Pierre. We would all have time to get to know each other better.

Three hours on it was almost dark. We were still sweating our way up the valley and beginning to feel pretty choked off.

"We should surely have got there by now," complained Alan. I had been thinking the same for the past half hour but, almost as he said it, I spotted the outline of a large square building perched on a spur above the lake – the Hotel Glère. With a supreme effort I managed to close up on Jean-Pierre.

"Jean-Pierre," I gasped, *"C'est le refuge, pres là tout n'est pas?"*

"Mais oui, bien sur," he replied, *"mais c'est ferme en hiver. Nous resterons en la caserne."*

Why the hell hadn't he mentioned this at the start and what the devil was a *caserne* I wondered. It turned out to be the deserted barracks that had once housed the cohorts of workmen who had built the Glère dam. It comprised two blocks, each 75 metres long with accommodation on three floors. The top floor was largely roofless while what was left of the bottom offered four metre free falls to the concrete basement through rotten floorboards. We chose the one dormitory on the top floor which still had a roof. The window frames had been sealed with blue plastic to give the impression of permanent sunshine outside.

A table, two benches and assorted iron bedsteads completed the ensemble and a rusting pot-bellied stove gave the clue why the walls had been stripped of their wood cladding.

So far as French Pyrenean huts went, this was superior to many and once Alan had got the stove working and we had settled down to supper, I envisaged the start of a happy relationship with the French contingent. Yet it soon became clear that communication was going to be a problem. Neither Jean-Pierre, Jacques nor Jean-Claude spoke much English while Janet and Colin had only the most rudimentary French. My French, once a superficially confident accent had been exposed, was execrable and Alan's not much better. On previous tours with Jean-Pierre, French had been the agreed *lingua franca* as a matter of *politesse* but on those occasions we had always had on board at least one bilinguist and Jean-Pierre had done us the favour of speaking at half speed. This time round, he was at full throttle and made little effort to include the Brits in his conversation.

Patently, it was essential that at least Jean-Pierre and I should be *d'accord* and working to the same agenda. I managed to catch his attention for long enough to establish that, weather permitting, we would be following our original plan of climbing the Pic de Néouvielle by the Brèche de Chausenque the following day and spending that night at the Orédon Hut.

"I hope this plan's okay with you and Jan?" I said to Alan who'd been sent the proposed itinerary weeks before.

"Fine by me," he replied, "but what exactly is involved in this Pic de Néouvielle?"

"According to Ollivier it's graded four star by this particular route. There's one passage of *alpinisme hivernal classique.* Maybe that's why Jean-Pierre's so keen to do it."

"That's pretty ambitious for a first day," said Alan. "We'll have to make an early start and watch the weather."

"Absolutely," I replied, "but Jacques and Jean-Claude are obviously extremely fit and, as Jacques's the guardian of the Orédon Hut, he must know this area backwards."

I then turned to Colin. So far this trip, I had been so preoccupied with getting on terms with Jean-Pierre that we had never managed to exchange more than a few words together.

"What about you, Colin. Are you happy about tomorrow's plans? It's likely to be a long day with some climbing involved but I imagine that you've done quite a bit of mountaineering."

"As a matter of fact," he replied breezily, "Although I've skied quite a bit, I've never done any proper mountaineering in my life. That's why I had to ask you to lend me an ice axe and crampons."

Alan was looking at me in amazement. We exchanged glances but said nothing.

After last year's bad experiences in *cabanes* and *abris*, I had brought with me my warmest sleeping bag plus sleeping mat and bivouac bag. This should have guaranteed a comfy night but I had failed to notice the hole in the roof just above my head which showered my face with spindrift throughout the night.

We never made Alan's early start. At 5 am it was blowing a blizzard so we all went back to bed. At 7.30 am there were patches of blue in the sky so we got up again and re-instated the original plan to climb the Pic de Néouvielle. However, over breakfast an impenetrable French debate delayed our departure by another two hours. By now Alan was pacing up and down in a black mood.

"What the devil's holding us up now, John?" he demanded. "This looks like another Jean-Pierre cock-up. It's already 9.30 am and if we're going to climb this mountain we're cutting things ridiculously fine."

The French got the message and when we started minutes later, Jacques shot into the lead. The rest of us followed in his slip stream but after an hour he came to an abrupt stop and went into a huddle with Jean-Pierre and Jean-Claude.

"*Quel problème. Qu'est-ce qui ne va pas?*" I asked Jean-Pierre after I had closed up.

"*Pas de probleme,*" he replied cheerfully, "*mais Jacques est deroute. Nous faisons fausse route. Ce n'est pas la bonne vallee!*"

Alan was at my shoulder and exploded.

"I really can't believe it. Jacques's supposed to be a local guide and he should know this route backwards. He's made a complete balls-up. We should have started this caper hours ago and now we've lost another hour thanks to his abysmal route finding. The weather looks dicey and I can't see how we can possibly attempt the Pic de Néouvielle this late in the day."

I turned on Jean-Pierre, "*Jean-Pierre – le Pic de Néouvielle. Ce n'est pas possible maintenant.*"

"*Bien sur, d'accord,*" he replied with a shrug, "*il est trop tard.*"

Jacques didn't appear to own a map so we spread out mine and revised the original plan there and then. The Pic de Néouvielle was scrapped and instead we agreed a new route to the Orédon Refuge some ten kilometres away and over two high passes – the 2,547 metre Hourquette de Mounicot and the 2,498 metre Hourquette d'Aubert.

Jacques was unabashed about his navigational nonsense and again rocketed into the lead as if a Yellow Jersey depended on it. Initially I tried to stay with him but his ability to execute effortlessly inverted kick turns on 40 degree slopes made it a no-match so I slotted in behind him with the rest as we zig-zagged up the steep north wall of the Hourquette de Mounicot. This experience may have been novel to Colin but he didn't appear in the least fazed and by 1.30 pm, a few wobbles apart, we had succesfully negotiated both *hourquettes*.

From here on, the 650 metre descent to the Orédon Refuge, past the frozen Lac d'Aumar and down the easy angled summer road, should have been plain skiing but I had forgotten about Jean-Pierre's first food cache and, at the south end of the Lac d'Aumar, we made a detour to retrieve it. After some prodding in the snow Jean-Pierre pulled out a large plastic bag with a triumphant *"C'est la nourriture. C'est indispensable!"* We were already carrying food but there was enough in that bag to see us through for the next three days.

"Bravo Jean-Pierre," I said encouragingly for he was now looking pensive and slightly bored.

He turned to me and with his hand on my shoulder said. *"John, je vous propose une bonne idèe – une route nouvelle au Refuge Orèdon. C'est plus direct et plus intéressante et la neige est très bonne."*

"Ou est votre route?" I asked him.

"C'est là," he replied pointing his arm in the direction of a dark forest, *"c'est très charmante, n'est ce pas Jacques?"*

Young Jacques, now at his side, was nodding approvingly.

Why not, I thought to myself. This might be yet another change of plan but a good run through the woods in powder snow was fine by me. The weather was still holding and we had made good time. Moreover, at the end of today there was Jacques's refuge to look forward to – no mere hut this but a full blown Touring Club Française *Refuge Hotel.*

"Okay, Jean-Pierre," I said to him. *"D'accord. Vous et Jacques êtes les guides. Nous vous suiverons."*

He plunged into the forest with Jacques on his heels but was stopped short when we came to the edge of a heavily vegetated rock escarpment.

"Une petite descente!" announced Jean-Pierre excitedly.

I peered over the edge of a near vertical rock pitch. We would have to scramble down this one and, as I chucked my skis over the edge into a snow bank at the bottom, I heard Alan muttering behind me – "Where the hell's he taking us to now?"

At the bottom of the escarpment Jacques, now on home ground, insisted on taking over the lead.

"Suivez-moi!" he shouted, *"c'est un short cut."*

I still have a vision of the Lac d'Orédon as I first saw it fleetingly through gaps in the pines of the Sapinière de Loste. The virgin snow on its surface winked and glittered as shafts of sunlight pencilled through the clouds. It presented a wonderfully tranquil sight to bring to an end what had been a thoroughly disjointed day. Soon, I thought, we would be sitting round the bar of the Hotel/Refuge Orédon swigging beer.

When I first awoke in Alan's arms, the immediate past was a blur of confused images. Lying prone on my back looking up into the sky, I could see slats of blue sky through the canopy of pines and could dimly recognise Alan's voice. It was soft and re-assuring but at first I couldn't understand what he was saying or what these other people were doing clustered around me talking in whispers.

My head was throbbing but, as I lay there frantically trying to make some sense of where I was and why, fragments of another life came back to me as if I had just woken from a dream.

The Pyrenees ... a ski tour ... Beyond this my mind was a blank. I felt totally bemused and disorientated.

"You're okay, John. Don't worry, you're going to be fine."

Alan's voice was unusually gentle and made me realise that something was very wrong. I made a huge effort to struggle to my feet and when I saw the others standing round in a circle staring at me anxiously, something clicked back into perspective.

"Take it easy, John," said Alan putting his hand round my shoulder. "I don't think you should be standing up yet. You're as white as a ghost."

"What happened?" I asked him.

"We found you in the snow. You'd gone slightly off route. Maybe hit something and then collapsed. There's absolutely no hurry. We're quite near the refuge so just rest here for a bit."

"I'm okay thanks," I replied. "Just feeling a bit wobbly. I'll be fine once we get to the refuge. Don't let's hang around."

I took a step forward and immediately felt sick.

"I don't think I'll ski this last bit," I said shakily. "I had better walk it."

Jacques had already strapped my rucksack and skis onto his own and beckoned me to follow in his tracks – *"doucement, lentement,"* he urged.

I gripped both ski poles tightly, planted them very deliberately into the snow and started to walk after him. It was like walking in a dream but even the simple task of fording a shallow stream became a superhuman task.

When I awoke in Alan's arms for the second time I was distraught and tearful. My mouth was filled with vomit but my head was clearer now and time fragments came flooding back to me – like falling into a hole, hitting something hard, staggering to my feet and trying to ski on.

"What happened Alan?" I asked, feeling totally dependant on him.

"You collapsed again. You must keep lying down. We'll soon sort you out."

I realised then that I had been concussed. I should have tumbled to it from the start for I had been concussed twice before playing Rugby in schoolboy matches and once through to the final whistle before waking up in hospital. I knew from those experiences that it was essential to rest, preferably in total darkness. It was so peaceful here in the forest. I didn't want to move but then my mind began working again.

"Alan, we can't just stay here. If we're so close to the Refuge Orédon we must get there as soon as we can. Has Jacques gone on ahead?"

"Jacques and Jean-Claude have gone to fetch help," he replied gently.

"From the Orédon Refuge?" I persisted.

"No," he replied, "from Fabian. Apparently, the Orédon Refuge is really a hotel and only open in summer."

I can't believe this, I thought to myself. Why didn't Jacques tell us this from the start. Fabian was miles away, right at the bottom of the Couplan Gorge.

The Couplan Gorge! That name brought me up short. The Couplan had never featured on my original itinerary because Ollivier had given it a health warning – *"une des souricières à avalanches les plus dangereuses qui soient!"*

I had always assumed that this was reason why Jean-Pierre had sensibly suggested that rather than go directly to Fabian from the Orédon we take a high route across the Hourquette de Cap de Long to the Refuge Sausset where he had made the helicopter drop. From there we could easily reach Fabian across the Campbieil Pass.

"My God, Alan, what route are they taking?"

"They've gone down the Couplan Gorge," he replied, "they should make it before dark."

I lay back and closed my eyes. There wasn't nothing I could do now. Everything had passed out of my hands and Alan, always rock solid in any crisis, had taken charge. Soon he was back at my side.

"How are you feeling now?" he asked.

"Not too bad," I replied, "but I feel a bloody fool to have had this stupid accident."

"Don't worry about it. We're now going to put you into your sleeping bag and take you to a little *abri* just by the lakeside. We're rigging up a rescue sledge."

I could never forget the diagramatic sketch of the SCGB approved rescue sledge that Susan Baldock had kindly sent me before that first tour with Alan, Nick and Richard. In theory the twin skis crossbound with ski sticks fastened with rope looked simplicity itself but even Alan, a maestro in all matters technical and mechanical, had to scrap this model in favour of the more practical method of slinging a bivouac tent between two skis and carrying me in the middle. Both Alan and Jean-Pierre were immensely strong men and neither Colin nor Janet slouches but it still took the four of them an hour and a half to carry me a mere 400 metres through thigh deep snow to the *abri*. It was now 6 pm and getting dark. I sank two bowls of soup and promptly fell asleep on the straw-covered floor.

It seemed only minutes later that the place was filled with a hubbub of loud voices, clumping boots and flashing head torches. Alan was shaking me very gently by the shoulder. "Wake up, John, wake up. The rescue party's just arrived."

I glanced at my watch. It was 1 am. I couldn't believe that I had slept for seven hours on the trot but my head had cleared and I was now feeling alert.

"They must have come by helicopter," I exclaimed, "how fantastic."

"No, there's no helicopter here," replied Alan. "Jacques has raised a detachment of Mountain Gendarmerie and they've brought a doctor with them. They've just arrived by ski from Fabian."

"Where are Jacques and Jean-Claude," I asked.

"No idea," he replied. "Probably gone home. But they did a great job. It took them three hours to ski down the Couplan but these people have come up in two and a half hours flat. That's some ten kilometres and uphill all the way."

The young doctor took my pulse, tested my blood pressure and my eyes and said in English: "I'm afraid you've been badly concussed. We must get you to hospital immediately. We can't wait until morning for a helicopter as the weather's too uncertain and it might not then be able to land. If we delay further and the weather breaks it will be impossible to take you down the gorge. Captain Fons of CRS Lannemazan is in charge of this rescue. You're in good hands."

I was trussed up in my sleeping bag like a chicken, strapped into a blood waggon and carried out into the night. I could only just move my head from side to side and could see nothing save a black void. There was no wind but the chill air took my breath away.

Alan was at my side.

"You okay, John? Jean-Pierre and I are going to come too. Apparently, it's a tricky descent and they need everyone available to help with the carry."

I blessed Alan then as I had done on so many occasions before.

By the angle at which my body was leaning outwards, pressed tight against the thick canvas sides of the rescue sledge, I realised that the ground must be very steep. What I couldn't see was the drama of ten men manoeuvering my sledge across a snow slope pitched like an Alpine chalet's roof. The sledge was belayed with ropes to the fore, aft and from above for, at this point, the snow was so hard that the sledge runners could get no purchase. Each member of the team had to move one step at a time with crampons stamping through the crusted surface, legs braced to take the strain and hands tortioning the ropes.

Further down when we joined the line of the summer road cut into the cliff face, I could feel the party's palpable strain as we traversed directly above the upper part of the Couplan Gorge known as Garganta. Here, the angle of the snow banked up against the rock wall was too steep to haul the sledge across so two men, each supporting one end of the sledge, lifted it shoulder high and tip-toed in and out of the bollards that marked the lip of the road and the abyss that sheered away beneath it. They moved like tightrope walkers and I could

Summit of Pic des Quatre Termes.   (L to R) – Jean-Pierre and Colin

smell their tension in the one word they both kept repeating *"précipice, précipice!"*

Alan told me about all this later. At the time I couldn't see a thing but felt everything. Yet my main concern was more mundane. Unable to move a muscle, my back had become excruciatingly painful. When we stopped for a moment and Alan asked me how it was going, I replied through gritted teeth:

"Okay but can't we go any faster?"

"I don't think so, John," he replied gently. "You should see what we've just come down and what's still beneath us."

Moving at this rate, I thought it would take us days to reach Fabian. Captain Fons must have thought so too for he suddenly switched tactics. The first I knew of it was when the blood rushed to my head and flurries of snow particles showered my face. The gallant Captain had decided to take the fall line to the bottom of the gorge down an avalanche cone. My head had become the blood wagon's prow as it sheered through the snow.

Level ground gave my rescuers new impetus and now the team raced the sledge across frozen avalanche slides and icy corrugations.

"For God's sake, Alan," I yelled out, "please get these lunatics to slow down. My head's bouncing around like a football."

He stuffed his duvet jacket between my head and the bottom of the sledge but the pace barely slackened.

By 5.30 am it was getting light. Now, for the first time, I could see the faces of my rescuers – dark, stocky, hard bitten mountain men. Two hours later we reached a police van parked on the far side of a monster avalanche which had swept down one side of the valley and then surged up the other.

It had taken ten men six hours to bring me down the Couplan and when I got to my feet for the first time in fifteen hours, I couldn't stand straight. Over black coffee and *petites beurres* at the St Lary Gendarmerie I talked things over with Alan and the doctor.

"We'll be taking you to the hospital at Lannemazan," explained the doctor. "Captain Fons will put in an official report about your accident."

"Where's Lannemazan and how long will I be there," I asked.

"Lannemazan is down in the plain," he replied. "But I can't say how long you'll be in hospital. Concussion's a serious matter. You'll have to take things easy."

"What about you and Jean-Pierre," I said turning to Alan.

"We've already discussed that," he replied. "We're going straight back up the Couplan to the *abri* to pick up Janet and Colin while the weather still holds so we had better get moving."

Suddenly I felt completely isolated.

"Keep in touch Alan," I said as we shook hands. "Thanks for everything. I'll do my best to join up again as soon as possible."

Even as I said it I didn't believe it. I had no idea how or when we would meet up again and, as my ambulance careered down the Aure Valley at a crazy speed, its sirens wailing and its lights flashing , I had resigned myself to my tour being at an end.

The nice young doctor who had brought me down the mountain wasn't part of the reception committee at the Centre Hospitalier, Lannemazan and sadly I never saw him again. I had been translated from a straw floored mountain shack into a luxurious double ward attended by relays of tight-lipped nurses who administered innumerable tests with brittle efficiency. I had no cause for complaint. My lunch of ham salad, pork cutlets, cheese, fruit and a carafe of wine was gastronomically worlds away from porridge cake and AFD stew but I would have preferred that any day and to be back with my friends.

This place wasn't much like an NHS hospital but it wasn't that friendly either. I tried to get a laugh out of the wizened Andy Capp lookalike with whom I shared a ward but he wasn't having any of it. He ate, washed and slept in his dirty flat cap and spoke an unintelligible patois. Once we had laboured through the story of how he had fallen off a ladder and bust two ribs, my attempts at further conversation were rebuffed with hostile incomprehension. Maybe I had lost cred on that first nursing round when he had spotted me stuffing an anal thermometer into my mouth.

Next day I was driven at breakneck speed to the regional hospital at Tarbes where fourteen electrodes were plugged into my head and a scan resembling a stock market index plotted on graph paper. Vainly did I try to get someone to explain my condition and progress. After the day's second major meal at 6 pm – soup, beef steak, apple purée, with another carafe of wine – the telephone rang. It was Martine Leire. I felt better after that and later that evening Alan rang too.

"How's it all going, John?" he began.

"Fine thanks," I replied, "I've had all the tests but I've no idea when they're going to let me out. Where are you speaking from and how are you all?"

"We're all at Fabian having walked down the Couplan this morning despite bad weather. We'll be staying at the Hotel Orédon tonight."

"You must go ahead and do your own thing from now on Alan but I'm still hoping to join up sometime."

"I've already agreed a revised plan with Jean-Pierre," he went on. "Jacques and Jean-Luc had to go back to Pau so that's left the four of us. We're going to return to the Orédon *abri* tomorrow night and have a bash at the Pic de Néouvielle the day after. We hope to be back at St Lary in three days time."

"Not the Couplan again I hope?"

"No chance of that," he replied. "Jean-Pierre says he knows of a much safer route back to Fabian."

"Best of luck and thanks again for everything, Alan. I'll get in touch when you're back from the Pic Néouvielle. After that it's probably sensible that I return to England."

It was a relief to hear that everyone was all right and heartening to have made contact again but deep down I was feeling bitterly disappointed. I cursed myself for this stupid accident and felt immensely depressed that I was now missing out on a tour that I had spent so much time planning.

Physically I was beginning to feel almost normal but I couldn't see that I would be anywhere near the Hotel Orédon in three days time.

That second day seemed interminable and it was no consolation to see the rain belting down outside. I had long exhausted the guidebook and map when my room mate decided to switch on the television to watch the *Grand Débat* between Giscard and Mitterand. That was it. I swore then that, whatever the cost and whatever the consequences, I would somehow get myself out of this place tomorrow, April Fool's Day.

Next morning the Duty Registrar discharged my nightmare ward mate with a wave of the hand but when I asked him for the results of my tests, he simply shrugged his shoulders.

"But I simply must get back to London," I protested. "My clients need me and I've got important meetings."

"Eh bien. Peut-être bientôt ... tôt ou tard."

He pushed off leaving me immensely frustrated that my French was not fluent enough to get anything but the most flaccid message across. I telephoned the Hotel Orédon and managed to catch Alan just as they were leaving.

"Alan, I just wanted you to know that I shall be making a bid to get out of this bloody hospital today come what may," I said breathlessly. "I'll meet you in St Lary in a couple of days time."

With the cunning of a POW planning an escape, I rehearsed how I would present my case for immediate release to the hospital's establishment. A crisis had arisen at home ... I must return to England immediately. I then dressed, carefully packed my rucksack and for the next three hours sat around the hospital's vestibule in my ski kit importuning doctors, nurses, administrators and orderlies, trying to pierce the impenetrable screen of French bureaucracy. Eventually I tumbled that cash on the table rather than insurance policy particulars, DHSS Forms E111 or simple pleading might do the trick. After an hour's bargaining with the *Section Administratif*, we settled for FF500 up front with the balance of FF1,077 payable later. Once money had changed hands, authorisation to leave the hospital took a ten second telephone call. My verdict on the Centre Hospitalier, Lannemazan, was: *Cuisine* Michelin; *Recommendable* standard; *treatment* efficient; *ambiance* unfriendly and *communication* non-existent.

Within minutes I was wobbling out through the main gates, leaning heavily on my ski sticks and wondering whether another day's expensive boredom would compensate for permanent brain damage. However, once outside, revelling in the sunshine and inhaling the fresh air, I reckoned that I had made the right decision. Buying the most expensive bottle of *anis* I could find – *Pastis 51* – I made my way to the barracks of 29 CRS Section Monatagne, Lannermazan, where I made a personal presentation to Captain Fons with a French *billet doux* I had painstakingly composed during yesterday's dog day.

My heart was singing as my taxi climbed higher and higher up the Aure valley to regain the heights so painfully lost three days earlier. While my driver soliloquised on the pleasures of *la chasse* I spoke of the joys of the mountains and, at St Lary, moved into the room that Alan had already reserved for me at the Hotel Oredon. I then had a bite of lunch before wandering out to explore the town.

Just as I was crossing the car park to investigate the cost of a day's ski pass at the Pla d'Adet téléphérique, I spotted a tall, familiar figure loping across the tarmac.

"Jean-Pierre, Jean Pierre!" I shouted, breaking into a trot to catch him up. *"Jean-Pierre, c'est moi! Merveilleux! Comment allez vous et qu'est-ce qui arrive?"*

I simply couldn't believe it. What on earth was he doing here when he was supposed to be up the mountain? But none of that mattered. I was already feeling inordinately pleased with myself for my escape from hospital. To run into Jean-Pierre seemed an extraordinary stroke of luck. I was delighted to see him and had so much to thank him for but then I thought, maybe something's gone very wrong ... I caught up with him and was about to seize his hand but, instead of stopping, he started back looking agitated and embarrassed. Then, after mumbling a cursory *"Une minute s'il vous plait,"* he dived into a *tabac*. He re-appeared some minutes later puffing furiously at a *Gaullois,* his composure restored but his expression incurious.

"Salut Jean-Pierre!" I began more cautiously. *"Quoi de nouveau chez vous?"*

"C'est bien, merci," he replied coolly without bothering to return my greeting.

I asked him if anything was wrong and what had happened to the others but he wouldn't be drawn except to say that he had just come off the mountain and was awaiting Jacques's arrival from Pau.

"Quoi, Jacques?" I asked him bewildered, remembering what Alan had told me.

"Parce que Jacques est indispensable," he retorted. Almost as an afterthought, he casually asked me if I would lend Jacques my Autophon, snow shovel and map, explaining that once Jacques had arrived in Jean-Pierre's car, they would both drive up the Espiaube Valley, take a ski-lift to the Col de Portet and from there catch up Alan, Janet and Colin. I had brought out from England a hired Alpine Ski Club Autophon specifically for Jean-Pierre's use and had already lent him a map. I had been assuming incorrectly that as a professional guide Jacques would be carrying his own avalanche transceiver. It was all very rum but I owed a great deal to both Jean-Pierre and Jacques so scurried back to my room to get what he had requested.

Back at the car-park a screech of brakes announced the arrival of Jacques. We exchanged cursory greetings as he and Jean-Pierre hurriedly strapped their skis onto the roof-rack. Just as Jean-Pierre was getting into the car I said, *"Bonne chance avec le Pic de Néouvielle. Au revoir – jusqu'a demain!"*

He swung round and faced me for the first time. *"Non, non – jamais demain. Ce n'est pas possible. Nous avons un projet nouveau. Demain nous faisons l'ascension de Pic de Néouvielle mais après ça nous grimperons le Pic de Campbieil – c'est une itinéraire très classique."*

"Mais quand retournez vous ici?" I asked him taken aback.

"Peut-letre après trois ou quatre jours," he replied with a shrug, *"cela depend du temps. C'est normale – Au revoir."* With that he and Jacques disappeared up the road in a cloud of dust.

I walked slowly up the hill on the far side of the Aure Valley to the village of Estensan. It was perched on a spur at the entrance to the Ourtrique, one of the many steep sided, heavily wooded side valleys that run up to the crest of the main range. This one takes its name from the bears that were once so common. Two kilometres below me, spread out across the Aure Valley like octopus tentacles, lay St Lary with its bars, hotels, teleskis, télépheriques, telecabins and ski boutiques with even the faint beat of a pop song.

A gulf of centuries separated St Lary from Estensan whose one narrow street was blocked by a flock of sheep with tinkling bells being shepherded to their spring pastures by a ragged old man and a pair of barking dogs. The wooden water troughs that lined the street were flushed with spring water gurgling an accompaniment to the rustic symphony. Cherry trees at the roadside were turning pink and, in the fields, old women in clogs were spreading steaming manure onto the moist, warm soil. The sun was shining and the air held the promise of Spring. I lowered myself onto a chestnut bench in the shade of a Romanesque church silhouetted black against the snows above and felt the pulse of the village beat slow and secure.

In the midst of Arcady my own world was in turmoil. The chance meeting with Jean-Pierre had thrown me and revealed how far the real world had moved on. After my schoolboy escape from hospital, I had naively assumed that I could pick up from where I had left off. I now realised that the accident had changed everything. I had put myself out of the running and no one was going to mark time. I couldn't blame Jean-Pierre for adapting his plans to changed circumstances.

Reason urged me to go home but instinct whispered that I might still carry on. It was this which caused such a bitter reaction to the news that Jean-Pierre was going out on his own. It wasn't just pique at missing out on the action that so upset me or that the contrived escape from hospital should now seem such a pointless and irresponsible exercise. I simply couldn't understand how Jean-Pierre, having gone to such trouble to organise food caches along the route, should now be reverting to four days of peak bashing in the Néouvielle. It seemed to indicate that our priorities were worlds apart and could only screw up any prospect of completing the traverse to Luchon.

When I thought about it, I realised that my own judgement was probably awry. Another interpretation of events was that Jean-Pierre had arranged this Néouvielle diversion to allow me time to recover. Even if he hadn't, the accident and its aftermath were my responsibility and the sensible course was to take the next train back to London. I felt thoroughly confused, unconfident and indecisive but I didn't want to give up.

That same evening I telephoned Georgina to talk things through and ended up with a compromise solution. I would try a test run on the piste tomorrow and, if that worked out, would wait another day for the others to return from the Pic de Campbieil. By then, I doubted that there would be anything left to salve of the traverse but it was still worth a try.

Early next morning on a beautiful day, I met my first fellow countryman in four days at the top of the Pla d'Adet's only red run. Francis Osmaston was on the last day of his skiing holiday and we found a common strand through his uncle Henry who had written the first climbing guidebook to the Ruwenzori. After one wobbly run, my confidence returned so we skied together for the rest of that day and dined that evening with his Chinese girlfriend.

Back at the Hotel d'Orédon I was just about to go to bed for an early night when I heard a murmur of familiar voices in the hall downstairs. I quickly dressed and rushed downstairs to the hotel vestibule to find Alan and Janet half sitting, half lying on a sofa, with their legs outstretched and their eyes closed.

"Alan, Janet," I burst out, "how marvellous to see you both!"

Neither made a move and when Alan looked up, I could tell that something was wrong. He was looking exhausted, strained and angry.

"What happened?" I asked fearful of another accident. "Why are you back today? What's happened to the others?"

"Frankly, John," said Janet, "we've just been through a pretty awful experience."

"Nobody injured I hope?"

"No, nothing like that," she replied. "Let Alan tell you the full story."

Alan broke in at this point: "After your rescue Jean-Pierre and I reversed the Couplan and spent the rest of that day sleeping off thirty hours on the trot. Next day, all four of us walked down the Couplan and holed up in this hotel from where I telephoned you in hospital. We reckoned that you couldn't possibly be out in under a week so we decided to return to the same *abri* by an altogether safer route and use this as a base to climb the Pic de Néouvielle.

"Over breakfast next morning, Jean-Pierre suddenly announced that Jacques would be joining us later that day. I can only assume that he must have telephoned him the night before from the hotel without telling us. He also told us that, as a consequence of your rescue, the Lannemazan Mountain Gendarmerie wanted us to try out some simple rescue techniques and a safer route up and down to the Lac Orédon to avoid the Couplan Gorge altogether. This seemed fair enough after all they had done to get you out so we agreed to take part.

"At Espiaube Jean-Pierre took on Pied Piper mode and picked up a crowd of giggling French girls ..."

Janet now chipped in: "For the next few hours, Jean-Pierre wandered aimlessly up and down the piste with the three of us in train followed by this posse of silly girls who were obviously finding the whole thing screamingly funny. Half way through the afternoon Jean-Pierre suddenly announced that the whole thing had been an April Fool and vanished down the mountain to pick up Jacques."

"So that's when I must have run into him in the car park at St Lary," I broke in.

"No doubt," growled Alan, "and having wasted the entire day hanging around for Jacques to join us, we then had to flog up to the *abri* late that same evening. I wasn't best pleased as you can imagine."

Janet continued the tale. "We could just about have worn the April Fool jape if it hadn't been for the resurrection of the lunatic Jacques. Next day he again assumed his role as guide but as before made a complete nonsense of the route finding. At the bottom of the Néouvielle couloir he had the cheek to tell Alan how he should tie on so Alan told Jacques what he could do with himself. Jacques then managed to turn our climbing rope into a cat's cradle. Alan untangled it and took charge."

"What happened next?" I asked agog.

"Just the sort of bloody shambles you'd expect," replied Alan bitterly. "Jean-Pierre never even made the summit. Half way up the couloir he said he had vertigo and wouldn't budge. Jan sailed up after me and Colin got there by sheer guts. When we all got back to the *abri,* I made it clear to Jean-Pierre that Jan and I had had enough. We both walked out down the Couplan yet again and have just got in. We're both pretty flaked and I've probably buggered my feet for ever."

"I'm appalled and very sorry," I said lamely, "but what's happened to Colin?"

"Colin decided to stay behind with the Frenchmen. Jean-Pierre had cooked up some half-baked scheme to climb the Pic Campbieil and Colin wanted to tag on behind. I've no idea when they'll be back but the best of Irish luck to him."

Early next morning Alan and I took a long walk in the hills above St Lary through sleepy villages with names from forgotten times – Ens and Azet. I wanted to talk things through to see where, if anywhere, we would be going from here. If my accident had thrown the programme, recent events had split the party. Whether anything was worth salvaging largely depended on Alan.

"I'm dreadfully sorry about all this, Alan," I began. "First my damned silly accident and now this Jean-Pierre nonsense. I simply can't understand his relationship with Jacques. He told me on that first day that he didn't even know the man's surname. I know we've lost four days but I still think we could make the traverse to Luchon provided the weather holds."

Alan turned to me in astonishment. "Do you really think so John?" he replied incredulously. "I think you're crazy to even think of it. You'll have to count Jan and me out. Her leave's expired anyway and I'm on borrowed time. But that apart, I can't possibly walk in those bloody plastic boots any more. They're half a size too small and five trips up and down that damn Couplan Gorge have ruined my feet. Anyway, who do you think will be going with you and when? I've no idea when Jean-Pierre and the other two will be coming back but, personally, I couldn't take a day longer with Jean-Pierre – or Jacques for that matter. Colin's a great goer but he's never climbed seriously. The Pic de Néouvielle fiasco was the last straw. If you want my candid opinion, it would be sheer lunacy for someone who's just had concussion to do anything but come home with us."

Of course Alan was right. I had been in cloud-cuckoo-land on all counts and had deliberately closed my mind to the seriousness of the Sobrarbe traverse and its lack of safe escape routes in bad weather. Yet, I still clung to the fiction that if there hadn't been this bust up between the two big personalities of the tour, we could still put something together.

Alan and Jean-Pierre shared certain physical characteristics but in other respects they came from different ends of the spectrum. Alan, born into and part of an intellectual and scientific elite, was creative and imaginative yet pragmatic and sensible. Jean-Pierre, the romantic Norman hotelier, was charming and generous yet fecklessly insoucient. Both were proud and could be arrogant. Last year, we had made good vinaigrette but this time the elements had never mixed. It wasn't simply lack of communication. Jean-Pierre's surprise additions to the team had created two camps. I realised that there was nothing more to be said and resigned to my two closest friends catching the train back to England the next day.

The three of us went out that night for our last supper together. It was a melancholy affair and, when we returned to the hotel, another surprise awaited us. Stretched out on the same sofa in the foyer as Alan and Janet had been the previous evening were Jean-Pierre and Colin. Both looked equally grey and exhausted.

"What happened?" I asked Colin anxiously "We didn't expect you back until tomorrow at the earliest. Where's Jacques?"

"Jacques's okay but he's gone back to Pau," Colin replied wearily.

"Did you get up the Campbieil?" I persisted.

"Yes, we climbed it today but we couldn't finish Jean-Pierre's circuit and that's why we're back tonight."

"What circuit?" I asked him.

"Jean-Pierre had intended that we would descend the south face to the Sausset Hut where he had made the helicopter drop and stay the night there. But when we started down, the visibility was so bad that Jean-Pierre decided it was too dangerous to risk without the rope he had left behind at the *abri*. So we reversed our ascent route and came back here."

"You've had quite a day," I said incredulously.

"Certainly was," he replied shaking his head. "I would never want to repeat that traverse above the Lac de Long in late afternoon. The snow was completely rotten."

There had been a perverse consistency in Jean-Pierre's plan. In effect, he had reverted to the programme we had originally agreed before the tour started but his mindset and mood swings were bewildering. Within the space of three days he had alienated half the British camp with his misconceived April Fool; inexplicably pulled out of climbing the Néouvielle half way up and, yet, been quite prepared to hazard a ski descent down the south-west face of the Campbieil, which the guidebook described as an *"itinéraire impracticable à ski"*, with an inexperienced stranger with whom he could barely communicate. The return journey to the *abri* above the rock ledges above the Lac de Cap de Long sounded nightmarish for it was here that the guidebook had warned: *"un plongeon avec skis aux pieds dans l'élément liquide avoisniant zero degrés peut s'avérer fatal."*

Colin was a survivor.

I made an effort to raise a laugh as we sat around the bar while Colin recounted these adventures but, with British hackles raised and French *amour propre* affronted, the *froideur* was as icy as the Lac. Next morning, after Jean-Pierre had presented his accounts, Alan and Janet left by bus to catch the train to England.

With Alan and Janet gone I abandoned any notion of pushing on with the traverse but was determined that the tour should not finish on a sour note. I wanted to re-build bridges with Jean-Pierre. He and Colin had evidently got on well together and both confirmed that they were happy to see out the time originally allotted for the tour. Our new plan was to complete a circuit of the Néouvielle, returning to Barèges by a different route.

Late that same afternoon, as the pine trees cast long shadows across the snow, we took a telecabin to the Col de Portet and headed northwards under the Crête de Craoues Blanques bound for the Bastanet Hut which overlooked a necklace of tiny lakes. After Jean-Pierre had gathered fire wood and I had drawn water from an ice hole, Colin cooked supper. Afterwards, we sipped *gluhwein* around a log fire and played Oh Hell while hail beat down on the shingled roof. Jean-Pierre had reverted to his old charming self and good humour had returned to our ship.

The wind of the morning had blown the clouds away and washed the sky blue when I peered out of our pretty little hut's doorway. The snow was frozen and the air clung like frost to my breath. Yesterday evening we had settled the details of our plan to explore the innermost Néouvielle. Today's objective was to reach the *cabane* at Aygues-Cluses some ten kilometres to the north west beyond a knot of pics and passes.

The first of these passes was the Hourquette de Bastanet, a postern gate walled between the cliffs marking the top of the steep snow couloir which closed our valley. For me, it was joy to be touring again and, as we slid away from that happy little hut, I felt totally exhilarated by the prospect of the day ahead. As the slope steepened, we zig-zagged upwards on snow so solid that we had to stab at it with our ice axes and use our *harscheisen* like crampons to get purchase. Within an hour we were at the top of the *hourquette* savouring the views.

Over the past nine days the mountain tops had usually been shrouded in cloud. Now all were visible and gleamed in the sunshine. To the south, I could see the three great cirques of Gavarnie, Estaubé and Troumousse and the crest of the main range like a wave of breaking white caps. To the north, the secret heart of the Néouvielle was revealed as a maze of porcupine ridges topped by spiky peaks and, in the valley of a thousand hollows at our feet, a profusion of tiny lakes merging imperceptibly into the snowscape.

An icy wind scoured my face as we weaved our way downwards by a series of steps past clumps of dwarf pines to the Refuge Campana de Cloutou sited beside another lake. Our route now lay due west up a deep shadowed valley hemmed in to the south by the Crête de Port Bielh. Somewhere high above, at the top of another couloir set squarely between the Pic du Contade and the Pic Des Quatre Termes, lay the Brèche du Contade. A steep sustained climb of 500 metres on skis and a final scramble led to the summit of the 2,714 metre Pic de Contade. From here we descended that same Brèche, where we had left our skis, then climbed the rocky south ridge of the 2,724 metre Pic Des Quatres Terms as a rope of three, making that another first for Colin.

We now stood on the pivotal peak of the Néouvielle. Five great ridges radiated from it like spokes and the entire Néouvielle Reserve was stretched out before us. Away to the south west, Colin pointed proudly to the Pic de Néouvielle's shapely summit pyramid and the more distant Campbieil behind it with every ridge, face, cirque and snowfield finely etched in the afternoon sunshine.

The day was drawing on yet we still had far to go. A spiralling 500 metre descent took us to the bottom of the Coume de Porteilh – oven hot, without a breath of wind. That final flog up its far side by another steep couloir to reach the last *hourquette* of the day, the Pas de Crabe, was also the most exhausting. Hot and dehydrated, we were beginning to tire but, from this narrow neck in the crête, the wide upland valley of the Aygues-Cluses and journey's end was spread out before us. The ground fell away steeply to the easy angled slopes of an enormous snow bowl dotted with solitary pines. At the edge of a snow covered lake was a tiny dot – the Cabane Aygues-Cluses.

"Watch this slope, Colin," I urged, "Undo your safety straps. The sun's been on this slope all afternoon and the whole lot could go from under us."

We skied it gingerly, one by one, without incident. Once esconced in the cabane, with the dead pine tree that Jean-Pierre had picked up on the way down blazing away in the granite fireplace, the day's dangers and difficulties were forgotten. We lay quietly in our sleeping bags on a dirty foam mattress which covered the raised stone shelf and sloshed down gallons of hot water to quench our raging thirsts.

Jean-Pierre's bizarre decision to appoint Colin as *chef de cuisine* was the evening's only glitch. He had left behind at the Bastanet Hut the prodigious quantities of tea, sugar and milk that he had bought at St Lary and his choice of pot noodles, two cubes of pasteurised cheese and a slab of porridge cake for supper set me thinking less harshly about the Centre Hospitalier at Lannemazan. But we had good reason to be thankful for a day in which we had climbed two peaks and three high passes and enjoyed the cameraderie of adventure.

All the old élan had returned to Jean-Pierre. At the start of the tour he had been gloomy about the weather but now he prophesied a week of sunshine. Yet next morning the sky was tinged with strange colours and the light on the hills had a muted quality. From this hut we could so easily have skied down the Valley of the Aygues-Cluses the easy way to Barèges but Jean-Pierre still had something to show us with a complete circuit involving a couple more cols. As he put it: *"C'est très classique avec deux hourquettes très raides."* He was right about both *hourquettes*. A hairy ice pitch below the Col de Tracens followed by a minor route finding hiccup above a vertical rock band just below the Hourquette de Mounicot left us quivering on the edges of our skis. Then, with both crises past, we were back on the same col that we had crossed nine days before. That fatal afternoon now seemed worlds away and I could barely recognise the place. The cornices had melted to reveal banks of prickly scrub about to burst into flower. We gazed across to the Turon de Néouvielle, a peak too far for today.

Once in the Glère Valley the snow turned first to mush and then a lethal porridge. Skiing was no pleasure as our ski bottoms juddered through a succession of partially melted avalanche cones embedded with stones. It was hot and humid work and when we reached the ski station of Lienz, we each sank three *citrons pressés* in quick succession.

We had been seven hours on the trot and, suddenly, the exertions of the past three days caught up with me. I felt an overwhelming sense of anti-climax and the effort of trying to converse amusingly in stilted French with Jean-Pierre was beyond me.

"John," said Colin quietly, "I think I'll be leaving you both now and be heading for home."

It came back to me that he had said something about this on that last col but I hadn't really taken it in. It also came to me that I knew little more about Colin now than I did when we first met. We should have had a lot in common as lawyers of much the same age yet somehow we had never touched base. I had been somewhat preoccupied with maintaining a relationship with Jean-Pierre but felt ashamed that I had not made more effort to get to know Colin better. We had shared the same adventure but had never exchanged a single personal experience. On this tour, he had climbed more peaks than any of us and this without previous climbing experience. He had always been in the thick of things, wholly dependable and cheerful throughout.

"D'you really have to go back to Ireland, Colin?" I asked him. "We've still got a couple of days in hand. I'm sure we could find something of interest."

"Thanks all the same, John, but I've made up my mind. I've had a good run and I had like to leave on a high note."

We walked together to the bus stop at Barèges where we had first started our journey together.

"Incidentally," he said, "thanks for all the equipment you lent me. You'd better be having it back now for I won't be needing it again."

I had forgotten all about the ice axe, crampons, snow shovel, slings and karabiners I had brought out with me. As he boarded the bus, he handed them over to me in a plastic bag. We then exchanged our last words.

"Goodbye Colin. Thanks for everything you did. You were a great companion."

"Goodbye John. Thanks for a great trip."

We corresponded briefly over some photographs he wanted to publish in an Irish mountaineering journal but, though our paths could so easily have crossed, I have never met Colin again.

Of the original seven who had started the tour we were now down to two. I still had a couple of days in hand and wanted to seal my friendship with Jean-Pierre with something special. His behaviour might have been idiosyncratic but we had now completed four Pyrenean tours together and had survived many incidents along the way. The previous day he had suggested that we might climb the 3,035 metre Turon de Néouvielle, a ski mountaineering classic which, in 1787, gained the distinction of being the first Pyrenean Three Thousander ever to be climbed.

When I got back from the bus stop, Jean-Pierre was propping up the bar smoking the inevitable *Gallois*.

"Jean-Pierre, as-tu envie que nous essayons de monter sur le Turon de Néouvielle?"

"Bien sûr, John," he replied enthusiastically. *"Bien sur, c'est une bonne idée, c'est une route classique."*

With that settled, *"le pere de Véronique"*, as he styled himself in Barèges, negotiated a deal with the proprietor of the Auberge Chez Louisette which included free board on the upholstered bar bench plus a discounted dinner. I thought I would be ravenous after three days' fresh air and exercise but Colin's regime of pot noodles had shrunk our stomachs. After a potato soup, assorted pâtés and charcuterie, steak and chips we staggered through *glaces* and *Tomme noire*. During that one meal we had consumed more calories than we had taken on board during the previous 72 hours. Before settling down for the night to the reassuring gurgle of the expresso coffee machine, Jean-Pierre added to our water bottles two full *gourdes* of *Cassis* to which he helped himself from the bar.

The Turon's ascent would involve a climb of 1,565 metres and with the weather forecast anything but settled, we slipped away from the Auberge at 5 am with the proprietor's dog. Charles Packe invariably climbed with his two Pyrenean sheepdogs, Ossoue and Azor, but this perky little chap was more like a scaled down husky.

The air was as muggy as on that first afternoon when we had skinned up this same valley and the snow was almost as slushy as on yesterday's descent. Our head torch beams steered a bumpy passage through the avalanche cones for only a glimmer of moonlight occasionally broke through the clouds. Dawn came up imperceptibly as we slid past the Glère barracks. I glanced at my watch and was disconcerted to note that our time to this point was no faster than it had been eleven days before. I was following Jean-Pierre like an automaton with leaden legs but, when we stopped for a quick drink, he too confessed that he was feeling completely washed out. Hardly surprising. He had been in the thick of the action throughout.

At the Lac de Glère, we branched westwards into the Coume Estrete which steepened into a gun barrel couloir marked on the map with the now familiar dotted lines. That zig-zagging climb seemed like eternity and the layer of new snow overlaying the older ice kept balling up under our *harscheisen*. When at last we were within striking distance of an elusive nick in the ridge, which had never seemed to get any nearer, I abandoned my skis in exasperation and kicked steps up the last 50 metres to the crest. At exactly 12 noon we reached the Turon's summit.

It should have been a moment to savour but we were both exhausted after seven hours of continuous climbing and the famous panoramic summit view looked lifeless in the flat light. The only feature I could take in was the thousand metre precipice that fell plumb into the inky waters of the Lac de Pic de Long at our feet. Black, baggy clouds were massing in the west and a cold wind had sprung up. We ate some chocolate on the snow encrusted rocks of the summit cairn, concerned now about getting down before the storm broke.

"*L'aventure est fini, John,*" yawned Jean-Pierre as he threw the last of his chocolate to the dog who had snuggled down in his own snow burrow.

"*Et maintenant – allez y, allez, allez!*"

We pointed our skis north and from that last mountain top plunged into a cirque of thigh deep snow. The break had re-charged my batteries and, as we powered down the Maniport Glacier, bashing through crust and crud in a race with the weather and the game little dog barking at our heels, I felt on equal terms with Jean-Pierre.

Exactly an hour and a half after leaving the summit, we were back in the bar of Chez Louisette downing another quart of *citron pressé*. I looked across to Jean-Pierre who was sitting back on his chair contentedly puffing at his *Gaullois*. Once again we had come down together safely from a high mountain. I was suddenly overwhelmed by a feeling of gratitude and achievement and, then, for a few fleeting moments, that rarest experience – unalloyed happiness.

An hour later as we half-walked and half-ran down the deserted streets of Barèges to catch the last bus to Lourdes, I slipped on a patch of ice and crashed head first into an oak doorway. The noise brought the householder to the door. Someone was trying to tell me that I had pushed my luck too far.

At Pau station, we were met off the train by Jean-Pierre's austere father and driven to Jean-Pierre's severely functional apartment at the top of a concrete skyscraper block on the outskirts of Pau. Martine had cooked us a delicious supper but we were both so tired that conversation was stilted and when Jean-Pierre pressed me with plans for next year, I was reluctant to be drawn.

There had been several pluses in this tour of incident, entrances and exits. The party had climbed five peaks and traversed at least a dozen passes in our passage through the Néouvielle. The *Régions des Lacs* had been as beautiful as Jean-Pierre had predicted but in terms of the Pyrenean traverse, my accident had meant that we had finished up at precisely the same place as we had started and of particular concern to me was the bust up between Alan and Jean-Pierre both of whom I admired and respected. Jean-Pierre admitted over dinner that this time he hadn't got on with Alan. I knew that the feeling was mutual and that they would not want to do another tour together.

This posed a dilemma. Alan was the closer friend, the joint architect of our first Pyrenean ski tour and the ultimate anchorman who you would always want in your corner and yet, for all his idiosyncracies, Jean-Pierre had proved a generous and stalwart companion for whom I retained warm feelings and with whom I wanted to remain friends.

For my part, I had felt exceedingly lucky to have survived concussion with no obvious ill effects but, before considering another Pyrenean tour with or without Jean-Pierre, I wanted time to think things over. As he drove me to Pau station, I promised Jean-Pierre that I would send him my photographs as soon as they had been developed and would also be writing to him about the future.

As the Paris Sleeper drew away from the platform I shouted across to Jean-Pierre and Martine from the open window as they both waved back: *"Au revoir Jean-Pierre ... Au revoir Martine! Merci mille fois ... A bientôt."*

It never once crossed my mind that I would never see or hear from either of them again.

Gèdre.   (L to R) – Julian Lush, John Wilkinson, David Williams, Alan Wedgwood and Nick Wedgwood

6   ACROSS THE SOBRARBE

Gèdre to Luchon

Reflecting on the Néouvielle episode after I got home, it seemed at first blush that, for all its scrapes and dramas, it could have ended up a lot worse. Feathers might have been ruffled but maybe, with time and goodwill, the rift between Alan and Jean-Pierre could be patched up. In the event, I was wrong. When I received no reply from Jean-Pierre to the sheaf of photographs and letters I sent to thank him for everything he had done to prepare the way and assist with my rescue, I assumed that he had simply been too busy to reply. He never did and although, for several years after, I regularly sent him a Christmas card, he never responded. Anglophobia or bruised *amour propre?* For whatever reasons he had taken against us and brought to a sad and incomprehensible end what for me had been a happy chapter of mountain cameraderie.

The *affaire Jean-Pierre* was a disappointment which took time to manifest itself. A more immediate psychological setback to my Pyrenean ambitions had come about through a chance discovery I had made in St Lary on the very day I had released myself from the hospital in Lannemazan. Browsing through the resort's only *librairie,* I came across a slim paperback entitled *Haute Route d'Hiver des Pyrénées – a ski de l'Atlantique a la Méditerranée,* published by the French Alpine Club and jointly edited by my old standby Robert Ollivier and another Pyrenean *Guide de Haute Montagne* editor, Jean-Louis Peres. It gave a detailed description of a 580-kilometre 34-stage traverse of the Pyrenees from Canigou to Arette Pierre Saint Martin first achieved by Charles Laporte of Pau in 1968 between March 3 and April 7.

In this book, *Les Pyrénées,* the distinguished French mountaineer Patrice Bellefon hailed Laporte's ski traverse as *"un des plus remarquables exploits de sa genre".* At first I almost willed myself not to believe it and only when I had studied the full description properly did its implications become clear. Until then, the mainspring for attempting my own Pyrenean traverse had been the complacent assumption that no one else had done it. I had seen the reference to an *Haute Route Pyrénéenne* from Fabian to Luchon in Ollivier's four-volume guide and had become aware of Robin Fedden's 1974 east/west supported ski traverse from the Pont d'Espagne to the Col du Somport only a year before Michael de Pret Roose's Eagles tour. Both Michael's intended route and our own unguided traverse from Urdos to the Pont d'Espagne broadly corresponded to Fedden's traverse in reverse but none of these traverses had covered more than one seventh of Charles Laporte's *integrale.* This was not a case of being pipped at the post. We had never been in the same race.

Initially I felt keenly disappointed but when I thought it through, it was some comfort that only ten years separated Laporte's pioneer traverse and our first unguided tour. It was also reassuring to learn that even Laporte, with all his local expertise, freely acknowledged his debt to the parties who first traversed sections of the Central Pyrenees in the 1950s. Before attempting the entire traverse, Laporte had made careful reconnaissances and had even skied the 350 kilometre stretch between Mount Louis and Gabas as a dress rehearsal before going the full distance. Although I never met Laporte, it created a retrospective bond that his team of four had also been dogged by avalanches, storms, cloud and mist and had been forced into route finding errors, impromptu bivouacs and dangerous late afternoon descents.

In terms of performance we were worlds apart. The average length of Laporte's skiing day was over nine hours. Nine of his 35 days had exceeded 11 hours. By comparison – and except for those two heroic 12 hour plus days with Walter Good – our daily average had never approached this and was reflected in the comparative distances we had covered. Although we had been travelling in opposite directions – west to east as opposed to Laporte's east to west – he had taken 35 stages to complete his traverse whereas we had already done the equivalent of 25 stages yet covered only 30 per cent of the distance. Some part of this discrepancy could be explained by my having strayed wittingly or otherwise into such unusual byways as the French Cirques, Spanish Canyons and the Néouvielle. These diversions had added colour but they had delayed our progress eastwards and I reckoned that, if there was any prospect of my finishing this Pyrénéenne traverse while I was still capable, I would have to take a more direct line in future and cut out the trimmings.

My belated discovery that someone had already done *La Haute Route Pyrénéenne* blunted an imperative sense of urgency. I was also concerned that my concussion might have a delayed reaction. Accordingly, when Alan Wedgwood wrote to say that his forthcoming Himalayan expedition would take up most of his next year's leave, I persuaded myself that a break from the Pyrenees might do me some good. Why not try a restorative Alpine ski tour after a six-year gap?

In the event, I left it too late to get my own team together but just when it looked as if I would miss a complete ski touring season, I learned that Alan Blackshaw and his wife-to-be Elspeth were planning to tour in the Pennine Alps. After a laconic telephone conversation; a one page manuscript Action sheet from Alan and a brief chat to fix the date and time when we were to rendezvous at Victoria Station, the scene was set.

Alan Blackshaw had a formidable reputation. He had been a founder member of the Alpine Climbing Group – the *corps d'elite* of British post-war mountaineering; had written Penguin's best selling climbing manual,

Mountaineering; was a past President of the British Mountaineering Council; had led the first British Ski Traverse of the Alps from Kaprun to Gap in 1972 with a team which had included Michael de Pret Roose and had made a pioneer north to south Nordic ski traverse of Scandinavia over four seasons between 1973 and 1977.

On our outward train journey to Switzerland, I warned Alan that I hadn't toured in the Alps for six years whereupon he confessed that he had done virtually no Alpine ski touring since his British Alpine Traverse ten years before. These lacunae may in part have explained our failure to reach a consensus on an agreed itinerary until we got to Martigny station. It was here that we also discovered that our skis, so confidently consigned by Alan to British Rail and SNCF at Victoria, had gone missing. Twenty-four hours later, by which time our options had been narrowed to Alan's preferred Little High Level Route from Verbier to Zermatt, we cut our losses by hiring skis at Verbier.

The prospect of another *Haute Route* over well honed ground didn't inspire me although this one was to prove instructive. Everything on Alan's agenda was completed within the prescribed time and his three targeted peaks – Rosa Blanche, Pigne d'Arolla and Tete de Valpelline – knocked off on successive days. We invariably got away first from the huts in the morning; successfully challenged all-comers to priority on all peaks and passes and always arrived at our next hut well before midday to ensure that we bagged the best bunk berths rather than having to sleep on the floor.

Alan's approach to ski mountaineering was strictly professional and made me realise that my own views on the subject were ingenuous. I listened agog to his *dirigiste* contention that the leadership of British Himalayan expeditions should be decided not by groups of individuals but by a continental style central committee. But it was when he gave a dismissive performance rating to the Wilberforce-Smiths' recently completed West to East ski traverse of the Alps in nine stages rather than by a continuous *intégrale* traverse that I went all quiet about my own Pyrenean traverse.

Alan's rate of uphill progress was only matched by Elspeth's. Fortunately for me, the speed which had been honed in pursuit of hares on Nordic skis across the remoter parts of Scotland most winter weekends was marginally reduced by an uncharacteristic lapse. They had somehow managed to allow the adhesive wrapping paper of their brand new Swiss skins to fasten itself onto their skins' adhesive face in such a way that nothing would shift it. Even so, Elspeth was oblivious to such handicaps. When on our longest day I eventually caught up with them on the Col de Valpelline, she told me that when one dud skin failed to stick, she had simply chucked it away and carried on with the other one.

Cheerful, *simpatica* and tireless, Elspeth was a joyful companion and the Alan/Elspeth combination *formidable*.

For all its seamless achievement, the flawless weather, the clarity of Swiss cartography (a marvel by comparison with most French and Spanish Pyrenean maps) and the sublime scenery of this most dramatic of *grandes courses,* the old Alpine magic was no longer working. My earliest ski mountaineering inspiration had been to read Robin Fedden's *Alpine Ski Tour,* the first full length description in English of the High Level Route on ski. When Fedden himself did the route in 1955, no British party had completed it unguided. Nine years later, in 1964, the route was still so unfrequented that Tony Delafield and I never met another party on it at any stage of our own guided traverse.

Eighteen years on, everything had changed. A photograph in Fedden's *Alpine Ski Tour* depicts its author wrapped in a blanket enjoying *"the friendly chiaroscuro of the best mountain huts"* which in those days were usually deserted, cold and damp. Sitting in a corner of the centrally heated Vignette Hut, attempting to read Robert Byron's *Road to Oxiana* amidst a babel of French, Italian, German and Japanese, I wondered what Fedden would have made of the solemn groups of skiers with their bored guides sitting tightly packed yet isolated as they waited to join the third sitting of the set Swiss supper.

Packaged guided tours, weight of numbers and the impersonality of modern huts had blown the intimacy of shared adventure. Long before we reached Zermatt, I had decided that Alpine high routes were no longer for me and that my wilder universe was in the Pyrenees.

The experience of playing tortoise to Alan and Elspeth's hares had shattered any complacency about my own fitness. It had been galling to have come in last uphill. Accordingly, before the next Pyrenean season I was determined to take a leaf from their Scottish training manual. For desk-bound types, fitness is a perennial problem. My regimen of bicycling from Putney to the City and back every working day was only a partial solution and had thrice landed me in hospital after brushes with motor cars. There is no substitute for the real thing but in Britain the only mountains that offer a reasonable prospect of winter snow are the Scottish Highlands, as Alan and Elspeth with their Edinburgh base, had long ago discovered.

Typically, Alan Wedgwood came up with the obvious solution. Taking advantage of a British Rail special offer to collectors of breakfast cereal coupons, he had worked out that, by catching *The Highlander* from Euston on a Friday night, we could cross Central Scotland on ski and be back at work by the following Monday morning. So it was that on the appointed date at the waking hour the original Pyrenean team of Alan and Nick Wedgwood and I emerged from the

David Williams in descent

cocoon of a BR sleeper – superior in every way to an *SNCF* couchette – to step straight into our ski bindings and steer an easterly course off the platform of Corrour, the highest and most isolated railway station in the British Isles.

Marching directly into the face of a bitter Arctic wind under a lowering sky, we poled past a herd of scrawny stags foraging in the snow and set off on a compass bearing towards a bleak and forbidding moorland. That same evening after knocking off a couple of Munros – Scottish peaks of over 3,000 feet as listed by Sir Hugh Munro in his 1891 *Tables* – we bivouaced beneath the flanks of one of Scotland's remotest peaks, the 3,757 feet Ben Alder. The following day we traversed this mountain on ski and reached the Grampian Hotel, Dalwhinnie, just in time for the high tea that Corrour's extravagently bewhiskered station master, James Morgan, had reserved for us by telephone. That same night we boarded the southbound sleeper at Dalwhinnie and the following morning I was back at my Bishopsgate EC3 desk well in time to start the weekly grind.

Both Alan and I had originally cut our mountaineering teeth in Scotland for, as many others have discovered, beneath those cold northern skies is country more remote than anything in Europe outside Scandinavia. This first Highland ski crossing was a revelation which was to serve as a precedent for many others to come and pre-requisite pre-Pyrenean training.

Alan and Nick had already agreed to provide the core team for the next critical stage of the Pyrenean traverse, which I was determined would take us all the way from Gèdre to Luchon across the Sobrarbe. Having heard nothing from Jean-Pierre, I decided to scrap the French connection and make this a True Brit affair. Alan insisted that one slot should be filled by his friend John Wilkinson – "an Alpine Climbing Group member and totally durable" – as he put it. That was good enough for me but I wondered what message John was trying to convey when he sent me a copy of an article he had written for the *Fell & Rock Journal* in which he evaluated the incidence of death caused by mountaineering activities. The thrust of the article was that accident risk increased with age but I was not re-assured that John's statistics gave a significantly lower accident rate for any age group than the 75 per cent average that had been par for my last four Pyrenean tours.

The party was brought up to six with the inclusion of Julian Lush and David Williams. Julian had been a Cambridge contemporary who had skied for the University. He was also an accomplished linguist, then working for Shell in Abu Dubai and had travelled mountains for most of his life. David Williams, on the other hand, was an unknown quantity. I had only met him once before on an Eagle Ski Club North Downs walk organised by his parents. He was unassuming to the point of reticence but professed to be a keen mountaineer and skier. I had taken to him from the outset and had been impressed by his quiet self-assurance and enthusiasm for the Pyrenees. Yet, at only 21, would he fit into this largely middle-aged party? I researched his track record but none of the Eagles I approached knew anything about him as he appeared to be the Club's youngest member.

To ensure that I wasn't making a disastrous mistake in selection, I suggested a weekend get-together before the tour began. However, when in early November I tried to contact David at home with suggested dates, he replied from Pau to say that he would now be living there for the next few months but had started to recce our proposed route with his Swedish girl friend Anna. The further information that this recce had been aborted by waist deep snow and avalanches and a subsequent telephone conversation during which David asked if the 20-year-old Anna could come along too sounded alarm bells. Swedish girlfriends in Pau? This had the makings of another Jean-Pierre/Jacques/Véronique situation. I really knew nothing about David let alone Anna. He might be a skiing whizz but, at 21, he still had something to learn. I kicked myself for being over-impetuous and shot off a very pompous letter to David about Anna:

"I should be delighted that she come provided that she is not only a good skier (which I do not doubt) but that she also has the right temperament and unflappability for an expedition such as this ... and can carry heavy loads. The first stage, Gèdre to Aragnouet, is to be regarded as a trial period and I reserve the right to decide whether Anna is likely to be able to cope with the remainder of the trip."

This was lawyer's stuff made all the heavier by my asking David if he would sort out certain administrative matters in Pau and report back. Not surprisingly, he never replied and for some weeks I wondered whether he and Anna had decided to cry off. No matter, the five of us should make a strong team.

If I had any doubts about the party, I had none about the route we would be taking across the Sobrarbe. Now that I had carefully studied the Ollivier/Peres *Pyrénéenne Haute Route* guidebook, I was reassured to find that the recommended daily stages were almost identical to those which Jean-Pierre and I had planned to do two years before.

Our starting point would be Gèdre where Alan, Walter Good, Jean-Pierre and I had exited three years before. From here, we had head up the Campbieil Valley, cross the Port de Campbieil into the Aure Valley, re-provision at St Lary and then push on through the Sobrarbe, weaving in and out of France and Spain until we reached Bénasque. As a final stage, we would again cross the main range back into France from Bénasque to Luchon.

According to the guidebook, the key passage was from St Lary to Benasque. This was the section that we had never got to grips with last time round. Once committed to the frontier ridge, it would be both difficult and dangerous to escape to France in bad weather. There would be none of Jean-Pierre's food caches on the way so we would have to carry seven days food in addition to tents, cooking equipment, stoves and fuel.

Came the date of departure with the David/Anna dilemma half forgotten, I had a shock at the Gare Austerlitz where I first met John Wilkinson. Alan, Nick, Julian and I had just flown in from Heathrow for a Paris rendezvous to catch the night sleeper for Lourdes. I had never asked Alan John's age but when this stockily built man with a determined jaw shook my hand, I was taken aback by his mane of grey hair. It wasn't simply John's 56 years that disconcerted me – on that first Eagles trip Robin Day had been edging 60 – but that 35 years separated him from the 21-year-old David Williams.

The following morning, the five of us emerged from Lourdes station blinking in the sun. Three weeks ago, the Wedgwood brothers and I had completed our Highland Crossing in Arctic conditions. Here, although it was only early March, the Pyrenean Spring had already arrived and the air felt positively balmy.

David Williams strolled across the car park to greet us with a boyish grin, accompanied by a blonde girl with saucer blue eyes. She looked all of seventeen. My God, I thought to myself, this must be Anna. In the rush of clearing my desk and last minute preparations I had forgotten David's earlier and unresolved suggestion that Anna might join the team. Standing there together they looked absurdly young.

After we had made our introductions, David took me aside.

"Anna's decided to stay behind," he said quietly.

I mumbled some trite commiseration but felt immensely relieved. Last time round, seven had been an unlucky number. This attractive girl was barely out of school.

"I'm so sorry that you can't come, Anna," I said hypocritically, "but what's the weather been like and what's the forecast?"

"It's been fine here for the last few weeks so the snow's settled and compacted," replied David. "It should be okay for the next couple of days but after that it's anyone's guess."

"Well then," I said briskly, "let's get going while it lasts."

We said goodbye to Anna, bussed to our starting point in the village square of Gèdre, shouldered our rucksacks and skis and set off up the Campbieil Valley for the Sausset Hut. The last time that Alan and I had been here was in early May three years before when we had retreated from the blizzard swept

Troumousse Cirque. Now, fully two months earlier in the year, the trees were in blossom and the sun so hot that when we took our first break above the Campbieil Gorge, we stripped to the waist to cool off and drained our water bottles. On the far side of the gorge, the shepherds were already moving their flocks up the hillside.

That first day's hut march was an instructive introduction to ski mountaineering for Julian. He had insisted on carrying a heap of unnecessary baggage but was learning the consequences.

That evening morale was high and when I stood outside the snug Sausset Hut before going to bed, the purple night sky twinkled with brilliant stars.

My original plan had been to make day two an easy one, climbing the Soum de Salettes en route to the Port de Campbieil from where we would descend to Fabian. Next morning Alan had other ideas.

"The weather's quite perfect, John. We can't waste a day like this. Surely we can do something better than your Soum de whatever-it-is. Why don't we climb the Pic de Campbieil instead? That's a 3,000 metre peak worth doing for its own sake."

"For a second day I would have thought that the Soum was a sensible option to shake down," I replied, "but okay, let's take another look at the map and guidebook."

The Pic de Campbieil originally featured on the Néouvielle itinerary two years before and had, of course, been climbed from the Orédon side by Jean-Pierre, Jacques and Colin. But its south face was a descent that even Jean-Pierre had sensibly backed out of. The guidebook described it as a *"très raide"* and *"impracticable à ski"*.

When I pointed all this out to Alan he was dismissive.

"I don't see any problem," he snorted. "We've managed plenty of these so-called *impracticable* passages before. Conditions are perfect and we may not get the chance again. Anyway, what does anyone else think?"

Only David spoke up. "I think it's an excellent idea," he said quietly. "I think we should give it a go."

We packed up smartly and dumped our heavy sacs at a rock band some 300 metres below the Port de Campbieil before starting the long grind upwards. As the slope steepened, I reflected that maybe Alan wanted to prove a point about this Jean-Pierre peak.

The climb was an uncomfortable baptism for the unfit and barely started, David Williams shot off on his own to take the lead. He had chosen a higher traversing line than mine and was moving upwards with an easy, economic rhythm. That's pretty cheeky of him, I thought to myself. Might this be another Jacques situation?

"David!" I shouted after him breathlessly, "Please let's keep together. You're taking a very steep line."

"Okay," he shouted back at me amiably, "I'll wait here for you to join up."

I felt a touch irritated that a new boy had taken it upon himself to lead but when we caught up with each other, it was even more galling to discover that he had chosen a better line than mine. Five and a half hours after leaving the Sausset we were all sitting in the sun on the Campbieil's summit enjoying a panoramic view of the Pyrenees with the peaks and passes of yesteryear spread at our feet. Alan had got it right and we felt proprietorial about the places we had been to on previous tours yet never properly seen.

"Look at them all," he exclaimed smugly, "There's Gavarnie, Perdu, the Col du Cylindre, the Cirques of Estaube and Troumousse ... the Brèches of Roland and Tuqueroye ... and now Campbieil!"

Yet even at this moment of triumph I was beginning to wonder how we were going to get down. The steepness of the face had forced us to step kick most of the upper section. To reverse this lot in the midday sun was a disagreeable prospect.

"We had better be on our way," I said to Alan after we satiated ourselves with a photographic orgy. "The sun's been on that face a long time. Reversing it will be tricky."

"Certainly will," replied Alan, "but why not go straight down the couloir?"

"What couloir?" I asked blankly.

"The one to our right as we came up. Didn't you see it?"

Shades of Walter Good? The only feature on that otherwise featureless face that I could recall was a narrow funnel of snow wedged between the Campbieil's summit ridge and the Arete de Lentilla. I had noticed it because a couple of climbers had left behind the imprint of their cramponed steps.

"Come off it, Alan. You can't mean that gulley with the steps going up it? You must be joking."

"Yes, that's the one," he replied. "I'm sure it'll go. The top bit's been in the shade so it'll be safer than the face."

"But it's diabolically steep," I protested, "and this is our first run."

"Can't be any steeper than Perdu or the Tuqueroye," he retorted.

There were any number of good reasons why I didn't want to ski this nightmare couloir and, apart from myself, wondered how everyone else would fare. Nick and Julian were good skiers. Alan would get down anything but what about John Wilkinson and David Williams? The others had overheard our conversation but no one said a word. David Williams was giving the snow an exploratory prod with his poles.

Reserve de Néouvielle

"Okay then Alan," I said. "Maybe we had better take a look at your couloir."

We walked down the narrowing summit ridge in file, skis over shoulders, to where a line of cornices ringed the top of the couloir.

"This must be the start of it," said Alan.

I peered over the edge into what looked like a plug hole which disappeared from sight round a sharp corner. Beyond that I could see nothing below but knew that a 800-metre vertical interval separated us from the place where we had left our rucksacks.

My stomach was knotted. Someone was going to have to lead this blind helter skelter but this time there was no Walter Good at hand. Please, I thought myself, not me. Yet I knew that as leader there was no face-saving alternative.

I tested the snow. At least it was firm – firm as ice. As I knelt down to re-adjust my bindings and tighten my boot clips, my mouth went dry. A surge of adrenalin made me feel as sick as I used to before a cross-country race. I hadn't noticed that David was standing at my side. Since our tiny contretemps earlier on in the day, we had hardly exchanged a word. As the *moment critique* approached, he said to me quietly:

"If you like, John, I'm perfectly happy to go first. I really dig couloirs like this."

For a moment I was taken aback. Who was this chap anyway? I looked up and stared at him. He returned my gaze assured and relaxed.

"Are you quite sure, David?" I asked him sharply.

"Certainly," he replied. "I'll be fine. No worries."

I knew I was chickening out but as I muttered. "Okay then, David, you go first. We'll follow you." I felt immensely relieved.

I had never seen him ski before but from that first choreographed sequence of clipped, linked turns, I realised at once that he was in a different league to the rest of us.

Then, as he vanished from sight down the funnel, I thought well here goes and launched myself after him. The snow was still rock hard with a film of melt overlaying it. If you slipped here you would never stop until you hit the bottom. I kept thinking to myself: just relax, hold your position, keep your nerve and get in that first turn. Why should this of all turns have to be the first of the tour?

I made it and once that was behind me everything else was possible. The couloir had looked impossibly steep from above but centrifugal force kept me glued to its walls as I spun on down before vanishing into its gullet. The snow was perfect, the ski edges were holding and, as the adrenalin pumped surges of energy through me, I took wings in pursuit of David's spiralling twists and turns. So this was how it felt to fly! I could never have matched his skill or style but sheer exhilaration made me travel ever faster until I lost control and shot past David as he paused to take stock of what was happening behind him. A little way below, I pulled up to a juddering halt, heart thumping, chest heaving and thighs locked solid.

"Tremendous stuff, David," I gasped. "Great lead."

We had stopped on easier ground. When I looked up the couloir I was amazed to see that we had already come half way down it. At the top, two black dots were moving purposefully down the top funnel like flies on a wall. Two others were still perched on its lip like divers about to take the plunge.

For a few vivid minutes each of us had lived out a personal drama on that upper section of that couloir but at 6.30 pm that same evening we were swigging beer in the comfort of the Hotel Terrasse de Fleurie's bar flushed with self congratulation. We had made the first ski descent of the Campbieil's west-south-west Couloir and, in David, had found a giant killer.

In my innermost anorak pocket, wrapped in cellophane, I carried photocopied extracts of the *Haute Route d'Hiver des Pyrénées* guide. The authors had devoted an entire chapter to the traverse of the Sobrarbe as it weaved an irregular passage around and over the frontier ridge. They stressed that this wild and unfrequented section from Fabian to Luchon posed *"sérieux problèmes"*. The French versant was a tangle of steep, transverse ridges dangerously avalanche prone in bad weather while the Spanish side was a *"réserve encore de bonnes surprises aux chercheurs d'aventure"*.

As always in the Pyrenees, the outcome depended on the weather. Over this section, if it did turn bad on us, we would have to choose between a French Charybdis and Spanish Scylla. On the other hand, if it held, we should be able to cross the Sobrarbe in five long stages, staying at the Trigonero Hut in Spain, the Hospice de Rioumajou in France and the Viados and Estos Huts in Spain before finishing up at Benasque. As bait to Alan, I had included in the draft itinerary the ascents of the second and first summits of the Pyrenees – Posets and Aneto.

Weather apart, the main problem was to keep weight to a minimum. As we would have to be totally self sufficient, food was the only area where there was scope to reduce so Alan and I had agreed to a basic diet of soup, porridge cake and an accelerated freeze dried food trade-named Raven.

After an indulgent rest day at the Hotel Terrasse de Fleurie, the six of us were picked up by a pair of taxis on March 10 at dawn. Pyrenean taxi drivers readily come to the aid of the party and in St Lary's Jean Palasset we had picked a winner – the very man who had ferried the *équipe* between Fabian and St Lary after my accident two years before. The road to the Bielsa Tunnel was officially closed for the winter but Jean kicked into the ditch a couple of *Interdit* road barriers placed in our way before dropping us off at the mouth of the tunnel. He had given us a flier.

The weather had looked promising when we first set off but, as I paused to photograph the party climbing steadily in tight column towards the Port de Bataillence, I noticed that straggly clouds were drifting across the higher peaks. When we had made our cracking start, I had reckoned that nothing would stop us reaching the Trigonero Hut that night but now some instinct told me not to be too cocksure. According to David, the fine weather had already lasted several weeks yet this was at total variance with my experience on five previous Pyrenean tours when we had never enjoyed more than three good days at a stretch.

The guide book had warned that navigation across this next stretch would never be easy because the route wandered up and over a series of ill-defined ridges with few obvious landmarks to guide. Even before we had reached the Port de Bataillance, a mere nick in the transverse ridge that runs northwards off its eponymous Pic, the clouds thickened and it began to snow. Up until then we had only had one minor-route finding hiccup but now the fun began. From the snow covered Lac de Héchempy, I climbed to a knoll from whose summit an awkward, slanting gully traversed across a snow face immediately above a rock bluff. The map marked this place *"passage délicat"* and indicated the precipice below. The slope shelved outward like a shallow roof and in that dull, flat light I couldn't get any feel for its angle. Even as I started I had a premonition of danger.

Half way across, both my skis slipped simultaneously from under me. The fall took me totally by surprise and the force of it broke the safety straps on both my ski poles. As they fell from my grasp, I lunged out desperately and managed to grab them before they rolled away down the slope but the effort left me unbalanced and then spread-eagled across the snow and I began to slide helplessly towards the lip of the bluff. Though I scrabbled frantically to get some purchase on the hard frozen snow with the tips of my poles, I simply kept on sliding and prepared myself for a hundred metres free fall onto the screes of the upper Héchempy Cirque below. Then, as unexpectedly as I had fallen, I stopped dead. Still spread-eagled but now stationary, I lay there panting and heaving for a full minute before getting myself together and crossing over to safe ground.

It had been another nerve wrenching experience but had happened so quickly that no one behind me could have seen what had happened. I yelled back up the slope into the murk:

"For God's sake, watch this place carefully – it's damned tricky."

Somebody shouted, "Okay, John, message over!" and then I saw Nick's familiar outline emerging through the mist above me. When he crossed this *mauvais pas* without faltering I assumed that I had simply lost my concentration at just the wrong time and thought no more about it. When he closed up we skied together diagonally down the hillside towards the Port de Héchempy to wait for the others. Stopping to glance back when we had reached easier ground I said to Nick:

"The clouds are lifting a bit. I can see them all now … They've got past that nasty sloping corridor but seem to have stopped. Can you see what's happening?"

The four of them were huddled together some way above us and out of shouting distance.

"I can't see what on earth's holding them up," Nick replied.

"This isn't the place to be taking a break," I muttered impatiently, looking at my watch. "Time's getting on. We must keep moving."

I sensed trouble. After a while David disengaged himself from the others and came snaking down the mountainside to stop at our feet in a flurry of snow. He was carrying a mound of extra kit strapped to the top of his rucksack.

"What's going on up there?" I asked anxiously.

"John Wilkinson's had a nasty fall," he replied. "He's dislocated his shoulder and he's badly shaken."

"We had better get back up to help him damned quickly."

"No, John," replied David. "I don't think that's necessary. He's managed to put his shoulder back himself. We've taken his kit off him and they're all coming down to join us."

It was ten minutes before the three of them started to ski down towards us. They were moving ultra cautiously and I could see that John was using only one arm with the other supported by a makeshift sling. Alan and Julian were carrying what remained of his equipment.

"How did it happen John?" I asked anxiously. "Are you all right?"

"I fell on that awkward sloping bit," he replied with a grimace. "Damned silly thing to do. It didn't do my shoulder any good." He looked dreadful.

"But how's your shoulder now?"

"Oh it's fine thanks. It has this irritating habit of popping out now and then but I've managed to push it back in."

He was still grinning as he said this but his face was ashen and his body lop-sided.

I checked the map and then looked at my watch yet again. 12 noon! My mind was racing but not properly registering.

"I don't believe it," I said to Alan. "We've already been going for over four hours without a break but, according to the map, have only covered five kilometres. We're not even half way to the Trigonero Hut."

"The map must be right," he replied gruffly. "John's in a bad way and this weather's getting worse by the minute."

"Let's get down to the Port de Héchempy out of this wind," I suggested. "We can discuss things better there."

As we all skied slowly down to the Port, I tried to think through the options open to us but it was David who first expressed what everyone was thinking: "We'll have to retreat," he said firmly. "There'll be a serious avalanche risk if we stay up here."

Retreat definitely and certainly we couldn't remain on this exposed ridge with the wind rising. John Wilkinson was now the first priority. Despite his fixed grin and jokey manner, he was obviously in great pain though, at this stage, none of us realised quite how badly he had been injured. When we sat him down on a patch of heather, a spasm convulsed his face. It then came home to me that we had landed ourselves in precisely the situation that the guidebook had warned – a retreat off the frontier ridge in bad weather.

"Let's take another look at the map," I said as we went into a huddle. "We must get John down ASAP but the Trigonero Hut's at least another six kilometres away over difficult ground on the Spanish side of the range miles from anywhere. The nearest place from here in Spain is Bordas on a road at the junction of two rivers due south of us."

"How far is that from here?" asked David.

"Maybe three kilometres direct and 1,000 metres below us. Trouble is that we would be off the French IGN map for much of the way and I've no idea what we would find when we got there."

My caution reflected a simple ignorance of the Spanish side of the range and the guidebook's warning of Spanish *"bonnes surprises"*. Wary of springing a trap for ourselves, I opted for what was becoming familiar ground.

"I think we should forget about Spain," I said decisively. "We just don't know what there'll be at the other end but at Fabian there's the mountain gendarmerie. Even if he can't make it himself, we can always get a proper rescue party to come up from the valley."

"That's probably right," agreed Alan who was about to make his second rescue mission to the Aure Valley. "But Fabian's a helluva long way from here and the map shows two tricky sections marked by dotted lines. I only hope John's up to it."

"I'm fine," chipped in John. "Don't worry about me."

Even before we started down, I had second thoughts about our decision. The Aure Valley was eight kilometres due north, over twice as far as Bordas, and to reach it we would have to descend two of the most avalanche prone valleys in the range – the Neste de Héchempy and the Val de Moudang. Both were off route for the purposes of the official *Pyrenean Haute Route* itinerary and when I had done my original researches into the Sobrarbe Traverse, I had marked down these sheer sided, enclosed valleys as no-go areas because Volume IV of Ollivier's Skiers Guidebook had described them as *"assez sèveres pour les skieurs"* menaced by *"dangéreux couloirs d'avalanches"*. However, I justified the decision because the weather had been settled for weeks and, provided we moved quickly, the avalanche risk was relatively low.

After a further redistribution of John's equipment between the five of us, the long descent to Fabian began. How he managed to negotiate that route with only one arm working will always be a thing of wonder. Our first hurdle was the Neste de Héchempy's headwall which provided thrills for all and spills for others, ending with a bumpy passage across frozen avalanche pack at the bottom. Further down the Neste, the second *passage délicat* became a helter skelter for Nick and Julian who tangled at the top of the exit couloir and finished the last 40 metres with Nick riding on Julian's head. These were difficult passages for fully fit men but John took them in his stride. His humour never deserted him and he never once complained.

Three hours after leaving the Port de Héchempy, we had our first tea break of the day in a deserted cowshed at the Granges de Moudang. We had made our escape from the frontier ridge just in time. The rain might be pelting down outside but up there it would be blowing a blizzard. The skiable snow had run out so here we changed into trainers. With skis strapped to our already overladen rucksacks and lanced through with icy rain, we stumbled down a rough, slippery track picking a tortuous way through massive boulders and avalanche debris.

We had been lucky in one critical respect: but for the exceptionally dry spell earlier in the season, the Moudang Valley would have been a walking death. Earlier snow and rock avalanches had scoured clean its side gullies and cut swathes through its forested flanks filling the valley bed with millions of tons of rubble.

Thirteen hours after leaving, we were back again to spend our third successive night at the Hotel Terrasse de Fleurie. John's arm was now grotesquely swollen. The French doctor made a quick diagnosis but only when John got back to England was it confirmed that he had broken his arm in two places. With the prospect of John's departure and the end of a record spell of good weather, a collective gloom settled on the party.

Alan said to me unhappily, "Why do we always fetch up at St Lary with some disaster on our hands? There must be some jinx on this wretched place."

I was becoming superstitious about St Lary myself for my own memories were not particularly happy ones. Here we were again only four days into a new tour, minus one team member, having got no further east than two years ago. As we sat around the bar, David brought more bad news from Pau.

"I've just spoken to Anna," he announced. "The short term forecast is for unsettled weather but the longer term forecast is for storms throughout the Pyrenees."

"What's 'longer term'?" asked Nick.

"Perhaps in three days time," David replied.

Two nights ago in this same bar we had been congratulating ourselves on a spectacularly successful start to the tour. Two nights on, morale had hit rock bottom. I felt paralysed and simply didn't know what to suggest for the best.

"Let's go to the Néouvielle for a few days," suggested Alan, suddenly breaking the spell.

At first I thought he must be joking. After the Jean-Pierre affair, I imagined that the Néouvielle would be the last place he would want to return to.

"Surely, you don't want to go back to the Néouvielle, Alan?" I asked.

"Yes, why not?" he replied. "It's much easier ground than the main range and the weather should be a lot better there."

This almost sounded like a re-run of conversations I had had with Jean-Pierre and I still couldn't believe that Alan was serious. Another Néouvielle experiment was precisely the sort of diversion I had sworn to avoid. This was also the type of decision best slept on but perversely I forced the issue.

"Personally, the last thing I want is to get side-tracked in the Néouvielle," I began. "We've only had one day's bad weather and it may clear tomorrow. I don't want to be diverted from the traverse proper. Alan's now suggesting that we spend a few days in the Néouvielle. I don't feel too happy about it so we had better put it to the vote. Let's start with you Nick. What d'you want to do?"

"I'll go along with Alan," he replied predictably.

"How about you, Julian?"

"I'll follow the majority vote."

"And you, David? Haven't you been to the Néouvielle recently anyway?"

"Yes I have," he replied. "Though not to ski. But it's a beautiful area and should have some great ski touring. I'm in favour of going."

"That's it then," I concluded sourly. "Four to one in favour of the Néouvielle."

Next morning when we awoke to a clear blue sky I immediately regretted last night's decision. Throughout the night I had been thinking back to our

Néouvielle adventures two years before and the way in which the original diversion had scuppered the Sobrarbe traverse. After breakfast, I took Alan aside for a chat.

"I reckon we were precipitate and over-cautious last night. The weather's cleared and the Néouvielle's really old hat for both of us. We came here to do the traverse. Don't you think we should have a re-think about the Néouvielle before getting bogged down there?"

In the past, Alan had always been my sounding board for both strategy and tactics. This time all he said was: "Make up your own mind!"

There wasn't anything to say after that. Maybe a spell in the Néouvielle would be good for everyone and put things into perspective.

I knew exactly how John Wilkinson must have been feeling as we sorted out his travel arrangements and said our goodbyes. After that, the five of us took the Pla d'Adet telecabin to the Col de Portet that afternoon. The pattern of the day was almost disturbingly familiar. John's departure reminded me of Alan and Janet's; our route into the Néouvielle was the same as that which Jean-Pierre, Colin and I had followed and, then as now, the weather was clearing.

Our skis glided effortlessly through the crisp, new snow, through glades of pine trees silhouetted black against the late afternoon sun and, as we climbed on, the tensions of the past 24 hours leached away. The Néouvielle was showing us its most attractive face and the contrast between yesterday's drubbing in the main range and this lovely peaceful evening could scarcely have been more complete. Even the steep zig-zagging climb to the Hourquette de Bastanet was a pleasure and from that col I stopped to gaze southwards towards the snow peaks of the main range shining palely in the fading light.

The similarities continued. Within five hours of leaving St Lary, we were sitting round another blazing fire of pine logs cooking supper. This time it was the Campana rather than the Bastanet Hut but, then as now, the Néouvielle was casting its spell. Amity seemed restored. Or was it? After we had eaten I tried to get a familiar message across.

"The Néouvielle's a most attractive area," I began, "but if the weather's really clearing we shouldn't hang around here for more than a day."

"Why not, John?" interrupted Alan, "What else do you have in mind?"

"The traverse of course," I replied taken aback. "That's why we're here. We're trying to get ourselves to Luchon. Everything else is a sideshow."

"But we're right in the middle of the Néouvielle just now," said Alan. "Why can't we make the most of it?"

"Because we've only got limited time and could easily get bogged down here," I replied. "My suggestion is that we climb the Pic de Portarras tomorrow

Posets from Port de Madera

and then ski down to Aulon. It's a *'très belle'* descent according to the guidebook so we'll get our Néouvielle money's worth. At Aulon we can ring Jean Palasset and get him to drive us up the Rioumajou Valley. If we can make the Rioumajou Hospice tomorrow night, we'll only have lost a couple of days of the traverse."

"Aren't you pushing it a bit?" said Alan. "What happens if the weather goes against us again? I think we should wait and see."

I left it at that. There was no point in arguing the toss about the weather but I was concerned that Alan and I seemed to be working to different agendas.

Alan didn't raise the subject again over breakfast next morning when clear skies foretold another fine day. Reversing yesterday's route to the Hourquette de Bastanet, we stormed up the south-east ridge of Pic Portarras with David in the lead and Alan glued to his heels all the way to the summit. The descent to Aulon was a ski run of dreams. On perfect snow in a remote setting, we coursed on downwards for eight kilometres through the beautiful Lavedon Valley, descending 1,350 metres before reaching a friendly bar in a shaded corner of Aulon's sunlit square.

With half the day still to run, the admirable Jean Palasset drove over from St Lary, squeezed all five of us plus sacs and skis into one taxi, whisked us back to St Lary for a pit-stop and then drove us twelve kilometres up the Rioumajou Valley to the Fredançon roadhead. In a normal year, the road up the Riomajou Gorge is impassable to traffic until early summer due to avalanches. Fortunately, this was an abnormal year and Jean's ferrying left us with barely an hour's walk to the Hospice de Rioumajou. For all that, it had been a long day and I was mightily relieved to emerge from the gloomy forest as it grew dusk to see, at the far end of the clearing, a dilapidated, single storey building backed hard up against the rock ribs of the valley's containing wall.

John Wilkinson's accident had brought us up short but, by reaching the Hospice de Rioumajou, we were back in the game. For years this place, tucked away in a recess at the head of an almost inaccessible valley, had been rooted in my imagination as the Pyrenean Shangri-La. In ancient times it had been the nodal point at which three historic mountain passages converged. By one such route Abdul Rahman's Moorish cavalry came from the south to pillage, murder and rape the Aure Valley. By another, Don Sancha's Aragonese made the revenge raid that cut the Moors to pieces at the battle of St Lary – a famous victory recalled in the hagiographies of three local Christian martyrs, Missolin, Calixte and Mercurial. The Hospice was built to commemorate those ancient battles and to succour Christian pilgrims on the high road to Santiago de Compostella to celebrate the *Reconquista*.

The reality of the Hospice was disappointing. Count Henri Russell once described it as "execrable ... but a marvellous place to spend a week". It can't have changed much since his time. One night was enough. Most of the roof tiles were intact but the barnlike building exuded an air of neglect. Except for one door permanently open to the elements, all windows were barred and shuttered. Russell probably slept in the same donkey stalls on the same crumbling straw as we did. After supper we huddled together before the wild fire whose flames leapt up from a grimy hearth, casting grotesque shadows on the wall. Apprehensive about tomorrow, I slept fitfully with the ghosts of a disquieting past.

Our passage from Rioumajou to the Granges de Viados held the key to the entire traverse. If the weather held and we got the route right, it would take us across the watershed of the main range into the remote upper valley of the Gistain and thence to Viados to spend the night. If the weather broke, we could be marooned for days at the end of one of the most inaccessible valleys in the Pyrenees.

At daybreak we crossed the foaming Cauarere River by way of a fallen tree trunk. The sky was flecked with high cirrus clouds but the air was crisp. Higher up, the forest thinned and gave way to a bleak valley closed to the east by an immense amphitheatre of snow and rock. The crux of this passage, which I had highlighted in yellow on my map, lay in negotiating one or other of two high passes. From where we stood, the ski route apparently went due east straight up the valley but still left us with a choice, higher up, of taking either the Port de Cauarere or the Port de Madera for the crossing into Spain. Yet, when I studied the ground ahead, I simply couldn't work out where or how the route could ascend the seemingly unscaleable headwall that closed the valley.

I took out my map and went across to Alan.

"What do you make of this? I can't see where the devil this ski route goes. According to this map it's dead ahead but that way looks impassable."

He stared at the ground ahead and then looked back at me quizzically.

"I can't see that there's a route there either. Surely, we can't be heading the right way."

"But it must go somewhere up there," I insisted. "Both the map and guidebook say so."

I took another hard look at the map. Unquestionably, the blue ski route was marked as running east-south-east up a feature marked Millarioux parallel to the summer walking route. Yet I still couldn't make out how it could get over the barrier of snow and rock ahead.

Alan was getting restive.

"I'm sure that it is the wrong way, John," he persisted. "I can't believe that there's any sort of ski route ahead."

He swivelled round and pointed to a steep forested spur that curled round an end of the valley behind us.

"Look over there, there's a perfectly good route going up the flank of that ridge. I can even see the line of a path quite distinctly."

This was definitely not the ski route shown on the map but it was clearly recognisable as the summer *Haute Randonnée* track doubling back along the ridge in a series of hairpin bends. This would eventually get us to the Port de Madera but by a more circuitous route. Never before had Alan and I seriously argued the toss over route finding but I could see that on this one he was not going to budge and was anxious not to make an issue of it. Although it is often the case that you can only assess a route when you've rubbed your nose against it, I was quite baffled by the line of the ski route as it didn't match the lie of the land.

"Okay, Alan," I said resignedly, "let's take your route."

The mystery of the ski route was never solved but it took us six long hours to climb a mere 1,000 metres to the Port de Madera. The ground was deceptive and it was as well that we had picked a good day for in any other conditions we would have been struggling.

My confidence too had taken a knock but as we breasted the port, my mood was transformed by the sight of a stupendous mountain which suddenly filled the entire eastern horizon. Taken by surprise I gasped, "That must be Posets! What a fantastic sight."

Posets had always been a mystery mountain. I had never even seen a photograph of it but the tableau now before us was as grand as anything in the Pyrenees. Six great ridges curved upwards to meet at the long undulating rocky crest which climaxed in a 3,375 metre summit pyramid rising sheer from a glacial cirque. A solitary white cloud overhung the summit. Seeing this mountain for the first time, I was stunned by its sheer size and wondered whether I had allowed enough time to tackle it.

We skied on down through a pine forest to the trough of the Cinqueta de la Pez and when we stumbled into the Granges de Viados in late afternoon, we had been off the French map for over an hour. This upper valley of the Gistain is the heartland of the Sobrarbe which until recent years was one of the remotest and most impoverished areas in the Spanish Pyrenees. I had expected a scattering of ramshackle shepherds' huts recalling J. B. Morton's dispiriting description of the place when he had stormed through here during his rumbustious trans-Pyrenean walk between the Wars.

Yet, as is so often the tale in Spain, these same valleys were once the seat of a proud mountain kingdom. Sobrarbe is still venerated by Spanish patriots as a centre of resistance to the Moors and the source of the *Fueros de Sobrarbe,* Aragon's eighth century equivalent to the Magna Carta. Sancho the Great was born here and his son, Ramiro welded Sobrarbe, Aragon and Ribargorza into the single kingdom of Aragon to dominate mediaeval Mediterranean but when Spain disintegrated during the seventeenth century so too did the Sobrarbe. Its valleys became the lairs of bandits who thought nothing of crossing the frontier to kill a Frenchman "for a sou". During the Second World War, the place again reverted to brigandage.

Old Sobrarbe is history but prosperity is better than impoverishment. At Viados, crumbling shepherds' crofts had been transformed into the summer retreats of Aragonese weekenders and one of these had been converted into a mountain hut. Its guardian was away for the winter but one room burrowed beneath the main building remained open. This former byre became our home. Alan ingeniously reconstructed a stove from odd fragments while the rest of us chopped up enough wood with our ice axes to generate what became an uncomfortably warm fug on a makeshift mattress of foam rubber.

It had been a taxing day but, as I had intended, had brought us within striking distance of Posets. This little known Pyrenean treasure, with its multiplicity of peaks, ridges, gorges, glaciers, rivers and lakes, covers an area nearly half the size of the Mont Blanc massif and is itself more a massif than a single mountain.

On account of its remoteness from France, French ski mountaineers have always considered Posets a plum because no sortie there and back can easily be accomplished within three days. The three ski routes that Ollivier describes are all *"sérieux", "difficile et longue"* with passages of *"alpinisme hivernal"*. In his book, the alternative of driving round to tackle it from Spain would not be playing the game for *"la facilité y gagne, l'aventure y perd."*

My original plan had been to climb Posets from the north using the Estos Hut as our base but this hut was another long day away from Viados across the Col Gistain and, remembering the forecast of impending storms that Anna had relayed to David at St Lary, I reckoned that we should strike tomorrow before the weather broke. But my proposals had a mixed reception.

"A ski ascent of Posets would be a great expedition," I had enthused after another indigestible supper of Raven AFD steak stew. "Ollivier particularly recommends this south-west route via the Col d'Eriste with a *'très belle'* descent down a *'véritable Vallée Blanche'.*"

"I'm not that interested in what Ollivier recommends," broke in Alan. "What precisely is involved?"

"It's a big day," I replied cautiously. "An ascent and descent of 1,725 metres."

"Crikey," exclaimed Julian, "that's one helluva big day."

"Yes," I replied, "but we can travel lightweight and leave all our heavy stuff here."

"That would mean spending another night at this place," said Alan unenthusiastically.

For so long my confidante, Alan's lack of enthusiasm left me with the uneasy feeling that we were losing touch but when David thought it "a great idea" the matter was settled.

Reveille was at 5 am next morning. After a mug of tea and a lump of porridge cake, we lumbered off across the Viados meadows in the general direction of the Col d'Eriste. It was still dark, the moon was shrouded in cloud and the air was muggy. We missed the foot bridge across the Anes Cruces river and wasted half an hour pacing up and down the bank trying to find another way across. As dawn came up, the clouds had a reddish hue and when we stopped for a breather a little way up the Millares Valley, I turned to David and said,

"D'you remember that conversation you had with Anna about the weather forecast? When exactly were those storms due?"

"Anna couldn't be that specific," he replied, "but I reckon they could be with us anytime. It's far too warm today and the snow's barely frozen."

It was Alan's turn to come in strongly. "I don't like the look of this weather either. We made a duff start and don't seem to be getting anywhere."

True. We had been going for an hour and a half but were nowhere near our objective. A collective lethargy seemed to have overtaken everyone except David. For the past six days we had been humping round packs weighing from 45 to 60 pounds, with skis and boots on top. We needed a break. Posets itself was in cloud. It was a mountain too far for that day.

"Okay," I said. "Maybe we should give this one away but let's get straight back to Viados and continue with the traverse to the Estos Hut rather than waste another day."

"Pity about Posets," said David. He was the only one who looked that disappointed.

"It's still a possibility," I replied. "There's nothing to stop us having a crack at it from the Estos Valley tomorrow when we're feeling stronger."

"That's entirely up to the weather," growled Alan, "but if we're going to reach the Estos Hut tonight we had better get moving."

Back at Viados, we packed up smartly and set course for the second time that day, pounding up what would have been the sunny side of the Cinqueta de Anes Cruces in our trainers. There was no sun but the very steep slopes on this side of the valley were mercifully denuded of snow. Only with the hardest set stuff would they have been safe to traverse. We were now making such good time that someone decided to cook up a packet of Raven mince and macaroni for brunch in the ruins of the Cabaña de Anes Cruces.

The notorious 2,572 metre Col Gistain still lay between us and the Estos Valley. Belloc and J. B. Morton, both intrepid walkers, had deliberately avoided it in summer because of its reputation for sudden storms. Preoccupied with forcing down a disgusting slug of Raven macaroni crunch while trying to work out the state of the snow at the top of the spiralling gun barrel *barranco* that led up to the col, I became conscious of the swelling cloud bank that had built up behind us in the west.

I was the last to tumble. The others were already moving off so I tagged onto the end of a flying column led by Alan, with David in hot pursuit. No lethargy now as we zigged and zagged furiously from one side of an ever narrowing couloir to the other in an effort to beat the storm. The black clouds billowed and boiled below but never quite caught up with us. We breasted the col and plunged down the other side, skiing through a mixture of breakable crust and liquid cement to safe ground.

Alan flung down his rucksack by a heap of grey stones marking the remains of a shepherd's *cabane* built at the side of a flat patch which, in summer, would have been a meadow.

"Let's call it a day," he suggested. "We could bivouac here and take a shot at Posets tomorrow. The summit must be pretty well due south of us."

Nick predictably agreed and David nodded his head in approval but I was far from happy. The route to Posets from here could only be up that steep, ice-glazed gulley leading to a rocky lip on the other side of the valley. The map marked this as the Coume de la Paoul and the guidebook described the gully as *"un goulet avalancheux et très raide"*. In no way was I going to be rushed into it.

"Look," I said evenly, "the Coume de la Paoul is a serious route. I don't think it's remotely sensible to attempt it from here. We could have a lousy night bivouacing in the snow and if the weather breaks it would be nightmarish. Let's stick to the original plan and spend tonight at the Estos Hut. After a decent night's sleep, we'll be in fine fettle for another crack at Posets tomorrow."

Alan made some inaudible comment and Nick suggested leaving some of the heavy stuff here to be picked up tomorrow on the way down from Posets.

"I would definitely advise against that Nick," I commented tersely. "It would be the worst of all worlds."

As we skied on down the valley, the clouds behind us began to lift and I wondered whether I had been over-cautious. The Estos Hut wasn't that easy to find and, when we did, all that remained was half a room covered in rubble and a fragment of roof. A vandals' fire had done for it but Alan immediately set to work rebuilding a rough terrace outside while the rest of us gathered fallen branches to make a fire in what was left of the grate. To the east, a brooding mass of cloud obscured the Maladetta Massif but at the close of day the sun came out to lighten our valley. As the shadows lengthened, I sat on the greensward watching a herd of forty chamois graze on a grassy alp and wondered about tomorrow.

That night was as wild as any I could remember in the Pyrenees. Snow poured in through holes in the roof and the wind was so fierce that I feared that the hut's shaky edifice would collapse and bury us in rubble. The storm so long forecast had at last broken and by dawn half a metre of new snow covered the ground. The wind blowing in from the north-east was cold enough to cauterize any exposed parts within seconds.

I had always set my cap at climbing Posets but from the moment I first saw it from the Col Madera, had a certain feeling that it wasn't going to be this year. With this change in the weather, there was no point in hanging around this miserable hut waiting for the mountain to come back into condition. As we stood in the snow on Alan's new terrace warming our hands on our mugs of tea and staring gloomily at a landscape totally transformed by heavy snow, I said to the others.

"I'm afraid that this puts out Posets so far as I'm concerned. We'd be crazy to attempt that gully with all this new snow. The weather's pretty dreadful so I suggest we simply get ourselves down the Estos Vallley to Bénasque."

"What are we planning to do then?" asked Julian.

"We've still got to get ourselves to Luchon," I replied. "From Bénasque we're also well placed to have a shot at Aneto. If the weather settles we could even get to the Rencluse Hut this afternoon. We've still got a few days in hand."

This and other plans were discussed at length but in the end there was no sensible alternative. What the Spanish map portrayed as a straightforward descent involved some gymnastic scrambles up and down thickly forested spurs to avoid a swim at the bottom of the vertiginous Gorgues Galantes. Lower down the valley Nick led a water skiing party to cross the river.

Four hours after leaving the Estos Hut, we clumped into Bénasque, dropped our skis and sacs on the pavement outside the Hotel Barrabes, the first hostelry we came to, and draped ourselves around the bar. After some initial language difficulties, Señora got the message and produced an endless lunch of soup, bread, salad, pork, chips and ice-cream to eat and *cerveza,* Rioja and a pint of olive oil to drink – this last item to re-line our stomachs after six days of Raven monosodium glutamate.

This feast did wonders for morale and, after a day which had started so badly, the party's mood demanded action. It was early afternoon and raining outside so the sensible thing would have been to call it a day and book ourselves into the hotel or, at least, get a weather forecast but the talk was all about Aneto and how we might climb it.

"Well, what about it?" demanded Alan. "You know the ground, John. What's the strategy?"

"The first thing is to get up to the Rencluse Hut," I replied.

"Have we enough time to get there this evening?" asked Julian very sensibly.

"It's quite a way from here," I replied breezily, "but if we can find a taxi to take us to the head of the Esera Valley, we could make it if we move like the clappers."

A Land Rover taxi was duly summoned by Senora and an exorbitantly expensive bargain struck. By 3.40 pm, when the last pair of skis had been lashed to the roof rack, I had sobered up sufficiently to realise that it was pre-posterously late for any sort of start. Yet thinking processes had stopped and no one suggested that we pull out.

Once beyond the shelter of Bénasque's narrow streets, the snow came billowing across the road from all angles. The sides of the Estos Valley were lost under its grey blankets as our morose driver hunched ever further over the wheel. Peering through the narrow slit left by his over-worked windscreen wipers, he swerved from one side of the road to the other to avoid the safe-sized boulders that littered it.

At the ruined Hospital de Bénasque the Land Rover slid to a halt, the driver switched off the ignition and ejaculated *"No mas – finish!"*

We clambered out, scuttled round the vehicle's leeward side to avoid the worst of the blizzard and made a half-hearted attempt to unload everything off the roof. Our clothing was already plastered in snow when I saw Alan shaking his head. I looked at him and he looked at me. We knew the game was up and clambered back into the Land Rover.

Back at the Hotel Barrabes we would have done better to have brought our own lavatory seats, plugs and soap. My tepid hip bath was caulked with a lavatory paper plug encased in a plastic bag. Dinner on the other hand was a jolly affair with Señora laying on our second feast within three hours. Olives, sardines, chicken'n chips, cheese and fruit and then more olive oil and raw, red local wine to shift the monosodium glutamate. For almost the first time on this tour we seemed to have relaxed. Conversation took on a lighter tone and we even played a rubber of Oh Hell.

The bad weather was forcing the shepherds to seek shelter for their flocks and by evening Bénasque's main street had become choked with bleating sheep. By next morning, the rooftops were covered in fresh snow with a mighty storm still raging up the valley. Albeit belatedly, we had made the right decision to retreat but now I was in a quandary as to our next move. Paradoxically, the sky in the south was ice clear blue and the sun was hot enough to burn but in the north the sky was blue black, the mountains were invisible and an icy wind blew down the valley.

Apart from John Wilkinson's accident, I reckoned that this tour had gone well. We had failed to get to grips with Posets but we had traversed the Sobrarbe and still had time to climb Aneto provided the weather held and everyone's heart was still in the game. Over breakfast I ran through the options.

"According to the programme, we've still got four days in hand. The original plan was to climb Aneto and cross the frontier into France to Luchon. However, after all this snow, all routes across the frontier ridge will be too dangerous for some days."

"What's the alternative," demanded Alan. "I can't say that I've read your programme."

"We could still have a shot at Aneto if the weather settles. We could get up to the Rencluse Hut today, climb the mountain tomorrow and be back here the following day. Maybe all the bad weather that was forecast is blowing itself out."

"Aren't you cutting things a bit fine?" replied Alan. "Even if it clears today you've only allowed us one day to get back to Luchon. I don't see how we can do that by public transport."

"Let me speak to the patron," volunteered Julian.

Alas the patron of the Barrabes could offer no advice on any useful subject so we wandered down the street to the new part of town and in a shiny modern bar talked it all over for the second time that morning. Nick bought a local newspaper and began studying the weather map's isobars with his airline pilot's eye.

"What does it look like?" I asked.

"The bad weather hasn't blown over. Look at the isobars on this weather map. Something very nasty's brewing. We could be in the middle of an Atlantic front within a couple of days."

Alan said, "If that's the case, I'm all for packing up and going home. Personally, I don't think that this weather's going to clear."

Nick agreed with Alan but David, like me, was all for having a stab at Aneto. Julian, who had been busy chatting up the locals while the the rest of us had been arguing the toss, broke what looked like becoming an impasse.

"I've got the answer how we get to France," he announced triumphantly.

"We can't get there by public transport without doing a round trip of at least 300 kilometres via Llerida and up through the Bielsa Tunnel. However," he continued pointing to a cheerful looking man in a leather jerkin, "that chap's a taxi driver who'll take us all to Bielsa for £35. It's a bargain."

"Where the hell's Bielsa?" asked Alan.

"It's on the north side of the range in the Val d'Aran. Think of it, we could be back in France this evening!"

I felt I had been hi-jacked.

"Actually Julian," I said to him evenly, "I don't want to be back in France this evening. I would prefer to be up at the Rencluse Hut ready to climb Aneto tomorrow."

David and myself apart, enthusiasm for Aneto was ebbing fast. When we took a vote, it was three to two against so we hired the taxi to Bielsa. The sun was hot but the air still cold as we sped down the deep cut gorge of the Estos Valley leaving the snow-capped mountains behind. Some 30 kilometres on, we swung off the main road and headed due east by a switch back road that ran across the grain of the land, climbing up and down a succession of rocky ridges radiating off the main range. The ground had a parched, dusty look and every knoll was capped by a half-ruined village. The people of these parts were forsaking the mountains for the plains.

When our road joined the Ribargorza Valley we swung north and again headed for the mountains through gaunt scenery, where colossal granite erratics were strewn about the valley bed like marbles. Then on through the Bielsa tunnel into the Val d'Aran and Viella where the snow was still falling.

From the time we had left Bénasque, I had been feeling frustrated and depressed. Retreat down the Estos Valley had been inevitable but we had quit Bénasque entirely of our own volition and I felt that my cup had been dashed. It was poor consolation to find the weather on this north side of the range equally unsettled but I hoped that the forecasters might have got it wrong and that somehow we could make a lightening strike on Aneto from France.

I had persuaded myself and half persuaded the others that from Viella we could gain a high point on the frontier ridge and get down to the Hospice de France as a launch pad for Aneto. Fantasy was replacing reality and we had reached the stage when much was left unsaid between us. From Viella we hired another taxi to Bosost and from there climbed out of the Garona Valley to the frontier by a twisting mountain road. We were now perched on the north/south ridge that separates France from Spain. Our taxi dropped us off at a side track and for the next two hours we skinned up a meandering snow track to a tiny *cabane*.

"It's already 6 pm and we've barely climbed 300 metres," exclaimed Alan. "Where are we supposed to go from here?"

"We had better call it a day and doss down here," I replied. "I had hoped we could have skied down to the Hospice de France from the top of this ridge but it's now too late."

The concrete Cabane de Barèges was a Cabane des Aires look alike. We were all tired and good humour had temporarily deserted us. When I walked inside with snow-covered boots Alan came out with a familiar expletive. We made a fire, ate the last of the Raven and I slept inside both my sleeping bag and bivouac tent on the cold concrete floor.

Next morning I was first up and, once through the door, stared around in disbelief.

"It's a fantastic day," I cried and, rushing back into the squalid little hut to rouse the others, called out, "Come and see for yourselves."

The sky was cloudless, the air was sharp and the world looked reborn. Everything seemed possible. The excitement was contagious and we were once again thrashing out a new plan to get across to the Rencluse Hut for a last shot at Aneto.

"The guidebook offers three routes to the Rencluse," I enthused, "but none are straightforward."

"Meaning what?" asked Alan.

"Two start from the Hospice de France – one goes up the Freche Valley and another across the Port de Benasque but both are long and subject to avalanche danger."

"That doesn't sound much good," he replied, "where does the third route go?"

"Straight along this ridge. It's the longest but probably the safest."

David said, "Let's stick to the ridge." No one demurred.

We were away by 7.45 am with David and Alan forcing the pace as we climbed towards the Col de Barèges. Their silhouettes were cast black against the pale blue sky and when we reached that col a wondrous panorama of peaks opened out to the south.

Now visible to us for the first time the elusive summit of Aneto, unmistakable for its granite comb, peeped up coyly from behind a jagged rim of peaks marking the frontier ridge. Every detail of the great whale back ridge that swelled away to the south bearing aloft a stud of peaklets had been sharpened into focus by the brilliant morning light. The way ahead looked straightforward and the foreshortened frontier ridge, beyond which lay the upper Estos Valley and the Rencluse Hut, looked ridiculously close. Ever since we had left Bénasque I had feared that caution had lost the venture. Now it seemed as if we might have a second chance.

David was standing next to me and I said to him, "I can trace a route along this ridge. I'm sure it will go. What do you think?"

When he didn't reply, I followed his gaze to Aneto and noticed for the first time that cursive wisps of cloud were forming a gauze halo about its crown.

Nick too was gazing at those wispy clouds intently. "Them be lenticulars," he muttered. "They're bad news."

Years before when climbing Mont Blanc on a morning which had promised fair, a lenticular cloud such as this had presaged a great storm which had sent us scuttling off the mountain.

Nick's voice rose a decibel or two. "And Jeepers," he exclaimed, "look what's coming in from the west. Here's the bloody great Atlantic front the weather chart prophesied!"

My concentration had been so fixed on the ridge ahead and then at Aneto that I had scarcely noticed anything else. To the south and east the sky was still unsullied but, when I swung round to where he was pointing, I saw a black band of cloud stretched taut across the western horizon. We pressed on hurriedly to the summit of the Pic d'Arres but I knew that our game was over.

The gauzy wisps that had first crowned Aneto had coarsened to thickening threads. These, in turn, gave way to flying columns of straggly cloud behind which followed a blanket of charcoal grey. For a few more minutes, a curious incandescent light glowing faintly in the east retained the promise of the morning. But then a pall fell about us and our sunlit world became grey monochrome.

"That's the end of it," I cried as a cold wind got up. "Let's get off this mountain while we can still see something!"

David led the way down for the last time of the tour. The rest of us followed in his wake with a wild spiralling descent through a powder filled gully. As we plunged down and down towards the Vallée de la Picque, I stopped for a moment to take a last look at Aneto but it had vanished into the clouds.

First sight of Aneto from Col de Barèges

Punta Alta in the Aigues Tortes

7

To the Enchanted Mountains

Luchon to Boi

T he journey of the depleted Sobrarbe team ended at Lourdes railway station where Anna Lindberg was on the platform to meet David. Our farewell dinner at the station buffet was a low key affair after which David and Anna returned to Pau while Alan, Nick, Julian and I caught the night sleeper to Paris.

Although we had completed the traverse of the Sobrarbe, a tour which had started so promisingly had ended on a downbeat. It had been frustrating to have backed off both Posets and Aneto but you can't win them all. The loss of John Wilkinson had had an unsettling effect but something else seemed to have gone awry and I realised that it was my relationship with Alan.

This had been our fourth Pyrenean tour together on which Alan had been the ultimate anchorman – dependable, resolute and unflurried. On previous tours we might have argued the toss but had never had any significant disagreement about overall objectives but somewhere along the line on this tour our relationship had altered. We hadn't laughed the way we had before and had only once relaxed over silly card games or Liar Dice. In the rush to catch taxis at Victoria Station to get ourselves back to work, Alan and I hadn't even managed to say goodbye to each other. We always remained good friends but, although I didn't know it at the time, our crossing of the Sobrarbe was to be the last time that we would tour the Pyrenees together. It took me years to accept that the old bonds had weakened. Maybe it was all in my mind. While I remained obsessed with the Pyrenean traverse, Alan had wider mountaineering aspirations. I often asked him to finish what we had started together but his interests had moved on to the Himalayas and his holidays were as limited as mine.

The *Affaire Jean-Pierre* had been a sadness but to have parted mountaineering company with Alan was another thing. I could never forget that our first Pyrenean tour together had given me the confidence to tackle the Pyrenees traverse unguided. Alan combined inspiration and imagination with pragmatism and common sense but he was always his own man, a natural leader who preferred to set his own agenda. I greatly missed Alan. We had shared so many adventures together.

At this stage, it never occurred to me that our partnership had ended. I was more concerned with the thought that in six Pyrenean tours we had barely covered half the distance to Canigou. Time seemed to be running out and I was also plagued by the married mountaineer's dilemma of balancing his sport's selfish needs with those of his family. For the next Pyrenean round I had banked on recruiting the same Sobrarbe team but Alan, Nick and Julian were otherwise engaged; John Wilkinson – now happily recovered – couldn't manage my dates and David Williams's job hunting only left him with weekends.

I had left it too late to form a viable Pyrenean team so I settled for another Scottish traverse. The previous year's Corrour to Kingussie crossing with the Wedgwoods had brought it home to me that ski mountaineering is one of Scotland's best kept secrets. Having crossed the Central Highlands from west to east last year, I now planned an east to west traverse of the Cairngorms starting from Lecht and finishing at Kingussie.

The Cairngorms held a special place in my heart. During my National Service days, I had been introduced to climbing there by the then padre of the Guards Training Battalion, Fred Jenkins and had discovered the temper of Cairngorm blizzards. I had proposed to my wife after a Cairngorm skiing weekend and it was on Cairngorm's White Lady piste that our three daughters had first learned to ski.

The Cairngorms are Britain's grandest range covering much the same area as the Mont Blanc massif. But whereas both the Alps and Pyrenees are pierced by motorways and tunnels and encroached on all sides by towns, villages, ski resorts and even factory complexes, the Cairngorms hinterland is almost as uninhabited and desolate as the range itself which supports only a handful of huts or bothies.

Structurally and scenically the Pyrenees and Cairngorms have nothing in common but both attract foul weather and the Arctic storms of the Cairngorm Plateau can vie with any Atlantic blizzard. As in the Pyrenees, weather would determine the outcome of my proposed ski traverse. Subject to that, I reckoned we could complete a 40-mile east to west crossing in five days climbing en route most of the highest summits of the range – Ben Avon, Ben a Bhuird, Ben Macdui, Carn Toul and Braeriach.

I took David Williams up on his promise to fit in a long weekend. He, in turn, made it a condition that Anna come too. I still harboured guilty feelings about my discouraging Anna to join the Sobrarbe crossing and remained wary of embarking on a serious ski tour with an unknown quantity but if David insisted that she come, so be it. I couldn't have known then that Anna would soon be my salvation.

Julian Lush couldn't come himself but warmly recommended a friend called Roger Childs. Although Roger had skied regularly, his ski mountaineering experience was limited to one guided *Haute Route* and in mountaineering matters didn't know the difference between a crampon and a chockstone. However, he had played flanker for Blackheath in its glory days, spoke the two Scottish dialects of French and Spanish and was also a keen sailor. I didn't apply the same qualifying criteria to Roger as I had to Anna on the basis that if

Roger was another sailor/skier in the Colin Chapman mould he was probably weatherproof.

At 12 noon on March 14 the four of us set off from Lecht, the smallest and most improbable of all Scottish ski resorts, in a south western direction with wispy clouds drifting over our heads and the mountain tops shrouded in mist.

Blonde Anna of the china blue eyes was as fresh and healthy looking as I remembered her from last year. She was also strongly built and from her first classy ski run I understood one reason why she was David's girlfriend.

On that first day we traversed two peaks, put up several brace of grouse, chased the odd hare through the heather and bivouaced for the night in a manger in one of the many disused barns at Inchory Lodge, a magnificent relic of Victorian stalking parties.

For the first two-thirds of our second day, cloud blotted out the landscape and for four hours we marched against a bullying wind on a compass bearing of 240 degrees, counting steps as we went before hitting off the massive granite pile of boulders that marks the 1,171 metre apex of Ben Avon. From this high point we set a new compass course south-westwards to reach the great neck in the range called Snecht. With the wind howling through the gap, we abandoned an earlier plan to climb Ben a Bhuird direct and set a new course due south. Through shifting cloud and billowing snow flurries we skied down a narrow valley and sought shelter in the Wood of Quoich. Here, as a watery sun made its first appearance, we pitched our tents by a frozen river amidst Scots Pines and made the heather our mattress.

The following day we were up at dawn but delayed while David made running repairs to Roger's glueless hired skins. A steep climb to Ben a Bhuird's South Top followed by a three kilometre traverse under threatening skies across a bleak, featureless plateau led to the 1,196 metres North Top. From here we skied another five kilometres westwards to Bheinn a Chaorainn Bheag to climb our last scheduled summit and third Munro of the day. It was now 3.30 pm. We had been on our skis for six hours since striking camp that morning.

For the past three days we had seen no sign of habitation save for Inchory Lodge. As I scanned the desolate landscape of heather, rock and snow from a summit as remote as any in the Highlands, I felt a flush of pride that we had cracked the trickiest section of the traverse in bad weather. From here I could look down into Glen Avon and, although still invisible to the eye, could identify the position of our intended destination for that night – the Falls of Avon Refuge. For the first time that day the sky was lightening; the cloud was beginning to clear and my altimeter indicated that barometric pressure was rising. Beyond this point, I knew something of the country that lay between us and Kingussie.

Everything seemed to be going our way when I said to David: "Can't be much further now to that refuge. Maybe two or three kilometres from here."

He took a quick look at his map. "Yup ... must be just round the corner hidden behind that spur at the junction of those four valleys. About 300 metres descent I reckon. Shouldn't take us more than twenty minutes to get down there."

Turning to Anna and Roger I said: "We're almost there. This is the last run down. David's going to lead the way."

On that first day David had sprained his thumb and had skied one handed ever since. Yet he snaked away with the effortless grace that marked his skiing whatever the snow conditions, whatever he might be carrying on his back and whatever his physical impairments.

"All set everyone?" I shouted behind me to the others as I pushed myself off to follow David. "Let's go!"

For all of thirty seconds I followed in his tracks as he flowed down the mountainside in a series of sweeping turns. Then, suddenly, he had to change direction to avoid a heap of granite boulders. Even as I watched him carve his turn I had a presentiment of disaster.

Over the years, I had had any number of spectacular skiing falls. Most had been harmless and others had resulted in broken ribs, torn muscles and bruised heads but nothing in my previous experience had felt like this one. The jarring wrench that followed the fall sent a shock wave of blinding pain throughout my body. It left me lying in the snow head down in a position from which I was quite unable to move. My right shoulder felt as if it had been plugged into a live electric socket.

Seconds before David had been drawing away from me. Seconds later he had somehow managed to climb back up the hill and was now kneeling besides me. The pain was so overwhelming that I could barely get the words out.

"David, for Chrissake get this sac off my shoulder," I choked.

As he and Anna gently eased the rucksack off my shoulder I almost vomited. Even without it the pain was agonising and remorseless. Falling at speed, a sudden twist from my 50 pound rucksack had jerked my right shoulder clean out of its socket. When eventually I managed to stand upright, my body had sunk several inches to the right and the arm which hung uselessly jangled with jabbing pain.

Only minutes before I had been a vibrant human being hurtling downhill on skis. Now I felt like a wounded animal unable to fend for itself with my world shrunk by a bewildered blur of pain. Yet my instincts were still intact and I knew what the consequences might be if we didn't get off this mountain to shelter before nightfall. I glanced at the watch on my good left wrist. 4 pm. We had two hours of daylight left. My mind was still working clearly in the small, selfish area of self-preservation. I couldn't be carried. Somehow, I had to get down under my own steam.

"David," I said through gritted teeth, "We must get off this mountain immediately. We must get to the Refuge before dark."

"Take it easy, John," he replied. "You're badly hurt. Looks as if you've dislocated your shoulder. Let's get your arm into this sling."

He had already whipped out a cotton sling and, while he and Anna put it on, Roger began to sort out the contents of my sac into three separate piles so that I had nothing to carry.

"Are you sure you can walk down?" asked David.

"Yes, I'm fine," I lied, "let's get going."

I grasped the ski stick in my left hand, took a first step downhill, cried out and almost collapsed. The simple effort of moving was excruciating and the over-whelming intensity of pain was outside my experience. Each downhill step required a prodigious effort of willpower and concentration to keep the body moving. Yet with so much at stake, every step became a goal in itself and I felt confident that I could negotiate this rough, snow covered ground without assistance provided I didn't faint in the process. My main worry was to avoid doing just that with all the consequences of falling on the injured shoulder.

With Anna at my side and my breath rasping out in hoarse staccato pants, I counted out twenty paces before stopping for a break. Every minute passed like an hour but after what seemed an eternity we reached the banks of the River Avon. I hadn't counted on crossing this river but, with Roger and Anna flanking either side, I braced myself to find a footing on the ice-glazed stepping stones that were half submerged in the water supported by my one ski stick. Halfway across, I faltered momentarily to balance myself. Roger caught my arm to steady me.

"Christ, that's my shoulder!"

An explosive flash of pain made me shout out involuntarily. I swayed and almost fainted but somehow managed to reach the safety of the grassy bank. For some minutes I trembled and retched uncontrollably before tackling the steep incline that led from the riverbed to the path above. The effort of climbing this called on my last reserves and when I eventually breasted the lip, I leaned on my stick and panted like a dog for five minutes.

My head and body were bowed but when David said, "Well done, John. Not far to go now, less than a kilometre. I think I can see the hut," I looked up to see that we had reached a rough stalkers' path. As I shuffled along like a broken old man with Anna at my side, I kept thinking about John Wilkinson. How on earth had he managed to reset his shoulder and keep going cheerfully for six hours with a broken arm?

It took another half hour for Anna and me to reach the refuge. As we approached it, the sun came out for the first time in three days to bathe the great hills in a golden light. David was standing outside what looked like a Pictish barrow, camouflaged by great granite blocks.

"Welcome to the Falls of Avon bivouac," he said. "This is it."

The exterior of the place looked more primitive than the scruffiest Pyrenean *cabane* but inside it was snug, roomy and windproof. They laid me down in my sleeping bag with a couple of sleeping mats as mattresses. At least we had got off the mountain but with that first hurdle surmounted, the prospect of how and when we were going to get out of here preoccupied my mind.

I was poor company for I couldn't stop groaning and was inwardly cursing myself for another damn fool accident when our traverse was all but in the bag. Lying there in the darkness, listening to the others discussing possible options in muffled voices, I also felt intensely frustrated that I could play no further part in proceedings.

"He's in a bad way. We must get help," said David.

"Could we put his shoulder back?" suggested Roger.

"No question of that," replied Anna.

"There's only one thing for it," continued David. "Anna and I will have to ski out and telephone the police to alert the mountain rescue people."

"How do you propose doing that?" asked Roger.

"The map shows there's a telephone at Luibeg near Derry Lodge. We can reach it by skiing across the Lairig and then down Glen Derry. Roger – you'll have to stay here with John."

"That's okay by me but how far is Luibeg from here?"

"Not much more than ten kilometres."

"That's bloody miles away! It'll soon be pitch dark outside and how the hell can you possibly ski in the dark with only one hand?"

"Don't worry Roger. We'll be okay. The weather's clearing and soon there'll be a full moon. We'll take John's bivouac tent just in case."

Within half an hour of our arrival, David and Anna had packed themselves up and, after a cup of hot soup, were ready to set off. I was beset by questions which I couldn't begin to answer and could only muster a feeble – "Good luck and for God's sake look after yourselves."

Inwardly, I was worried sick. David would have to ski single handed in the dark. They couldn't possibly get to Luibeg in under three hours – more likely four. What happened if either of them had an accident on the way down? What if the telephone at Luibeg was out of order? How long would it take the mountain rescue people to get up here? The prospect of another blood wagon

Rupert on the Crête de Crabides

evacuation with a dislocated shoulder didn't bear thinking about. Like a coward I began to wonder whether I would be able to survive even one night enduring this awful pain.

From the bobbing arc of his head torch I could see Roger busying himself about the hut, making brews and preparing a hot meal. He was understandably disappointed that I could only force down a cup of soup and must have thought I was hallucinating when I told him that my arm had taken on a personality of its own. Certainly, it felt a limb apart.

"Roger, any chance of your doing anything about this wretched arm? It's sticking out from the rest of me and its gone icy cold."

He shone his torch on me and replied gently, "It's still strapped to your chest, John. I can prop up your sleeping bag but the arm looks fine to me."

I wasn't up to proper conversation but any sort of communication was becoming essential for morale.

"Roger," I began again, "I don't suppose you've got any sort of pain killer with you?"

I knew that we had only brought Aspirin and what I had taken of that had had zilch effect.

"Sorry, John, I'm afraid you've had it all."

So it went on with the seconds dragging by like minutes and the minutes like hours. Time and pain had become my sole pre-occupation but I kept putting off the one question that I hardly dared ask. I couldn't see my own watch but I had been making my own calculations of what I reckoned the time must be. Eventually, I could wait no longer.

"Roger, what do you make the time? Must be getting near morning now."

He switched on his head torch with a grunt. "Bit earlier than that I'm afraid, John – I only make it 10.45 pm."

"Are you sure?" I stammered, "Perhaps your watch has stopped."

Endless night had become eternity itself but aeons later I thought I heard a buzzing sound.

"Roger, Roger, I think I can hear something … Listen, it's getting louder!"

He had been dozing in a corner of the hut but was on his feet in seconds and, lurching towards the doorway, walked into its six-inch thick oak lintel for the third time. His head torch took most of the impact but by the time he had recovered and got outside the noise had become fainter. Whatever had caused it had gone away down the valley. Hopes so suddenly raised were as quickly dashed.

Then the noise returned and as it grew louder Roger dashed through the doorway. "John – it's a helicopter! It's a bloody great helicopter!" I heard him bawling out as his voice was drowned by a deafening roar and a wall of snow burst through the open doorway with the force of a water cannon. Within minutes a hubbub of voices filled the hut and I was dazzled by flashing torches.

"What's all this kit then, Mister?" a man yelled out. "What the hell have you lot been up to then? We'll need another 'copter to cart away all your rubbish! You'd better come along with us to avoid further mischief."

Two jollyboy RAF crewmen had already cleared the hut when I levered myself off the floor and crawled outside. The sky was pitch purple and glittered with the diamond points of a million stars. An enormous silver moon hanging pendant lit up the encircling white peaks with a cold incandescence. Ice cool air filled my lungs and the snow squeaked under my boots as I made my own way towards the ladder of a bright yellow Sea King helicopter which was quivering on the ground like some gigantic bird poised for lift off. I was oblivious to pain as the crew helped me through the door and chucked in after us our ragbag equipment. The engine's roar crescendo'd to ear splitting pitch and dense plumes of snow billowed up from under whirling rotor blades as we rose up vertically from the valley bed before heading north westwards for Inverness on our magic carpet.

The Sea King had landed at the Falls of Avon at exactly 12 midnight. Half an hour later we touched down on the roof of Raigmore Hospital and at 3 am the anaesthetist's needle put me into a wonderful sleep. Ten hours after the fall, my shoulder was back where it belonged.

Next morning Roger picked me up from the hospital. He had been my stave throughout last night. I thanked him in the laconic, half embarrassed way one adopts to someone whose probably saved your life and then asked anxiously, "What happened to David and Anna?"

"We're all going to meet up to have tea in Braemar this afternoon," he grinned.

All four of us were re-united five hours later to eat toasted teacake and swop tales of wonder.

"Anna and I eventually reached the telephone at Luibeg at 10 pm," recounted David. "It would have taken us a lot longer if it hadn't been for the full moon. When I got through to the police and explained what had happened, the first words of the Sergeant were: 'I'm afraid your friend's out of luck. The RAF Lossiemouth's helicopter's somewhere off the Beauly Firth looking for the body of some lunatic who threw himself off the Keswick Bridge'. Luckily for you, they then decided to call off the suicide search until morning and pick you up instead."

Both incidents made the front page of that evening's edition of the Inverness

Evening Express. The caption *"Middle-aged hillwalker on the mend"* said it all.

I would never again try to follow David Williams in hot pursuit. That mistake had cost us a rare prize. During the last two days of our Scottish visit, when we should have been completing the Cairngorm traverse, the Highlands had their best weather of the season. Yet I could count my blessings. The courage of three stalwart companions and the speed and efficiency of the RAF's helicopter rescue had probably saved me from permanent incapacity. Physiotherapy and a swim-a-day regimen eventually got my shoulder working again although the nerve endings in my fingers were never the same again.

Later that year, to dispel old spectres, my family and I joined David and Anna for a few days walking in the Pyrenees. Over Christmas I took the family skiing and, after surviving an Eagle Ski Club weekend meet in the Cairngorms, I was convinced that my shoulder would take the strain of another Pyrenean joust.

So it was that almost a year to the day after the Cairngorms débacle another Pyrenean roadshow foregathered at the faded *Fin de Siecle* Hotel des Bains, Luchon, where our Sobrarbe traverse had finished two years before. Yet, although I was reluctant to admit it, the Cairngorm accident had given my self-confidence another knock. Now over fifty, I had begun to wonder whether I would ever complete this potty traverse. Virtually every visit I had made to the Pyrenees had involved some scrape or accident – John Blacker's fall after climbing the Vignemale, Richard Morgan's back injury on the Col Suzon, my avalanche escape in the Val de Gaube, Alain's death in the Vignemale avalanche disaster, my concussion in the Néouvielle, John Wilkinson's dislocated shoulder and broken arm ... and any number of minor mishaps best passed over. To have been the subject of two major mountain rescues within four years seemed to confirm that I was accident prone. I wondered whether this was the reason why neither of the Wedgwood brothers, nor David and Anna, John Wilkinson and others had been takers for this latest tour.

The team this time reflected the changing scene. Apart from Julian Lush and Roger Childs, I had never toured with any of the other three whom I had met only briefly or knew by reputation through the Eagle Ski Club. Patrick Bailey, an accountant, was the editor of the Club's Yearbook; David Seddon was a youthful geriatrician who rowed a lot and Rupert Hoare was a Seismic Geologist with a competitive urge and a penchant for oil or weight bearing rocks.

Without a nucleus of old and tried companions, I wondered how far we would get with my plan to push the Pyrenean traverse another 90 kilometres eastwards. Starting from Luchon, I intended to cross into Spain; steer a course through the Aigues Tortes National Park and then cross the remote Pallars-Sobira region to

Andorra. This tour was scheduled to last a full fourteen days so, thinking that we had time in hand, I couldn't resist another shot at Aneto.

Luchon is the sort of place best experienced at the end of a tour rather than at its beginning. It takes its name from the Dionysian deity Lixon whose naughty rites would have surprised Bunny Club members and to whom a local pin up, Fabia Festa, dedicated her festive alter. Lixon was the most famous Pyrenean spa in Roman times, warmly recommended by both Strabo and Pliny, when public bathing was almost as popular as football is today. The scale and sophistication of the biggest imperial baths – incorporating gymnasia, theatres and libraries – would beggar modern Health Centres. The bath culture took a dive when the early Christians, more concerned with moral cleanliness, prescribed mixed bathing but, after centuries of decline, the baths of Luchon were revived when Baron d'Etigny, the Steward of Gascony, persuaded de Richelieu to take the cure. By the early nineteenth century, when Pyrenean spas again became fashionable, Luchon boasted 98 baths and 42 separate springs.

Luchon has sometimes been described as the Chamonix of the Pyrenees but you can't see Aneto from any part of the town and the Victorian traveller Charles Blackburn more accurately likened it to *"Chamonix without Mont Blanc . . . a place where guides are 'rarae aves' and ice axes almost unknown."* Blackburn was also unimpressed by poncey Frenchmen riding around on diminutive ponies, wearing kid gloves, with their dogs wrapped in flannel being carried round in baskets. But the types who really got up his nose were the whip crackers – nineteenth century skate boarding equivalents who roamed the streets from morning to night making sleep impossible. Arriving at Luchon of an evening in early March in Childs' luxurious Citroen Safari, I soon discoverd that the Childs/Lush axis was more interested in Luchon's sybaritic delights than hairshirtery. However, the only available entertainment remotely Roman or *risqué* came in the form of a metre high phallic shaped, bulbous bottomed bottle of plonk masquerading as Chianti. This we drank in the dingy pizzeria which happened to be the only place still open in Luchon that evening.

"Why *Chianti* and why *pizzeria* here in Luchon?" queried Julian.

"Don't worry Julian. We'll do a lot better when we get to Spain," replied Roger with the assurance of a man who evidently knew that country better than his native Greenwich.

At 7 am next morning, we emerged from the Hotel des Bains expecting the worst only to be confronted by a clear sky and a tantalising view of the frontier ridge framed at the end of the famous Avenue Etigny. Rupert immediately

Early morning at Pic Montjoie

betrayed something of the enthusiasm for getting to grips with the mountain that was to characterise his contribution to the party's momentum. Unfortunately, delaying action by Childs ensured a belated start and to get the show on the road I had to hire a taxi to get us as far as possible up the Pique Valley in order to "extract some of the sting from the first day", as Childs put it. Journey's end came where an enormous avalanche had demolished the road and dumped what remained of it at the bottom of the gorge.

"When will they repair this?" I asked the taxi driver.

He shook his head philosophically: *"Cette année, l'année prochaine – peut etre jamais!"*

We watched transfixed as he made a series of tightly calculated turns on the edge of the crumbling precipice and then walked slowly on up the valley trying to acclimatise to the weight of over-loaded rucksacks.

Before the Viella Tunnel was opened in 1955 to link this neck of France with Spain, the Hospice de France had been the main French staging post between Luchon and Bénasque for as long as history records. When the British Alpinist Spender passed this way in 1896 during his Pyrenean traverse, he found a "perpetual flow of humanity" passing through what was then a sizeable inn. When we saw it, the Hospice was just another ruin shortly due for demolition.

Yet this building marks the spot where the ancient routes to Spain divide and here it was that I would have to make the critical decision as to where we would cross the frontier ridge to reach the Rencluse Hut. The guidebook offers three options and forever imprinted on my mind was the bird's eye view we had had of all three from the Pic d'Arres two years before.

The traditional summer route across the Port de Bénasque has been used for thousands of years but becomes an avalanche gauntlet in winter and, as the guidebook cautioned, should only be attempted in settled conditions with the full paraphenalia of crampons, ice axe and ropes. A less frequented route follows the U-shaped trench of the Freche Valley but this had looked even more dangerous than the Port de Bénasque with its floor littered with avalanche debris.

Even before we had arrived in Luchon, I had plumped for the third option. This followed a longer but safer route along the north/south frontier ridge that divided the Val d'Aran from the Freche Valley. We had recce'd the first part of this rolling ridge as far as the Pic d'Arres two years ago before being forced off by storm. However, whereas on that occasion we had merely had to step out onto the ridge from a high cabane at 7.45 am, this time round we were still 800 metres below the crest of the ridge and it was already 10 am.

"I'm afraid that there's nothing for it but to get ourselves onto that ridge above us," I said to the others while we took a short break at the Hospice. "The other routes are altogether too dangerous but once we're up on top it should be easy going."

"I hope you're right," grumbled Roger. "That looks a helluva long way to climb and it's already damned hot."

First days are always bad but this one was a corker. The sky was blue but the air was windless. Getting up the west flank of the Freche Valley by a succession of grassy spurs studded with rocky outcrops overlaid with snow and ice involved a prolonged and exhausting scramble. The additional weight of skis shifted the balance of our overladen rucksacks and, as the sun waxed, our shirts became sweat sodden. Sweat mixed with sun cream also produced a particularly astringent eye wash: as I peered skywards through my fogged sun-glasses, I prayed that once we had reached the crest of the ridge the going would be easy.

Two hours later, a tetchy party foregathered on the ridge with the sun at its zenith. The going wasn't as easy as I had imagined for the snow kept balling up in thick wadges under our skis. At 1 pm the six of us were strung out along the ridge in a line so distended that I called a halt. Most people were too knackered and dehydrated to complain but not Roger.

"I don't call this an 'easy' route," he muttered, "and we've still got bloody miles to go to reach your frontier ridge."

From this vantage point I carefully noted an ugly lump half way along the ridge which the map identified as the Pic de Montjoie. The guidebook had warned that the quick way around this obstacle, involving an airy traverse across a 40-degree slope of coarse, long grass overlaid with snow, was liable to *"glissements de neige"*. The consequences of a 600-metre free fall into the Freche Valley were so obvious that I made a quick re-appraisal.

"I don't like the look of that slope," I said to Rupert.

"What's the problem?" he replied.

"The snow overlaying it looks dead rotten. I wouldn't chance us traversing it. We'll have to stick to the ridge even if it means climbing over that little peak."

"Fine by me," said Rupert. He had been shadowing me all the way and relished the prospect of action.

There had been rumblings and grumblings from behind and I feared that this tactical change would be unpopular. The flog up the Pic de Montjoie in the afternoon sun confirmed my fears but the sight that greeted Rupert and me as we breasted the summit was even more depressing. I had wholly under-estimated what was still involved to get from here to the Pas de l'Escalette on the watershed ridge which led into the upper Esera Valley. First, we would have to descend 100 metres into a gap and then climb on for another two kilometres along the snaking whaleback of the Crête de Crabides to the pas itself. And that was only the start of it. From the pas we would have to cut across to the Port de Picarde; descend 600 metres into the Esera Valley and finally climb another 300 metres up the other side to the Rencluse Hut which was three kilometres distant from the port.

I looked at my watch and again at the relevant page of the guidebook I had photocopied and painstakingly cling-filmed. Ollivier's estimated time for this route was six to eight hours. We had already been going for close on five but had barely covered one third of the distance.

When we had started out I had rejoiced at striking a spell of good weather. It had never occurred to me that we would be stopped in our tracks by heat and dehydration – still less that we would be spending the night anywhere but at the Rencluse. For a minute or so I was flummoxed. The guidebook hadn't mentioned any intermediate huts. The prospect of having to retrace our steps even to the Cabane de Barèges was simply appalling.

Turning to Rupert I said, "We're not going to make the Rencluse Hut. Not tonight at any rate. This is a very tired party and there's still a long way to go to the Port de Picarde let alone the hut. In any event, I wouldn't fancy skiing down the north side of the Esera Valley after all this sun."

"Dead right," said Rupert. "We started much too late. That first climb to the ridge took the stuffing out of most of them. Okay, but where do we spend the night?"

"We had better start looking," I replied as we started to scan the flanks of the ridge we had just struggled up and then downwards towards the dark forests of the Val d'Aran.

"What's that down there then?" said Rupert excitedly.

I followed his arm to the outline of a building tucked away in the shadowed folds of a small side valley.

"Must be a hut of some sort," I replied, pulling out from my pocket the map which I had scarcely bothered to look since we had scaled the ridge. "Yes, it's a hut alright. Marked on the map near a tiny lake which we can't quite see from here."

Providence had stepped in to bail me out. When the rest of the party joined us on the summit in various stages of disgruntlement, I broke the news.

"We're going to have to call it a day. There's no way we'll be able to make the Rencluse tonight."

"That's damned good news," panted Roger, "where's the hotel then?"

"There's a hut just down there in the valley," I replied, pointing it out. "It's only a short ski from here."

"Jolly lucky it happened to be there," Roger snorted.

The Spanish plaque above the doorway proclaimed the hut to be the *Montane Poulane Las Bordas*. Since its construction in 1957, successive generations of vandals had cannibalised the wooden sleeping platform for firewood leaving room for only three. We tossed for the privilege of sleeping on wood with the losers settling for the stone flagged floor. Morale took a boost when the still lively Rupert announced that he would take charge of the cooking from now on.

It snowed a few centimetres during the night but dawned a beautiful day with a silver moon still riding high. Rupert had already boiled a billie when I first poked my head outside the door and, when my breath froze cloud-like on the air, I knew that things would be going our way. There was a new spring to our skinning as we criss-crossed the northern flanks of the Pic de Roye in long zig-zags to recapture the ground surrendered so reluctanly yesterday evening. Within an hour of leaving the *cabaña* we had regained the Pic Montjoie's summit.

Only yesterday, the effort of reaching this insignificant bump had been a penance. Today, our breathing was steady and our hearts sang. The early morning mists had evaporated leaving only the Garona Valley covered by a grey duvet of cloud while all about and above us great snow peaks sparkled in the sun. From this vantage point, the snaking Crête de Crabides, which had looked so discouragingly long the previous day, now became a thing of beauty and the path to Spain.

Rupert was looking southwards in the general direction of the frontier ridge like some climbing Cortez.

"Look over there, John," he cried imperiously. "D'you see that nice little peak ahead of us. Must be the Pic Escalette. Definitely worth going for I think."

At this early stage of my friendship with Rupert, I hadn't appreciated that to him almost anything inclined to the vertical presented a challenge. I glanced at my photocopy guidebook map.

"That's the Escalette alright," I concurred. "but it's not where we want to go. The guidebook shows that our route to the Pas de l'Escalette veers west of the pic. The peak itself is quite a bit off our route. We've already climbed Montjoie twice so we don't want to bag another pimple just for the sake of it."

I wrongly surmised that Rupert's silence denoted acquiesence so skied off the summit by a narrow corniced ridge down into the Pas de la Montjoie gap before climbing up the other side to join the Crête de Crabides. As Rupert and I forged on ahead along its rolling crest, I realised that in my pre-occupation to match him stride for stride, we were heading straight for the Pic de l'Escalette rather than in the direction of the pas. When I stopped to double check the map, Rupert shot into the lead and when I next looked up, he was way ahead.

"Rupert," I shouted after him, "we're off route. You must bear to your right. The pas which is west of the pic."

I might as well have whistled in the wind. Once established in the lead, there was no reining in Rupert. Having slipped the leash he was now making a characteristic dash for the summit. I couldn't catch him and I couldn't split the party but when I joined him on the summit of the Escalette I could see exactly why the ski route by-passed it. We had reached a dead end. To get off the pic would either involve a tricky little descent or we would have to waste a lot more time retracing our steps.

"You've bagged your peak, Rupert," I began testily, "but we're now way off route. The pas is 600 metres to the west of us and somehow we're going to have to get ourselves off this bloody little peaklet."

"No worries," he replied unconcernedly. "I don't see the problem. I'll just nip down this rib to see how it goes."

With that, he shot off down the spine of a rocky ridge and finished the pitch by kicking a ladder of inward facing steps into a steep slope of *névé* with his feet moving in and out like pistons.

"It's fine," he shouted up from below, "a piece of cake."

Unfortunately, not everyone possessed Rupert's climbing skills. An hour later a chasened party re-assembled on a patch of level ground at the foot of the ridge where Rupert had been sitting it out. As I re-coiled and re-packed the rope I lamented lost time and did so again as we blundered around the frontier ridge searching for the Port de la Picarde – a classic example of a Pyrenean "double col" which so often confounded Belloc.

However, reaching the port had rewarding compensations for at its threshold there burst before us one of the great spectacles of the Pyrenees – the north face of the Maladetta massif crowned by Aneto. We had had tantalising glimpses of Aneto's coy summit all day long as we had climbed higher and higher up the Crête de Crabides, with more and more of its shattered granite spine coming into view but, until we finally emerged at the port, the body of the mountain had stubbornly remained hidden. Now the whole sprawling mass lay outstretched before us. Its roots were buried in the pine-forested trough of the Esera Valley from where it rose in one tremendous 1,500 metre sweep of snow and ice. With the noonday sun directly above its glacial sheaf, dark shadowed steps and troughs alternated with aproned folds of dazzling white.

As a set-piece this rivals any other in the Pyrenees and has caught the imaginations of artists and engravers, writers and poets, scientists and savants,

travellers and climbers ever since the cult of mountain scenery began. Professor J. D. Forbes, the Father of British mountaineering and the most eminent glaciologist of his day, was so moved when he saw it in 1835 that he wrote of "prodigious glaciers which seem to me to rival those of Mont Blanc and to vie with the icefields of Grindelwald." Count Henri Russell, who had travelled the world from New Zealand's glaciers to the Canadian Rockies and visited the Gobi Desert in between, curiously likened it to Siberia. The French Pyrenean chronicler, Beraldi was so enraptured that he made fifty pilgrimages to feast his eyes upon it between 1886 and 1906.

Ours was a grandstand view in perfect weather and from this vantage point I could trace tomorrow's intended route up and down Aneto following a line just to the west of the rocky Portillones Ridge, through the famous Portillon Inferior gap and thence up the Aneto Glacier to the summit itself. Eleven years before I had climbed Aneto from the Vallibierna on a lovely summer's morning with John Blacker. The prospect of a 1,264 metre ski descent promised something special.

The Rencluse route is now the *voie normale* which in summer carries a caravan of trekkers. Benign and tranquil in the sunshine as it appeared, Aneto can be as treacherous as any high mountain in bad weather and in earlier years, the dangers posed by its glaciers so terrified local guides that they actively discouraged attempts to climb the Accursed Mountain. Yet the very name Maladetta is probably as misleading as the perceived difficulties of the climb. Romanticism has strained etymology for unlike Mont Blanc's Mont Maudit, Maladetta is more likely to be a corruption of the local Catalan *Mal Hetta*, which simply means the highest.

Myths of inaccessibility attach to all great mountains but the evil reputation of Aneto was artfully used for some forty years to further the commercial purposes of the man with whom it is most closely associated. Pierre Barrau, a local chamois hunter, made his first appearance on the Pyrenean scene when he was hired as a mountain guide by Ramond de Carbonnières, the pioneer of all Pyrenean mountain exploration, when making the first serious attempt to climb Aneto in 1787.

On that occasion, Barrau refused to accompany his employer beyond a certain stage, leaving Ramond to carry on alone to what was then the highest point attained in the Pyrenees, the 3,020 metre Col de Alba. Nothing daunted, Barrau now set himself up as the local expert on the Maladetta Massif yet, at heart, he remained a superstitious *montagnard* with all the qualities and defects of that breed. Deep down he implicitly believed in the Maladetta's inaccessibility and the ancient legend that the boulders that litter its slopes were the petrified relics of the shepherds and their flocks who rebuffed Christ when seeking shelter from a storm.

Barrau's knowledge of the lower Maladetta derived from his hunting experiences but thirty years on from that first encounter with Ramond, his skills as a mountaineer were put to the test when the young German scientist Von Parrot passed through Luchon during his pioneer foot traverse of the Pyrenees in 1817. Von Parrot, another Pyrenean unsung hero, was already an accomplished mountaineer. Six years before as a 20-year-old, he had bravely attempted solo first ascents of two Caucasian giants Mounts Elbruz and Kazbek and earlier that same year had narrowly failed to make the first ascent of Monte Rosa, the second summit of the Alps.

Von Parrot had hired Barrau as his guide on the basis of the latter's reputation but high on the mountain it had become obvious that Barrau was basically ignorant about glaciers, employed a naive technique on snow and ice and evinced an unswerving antipathy to using a rope. True to form, he refused point blank to budge beyond a feature he recognised, leaving Von Parrot with no option but to solo the 3,308 metre Pico de Maladetta. Technically, the pico is a more difficult climb than Aneto itself but on reaching its summit Von Parrot realised that Aneto was unquestionably the higher peak. Unfortunately, the difficulties of the ridge that linked the two peaks were beyond him so late in the day though, from this viewpoint, he traced an easy route to Aneto's summit up the Aneto Glacier.

Von Parrot magnanimously passed on his discovery to Barrau who now had the Crown of the Pyrenees for the taking. However, instead of doing something about it himself, he allowed another seven years to slip by before accepting another serious engagement to climb the mountain. The offer came when two young Frenchmen, Blavier and de Billy (who later became the first President of the French Alpine Club) hired him as their guide in 1824. Barrau, now aged 68, remained ambivalent about the Accursed Mountain and when his clients noticed that he had brought no rope, he told them that what had been satisfactory for "the German" was good enough for them. High on the glacier, Barrau disappeared down a crevasse. In 1931, 107 years later, his remains were disgorged from the blue ice of the glacier's snout.

Like the legend of the petrified shepherds, old Barrau's end became the stuff of myth. His unseen presence, lodged somewhere in the depths of Aneto's malignant glaciers, was seen by locals as divine retribution. Potential clients now shied away from the Maladetta, as did their guides, and not until 1842, eighteen years after Barrau's death, was Aneto first climbed from the Vallebierna on the south versant by a French count and a Russian Imperial Officer.

Mont Blanc, an altogether more serious undertaking, had been climbed 56 years earlier.

Although the *Affaire Barrau* may partly explain Aneto's belated first ascent, it did wonders for Luchon's tourist industry. For years after, timorous Luchonese guides would bring their clients to the Port de Bénasque, extend their arms towards the Accursed Mountain and cry tearfully, *"Il est là, Barrau ... il est là, le pauvre Barrau!"*

Local legend has it that Hannibal crossed the Pyrenees en route to the Alps by either the Port de Bénasque or Picarde or maybe both. Given the difficulties of Hannibal's likely Alpine passes, neither of these would have given him many problems but, fact or myth as the case may be, the zig-zagging track that crosses the Pyrenean chain at this point follows a route that pre-dates both Carthaginians and Romans and has been used ever since commerce across the Pyrenees began.

Had we only reached the port a couple of hours earlier, the 600-metre descent to the valley bottom would have given a memorable ski run. But ski mountaineering is all about timing and thanks to the Escalette diversion we had arrived too late. The sun had reduced the snow to a treacherous mush and by the time the vanguard reached the Rencluse, we had been on the go for over eight hours. As the last man staggered in twenty-five minutes after the first, I pondered on the seriousness of this crossing in anything but settled weather.

Before the upper Esera Valley was desecrated by the building of a motorable track up the middle of it, this was one of the most beautiful and remote places in the Pyrenees set betwixt its two grandest massifs – Maladetta and Posets. The Catalan Mountaineering Club's spacious hut was built in 1917, the same year as a famous local guide Jose Sayo was killed by a lightning bolt on Aneto's Pont de Mahomet. In summer, it is a favourite tourist destination. In winter it is closed. Yet there's probably been some rough shelter on this site open to all ever since the petrified shepherds first pastured their flocks and not far from the newer hut we located something altogether older under a snow drift. We promptly took possession and, while Julian and David tried to light a half-burned pine log in the fireplace inside, the rest of us prospected for firewood outside. Neither party was successful but, although the hut remained cold and dank, good cheer was restored with Rupert's cooking.

When I went outside the hut before turning in that night, the sky was ablaze with blinking stars, there was frost in the air and the weather promised fair. A rare mood of optimism overcame me. Here we were at last, secure in a forward base for our tryst with Aneto in the morning. By this time tomorrow, we would surely have it under our belts and have completed a memorable ski descent.

"John. Wake up. It's already 6 o'clock!"

Rupert's insistent voice was buzzing disconcertingly close to my ear and his bustling presence confirmed by an intermittent head torch beam focused over the stove.

"I've got a brew going," he announced tersely. "We had best be up and get going as soon as we can."

I wasn't yet acclimatised to Rupert's early starts and should have congratulated him for his enthusiasm but this frenzied burst of activity and the hissing noise of the Gaz stove merely irritated me. I had had a lousy night having discovered half way through that my number two sleeping bag had been too thin to repel a liquid substance that oozed from the hut's cotton waste blankets. I had also had a disturbing nightmare about helicopters, broken skis and blood wagons. Furthermore, I was quite certain that I hadn't been dreaming about the wind which had howled around the hut throughout the night.

"What's the weather like?" I growled.

"Not entirely good," he replied Delphically. "It was too dark to see anything much when I first got up but it may well be clearing now."

I pulled on my anorak and padded across the icy floor barefooted to check for myself. The door had become so blocked with snow that I had difficulty forcing it open. When I did so and peered outside, I shut it almost immediately. Black, baleful clouds hung low about the valley and heavy, wet snowflakes were falling. High above, the wind was gathering strength.

"Rupert – just hang on a moment. In this weather we won't be going anywhere fast today."

He had already done his round of the bunks Epp-style prodding the unwilling troops into action.

"I'm sure it will clear soon," he replied confidently. "Breakfast's almost ready. I'm already packed and prepared for the off."

"Okay then, we'll just enjoy your breakfast."

We ate it and then, to a man, went back to bed as the wind increased its intensity. For the next four hours I dozed off and on. When I next got up, at 11 am, it was still as dark as night inside the hut for the snow had banked up to window level outside. The wind had moved down into the valley and was now roaring round the hut like a train emerging from a tunnel. Spindrift was blowing in through every crack and crevice of the old timber cladding. Autophon practice was abandoned after a few minutes in the open but, with no heating in the hut, we kept active at intervals throughout the day with water collecting sorties; prospecting for firewood in waist deep snow and trying to clear the drifts that kept piling up against the hut's only window.

Roger raised morale with an omelette of seven eggs, a tin of tuna and a slug of *chorizo* left behind by the Spaniards who, according to the hut book, had climbed Aneto on ski in perfect conditions only the day before. When Julian and David finally gave up trying to light the log in the grate, reading, skin patching and cards were successively abandoned for our sleeping bags from which we told each other stories which in any other circumstances would have meant instant relegation to Bores Corner. Roger and Julian shared an interminable yachting yarn; Rupert explained how geophysicists dispose of their faeces in outback Australia; Patrick remembered how the ashes of his relative sent over with an American wartime food parcel had been eaten as soup; David told of a geriatric returning from the dead and I recalled an incident from Arabia Deserta.

Throughout that day, throughout the next night and on into the following morning the wind crescendoed and diminuendoed. You couldn't see much through the narrow slit of window beyond the horizontal and vertical sheets of snow that came billowing past us like clipper's sails. Spindrift blowing in from a particular crack in the roof had covered my bunk and much of the kitchen range. I had little doubt that our stoutly built Catalan hut could take any amount of buffeting but by the morning of the second day I knew that my original plans would have to be re-cast.

During that night I had been rehearsing the options in my head and again in the early morning with map and guidebook. When Julian popped the familiar question over breakfast, "What are the plans for today?" I was ready.

"It's been snowing continuously for the past 24 hours and the barometric pressure's still falling. Even if it stops snowing now, we would still have to give it at least a day to settle before we tackle Aneto."

"Can't we carry on eastwards into the Aigues Tortes as originally planned?" chipped in Rupert.

"I would have liked to have done so," I answered, "but all the routes eastwards to the Val d'Aran or the Ribargorca are long and complicated. I wouldn't want to try any of them in this sort of weather."

"How's the food situation, Rupert?" asked Roger. "How long can we last out. I'm starving."

"You've been fed like a fighting cock," Rupert shot back. "We can easily last another day, maybe two."

"Personally," said Julian, "I'm getting bloody cold in this miserable hut. We've totally failed to get the fire going and anyway there's nothing to burn. I agree with Roger about food. Frankly, I can't see the point in hanging around here."

"What does anyone else think?" I asked. Privately, I had already reached the conclusion that there was probably only one sensible course of action left to us.

The general consensus was to get out while we still could rather than stick it out in the hope that the weather might improve.

"Okay then, we must retreat to Bénasque. Once we're down there we can take stock and re-provision. Maybe we might even have another go at Aneto if the weather settles."

Roger said, "Thank heaven for that," and Julian, "We must bend to the wind."

In my own mind I took this sensible decision less philosophically. I had set my cap at Aneto but once again we were pulling out. We had got the worst of both worlds by securing a strategic position at the base of the mountain but at the expense of two traverse stages. If we had only by-passed Aneto completely during those first two days of good weather we should now have reached the Aigues Tortes. Retreating to Bénasque was a step backwards yet I couldn't think of a better alternative.

By 9.30 am we had broken cover and were edging our way down the steep upper slopes of the valley through the blizzard. I was a touch less reluctant to leave the hut when I saw that during the night the snow had drifted right over its roof. The route down the Esera would normally have been a doddle but the depth of new snow made for classic avalanche conditions and early on I set off a small slab avalanche where an accumulation of new snow covered an icy base. Thereafter we moved very cautiously, slowed by lack of visibility, which gave even minor features an exaggerated perspective. When the valley flattened out the problem was how to make progress through the thigh-deep snow against a head wind.

We passed within metres of the Hospice de Bénasque, a grander Spanish equivalent of the Hospice de France originally built for the Knights Hospitallers of St John of Jerusalem, but our minds were so totally focussed on finding the way down that we failed to notice it. Four hours after leaving the hut we made our first stop at the baths of Bénasque, once the highest Roman spa in the Pyrenees. At this same spot two years ago the Sobrarbe party had been dropped off by a Land Rover taxi, only to turn tail to escape another blizzard. As we strapped our skis to our sacs to begin the long march to Bénasque a flight of eleven Griffon Vultures wheeled above us through the scud in languid spirals.

I had become inured to the inevitability of forced retreats from Pyrenean huts in bad weather. Whatever disappointments these might have involved, there are few keener pleasures than the experience of emerging unscathed and then fetching up at a congenial Spanish hostelry. The Hotel Barrabes with its cold, tiled floors, tepid showers and non-functioning radiators, rated a low category in the scale of such things but our happy landing two years before was reason enough to give it another try.

Retreat down the Esera Valley

With Childs on board, the Spanish experience was to take on another dimension. This Spanish speaker and landowner was by inclination and occupation a "Mr Fixit" with a highly developed bargaining instinct. Back in Luchon, he had promised that things would be better in Spain and, from the moment we burst in through the door of the bar bedraggled and sodden, Childs's rapport with the Hotel's *Señora* was immediate. At the drop of her mantilla this aloof lady produced litres of ice-cold *cerveza* and endless platters of *tapas* – *calamares,* ham, olives, anchovies and potatoes in mayonnaise.

Since my last visit the hotel had evidently become the local climbers' pub. Displayed behind the bar was an extravaganza of mountaineering club badges from every part of the world which gave the Barrabes a reassuring familiarity. Now on my third visit, I had come to have a special feeling for Benasque for it was here that my own Pyrenean pilgrimage had begun. Proximity to the new ski resort of Cerler had wrought changes but at heart it remained the quintessential mountain redoubt of the Pyrenees.

Remote from the Spanish plains at the head of the Esera Valley yet within sight of the French frontier, Bénasque was always more than a mountain village. The thirteenth century church of St Marcial is built like a garrison fortress and Phillip II personally commissioned the once formidable castle to be a forward bastion against the French. Benasque reached its apogee at the time of Spain's greatness. The decaying sixteenth and seventeenth century stone houses built in Gothic and Renaissance style with galleried courtyards that abut its cramped, cobbled streets were once the summer villas of the Aragonese nobility. Massive stone portals still bearing the escutcheons of the Faures, Conques, Cornels and Inllades recall the time that when "Spain moves, the whole world trembles." The French spas of Luchon, Barèges or Cauterets have elegance but nothing that matches the muscular Palace of the Counts of the Ribargorza, a Italianate mansion set square in the middle of the old town and set off to perfection by its mountain backdrop.

Robin Fedden describes in *The Enchanted Mountains* the architecture of Bénasque with the enthusiasm of a devotee and an expertise befitting a former Secretary to the Historic Buildings Committee. Yet these laudatory passages would have surprised earlier English travellers. Spender's verdict on Bénasque was scathing – "typical of Spain ... with the sordid squalor of its filthy streets" – and J. B. Morton, some twenty years later, wrote in his *Pyrenean* of its "oppression and ... impending doom".

Morton might not have been quite so gloomy about Bénasque had he known that his exemplar Hilaire Belloc chose it as the setting for his most famous lyric poem, *Tarantella*. Belloc wrote *Tarantella* long after his earlier essay, *The*

Pyrenean Hive which recalls a youthful visit to Bénasque with two male companions after crossing the mountains from Luchon. That lesser known piece describes the clattering of the mules' hooves, the drivers' argument, the wine which tasted of old saddle, the noise of insects buzzing, a wild-eyed gypsy woman's outlandish singing in the quarter tones "not so much of music as of fire" and the man who cried in accompaniment to her dancer's gyrations with his "hap! hap!" while "beating his palms together rhythmically and driving and goading to the full limit of her power."

The Pyrenean Hive is *Tarantella's* prose prototype but the inn where he slept on straw "with the fleas that tease in the High Pyrenees" is unlikely to have been at Bénasque for in those pre-First World War days, the popular local hostelry was the Posada del Casino with its eschutcheoned doorway and a bedroom which Lord Schuster, latterly a president of the Alpine Club, described as being "gorgeously upholstered with red damask hangings". The wine Belloc drank may have tasted of tar but he never walked the Pyrenees with anyone called Miranda for, according to A. N. Wilson, Belloc probably lifted this name from the Duke of Miranda, a Spanish diplomatic acquaintance in London. *Tarentella,* Belloc's most famous poem, is a sad, nostalgic evocation of male companionship written long after he was capable of the prodigious walking feats of his precocious youth but it was his visit to Bénasque that inspired it.

It snowed again in the night leaving the roof tops of Bénasque encrusted in white. The sky was brightening in the south but, although the weather looked as if it might be improving, the forecast remained unsettled and this compounded my dilemma of what to do next. It was tempting to stay longer in Bénasque so as to take another shot at Aneto from the Rencluse but this would use up at least three more days and take us no further eastwards than where we had started. In the event, I compromised by agreeing to half a day's skiing at Cerler but, as the clouds began to lift, I was left wondering whether we shouldn't have stuck it out another day at the hut and gone for the summit today.

By mid-afternoon, everyone had tired of the piste so we returned to Bénasque to hire a taxi and repeat the trick of driving round to the Val d'Aran. I had put my frustrations behind me but made a private vow that one day I would return to this gem of a mountain village to climb both Aneto and Posets on ski. The day was already fading when we made our *"Adios"* to the Barrabes's two lady bartenders and, with Angelo at the wheel, once again headed down the narrow *garganta* of Congosto de Ventamillo before swinging eastwards as the sunset turned the barren hills from faded ochre to red.

On reaching the Val d'Aran Childs took it upon himself to set the tone of the tour. That short spell at the Rencluse had involved no real privation and any perceived calorie deficiency had been more than made up at the Hotel Barrabes but Childs insisted that, to get back into shape, it was essential that we spend a night at Arties in the Parador Don Gaspar de Portola, the birthplace of the eponymous conquistador Don who had gone one better than Belloc by walking across America in a suit of armour to found San Diego in 1781. Patrick questioned the cost of this extravagence but when Childs negotiated a bed-and-breakfast package which included dinner, three bottles of Spanish bubbly plus sherry, port and assorted wines at £20 a head, no one demurred.

The Val d'Aran is another Pyrenean jewel made for the pursuit of man's happiness. More French than Spanish in character, it is the only Pyrenean valley north of the watershed that runs on an east/west axis. Its neat fields are watered by the upper Garona which, by a geographical fluke, originates in Aneto's glaciers yet reaches the north side of the watershed through a subterranean passage. With its cool, fresh climate and stylish slate roofed stone houses, the Val d'Aran appears to be more Alpine than Pyrenean, yet apart from Napoleon's brief annexation at the beginning of the nineteenth century, it has never belonged to France. From feudal times, it was ruled by the Kings of Aragon and when, in 1659, the Treaty of the Pyrenees was concluded between what were then the two most powerful countries in the world, the Val d'Aran inadvertently became an exception to the general rule that the Franco-Spanish frontier would thereafter follow the watershed. The French negotiators had been badly briefed for, when the Spanish envoy de Haro said to his French counterpart Cardinal Mazarin: "The Val d'Aran of course you regard as Spanish", Mazarin replied: "Of course!" And so it has remained, a Catalan enclave within the geographical ambiance of France.

The Val d'Aran also forms the northern boundary to that most delectable of Pyrenean national parks – the Aigues Tortes wherein are found the *Encantados* – the Enchanted Mountains. It was now my aim to push the route as far eastwards through this area as time would allow. Last night's binge on artichokes, veal steak and ice-cream pie had been too rich to sleep well on but the four-and-a-half-hour climb to the Restanca Hut from the Pont de Ressec dissipated any after effects. At this warm, friendly hut run by a hirsute guardian, his wife, his girl friend and his dog, we were soon tucking into a gargantuan meal of ham and eggs round their pot-bellied stove.

Now for some surprises. Although I had half forgotten about it, both Rupert and Julian had warned me at the outset that they would have to leave early. Apparently their time had come.

"Tomorrow's going to be my last day of the tour," announced Rupert.

"Very sorry to hear that, Rupert," I replied taken aback. "We're just about to start the most interesting part of the tour. Can't I persuade you to change your mind?"

"No hope, I'm afraid. I've simply run out of leave."

"I'm sorry to say that I'm also going to have to cut things short," broke in Julian." As you know John, I flew straight in from Abu Dhabi to join this tour. I really must see something more of the family before my leave ends. Incidentally, I would also like some pesetas from Patrick to help me get home."

This doubly bad news stunned me but the mention of pesetas brought Patrick, the tour's treasurer, to life.

"I would like each of you to contribute 5,000 pesetas to the kitty right now," he demanded. "If these two are leaving we must sort out the Parador bill."

"But I haven't got pesetas on me," retorted Julian. "That's precisely why I'm asking you to lend me some. Wouldn't it be altogether simpler if I settled up in England?"

Patrick would have none of it and, though the pros and cons of this supremely unimportant argument kept some of us entertained for days, it was never resolved. To maintain *bonhomie* I suggested a game of Hearts but Rupert tired of this when he discovered that the Restanca Hut's only other guest, a stoney eyed Catalan, was a genuine rock jock like himself. For the rest of the evening this hapless man with only a smattering of English was bombarded by mountaineering mono-talk.

With only half a mountain day left, restless Rupert was up at 6 am only to find that it was snowing. After a bad night crowded with boorish and depressing thoughts I got up at 7 am to find that it was still snowing. Rupert's energies were now directed at levering Childs out of bed and by the time we had embarked on a traditional Catalan breakfast of two eggs and half a pound of bacon apiece, he could scarcely contain himself.

"What's up, Rupert?" I asked him innocently knowing that he was dying to get to grips with a mountain.

"I don't know why we're all sitting around in this hut," he burst out, looking at me accusingly. "You included Montardo in your original programme and I very much want to climb it before I go home."

In Rupert's climbing canon, that first day's bag of Montjoie and Escalette didn't really count. Patently, our failure to so much get close to Aneto still rankled. Montardo was the shapely pyramidical peak at the head of the Arties Valley that we had briefly spotted yesterday during our march up to the Restanca. It was a mountain altogether more worthy of the man.

"But we can't beat the weather, Rupert," I reasoned. "It's still snowing hard outside and the visibility's appalling. We really must wait until it clears up."

"But we must do *something,* John," he retorted. "You surely want to climb Montardo? It's a fine looking peak."

"Let's give it an hour or two," I suggested mollifyingly.

As we hung around the hut watching the clouds go by, with Rupert's adrenalin count ever rising, conversation inescapably turned to equipment.

"What's that extraordinary *Alpenstock* you've got there John?" was Rupert's opener.

"Are you referring to my ice axe?" I retorted. "I'll have you know that it was made by Simond of Chamonix."

"My God! it's even got a wooden shaft!" he chuckled, "I thought people only used those things as walking sticks. Anyway they're very dangerous. Wouldn't do for a proper belay. Wood breaks quite easily you know."

"You're just a creature of the utilitarian modern school, Rupert," I replied airily. "This ice axe is a work of art in the right hands."

With such pleasantries we passed the time, with Rupert crowing at the age and provenance of my equipment. By 11 am he had tired of this game and his pressurising to move had became irresistible.

"We're heading for the Ventosa Hut across the Col de Crestada," I told the guardian as we paid our bill. "If the weather improves we'll try to climb Montardo but my friend here has to return to Arties on his own."

"Oh yes?" he replied looking dubious. "I'll telephone the guardian at the Ventosa to say you're coming. I'll also ring the Fire Brigade at Arties to make sure your friend arrives safely."

"But I don't need the Fire Brigade," protested Rupert, "I can get down to Arties perfectly well without them."

"Rupert," said Roger sternly, "in Spain, the Fire Brigade also runs mountain rescue. Anything might happen to you and we don't want to pick up the pieces."

In a final push to leave his mark, Rupert took the lead from the start and headed straight for the Col de Crestada by a brutal line which made no concessions to the art of contouring. As we followed a respectful distance behind, a speck appeared on the skyline which transformed itself into a lone skier. Rupert was concentrating so hard on getting to the col that he didn't notice this new arrival on the slopes. The rest of us waited expectantly as the skier came spiralling down the mountainside in a sonata of elegant turns.

"Must be the guardian of the Ventosa Hut. The Restanca lot said they might be expecting a social call," said Patrick knowingly.

The skier came to a graceful stop at our feet like some bird alighting.

"Hi! I'm Carmen," a woman's voice volunteered. "I guard the Ventosa. You come and stay with me tonight? See you later!"

Before Roger could say *"Adios"*, she had swooped away again like a chough. Muffled up and be-goggled we hadn't even see her face.

"Who on earth was that?" asked Patrick.

"That was Carmen, silly," we chorused.

Rupert's forward-at-all-costs policy had missed him a trick. His bid to climb Montardo was time expired long before he reached the col. I often pondered on what might not have happened if he had been less interested in mountain conquest and had instead joined up with Carmen. Presumably, they would have skied down to the Restanca together though not necessarily in tandem. It would have been a fastish run, for Rupert is nothing but competitive. Yet observing Carmen's skills and knowing Rupert's *kamikaze* instincts, it was probably as well that he went solo. After that? A chat over a cup of coffee perhaps? We shall never know.

Saying goodbye to Rupert on the Col de Crestada was a mournful business. His energy, enthusiasm and mountaineering skills had boosted our performance no end. Had he stayed on to chide and drive us, we might even have conquered Montardo but the clouds never lifted and as the ground steepened and the snow got deeper, I felt ill at ease. The summit was no more than 160 metres above but I couldn't see a thing and, after discussing the matter with David, my new climbing confidante, we agreed to call it off.

It wasn't the bravest decision of the tour and, to rub the point in, the clouds had started to lift by the time we had got back to the col. Until that moment, the mountains of the Aigues Tortes had been hidden by clouds but now, as we coursed gently down a wide, open valley by a series of shelved steps and hollows, the sun blinked and the mists rolled back. A wonderland of spiky granite peaks, clumps of dwarf pine and snow-covered lakes flung broadcast like cloths of damask unfolded before us. To the east the saw-toothed ridge of the Aiguilles de Travessani emerged from the mist and directly to the south the summit pyramid of a solitary mountain thrust through a ruff of feathery cloud – the Punta Alta. The ensemble reminded me of a starker grander Néouvielle. I had seldom seen anything more beautiful.

As we approached the Ventosa Hut, the western sky became streaked with hues of salmon pink as the last of the clouds streamed off the crests of the Besiberri like crusaders' banners. The hut was perched above a rocky basin cupping the Lago Negre. Twists of gnarled pine, finely etched as if in steel, protruded from the crevices which seamed its granite walls. Fedden had written lyrically about this place and Julian, long resident in Japan, exclaimed: "Breathtaking. Just like a Hokusai print. One of the finest views I have ever seen!"

Carmen was not long behind us. Our march she had doubled but our time she had halved. She walked into the hut proprietorially, kicked the snow off her boots and slowly peeled off her gloves, ski hat, anorak and over-trousers as she shook out a cascade of curly black hair.

Suddenly, the atmosphere became charged as if she was about to start a strip tease. This was no leathery *montagnarde* but a shapely young Oread!

"Your friend Rupert is safely down in Arties," she announced with a smile. And that was the start of it. Julian was first to introduce himself but soon enough everyone else was in on the act.

"Carmen – can we help cook, clean the potatoes, wash up or do *anything* to help?" they pleaded pathetically.

Mercifully, she wouldn't allow these duffers near her kitchen while she fried veal steaks and made a "special" pudding for *"zee Enghleesmen"*.

You would never have thought that they had seen a woman before as they ate their supper like hungry dogs. After the meal, it was Childs's turn to play sink macho. He might have made that omelette at the Rencluse but I had never before seen him wash up. Now he was in the thick of the suds after manoeuvering himself into pole position by the sink. Disloyalty to friends is inexcusable but this uncharacteristic display of servile domesticity was sickening.

After they had finished this absurd pantomime and another couple of bottles of house Rioja, it dawned on me that the tour's momentum was about to take another knock.

"I think we should all turn in now. Weather's clearing and we've a long way to go tomorrow," I ventured.

"Oh please don't be so boring, John," said Julian. "I don't feel in the least tired. Why don't we teach Carmen how to play Hearts before we go to bed?"

"Julian," I interposed, "Carmen's already had a long day and we must make an early start tomorrow."

He pretended not to hear me but, turning instead to Carmen, said with a nauseating grin: "Carmen – would you like me to teach you how to play Hearts? It's an English game of cards and good fun."

Carmen, smiling, archly replied: "But of course Julian! I do not know your game but I too like cards and I would like you to teach me."

By now Roger had surreptitiously squeezed himself onto the bench beside her and began to use all the advantages of a Spanish speaker.

"Let me have a look at your hand, Carmen," he insisted. "I can teach you some tricks."

I looked across to David who had gone into a trance-like state of mystification. We were in for an unedifying evening. Last night, Patrick had easily won the Hearts rubber but tonight, with Childs's sycophantic assistance, Carmen came in first at a canter. It was probably harmless enough but the spectacle of heavily married, middle-aged men reverting to type was ridiculous.

"Carmen," teased Roger with a leer, "how old d'you think I am?"

I was about to say, "old enough to be your grandfather", but assumed that she had rumbled him by now.

"Perhaps about thirty-seven?" she murmured demurely. "And I am twenty one."

So this was the reward of the man who had coined the adage – "I've got her exactly where she wants me."

Somehow I had to wean them away from this preposterous line of enquiry and get back to the business of ski mountaineering and tomorrow's programme.

"Tell us something about your life Carmen," I interjected. "Where were you born and how did you come to run this hut?"

"I was born in Barcelona," she replied, "but now I live in Lerida and work in Viella in the winter. I have been the guardian of this refuge for two seasons because I love zee mountains. There are many huts like this in the Aigues Tortes owned by the Catalan Mountaineering Club – Santalo, Blanc, Amitges ..." she rattled off a list of names.

"Your Catalan huts seem much better than those I've used in France," I said. "Are they always guarded in winter?"

"Oh yes," she replied, "most of them are for some part of the winter season."

"The French guidebooks don't mention any of that."

"Oh no," she smiled, "but we have our own guidebooks covering the Catalan Pyrenees – you should read them."

"How d'you manage on your own?" chipped in David Seddon.

"No problem," she replied swiftly, "but normally my boyfriend helps me. Sadly, he's not here now – he's hurt his knees skiing."

I glanced at Roger and Julian. A warning shot perhaps?

"Poor chap," I commiserated. "I'm so sorry. I wouldd very much like to meet him."

"I think we should ask Carmen about the weather," Julian suggested with his most ingratiating smile.

"Will it be fine tomorrow, Carmen?"

"Maybe," she replied, "but probably not. You never can tell in zee mountains. Perhaps tomorrow, I climb Punta Alta. You would like to come too? Okay? But I must be back early."

"Of course we would like to come with you," chorused Roger, Julian and Patrick in unison.

In Bénasque after the retreat.   (L to R) – Patrick Bailey, Rupert Hoare, Roger Childs, Julian Lush and David Seddon

"Then no problem," smiled Carmen. It was her favourite expression.

After such a delicious meal it seemed churlish that I should have to point out to Roger, Julian and Patrick that we were not in the business of being led up mountains by twenty-one-year-old Catalan chicks.

"The Punta Alta was never on our programme," I remonstrated. "The object is to get to Espot not stick around here. We must keep pushing on with the traverse."

At this, they reacted as if the lady's honour was at stake.

"But Carmen's been very kind to us," said Roger indignantly. "Nobody knows what the weather's going to be like tomorrow and this hut will make an excellent base if it turns bad on us."

Julian blurted out, "Anyway, I would really like to climb the Punta Alta with Carmen. She's the guardian here and must know exactly what she's doing."

"Yes, Julian, I've no doubt about that," I retorted sourly.

I gave up after this exchange. They were like dogs searching for something more than water with their "Carmen this" and "Carmencita that". I thought back wistfully to those golden days when a diet of porridge cake had sufficed; when we had rejoiced in the hair-shirtery of miserable bivouacs and had thought of nothing but the way ahead. Or had it really been like that? No matter. What was for certain now was that somehow I had got to break the spell of this Catalan Circe. David, I knew, would always be right behind me but I was beginning to miss Rupert.

Twice that night I was up with diarrhoea as a consequence of Carmen's cooking and almost forgave Childs for his earlier performance when, at 3.30 am, he sacrificed his personal supply of lavatory paper towards my cause. By then I had decided that if it stayed fine, I would scrap the Punta Alta caper and revert to the original plan of getting to the Colomers Hut. However, by 7 am the weather looked anything but settled so before the others could get at her, I asked Carmen for a forecast.

"No good weather today – but maybe okay this morning," she advised. "So now we climb Punta Alta? No problem."

In the circumstances, there was no point in standing in the way of Childs and Lush or indeed denying Carmen whatever pleasure she might derive from their company. When I thought about it dispassionately over breakfast, I took comfort in the prospect of an agile Carmen leading a party which included four 50-year-olds up a mountain that she must know like the back of her pretty hand.

"All ready?" cried Carmen as she took off from the steep slope behind the back of the hut as if she were racing a Womens' Downhill. Trying to keep up with her, I set the party's tone with a dramatic but harmless fall above the inky waters of the Lago Negre. There was something feral about the way she slid across the snow smooth as a stoat. There was also something animalistic about the rag-bag pack that followed her. Roger ungallantly hinted that she might possess some undisclosed stoat-like characteristics yet confessed that it was under Carmen's aegis that he had discovered a new interest in equipment.

We closed the gaps as the ground steepened and the weather worsened, with Carmen always in front weaving her way upwards. When it came to technique Julian was her most assiduous pupil and stuck doggedly to her tail while attempting to emulate her effortless inverted uphill turns executed with a hip swinging tango-like motion which he christened the Carmen Flick.

With 200 metres still to go to the summit we cached our skis under a rock as the wind gathered force and the snow fell thicker.

"You'll need ice axes now," shouted Carmen above the din as she began to hack steps out of a steepening slope of *nevee*. I wished that Rupert had been there to see ice axe woman in action. Her textbook exhibition continued for the next forty minutes until we reached an ice encrusted cairn and could climb no longer.

"Thank you, Carmen, thank you so very, very much," gushed Julian. Then to confirm the message, came out with *"Muchas gracias, muchas gracias Carmencita"* and flung his arms around her. The rest of us got handshakes and the proclamation "That was my first 3,000 metre Pyrenean peak!" I was genuinely delighted to witness Julian's triumph but found its manifestations disconcertingly un-traditional.

"And now we go down," announced Carmen. "No problem!"

Actually, with the weather worsening by the minute there were *muchas problemas* in the offing. Carmen was in a hurry to get back to her hut to deal with the influx of weekenders. As a result, descent from the summit was disordered with Patrick adopting the *bumsitz* position for the final run down to our skis. At this point Carmen announced that it was too cold to hang around so was off down the mountain before Roger could get his skis on. The snow was deep, visibility was deteriorating fast and, although retreat never quite became rout, there were *muchas* falls on the way before we foregathered back at the hut. Carmen had been in situ for some time and was now back in control dealing with a gaggle of locals up from Boi who clamoured for her favours. Julian's bubble had burst. From now on, it would be business as usual.

"Never mind," I comforted. "The spell had to break sometime but you've had some fun. Thanks to Carmen, you've also climbed your first Pyrenean three thousander."

"I really must make tracks for home tomorrow," he replied gloomily, "but Carmen says that the weather's going to be bad for the next few days."

I didn't try to dissuade him from leaving for I knew that he desperately wanted to be re-united with his family. However, his departure at this stage posed problems for the rest of us. We still had several days in hand. If the bad weather persisted how would we get Julian safely down to a roadhead without prejudicing what remained of the tour?

"We'll think of a plan," I reassured him, "but let's all sleep on it tonight and see what tomorrow brings."

We didn't have Carmen to ourselves that evening but her personality suffused the hut and a warm feeling of cameraderie prevailed. Until she put me wise to it, I had neither realised that Catalonia boasted the best system of huts in the Pyrenees nor that the Editorial Mont Blanc of Barcelona published a comprehensive range of Pyrenean ski mountaineering guidebooks. But, then, I was still learning about Catalonia and shouldn't have been surprised at this efficiency.

Catalonia owes something to both France and Spain but bows to neither and ever since feudal times, when Catalonia's commercial empire encompassed the Mediterranean, commerce and trade have been its hallmarks. Catalonia withered when Aragon and Castille united to turn Spain's face against the Old World to conquer the New. Now, after years of decline, Catalonia is again at the heart of Spain's economic renaissance.

After yesterday's climactic conquest of the Punta Alta, post-summit detumescence was inevitable. I had another sleepless night racked by diarrhoea but could scarcely believe our bad luck when Carmen confirmed that the blizzard which had started yesterday was likely to continue for another three days.

"Carmen's just passed on some bad news about the weather," I told the others glumly. "Forget about the original itinerary. We haven't a cat in hell's chance of reaching Andorra. We'll be lucky to get back to the Val d'Aran."

"What's the plan then?" asked Roger.

"We've got to get Julian to a roadhead somehow so I suggest we make for the Colomers Hut across the Port de Caldes and stay there tonight. We can then put Julian on the road to Salardu and even reach Espot ourselves if the weather clears."

Julian was looking unhappy. "That's all very well, John, but there's a bloody great storm raging outside."

"We can always turn back if things get too bad," I replied. "Let's make a start anyway."

We paid Carmen the equivalent of £13 a head for two nights accommodation, two dinners and miscellaneous food and drink.

"Are you sure you should try to cross to Colomers?" she asked anxiously. "This is a bad storm. The snow on the pass will be very deep."

"We'll be fine thanks, Carmen," I replied nonchalently. "Don't you worry about us."

She gave me a strange look and shrugged her shoulders. This time, she didn't say "no problem".

Outside the hut successive sheets of snow came sailing down the valley to reduce visibility to a few metres. Our route, such as it was, lay under the Aiguilles de Travessani and along the edges of its twin lakes but, with the blizzard blowing straight into our faces, I couldn't make out the difference between snow and sky, lake and shoreline. At the edge of the first lake I fell through the ice and emerged dripping. The water quickly froze to ice. By the time we reached the Col de Travessani, the snow was waist deep just as Carmen had predicted.

"We're going to have to call it a day and get back to the Ventosa," I shouted hoarsely. "The weather's getting worse. It would be madness to cross the Port in this weight of snow."

"I think we can all see that," said Roger.

On the way down, I managed to repeat my ice-breaking trick but this time I fell into the lake backwards and couldn't get up unaided. The water froze my clothing solid and jammed my bindings. We fought our way back to the Ventosa and at 12.15 pm I had another session with Carmen.

"You were absolutely right about everything," I began sheepishly, "but somehow we've got to get Julian to a roadhead and ourselves back to Luchon."

"You'll never make it to the Val d'Aran today or tomorrow," she replied. "This is crazy weather and I don't know when it will stop."

"What do you suggest then?"

"You must ski out south down the Malo Valley. There's a roadhead just beyond the dam. I'll telephone a taxi driver at Boi. He'll pick you up at the dam and take you to Luchon."

"A taxi! To Luchon! Carmen – *Phenomenale*!" they chorused.

"No problem!" beamed Carmen.

Once again, with a wave of her wand, she had reduced Roger, Julian and Patrick to grovel mode. They made the usual protestations of eternal friendship but as they were packing up, I took down her name, home address and telephone number.

"Thank you for everything Carmen. *Muchas gracias.* We must keep in touch and meet up again next year."

When the sun shines, the scenery of the upper Malo Valley is as idyllic as that of any place on earth. Robin Fedden had once retreated down this same valley in summer in torrential rain after an entanglement with a Spanish Captain of Militia whose passion for painting aborted Fedden's first attempt to climb the Enchanted Mountains.

Our winter descent on ski through the eye of the storm was every bit as dramatic. Half blinded by whirling spirals of spindrift, we all had more spectacular falls and at one stage were blown helplessly across pavements of snow-stripped *roches moutonnées* like feather down. Snow, rock and sky seemed to have merged into a grey blur when we reached the Lake of the Cavaliers to be confronted by a palisade of up-ended slabs of pancake ice two metres thick and wide as tennis courts.

These walls of ice, flaring like the sails of the Sydney Opera House, proved impossible to cross on ski and we were forced to switch direction sideways and head for an indistinct shore line marked by more crumpled folds of ice where the lake was bounded by cliffs. In this hostile world, we progressed like ants under beetling walls of white granite festooned with monstrous icicles until, suddenly and unexpectedly, a blank, grey wall as tall as a skyscraper emerged from out of the clouds to block the way ahead. We had reached the Cabelleros Dam.

Clambering up a steep path we came out at a car park deserted save for a solitary diesel Land Rover. Its roof was buried under a foot of snow but its engine was still running. The driver disengaged himself from the front seat and walked over towards us with an engaging grin.

"Your taxi to Luchon, Señores. Carmen Valldosera sent me!"

8

HIGH ROUTE TO ANDORRA

Salardu to Arinsal

"I prefer to receiving English letters than Spanish ... I'm very happy because I have very good remembrance of those days ..." Carmen's letter brought it home that it might take some time to extirpate the Carmen Factor on any future Pyrenean tour involving members of the most recent party. On behalf of the others, I had taken it upon myself to send Carmen a coffee-table book about the English countryside "in sincere appreciation of all you did for us". Later I discovered that Julian had been conducting his own correspondence and that Roger had been telephoning her. Shortly after our return to England, our seemingly reticent batchelor Patrick asked me to vet a draft article he proposed writing about our trip in the Eagle Ski Club's Yearbook in which he had described the Ventosa Hut as "notable for its captivating twenty-one-year old guardian, Carmen". I told him politely not to bother and that as leader I would be submitting the official report in due course.

Even discounting the Carmen factor, I had to conclude that this foreshortened tour had been a damp squib. We had had 50 per cent foul weather in nine days and only progressed ten kilometres further east. If we were going to get anywhere next time, we would have to have our fair share of decent weather and a committed team. More specifically, I wanted both David Williams and Anna Lindberg on board. Unfortunately, having abandoned a promising career as a marine engineer to spend more time in the mountains, David had signed up for the Eagle Ski Club's expedition to attempt the first ski crossing of Alaska's Hayes Range. Both Roger and Julian impressed upon me how much they wanted to re-visit this area but when Roger suggested bringing Carmen on board for the whole tour, I reckoned that a cooling off period was necessary. Middle age might provide ballast but the accent had to be on youth. The Pyrenean High Route would have to wait another year.

In recompense, I set my sights on a ski crossing of the Picos de Europa, the highest and most spectacular range in Spain's Cordillera Cantabrica, with three of last year's Pyrenean team, Roger Childs, Rupert Hoare and David Seddon. At that time the Picos were virtually unvisited by British climbers. I knew of only one party, the French duo of Berreux and Parmentier, who had traversed them on ski. Geologically and geographically they form a western extension of the Pyrenees but as we discovered for ourselves, the combination of dizzying limestone gorges, chasmic sink holes, Atlantic weather and wholly inadequate maps didn't lend itself to an easy ride. Grandiose plans were modified en route and we left this fine range impressed by its scenery but chastened by the experience.

Come the summer of that same year, I was determined to pre-book a committed team for next season's Pyrenean round. Childs and Lush were still

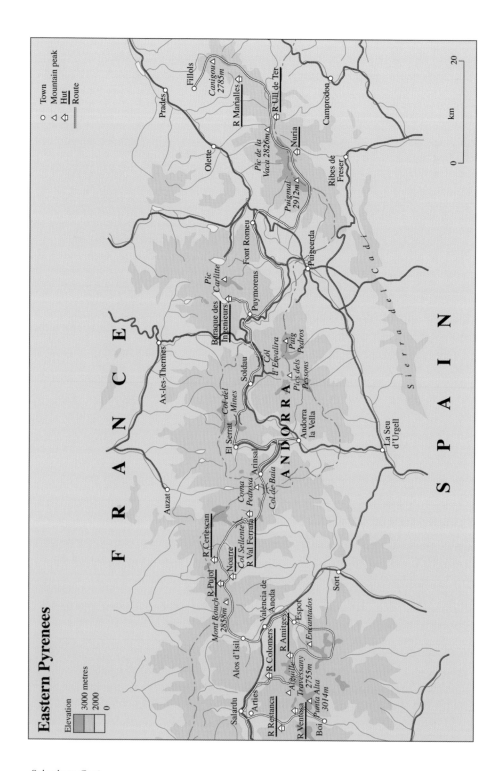

Salardu to Canigou

going on about Carmen; Rupert Hoare had committed himself to climb in the Karakorum and David Seddon was unavailable for professional reasons. David Williams had previously confirmed that he and Anna would be starters provided he could find himself a new job in North Wales to where he had recently moved but, in early September, wrote to say that he was recovering from meningitis contracted in Chamonix after a strenuous Alpine season. This was the worst possible news. I went into overdrive to find replacements from old *compagneros* and even approached the Dutch Seven Summiteer Ronald Naar whom I had recently met on Mont Olympus but drew a complete blank.

Faced with the prospect of another no start, there seemed nothing for it save, in the argot of *Childspeak*, "to bring Carmen on board". I wrote her a couple of letters in English but when I got no reply was forced to the expedient of asking Childs if he would kindly get in touch with her by telephone. On a postcard-sized memorandum portentiously headed "Note from Roger Childs" he wrote. "Your beloved Carmen has been away and only just got your letter."

Carmen sent me a postcard depicting a lone member of the Second Barcelona Everest Expedition grinding his way up to the South Col. I concluded that this must be her boyfriend Miguel – the man with the "bad knees". She had kindly spelled out the dates on which her Ventosa Hut would be open and invited me to "write a letter too". I did so by return and got her reply on Chartreuse yellow and green notepaper in Catalan. Reluctant to pass this one on to Childs for translation, I managed my own and gleaned that Carmen was now an instructress at the Baqueira Beret Ski School in the Val d'Aran and that Miguel came as part of any package.

This was fine by me and might even guarantee momentum but, as I discovered much later, I had misinterpreted a critical supplement to Carmen's letter detailing which of the huts along our proposed route would be guarded and which not. This was to have some unfortunate repercussions.

According to the Ollivier/Peres Pyrenean *Haute Route* guidebook, our route from the Val d'Aran to Andorra through the Catalan Aigues Tortes and Pallars Sobira was likely to be the most serious and remote of the entire Pyrenean traverse. We would have to carry basic rations, fuel and bivouac equipment but, on my reading of Carmen's letter, at least two of the huts we would be staying at en route would be guarded. I therefore decided that we would cut food to the minimum and rely on the excellent Catalan hut guardians to provide the rest.

Remembering the speed at which Carmen covered ground on ski, Roger and I, accompanied by Rupert Hoare, fitted in five training days in Spain's Sierra de Gredos based on Roger's *finta* in sight of Al Mansour. As matters now stood, the team had shaken down to Roger Childs, Julian Lush, Carmen, Miguel and myself but I was still praying that David Williams would have recovered from his meningitis and that both he and Anna would come on board. The success of the tour might hinge on their participation.

Three weeks before we were due to drive out to the Val d'Aran in mid-March, David wrote to say that he was feeling much fitter after five days ice climbing in Scotland and that he and Anna were definite starters. I almost went down on my knees. The scene was now set save for one detail – the precise roles of Carmen and Miguel. I had been frantically busy in the office so liaison had been sporadic. Further, when our travel agent informed me that all the hotels in the Val d'Aran were fully booked, I couldn't give her a definite rendezvous location for our proposed dinner date. Somehow we would have to make contact on arrival.

Transport arrangements for this trip were unusually complicated. Julian and I were to fly to Paris to meet Roger, David and Anna at a bar near the Gare d'Austerlitz from where we would put Roger's stretch limousine Citroen on the night train to Toulouse and then drive out together to Salardu in the Val d'Aran. After some hiccups finding the Paris rendezvous, things fell into place and next morning we were speeding southwards across the plain of Haute Garonne towards the Pyrenees under a tumultuous cloudscape of racing black galleons and spiralling cloud towers. This was the first time on any Pyrenean stage when I had already toured with every other member of the party. The optimism that this engendered dispelled the minor irritation of Julian forgetting his ice axe and snow shovel.

Although I had learned some lessons from sampling the peripheral attractions of the Pyrenees, I was determined to see something more of the Aigues Tortes National Park even if this meant departing from the strict line of the traverse. As we had discovered two years before, this magical stretch of country south of the Val d'Aran has some of the finest scenery in the Pyrenees and the best appointed huts.

For me, there was also a special significance in starting from Salardu for it was here that Robin Fedden had rendezvoued with his Pyrenean mentor the lame Don Miguel before beginning his quest for the Enchanted Mountains. It was here that I hoped we would cap coincidence by meeting Carmen and her Miguel. Not everyone felt the same.

"I really don't know why you old roués go banging on about Carmen," grumbled David when we reached Viella somewhat earlier than expected before midday. "I've no doubt that she's a great goer but to take her on board with her boyfriend whom you haven't even met could lead to some almighty complications."

"I don't agree," said Julian leaping to her defence. "We should try to make contact as soon as possible. She would be a tremendous asset to any party."

"How d'you propose getting in touch with her?" asked David.

To this there was no simple answer and when Roger's enquiries confirmed that not a single hotel had rooms available, David returned to the attack.

"I really can't see any point in hanging around here," he protested. "If we get started now we can easily get up to the Colomers Hut this evening and be on course for an early start tomorrow."

"Personally, I don't see much point in going anywhere just now," broke in Roger gloomily. "I can't see a vestige of snow anywhere."

So far as we could see anything above a pall of low cloud that masked the peaks, David had a point. But I was beginning to have doubts about Carmen's plans and was wise to Roger's delaying tactics.

"David's probably right," I said. "Carmen never made a firm commitment and it might take all day to find her. She's probably busy anyway. I think we ought to forget about her for now and get up to that hut tonight."

Julian and Roger made protesting noises and Roger burst out,

"But you said we would be staying this first night in a hotel. It's written into your programme."

"Correct," I replied, "but there's nowhere to stay. We'll try to meet up with Carmen on the way back."

"Okay then," he grinned, "but let's just hope there is some snow higher up or we'll be walking all the way to Andorra."

We drove on cautiously up the Tredos Valley. The lower roads had been clear but five kilometres on this one was blocked by snow. Now in a more positive frame of mind, we spent the next fifty minutes unloading, sorting out food and kit and re-packing.

"Roger and I will nip down to Salardu to park the car," I told the others. "We will be back in about twenty minutes by taxi."

I had never known Childs to be at a loss in Spain or anywhere else for that matter but for the next two and a half hours we traipsed from hotel to hotel and bar to bar down the length of the Val d'Aran leaning on landladies, barmaids and anyone else who might be on hand to help us find a taxi. Starting at Salardu, we moved on to Arties and finally fetched up at Viella. This fatuous search became an end in itself and by the time we returned to the others in the one taxi operating that day David was looking extremely po-faced.

"What on earth happened to you two then?" he demanded. "We had been wondering whether you'd had an accident. If you'd only walked back up the road from Salardu, you could have been back here within thirty minutes."

"Just looking for Carmen," grinned Childs unabashed but I felt sheepish. Having started the day so well, we had now left barely enough time to get to the Colomers Hut before dark. As we slid away up the valley past the ancient baths of Tredos, it had already started to snow.

It took three hours to reach the Colomers Hut, prettily sited at the edge of a dam, by which time we were completely coated in snow. Apart from a friendly bearded guardian, the only other occupants were a French ski mountaineering trio. I was feeling tired and like Roger and Julian didn't hesitate about ordering the guardian's *plat de jour* of soup, beans, trout and peaches. I was then dismayed when David and Anna insisted on cooking their own supper. Roger, Julian and I were middle-aged and prosperous. David and Anna were having to count the pennies. Having separate messes was no way to build team unity. I kicked myself for my thoughtlessness.

I had planned that the traverse to Andorra would comprise two phases. The first would involve a three-day journey from Salardu to Espot through the Aigues Tortes, spending nights at the Colomers and Amitges Huts before fetching up at the Hotel Roya in Espot. The second phase held the key to the whole venture. Starting from the Noguerra Palaresa Valley, we would hug the frontier ridge and steer a course through the steep, unfrequented highlands of the Pallars Sobira all the way to Andorra. I had reckoned that we would be pushed to complete this section within five days even in good weather.

The Pallars Sobira had remained virtually unknown to such earlier British Pyrenean pioneers as Packe, Russell and Spender and was only traversed on ski during the late 1950s.

In 1974, starting from Arinsal in Andorra, Robin Fedden attempted to make a first British ski traverse of the Central Pyrenees with mechanised transport backup but his party of three was beaten back by storm before they had even started to cross the Palars Sobira and had to drive round to pick up their intended route westwards from the Lake of St. Maurici. From there they reached the Besiberri Hut on the Western approaches of the Aigues Tortes only to be forced to abandon the next section of their traverse by more bad weather.

I was wary of what might lie in store for us in Pallas Sobira but had no particular worries about our crossing to the Amitges Hut. However, when we awoke the following morning, I could tell that the original plan might not be enough to satisfy David Williams. He was up first and came bursting back into the hut with, "You won't believe this but we're in for a fantastic day. The sky's crystal clear and the guardian says the good weather's going to last. I've had a word with the French party. They're already having breakfast and going for the Point Luccia. We might go one better and climb the Aiguille de Travessani."

Fedden's *The Enchanted Mountains* contains an evocative photograph of the Travessani's smooth granite slabs plunging into the same lake that I had twice fallen into two years back when trying to reach this same hut in a blizzard. The ascent of the Aiguille was dear to my heart.

"Okay, David," I replied, "Great plan. Let's give it a go but we'll have to get moving smartish if we're going to make the Amitges this evening."

"Slight change of plan everyone," I announced to two recumbent forms in the bunkroom. "It's a perfect day and we're going to climb a fine peak before pushing on to the hut."

After overcoming initial reluctance to get started, we dumped surplus kit at the hut and left at 9 am a full two hours later than the better disciplined French. Their syncronated spiralling descent tracks coming down the Point Luccia were clearly visible as we skinned up to the Col Travessani where four of us dumped our skis and followed in David's slipstream up the narrowing snow ridge, which terminated in the teetering cornice marking the pic's 2,755 metre summit.

The air was crisp, the sun shone bright and the snow crystals sparkled. All about us shapely mountains glittered white. Most prominent was the Punta Alta rising keep-like from its mountain moat but further west I could recognise the peaks and passes of yesteryear fresh painted with new snow. The Pyrenean magic was working its spell. This was as good a start as any I could remember.

As if to capture the mood, David took off arrow straight from the summit and skied down the narrow rake up which the rest of us had just been kicking steps puffing and struggling all the way. Where the ridge dipped sharply he momentarily slowed and then, twisting and turning into the slope like an eel, spiralled down to the col from whose corniced lip he launched himself off like a ski jumper before landing like a bird. "Bravo!" we shouted as he snaked downwards through a metre of fluffy powder snow to the depths of valley.

By the time we were all back at the hut, four and a half hours' worth was on the clock. I thought that it had been worth every minute but it was now early afternoon, the sun was at its hottest and the day's real business had scarcely begun. We skated across the frozen Colomers Lake and then began the four kilometres climb to the Port de Ratera de Colomers some 400 metres above us. As my pack began to feel like a sack of stones and my shirt dripped sweat, I fell behind the others. Retching and heaving, I only caught up with them when they stopped for a short break before tackling the steepest part of the climb.

By the time we had reached the Port at 5 pm my energy had leached away. The sun had already disappeared behind the western peaks and the dreary landscape of shale and scree now confronted us. That ridiculously late start was catching up with us. We had reached another of those curious Pyrenean double

En route to Andorra

cols which make route finding confusing and had gathered together in a huddle to consult the map.

"Where the hell are we," grumbled Julian. "It's getting jolly late. Are you sure we are going the right way?"

Even in good light, the business of deciphering the contouring of French IGN maps is never simple. Struggling as I had been to keep in touch with the pack, David had taken over the lead and had shown an almost uncanny instinct for route finding.

"I'm sure David's got the direction absolutely right, Julian," I broke in quickly. "This isn't easy country to navigate and the route to the hut's not obvious. We've still got to get across this next stretch of high ground to the Port de Espot before we can ski down to the Amitges Hut."

"How far away's this bloody hut anyway?" demanded Roger. "We've been going all day virtually without a break and now it's almost dark."

"I can't say precisely," I snapped back, "but it's downhill all the way from the next col. Let's not waste any more time talking about it and just keep moving."

Tempers were getting frayed. The spark of enthusiasm with which we had started the day had long been extinguished. Save perhaps for David, we were all tired and beginning to look ragged. It had also started to snow.

We reached the Amitges Hut as the last light of day faded. Once inside Roger turned on me accusingly:

"That was far too long a day and this is a hut too far. You never properly discussed your change of plan with anyone but David. We shouldn't have added a peak like that. We've been going virtually non-stop for almost ten hours."

"Okay, Roger," I replied wearily. "I'm sorry. It has been a long day and I'm bloody tired too. Maybe there should have been more consultation back at the Colomers but when there's fine weather we've got to take our chances. We've bagged a fine peak, had a great ski descent and we're dead on target. Thanks are due to David for his excellent route finding."

"And what do you propose for tomorrow?" he countered unmollified. "My feet are buggered and I had like to make it a rest day."

"I'm right behind Roger," chipped in Julian. "You should have let us know what we were letting ourselves in for."

Throughout all this, David and Anna had said nothing but I could see that David was uneasy and embarrassed. His quiet and unassuming exterior concealed a steely and determined man with a true mountaineer's ambition. It would never have occurred to him that this had been anything but a entirely successful ski mountaineering day. He was patently mystifyied by this outburst.

"Tomorrow's another day," I said gently. "We're all tired. Let's sleep on it and see how we all feel in the morning. If needs be, we can always re-vamp the programme."

As Pyrenean huts go, the Amitges had every possible mod con. For all that, ours was not the jolliest of suppers and nobody spoke much. There had plainly been a breakdown in communication for which I felt responsible. Yet the *froideur* also reflected a difference in mountaineering philosophy. This wasn't a guided party bound by a rigid programme but a group of friends, fellow *montañeros* following a common purpose. Nothing is for certain in the mountains. You must improvise as you go along. The adventures and setbacks of any particular day fall with the dice.

Next morning snow was falling lightly but persistently. After our exchanges yesterday evening, I wondered whether we still possessed the collective will to reach Espot by a circuit of the Encantados. There was always an easier alternative.

"Well, John," asked Roger over breakfast, his natural good humour restored, "What have you got in store for us today?"

"If we're all feeling up to it and weather permitting," I replied, "I would like to complete this Encantados circuit. It's not part of Ollivier's Pyrenean *Haute Route* but it looks perfectly feasible from the map."

"What exactly's involved?" asked Julian.

"First we'll drop down to the Lake of St Maurici and then climb the valley opposite to cross the Col de Monastero. After that we swing round east-north-east behind the Encantados before descending the Peguera Valley to Espot."

"How long will that lot take us?" asked Roger.

"Certainly the whole day," I replied. "It's 16 kilometres worth and involves 800 metres of ascent and over 2,000 metres of descent."

"Phew," whistled Julian. "I hope your Encantados are worth it."

"Sure to be," I said, "with a hotel at the end of it."

The Encantados had been a goal of mine ever since I had first read Robin Fedden's *The Enchanted Mountains* thirty years before. For Fedden, their ascent had been the summation of his Pyrenean quest. Our mountain paths had only crossed once on parallel mountaineering expeditions to Turkish Kurdestan but I felt an empathy in sharing his love for unusual mountain ranges. Like him, I had spent the early years of my working life in the Middle East. Like him, I was on a quest.

Fedden was a fastidious aesthete with an iron core. He had been an artist like his father Romilly; a poet and promoter of British Forces poetry in wartime Cairo; the author of over a dozen books and a campaigner for the preservation of Britain's historic houses during his thirty-year association with the National

Trust. An expert skier, he embraced mountaineering in his middle years with a convert's zeal and was elected to the Alpine Club largely on the strength of the three Pyrenean climbing seasons during the mid-1950s when the range was little visited. His mountain genius was for exploring and writing about unconventional ranges in Lebanon, Greece, Spain, Eastern Turkey and the Andes.

Fedden's writing combines a gem-like style with scholarship and inspirational enthusiasm. His description of the High Level Route from Chamonix to Zermatt in his *Alpine Ski Tour* opened my eyes to ski mountaineering though this magisterial book was actually written on the basis of a single High Level Route and fifteen days' guided ski touring. In *The Enchanted Mountains,* he reveals both his own soul and that of the Pyrenees in a prose poem.

Fedden's only rival in English for conveying the genius of the place was J. B. Morton, the Francophile disciple of Belloc, who for 51 years wrote the *Beachcomber* column for the *Daily Express.* Some time during the 1920s Morton walked from one end of the range to the other and recorded his swashbuckling adventures in his rumbustuous *Pyrenean.* Yet Morton was an honest walker who never aspired to the heights whereas Fedden carries his readers on a pilgrimage to unimagined horizons through the dream-like world of the Spanish Pyrenees.

In 1977, at the age of sixty-four, seventeen years after he had first climbed his enchanted mountain, Fedden returned to the Pyrenees to attempt the first British ski mountaineering traverse of the central section from Andorra to the Somport Pass. Bad weather aborted most of the first phase but after re-commencing at the Pont d'Espagne, Fedden's party reached the Somport seven days later after a straight run in perfect weather. He died three years later.

The Encantados circuit was going to be a long haul but there was no point attempting it in bad weather and, after yesterday's ruffled feathers, I didn't want to push anything too hard. I delayed our start until 9.20 am when we quit the hut by an icy path through flurries of snow towards the Lake of St Maurici. Somewhere ahead in the clouds, four kilometres across the valley, were the twin peaks of the Encantados but the cloud was low and I began to wonder whether we would ever get a sight of them. Even if we did, would the view match my mind's eye picture?

The early British pioneers missed out on this part of the Pyrenees. J. B. Morton deliberately avoided what he had heard of as "terrible mountains ... of jumbled rock, with high lakes where no footfall comes, and enormous chasms brimmed with mist and torrents which plunge from inaccessible cliffs and fill the air with ice cold spray ..." Fedden's lame mentor, Don Miguel spoke of its unvisited valleys and mountains, with lakes filled with trout "big as dogs".

To Fedden himself they assumed a mystical perfection with "no deficiencies or faults". How could any mountain fulfil such high expectations?

As we coursed down the rocky path fearful of tearing our out ski bottoms, the clouds began to lift, the sky lightened and, then, like shadows emerging through a gauze of mist, the faint outlines of the Encantados became visible framed between converging ridges. By the time we had reached the lakeshore, their mysteries were revealed spiralling into the clouds in whorls of slabby rock riven by snow gullies. Their heads remained in the clouds. They were as beautiful as I had expected.

Guidebooks ascribe the first ascents of the Grand and Petit Encantados to a French dandy, Colonel Brule, and his aristocratic compatriot Count d'Astorg in 1901 and 1902 respectively but legend prefers the claims of two shepherds from Espot who became petrified as the twin summits for failing to attend mass. The first Spaniard to climb both peaks, Jaime Oliveras, was a priest who celebrated his triumph by granting the shepherds absolution.

Down at the lakeside a fleet of Land Rover taxis was disgorging a shoal of fat ladies for their constitutional before being ferried back to Espot. This alarming sight alerted me to the realities of our own situation.

"We're right off schedule," I burst out. "It's already 10 o'clock. Unless we get a tremendous move on, we'll never do this Encantados circuit."

"But where have all these people sprung from?" asked Julian.

"From Espot," I replied.

"But isn't that where we're supposed to be going?" asked Roger. "It can't be that far from here."

"Not if you go straight down the valley but we're not going that way. Our route goes 16 kilometres round those bloody great mountains in front of us."

"Good grief," murmured Roger with a despairing gesture,

"Not another marathon please. Not with this load."

When push came to shove, he would be with you all the way though not until he had floated some energy-saving wheeze.

"Look, John," he said suddenly. "I've got a good idea. There's a hut on the other side of this lake called the Mallafre. Why don't we dump all our heavy stuff there and when we reach Espot pick it up by taxi?"

"What d'you mean by *heavy kit*, Roger?" asked David suspiciously.

"Oh ... all that extra rubbish we've been lugging round these past two days – sleeping bags, bivouac sacs, slings, spare food, cookers, crampons etc," he replied airily.

"You could make a big mistake getting parted from equipment on the mountain," David retorted. "I'm hanging on to what I'm carrying and I would advise you to do the same."

David already carried the heaviest load. *Wedelning* through crust and crud with a 50-pound load never seemed to bother him but for lesser mortals I was certain that in no way would the Encantados be circuited within a day without shedding some weight.

"I think Roger's got a point," I said. "Let's get to the hut first and see if it's guarded. If it's not we may have to think again."

We reached the Mallafre Hut by diverse routes and found it empty save for a predictably hirsute guardian. Some British climbers sport beards as others wear ringlets but for male Catalonians they're *de rigueur*.

"We want to do the Encantados Circuit across the Col Monastero," I said in English. "How long will it take us to reach Espot from here?"

He looked at us quizzically not sure what to make of the age disparity.

"It all depends how fast you go," he replied glancing at his watch. "There's not much snow this year so you'll have to walk a lot – especially down the Peguera Valley. You certainly won't get there in under eight hours. A much quicker way is to go back to the lake and walk down the Escrita Valley."

Eight hours …! It was now 11 am so, at best, we couldn't reach Espot before 7 pm by which time it would be dark.

"I just don't think it's on," broke in Julian. "We've left it too late. What happens if we can't reach Espot tonight?"

"There's always the Blanch Hut," I replied and then, turning to the guardian, "Can we leave our heavy kit here with you?"

"Certainly," he replied, "but please collect it before tomorrow night. I'll have a full house by then."

I was wearing a double face. Julian could well be right. Given an already tight schedule, this diversionary circuit was an indulgence. If it took more than a day we would be cutting fine the more serious passage across the Palars Sobira. David must have sensed an impending wobble and now came in strongly.

"Come on Julian," he said. "We'll do this circuit easily provided we start now and don't hang around debating the point."

David's confidence and enthusiasm had settled it. I felt wimpish that the thought of an easy option had ever entered my head.

"Okay everyone. Let's leave all unnecessary kit here and get moving PDQ."

Luxuries to some are necessities to others. Julian's three different types of toothbrush and range of toiletries wrapped in individual containers went some way to solve the mystery of his outsized pack.

The guardian's assessment of snowcover was broadly accurate. There was

Lunch at Espot.   (L to R) – Anna, Roger, Julian and David

never quite enough of it to put on skins for the length of the Monastero Valley but where the ground steepened on the way up to the Monastero Col, a thin layer of snow overlying frozen ground made for precarious scrambling. From a pronounced rocky lip we dropped into a boulder strewn basin which led to the base of a steep snow couloir that disappeared into the clouds.

"Must be the Col Monastero up there," remarked David.

He had been forcing the pace out in front. For the second day in succession I had been suffering from Mountaineer's Foot, a condition which impedes the placement of one foot in front of the other. However, from my vantage point at the rear, I could see that, without the ice axes and crampons that had been incautiously dumped at the Mallafre Hut, Roger and Julian might have difficulty following David and Anna up a slope which the map marked as a *passage delicat*. Moving with no protection other than their ski poles, David and Anna were already nearing the top while Julian and Roger were teetering on tiny footholds half way up. I unsheathed my ice axe and followed at a circumspect distance.

No one came to grief but the climb slowed us. By the time we had fore-gathered in David and Anna's cornice snow cave it was already 3 pm. It had taken little short of four hours to climb a mere 800 metres with almost two-thirds of the distance still to go. At least from now on we could ski.

A long passage over broken ground under lowering cloud, through a familiar landscape of granite peaks, snow-covered lakes, past clumps of gnarled pines, took us up, over and around a succession of switch backs, bowls and inclines, with attendant skin stops and swops before we reached the thickly forested lower Peguera Valley. Here the snow gave out precisely as the Mallafre Hut's guardian had predicted and now the business of finding a path through thick forest was a puzzle.

Unflurried by a stream of unsolicited rearguard advice as to where we might or might not be going, David's route finding got us to Espot's Roya Hotel at exactly 7 pm. By beating guidebook time by fifteen minutes and completing our second successive ten-hour day I thought we had done pretty well until I noticed that Anna was limping.

"Everything okay, Anna?" I asked her as we went in for dinner. "You're limping a bit. Nothing serious I hope?"

"I'm fine," she beamed back. "Just a little tired that's all."

But David was looking glum. "I'm afraid her knee's playing up," he said gruffly. "It's an old injury. All that walking today did it no good."

Anna's knee was a worrying development. As I lay in my bed that night listening to the bells ringing out from the whitewashed belfry of the village's

Romanesque church to strike midnight, I remembered the punishment of the two shepherds for disregarding this call to comply with the canons of their faith.

The Hotel Roya was the ideal place for Anna to rest her knee and for the older generation to recuperate. As Childs expressed it over his bacon and three eggs breakfast, it would "make up for my deprivations of the past three days." We spent the morning wandering round dusty, cobbled lanes, past cows foraging in the tiny back gardens of low slung houses whose circular slated roofs reached down to the ground. We wrote postcards sitting in the sun on the humped back bridge that spans the Rio Escrita and then gorged ourselves at the Restaurant Juquim on grilled trout caught in the river that same morning. Sitting outside sipping ice-cold lager and watching the world of Espot drift unconcernedly by, I felt that another spell was being cast.

"Don't you think we should be making a move soon, John?" David's voice broke my reverie. "Alos d'Isil's still a good way up the valley."

"Yes, of course," I replied, starting suddenly, "but how's your knee, Anna? Don't you think you should rest it a bit longer? We could easily stay here another night."

"I'm fine thank you, John," she replied with her usual smile.

"Surely, we don't have to move just yet," broke in Roger. "I'm sure that Eduardo can take us to Alos d'Isil in his taxi."

Eduardo Roya was the third generation owner of his family's hotel and had already rescued our heavy kit from the Mallafre Hut. Alos d'Isil, a tiny hamlet some 20 kilometres up the valley of the Noguera Palleresa, was our scheduled roadhead and launch pad for the trek across the Pallars Sobira.

"Certainly, I can take you up the Noguera Palleresa," Eduardo assured us with a grin, "but Alos d'Isil is deserted. The mountain people are leaving their villages to work in the big towns. You had better stay at Isil o Gil where there is a *hostal*."

We left Espot in late afternoon as the sunlight softened the harsh winter colours on the flanks of the Noguera Pallaresa to pale gold. Pointing airily with his free hand as we drove up the valley, Eduardo was moved to soliloquise.

"There, they are breeding *Urogallo*," he said with a proprietorial gesture, "to re-introduce it into our valley."

"We call it the Capercaillie," I replied. "It still lives in Scotland."

"Ah yes," he said, "Scotland ... They say it has mountains too."

"You must come over and see them some time," I replied.

"Maybe I will," he went on. "My hotel has made me a successful man and I love the mountains – yet those who live in them never truly appreciate them."

"What d'you mean Eduardo?"

"Well," he replied with a conspiratorial chuckle, "let us say that these mountains have helped me pursue my other interests – interests which involved a certain trade with France. You may have heard of the *contrabandistas*?"

A vision of *Jamaica Inn* crossed my mind and I glanced across to take a closer look at Eduardo's hard-nosed profile.

"But we have our problems too," he continued. "Ten years ago that village we've just passed supported ten families. Now it has only two. We need tourism to support these mountains."

"Then what about those other interests?" I asked him.

"Ah that!" he sighed with a shrug. "The trade's almost finished. With tariff harmonisation the margins are gone. We used to cross the mountains with mules but now its cheaper to bring the stuff round by lorry."

The last of the evening sun shone faintly on the austere mountain wall that formed a backdrop to the village. The Land Rover bumped across the cobbles of a stepped, hump back bridge flanked by ancient oak trees that spanned the Noguera torrent and led us into a broad, elegant square.

"Here we are," said Eduardo. "Isil o Gil."

Enclosing the square were substantial three-storey houses built of stone with wrought iron balconies. The Romanesque church was altogether grander than Espot's for we were now in the heart of Pallars, a district known to Catalans as the "heroic masculine country of the Sun". Three centuries ago, this remote mountain village had been a summer resort of nobility like Bénasque. Long before that, even before the decline of Rome and after the unification of Aragón with Castille, the people of these remote valleys boasted their own customs and made their own laws. The Romanesque church, like so many others which penetrated the furthermost recesses of Pallars, attested to a rugged independence and a robust faith. Yet the place had a curious atmosphere. Isolation, poverty and rural depopulation can breed bigotry, xenophobia and vendetta.

Eduardo stopped the Land Rover outside an impressive mansion bearing a sign *"Refugi Can Trucs"*.

"This is the *hostal* I told you about," he said. "I'll leave you here. The guardian will look after you well. I'll get my friend José to pick you up early tomorrow in his taxi. He'll take you further up the valley beyond Alos d'Isil to the entrance of the Comomala Barranco. You can start skiing from there."

Just before leaving, Eduardo whispered in my ear: "José's okay. Don't worry about him. But he's a real *contrabandista*."

The Refugi Can Trucs, originally built as a private house in 1827, has successively been used as a police barracks, school and mountain hut. The enterprising young couple from Barcelona who now ran it had decorated the dining-room with wooden skis and ice axes of a vintage that I recognised as my own. Skiing and school party holidays had rescued Isil o Gil's economy from collapse and the village now marked the start of the 24 kilometre langlauf course making a semi circular sweep round the upper Noguera Palleresa.

At supper we stuffed ourselves with a thick vegetable soup and a dozen of the region's speciality pork sausages at a communal table shared with fourteen school children. They made conversation impossible during the meal and continued their racket until 3.30 am next morning when Anna finally lost her Swedish cool and shut them up. With only two hours sleep before reveille at 5.30 am, breakfast was a subdued affair. Julian was looking anxious.

"I hope we've got enough food for this trip, John," he blurted out suddenly. "I haven't brought any spare with me and you didn't ask me to carry any. Why didn't we re-stock at Espot?"

"The simple answer to that, Julian," I replied, "is that both the Certescan and Ferrara Huts are guarded. The last thing we want on a tough passage is to over-burden ourselves with surplus food."

"Who told you that about the huts?" he retorted.

"Carmen," I replied wearily.

"Okay then," he conceded. "but your views on food are very different from mine. I just hope we have enough to eat."

During this exchange, I had barely noticed the man who had slipped through the dining-room door and was now staring impassively at me from a dark corner. I walked across to him.

"José," he said with just the hint of a bow, "Taxi."

José had coal black eyes, a challenging look and an off-hand manner. He spoke a brogue Catalan which resisted even Childs' attempts at conversation. Yet he was not wholly uncommunicative and when we passed through his own village of Alos d'Isil, built in much the same style as Isil o Gil with its own fine church and solid houses, he spelled out on his fingers that only eighteen people were now living there.

The young guardian of the Can Trucs had told us that in early January life in the valley had come to a standstill after a metre of snow had fallen. Now, as we drove up the dark, narrow valley, there wasn't a vestige to be seen and it worried me to think what the long, jarring walk to the snow line would do to Anna's knee. More than that, how she was going to cope with at least five tough days ahead? There were no break points along this section. None of us had experienced the Catalan Fire Brigade's rescue service.

It was 7.20 am when José dropped us off at the mouth of the Comamala Gorge, a densely wooded side valley off the Noguera Pallaresa. With skis on

Across the Palars Sobira

sacs, we headed due east along the line of a footpath which threaded its way up the valley's steep flanks through dark groves of beech wood. As the first rays of the sun lit up the mountains behind us, I spotted an isard watching us from a ridge high above.

The team was fitter now and climbing with less fuss but when, after an hour and a half's humping, we reached the snowline, David came over to me with a worried look.

"I'm afraid that we'll have to take a break here. I've got to do something about Anna's knee. It's badly swollen and she needs a rest."

"Time for a pit stop anyway," I replied.

I walked over to where Anna was sitting on her rucksack with her unzipped ski trousers pulled up over the knee. It was red and swollen. David was tenderly applying snow compresses.

"That knee looks very painful Anna," I said. "D'you really think you should carry on?"

"I'm fine thanks," she beamed back. "David's an expert with cold compresses."

"Today's a crux passage," I continued unconvinced. "We've got to climb 1,650 metres to the Col Galina and then descend another 1,100 metres to Noarre with two tricky cols to negotiate in between. Guidebook time is ten hours and we're only at the start of it. Before we're really committed we can easily retrace our steps back to the valley and give your knee another day to settle."

They both knew all this. We had been over the route before. They also realised as I did that retreat to Isil o Gil at this stage was tantamount to abandoning the traverse. We would have lost two days that weren't scheduled and thus run out of time.

"No question of that, John," replied Anna with her most beatific smile. "Don't worry about me. The knee's not that bad. I promise you that I'll manage."

"We both want to carry on," said David.

After a further re-distribution of the contents of Anna's rucksack we continued on up the valley. David had insisted on taking the bulk of her equipment. His sac was now ridiculously heavy.

Breasted the lip of a wide, shallow basin we saw for the first time an enormous mountain that filled the head of the valley.

"Cripes – what's that bloody great thing ahead of us," exclaimed Roger.

"That's Mont Rouch," I replied slowly. "Somehow we've got to get round that brute."

The sight of Mont Rouch had taken me aback. Before planning this route, I had never even heard of the mountain. It scarcely figured in any of the British books that I had read on the Pyrenees although, from the map, it was clearly the pivotal peak of the Palars Sobira with four great ridges radiating from its apex. The reality was daunting. It now stood four square before us with its bulky shoulders silhouetted in the morning sun. Its deep cast western flanks were still in shadow but the morning sun had set light to the icy crest of its serrated south-west ridge that soared to a pointed summit.

"Well now, Maestro," groaned Roger, "what's your plan for this one?"

In my mind, I tried to match the guidebook's sketchy description of the route with the reality before us.

"We've got to turn it to the south," I replied hesitantly. "There's a high col called the Puerto on that south-west ridge in front of us – the Serra de Pilas. From there we've got to drop down into another valley and then cross another high col across the Serra de Mitjana before climbing to the Col Galina ..."

I tailed off there. Quite enough to take on board for the time being. Just to reach that first Col Puerto, we were going to have to climb some 1,200 metres from the roadhead and we had barely done a third of it. I didn't remind him that, according to the guidebook, that second col, the 2,767 metre Col de Mont-Rouch, could only be reached by a rocky chimney which was usually *verglassed*.

"But which valley do we follow?" asked Julian.

From this point, there appeared to be a choice between two valleys, both of which ran steeply upwards towards Mont Rouch. David and I conferred with the map.

"Must be the right fork," I pronounced.

"Are you sure?" queried Julian. "The left looks more direct and not as steep."

"But it doesn't take us to the right place, Julian," snapped David.

"I don't see why not," Julian retorted, "I can't see any named col marked on my map. The left fork takes us higher up the ridge."

The argument rumbled on. Julian would not be convinced and I could sense David's growing irritation.

"We must get on in any event," I broke in. "The *Haute Randonee Pyreneene* definitely follows the right hand valley so it must be the safer bet."

We put on skis for the first time and began to zig-zag up a series of ever steepening snow bowls to the 2,500 metre Col Puerto. The last bit was so steep that we had to take off our skis and kick step up it.

"It's 12.50 am," I announced looking at my watch. "It's taken us five and a half hours to get this far but that's the main bit of climbing under our belts."

"How are we doing on distance?" asked Roger.

"Probably done about a third," I replied.

"Well, I only hope we've come to the right place," said Julian. "It's a bloody steep descent into the next valley."

David's brow was furrowed as he and I peered down from our notch in the ridge into the shadowed Nyiri Valley. He wasn't just worrying how Anna's knee would react to a near vertical descent through deep snow.

"The sun's been on this slope a long time," he muttered. "It could easily avalanche."

"Let's not hang around," I urged. "We must just keep going."

It was certainly steep but the snow at the top held well and the greater risks to Anna's knee came as we skied down to the valley bottom where crust became treacly porridge. At a brief lunch stop David applied more snow poultices to Anna's knee. I thought to myself that in anything but fair weather it would have been madness to attempt this passage.

We crossed the Serra Mitjanna by another steep col but never noticed the difficulties of which the guidebook had warned. Throughout that long morning we had been eye-balling the west face of Mont Rouch but now, as we climbed out of the trough of an un-named valley towards the Col Galina, the great triptych of its south and east facing ridges began to recede. It had clouded over towards midday but, as we reached easier ground high on a ridge, the sun came out and I paused to look down into the Pallars heartland to the south across a maze of dark shadowed crests and troughs of *serras* whose names were unknown to me – Pilas, Mitjana, Mascalida.

I had thought we had been making good progress but by the time we had reached the Col Galina at 3 pm, we had already been going for seven and a half hours and were still nowhere near the chalets of Noarre, our ultimate destination.

"Let's take a break and a bite here," I suggested, and, going across to David and Anna, I asked, "How's the knee holding up?"

"Fine thanks," said Anna with her usual smile but this time she looked strained and I had noticed that her normally fluid skinning action was becoming laboured. We had already climbed 1,650 metres. That couldn't be doing her knee any favours.

"That's great," I said without conviction. "Even so, I don't think we can make the Noarre chalets tonight. Noarre's another nine kilometres away and I've no idea what we'll find when we get there. There's no proper hut and all the barns may be locked up."

"What are you suggesting then?" asked David.

"There's this refuge marked on the map which isn't mentioned in the guide-book. Maybe it's just been built or maybe it's just a shack but it's only 430 metres below us behind that spur beyond the lake."

"Okay," said David. "Let's take a look at it. Anna's got to give her knee a rest whatever she says. She shouldn't go any further tonight."

We skied circumspectly down a steep-sided hanging valley hugging the contours of a succession of snow-covered lakes. There, secured by iron stanchions driven into the rock, stood a silver aluminium box. It was perched on the lip of a spur which jutted out into the valley like a ship's prow. The Refugi Enric Pujol was a hut of dreams. Overlooking the wooded Mollas Valley, its panoramic views lead the eye ever eastwards to ridge after pine-covered ridge. We threw off our sacs and burst inside.

"Hey!" cried Julian, "this place was only built three years ago. It's got the lot – bunks, clean blankets, everything! I vote we stop here."

No doubt about that. Roger had already bagged himself a strategically placed bunk near the door. Nothing would have moved him.

Our supper that night was meagre but we ate in style on solid pine chairs around a matching table by the light of an wooden candelabra. According to the hut book we had just missed the Italian ski mountaineer Sergio Serra of Trieste, who had passed through only two days before on the sixteenth day of his east to west solo *integrale* ski traverse of the Pyrenees. We had spotted what appeared to have been ski tracks on the way up to the Col Galina and now the mystery was solved. Anna had been heroic but Sergio put our day into perspective.

Next morning we were up at 6.30 am to see the dawn break over a flawless sky.

"How's the knee today?" I asked apprehensively.

"Just fine," she replied.

"Do you really think you can take another long day, Anna?"

"Yes, of course," she replied as if I had asked a silly question.

"What's the plan today then?" broke in Roger.

"First we'll ski down to the Noarre chalets and, if Anna still feels up to it, we'll push on to the Refuge Certescan. According to the guidebook, we should make the Certescan in about five hours."

"Piece of cake then," grinned Roger.

"I only hope we'll get something decent to eat there," said Julian. "I'm beginning to feel jolly hungry."

"Don't worry, Julian," I replied, "the Certescan's guarded."

We were all beginning to relax again. Julian and David made a pantomime of burning every single piece of rubbish they could find outside the hut before we all skied off the lip of the Mollas Valley's headwall. Down into its shadowed gulf and through mixed woods of beech, silver birch and pine by the riverside, with the sun blinking through the trees, we had to cross a log bridge and walk the last stretch on foot before reaching a cluster of slate-roofed stone houses by a grassy path lined with silver birch.

Noarre, lying at a junction of three valleys, seemed as much rooted into the

Julian approaching the Col Puerto

landscape as the snow capped mountains that surrounded it. The shepherds' summer houses had not long been converted into weekenders' retreats but the neat ensemble delighted the eye and we could easily have whiled away the rest of the day lounging around in shaded gardens. But we had allowed our guard to slip: when we eventually got moving again, it was midday. The lower part of the Noarre valley up which our route now lay was entirely bare of snow. The sun was high and the trees, leafless in winter, offered no shade. Where the path crossed beneath a broad waterfall, we stopped to soak our sweat-sodden shirts in the icy water and fastened dripping handkerchiefs over our heads for relief.

Two and a half hours after leaving Noarre, we were still struggling up the stony hillside on foot in the heat of the afternoon. Just beyond the treeline a suspicion of the summer path we had been following bifurcated. David hesitated and stopped to take a quick look at the map.

"According to this map, we could go either way," he said.

"Agreed," I said, "but I'm in favour of sticking to the main valley."

"Yes, I think that must be right," he agreed.

"Are you sure about that," came in Julian quickly. "That doesn't necessarily look the right way to me."

"Are we even in the right valley?" quipped Roger.

During most of this trip, the more serious leads whether uphill or down had fallen on David. As the party's fittest and strongest member and unquestionably its best skier, David spent most of his time out in front with me as backup. He possessed an almost uncanny navigational sense but, for some perverse reason, both Julian and Roger seemed determined to convert any route-finding decision into a question and answer session. David was amazingly tolerant but today his patience was wearing thin.

"I can't think what you're talking about, Julian," he snapped. "The right-hand route's a summer path which goes over a bloody great spur. The one we've chosen carries on straight up this valley."

"We can't hang around arguing the toss like this," I broke in, "We've already fallen behind schedule and must push on to the hut." In any event, David had already pushed on.

Having spent the better part of a very hot day walking in plastic boots with heavy loads, there still remained a 1,000 metre climb on skis through heavy snow to reach the Col Certescan. That stretch seemed endless and by the time we had descended to the Lac de Certescan and spotted the hut on the other side even David, struggling under his huge load, was looking tired. Now, with the evening closing in and the sky becoming murky and overcast, I began to feel uneasy as we approached the hut.

"Can't see any signs of life in this place," rumbled Roger as he looked through a window.

I kicked my skis off, pushed open the heavy wooden door and stared into a sombre living-room. Blackened exposed beams supported a stone-tiled roof.

"What's happened to your guardian?" asked Roger accusingly.

"I've no idea," I snapped back. "All I know is that it's supposed to be guarded. Carmen said so."

"There's clearly nobody here," cried Julian, flinging down his rucksack. "What sort of dump is this and what on earth are we going to have to eat? I'm bloody tired and practically starving."

"I'm just as disappointed as you are, Julian," I said. "I'm very sorry about the guardian too but we've just got to make the best of it."

He wasn't the only one who had been sustained by the prospect of a curvaceous Catalan guardienne awaiting our arrival with bacon and eggs and cold beer. I wanted a break from these grumbles and said: "If you'll all give me your water bottles, I'll get them filled at the lake for a brew."

I marched out of the hut and plodded through the snow to the lakeside to cut through the ice to draw water. Suddenly, I felt intensely cold. I was tired. This had been our fourth big day in five.

When I got back to the hut, I noticed a change in the atmosphere which had nothing to do with the cold. David and Anna were sitting stiffly on one side of a rough hewn wooden table with Roger and Julian on the other. No one was talking.

"What's the problem?" I asked ingenuously.

"We've just been discussing where this tour's going," David blurted out, "and there's a big difference of opinion between us. As far as I'm concerned, we're dead on schedule. There's one reserve day in your programme and I've just been suggesting to Roger and Julian that if we make the Val Ferrara Hut tomorrow, we could climb Pic Noris the following day."

Earlier in the tour I had shown David a Catalan route guide illustrating a route up this attractive peak and we had discussed it as a possible objective. I hadn't given it a thought since.

"But what about Anna's knee?" I asked, still bemused by the strained atmosphere.

"My knee's fine," she replied crisply, without her usual smile.

"Anna's knee is not the problem," broke in Roger curtly. "Frankly, I'm not in the least interested in climbing Pic Noris. I don't want to extend this tour any longer than I have to. I've got work to do and I wouldn't mind getting back to London early."

"I entirely agree with Roger," came in Julian. "I think we should finish this tour as quickly as possible. Quite apart from anything else, we've almost run out of food."

Earlier in the day I had had a certain feeling, never previously experienced on a Pyrenean tour, that the Pyrenean High Route was at last within our grasp. During the three hours we had been flogging up that endless twisting valley to the Col Certescan, I had been running over in my mind the catalogue of disasters, accidents, set-backs and disappointments that we had had in getting this far. I had been delighted with our progress and, though I suspected that something had been building up between David, Roger and Julian, I was completely taken aback by this spat.

"Look, Julian," I said, trying to pull the loosened strands together, "I'm very sorry about the food. I thought that this hut was going to be guarded and organised our rations accordingly. Okay, I've got it wrong and I apologise but we're not going to starve and we can certainly last out until we get to the next hut."

"That's all very well," he replied, "but I'm in the same boat as Roger. I don't want this tour to last any longer than it has to. I would like to get back to our house in Foix and I don't see why we can't cross into Haute Ariege from where we are now. It's just across the frontier ridge. I'm sure you could get a taxi back to Salardu from the nearest French village."

"Sorry, Julian," I replied, "that's simply not on. I'm not prepared to pull out of the tour at this stage with Andorra only two days away. As David says, we're bang on schedule. Even if we weren't, I would be dead against trying to cross the frontier ridge into France as all those routes are dodgy. We're miles from anywhere and it would be madness to split the party. Having got this far we should continue as planned. If the weather holds, we'll be in Arinsal the day after tomorrow."

Even before I had finished this spiel David had got to his feet. "I don't understand you two," he said, turning on Roger and Julian. "Anna's got a lousy knee yet she's perfectly willing to carry on. I totally agree with John that we would be crazy to stop or split at this stage. If you'd only bother to study the map you'd see the reason why for yourselves. There's no easy way out from here but if we do reach the Ferrara Hut tomorrow I would still like a shot at Pic Noris."

He was already half way out of the door when he said, "And now I'm going out to get some fresh air."

Early on in this tour I had realised that our various objectives were not identical. It wasn't just a question of age so much as a difference in mountaineering philosophy. Roger and Julian were both experienced travellers and good companions. When it came to the crunch they would come up trumps, but they were too worldly and pragmatic to possess the mountaineer's obsessive and sometimes perverse ambition to push the route regardless or to wear willingly the hair shirt that often goes with it.

David had been the tour's outstanding contributor. I might have planned the overall strategy and day-to-day itinerary but David had been our spearhead, shouldering by far the biggest loads with the courageous Anna always at his side. I shared his ski mountaineering aspirations and although his parting shot about the Pic Noris was stubbornly undiplomatic, I understood how he felt. With Andorra only two days away, this collision course was ridiculous. We were *companeros* who had done so much together and I was determined to avoid another Alan/Jean-Pierre style bust up.

I followed David out of the hut. He was sitting on a rock staring into the middle distance.

"David," I began, "I'm very sorry there's been all this fuss. As far as I'm concerned you're the key person on this tour. None of us could have done without you. You've just got to make some allowances for us old men."

He was only partially mollified. Although Anna did her best to jolly things along and unearthed two packets of bacon left behind by Sergio Serra to which she added salami, Pom and a cube of cheese to go with two ship's biscuits for our supper, the atmosphere remained sour.

"Sergio's certainly saved our bacon," cracked Roger but even this dreadful joke failed to raise a snigger for we had descended to eating at separate tables. But patience and humour will ever be the traveller's companions and by next morning a decent night's sleep had miraculously dissolved last night's ill humour. A pencil of sunlight stabbed through the low window to light up the drab room as we all gathered round a single table for tea and a wad of Anna's unaggressive flapjack leavened with raisins, sesame and sunflower seeds and honey. That tiff might never have been and with *bonhomie* restored my optimism came flooding back.

"Weather's looking great," chirped up Julian, the charms of Foix forgotten. "What sort of day have you got in store for us John?"

"The guidebook's not very helpful about this next section. We've got a good way in distance but as we're a lot fitter I reckon that six to seven hours should see us to the Ferrara Hut. The key will be the Col Sellente. It's about 12 kilometres due south but to start with we just follow our noses and ski straight down the Certescan Valley."

David had been poring over the map and now joined in. "There's no sort of route or path down the Certescan Valley that's marked on my map and the bottom bit looks very heavily forested. Why don't we follow the line of the *Haute Randonnee Pyrénéenne*? It's clearly marked and keeps to the open ground past these two lakes."

Describing a neat arc on the map with his finger to illustrate his point, he went on. "It's quite a bit longer than your route down the valley but it looks more scenic and should give us a decent ski run."

"For that matter, David," I replied dubiously, "there have been no ski routes marked on either of the IGN maps we've been using to cross Pallars. I'm all for avoiding the forest but I'm reluctant not to follow the guidebook's direct route. What does anyone else think?"

The verdict went to David four to one. There's a time to assert and a time to assent. We chose David's route.

Relaxed and happy again, we left the hut a touch later than I had intended and initially it looked as if David had got it right yet again. The day started fine as we wove our way through open country past the upper Romedo Lake, although the going became sluggish as the snow had barely frozen last night.

Above the lower Romedo Lake David and I climbed steeply to the top of a rocky spur to be confronted by a *mauvais pas*. Walking routes don't necessarily make good skiing routes. Although in summer you would have given little thought to crossing the rock bay overlooking the lake by what would have been a narrow path, snow had transformed the place. The rocks above were too steep to climb over and the bay across whose face the path descended diagonally to lake level was now covered by a snow bank. This sloped steeply to a rock lip before dropping ten metres sheer into the lake whose surface was covered by a thin veneer of ice. To have fallen into the freezing water at this point with skis and a heavy rucksack would have been a one way passage.

We formed a cluster on the top of the spur and pondered on how to tackle this obstacle.

"I don't like the look of this one bit," I began.

"You can say that again," said Roger. "It looks deathly."

"What d'you think, David?" I said.

He paused for reflection. "Certainly looks nasty but if we don't cross here, we'll have to retrace our steps all the way round the lake. It can't be as bad as it looks. Let me see how it goes."

"For God's sake watch yourself," I muttered as he began to side slip diagonally down the slope testing the snow with ski and poles as he went. I had never seen him ski so gingerly and was not reassured when he reached the bottom and shouted back: "You must take this one very carefully."

David could do things on ski not vouchsafed to others.

Towards the Port de Baiau

Taking a deep breath, I began to follow his tracks across the slope with my heart pumping and, once started, realised why he had sounded a warning. The snow was wet and unconsolidated and, as I slid across its surface, slabs of the stuff rolled away from under my skis to fall into the lake below with a dull plop. I came to an inelegant halt at the lake's edge beside David. My legs were quivering as I looked hard at him but he was now looking over my shoulder to where I had just come from.

"My God," he muttered. "Roger's just about to come."

"Bloody Hell," I said.

Without another word, David kicked off his skis, pulled out his ice axe and began to clamber back up the snow slope to where Roger was about to start his run.

"Hang on Roger," I yelled up to him, "just wait a minute."

Maybe he was too psyched up to hear. Maybe he simply didn't care but barely had I flung off my own sac and begun to rummage around frantically inside it for the climbing rope, than he had started to move down the fatal slope in an exaggerated crouch position.

There are times in skiing when you least want to lean outwards from the slope even though you must. This was such a time. At the *moment critique*, just as he was gathering momentum, Roger leaned into the slope. His skis shot from under him and I caught my breath. Childs was long past the fighting weight of his youth. To stop in its tracks the six-foot-two-inch frame of this ex-Blackheath flanker with the added weight of skis and heavy rucksack was the equivalent of halting Jonah Lomu in full stride. By the time I had whistled "Christ" and frantically tied a loop into the rope ready to pull out a water-logged Childs, David's lunging tackle had done just this.

"Nice one, David," I shouted with my heart still thumping.

"Thanks for that David," croaked an ashen-faced Roger as the two of them collapsed on safe ground.

"Close thing, Ruggero," replied David grinning wanly.

Another drama had been played out to be the talk of Greenwich for months to come.

Anna and Julian followed cautiously but without incidence and we recuperated awhile at the far end of the lake, sitting on our sacs in the snow with a bird's eye view of the ground ahead.

"That's the way we go," I said jocularly. "Our route goes down the Romedo Valley before it swings out of sight behind that great spur and then follows the Ribera de Sellente to the Col Sellente. Must be that faint nick on the skyline."

"Looks like a damned thick forest down there," said Julian, peering down at a confused tangle of valleys below us.

"And one helluva long way to that col," added Roger. "Seems we've only just started."

With the benefit of hindsight, I can categorically state that the lower Romedo Valley is not suitable for ski touring. After negotiating successive bands of heather, bush and rock, we hit the forest proper as the snow gave out. If there is a path, we never found it. The lower we went the thicker grew the forest. With skis atop sacs, we plunged and thrust, reared and backed, weaved and wove our way over fallen trees, hidden holes and thick undergrowth, battling on downwards through beech, birch and pine thicket, with our skis waving and tossing like antlers as they repeatedly tangled and snagged in the overhanging branches. It was tiring, back wrenching stuff and rather than continue this snail like progress to the valley bottom, we tried to break out of the forest by taking a higher traversing line across the head of the main valley. This proved a futile strategy for the way became barred by an impassable gorge so we had to retrace our steps and, after another exhausting brush with the forest, eventually discovered the bridge which crossed the river at precisely 12 noon.

We had now reached the confluence of three spectacular gorges. At the bottom of each, thunderous torrents raged and tore at massive boulders lining their banks. No hint of the existence of this tremendous spectacle was indicated on our map. We felt like explorers and were tempted to investigate further but this diversion had already put us two hours behind schedule.

"We're going to have to get a tremendous move on," I said to David. "The Col Sellente is six kilometres from here and another 1,000 metres above us. The Val Ferrara refuge is another six kilometres beyond that."

"Dead right," he grinned wryly.

For the next four and a half hours we skinned up the Ribera de Sellente without once stopping, save when a slab avalanche peeled off the underside of the Col de Becero and almost took Roger with it.

At the Col Sellente we stopped for a short break. The Val Ferrera was now at our feet and away to the south the rugged peaks of the Serra de Monteix shone palely in the afternoon sun. Breaking the eastern horizon under a lowering sky, the serrated ramparts of Andorra were visible for the first time. It was a lovely tranquil evening. The valleys were darkening in shadow with the mountains at peace. As I sat on an isolated patch of yellowed grass munching a piece of chocolate, I experienced another fleeting moment of happiness. We weren't there yet but in my bones I felt that we were about to crack the most critical stage of the Pyrenean High Route.

I glanced at my watch. 4.30 pm. Still a long way to go. When we left the Col Sellente and slipped past the Baborte Lake on our way down the valley, Julian shouted: "Look, John, there's a hut just above us on that spur. We could easily stay there tonight."

The newly built Baborte Hut shone silver in the last of the sunshine, a replica of our favourite Pujol Hut. It was tempting to stay there but I had the bit between my teeth and was determined to reach the Val Ferrara Refuge that night or bust.

"We must press on to the Val Ferrara, Julian," I shouted back and then to spur him on: "The hut's guarded so we should at least get a decent supper if we're not too late." Food had become everyone's preoccupation.

Beyond the lip of the lake David found a thread of slushy snow, which led steeply down through clumps of pine trees to a small hut near the valley bottom. While I changed into trainers to give the ballooning blisters running the length of both insteps a break, Julian and Roger engaged David and me in another route finding pantomime.

"What's the altitude of this place?" asked Julian.

"Does it matter?" replied David.

"I want to get my bearings," retorted Julian.

"The hut's straight up the valley," I told him. "All we have to do is to follow the stream or the track to get us there."

"I can't see either," grumbled Roger. "Are you sure we're in the right valley?"

"For God's sake," I exploded. "Let's stop talking and just keep moving."

We were tiring now. Down in the forest with dusk falling it was easy to find the stream but not the track which lay somewhere on the other side. By the time we had found a crossing it was pitch dark and, though we located the path, it now slewed round on itself to terminate in a dead end. Retracing our steps we missed the foot-bridge, waded through the stream and stumbling along by head torch light, eventually blundered onto a high-eved building.

"It's the hut!" cried Roger.

"But no lights on here, John," groaned Julian. "Let's hope the guardian's still awake."

We barged through the door into the living-room-cum-dormitory without bothering to remove our boots and dumped down our sacs and skis on the floor with an almighty crash. Flashing my head torch around the room, I picked out two sleeping bagged shapes stirring on the bunk.

"Guardian, guardian?" Roger demanded. "Where's the guardian?"

"No guardian," came the reply. "Who you?"

We didn't bother to explain but gathered that they were students from Barcelona trying to get some sleep.

"No guardian, no supper," exclaimed Julian bitterly, "There's the rub of it, John. You said that this hut would be guarded but patently it's not. Can we at least brew ourselves a hot drink and try to get some heat into this place. We've been on the go for twelve hours with scarcely a break."

We were all wet, tired and hungry. We should have been celebrating the completion of a great day. The last thing I wanted now was another *Affaire Certescan*.

"Sorry Julian, I'm really very sorry about the guardian. Once again, I was relying on what Carmen told me. It really would be a bit anti-social to light the stove this late. Let's just pool our resources to see what we've got to eat."

We pulled out every scrap of food stashed away in our rucksacks and laid it out on the table for Anna to concoct supper. It didn't take much preparation. Each individual's ration consisted of one cup of soup, a sliver of salami, one oatcake, a tiny cube of cheese and a taste of Sergio's bacon.

Julian kept on growling: "Just wait until I see Carmen ..." while I remonstrated: "Just think of Scott and Fiennes. Healthy people like us can survive for days, even weeks, on short rations."

"So much eyewash," he replied, "but wait till we get to Foix. You can make up for this by taking us all out to *Le Grand Gousier* where I can guarantee a *grande bouffe*."

We did indeed have such a meal at *Le Grand Gousier* where Julian, generous as always, let me off my forfeit. Yet many weeks later, when appetites had long been satiated, Roger confessed that he had never felt better on that diet. Julian never wholly let me forget his privations and I, in turn, never had the courage to confess the awful truth that I discovered years later on re-reading the Carmen correspondence. I had failed to notice an addendum to her Chartreuse *billet doux* in which she had clearly given the dates on which both the Certescan and Ferrara Huts would be guarded that season. None coincided with our own dates. I realised only then that I had committed a monstrous slander.

"Mea culpa, mea culpa. Perdona Carmen, perdona."

It snowed again in the night but next morning we woke to a glorious day. Even without the comfort of breakfast, our spirits soared. In the closing stages of yesterday's trek the hills had become drab and lifeless but now, under a dusting of new snow, they looked like ancient monuments restored by a fresh coat of paint. The mountains were on song as we were. Nothing was going to stop us reaching Andorra.

Like the mountain states of Liechtenstein and San Marino, the autonomous principality of Andorra owes its historic survival and independence to its physical inaccessibility. Early Pyrenean travellers tended to avoid this mountain fortress on account of its primitive ways and difficulties of access. We were to experience the same problem.

"How exactly do we get into Andorra?" Roger had asked me.

"The guidebook offers two alternatives," I had replied. "Neither is straightforward but the one I've chosen goes up the Baiua Valley due east of here and crosses the frontier at the 2,790 metre Port de Baiau."

"Surely, that's higher than we've ever been before on this trip?"

"Precisely," I replied, "and just before we reach the port we've got to climb one tricky pitch with some exposure."

"Then why are we taking this route as opposed to the other?" broke in Julian.

"Because we want to climb the Coma Pedrosa as per the itinerary," I replied.

David at least looked pleased. He was still smarting at having to forego his Pic Noris.

With the weather so fine and settled our delayed start didn't seem to matter and early on I felt full of fizz as we skinned up the Baiau's long, enclosed valley but, as the morning wore on, the heat, reflected like a mirror off last night's new snow, became almost unendurable. I had made trail for the first part of the day with the snow balling up under the skis but when I handed over to David felt completely spent and took my place at the back of the line.

There's a pyschological catch about going last. Once you've fallen behind, it's sometimes difficult to catch up again. As we laboured on upwards in seemingly endless zigzags, I never appeared to be getting any closer to the person ahead and never before had the sun so completely leached my strength. I kept stuffing lumps of snow down the front of my shirt and then inside my handkerchief hat to make an icy pancake but the melted water evaporated long before reaching the parts for which it was intended. Gasping for breath at every bend, slumped over my ski poles, I kept glancing up the blazing white slopes above me to where a distended line of black figures seemed to have frozen into the snow. They never appeared to move but never did I gain on them. Dehydration was exacerbating Mountaineer's Foot.

The Port de Baiau had been visible throughout our ascent as a nick at the head of the valley and the only possible point of weakness through the line of jagged peaks that marked the frontier ridge. Yet it never seemed to get any nearer and, as morning merged into afternoon, I began to wonder whether we would ever reach it. Eventually, I caught up with the others where the upper valley narrowed into a steep snow couloir before merging into a near vertical rock wall split by a shallow corner.

"Bloody hell, what a ghastly slog," I gasped out, still panting like a dog. "The port must be just above us now, marked by that cornice."

"The sting's in the tail," said David, straining his neck upwards. "This rock pitch is a good 20 to 30 metres."

"That's the one," I replied. "This must be the technical bit the guidebook refers to."

By the time the rest of us had strapped our skis onto our sacs, David had climbed the corner by a series of bridging moves. I followed him less confidently to easier ground where he had prepared a belay for anyone who wanted a top rope. After some struggling, scrabbling and hauling the whole party were assembled on the corniced col.

"Well done, well done, everyone," I shouted excitedly.

"We've done it. We've made the Port de Baiau. We've reached Andorra. Well done, Anna – a fantastic achievement!"

Then, looking back beyond the valley that had taken us most of the day to labour up, I took in for the first time the view that had always have been behind us but which I had been too tired to notice.

"Look at this amazing view," I cried to the others. "We can virtually see the whole of the route we've done this past week."

"I believe you're right, John," said Julian. "With the eye of faith I can almost see our tracks."

The mountains and valleys of Pallars Sobira were now spread out before us like a map. Every facet and feature of the sweeping arc of peaks that stretched back to Mont Rouch was brilliantly etched black or white, with the triangular ridges of that fortress-like mountain dominating all else. Beyond Mont Rouch, indenting the far horizon, rose the peaks of the Encantados and Aigues Tortes. For the past eight days, these hills and valleys had been the stage of our lives. Their crossing had been the most demanding stage of my Pyrenean High Route. On no other tour had we experienced such a continuity of hard, long days. That Anna's knee had lasted such a course was a minor miracle.

Andorra had become something of a quest in itself and to have reached it on this lovely, sunny afternoon gave me another moment of pure elation. The Port de Baiau was the climax of our journey marking both the tour's high point and its effective end. For a while I stood motionless on that windless col gazing westwards at the endless panorama of peaks that stretched away to a dim nothingness. Something told me that I would never see such a sight again.

We took a round of photographs and, when I looked at my watch, couldn't believe that it was already 4 pm. Had we really taken seven hours to get here? I turned to David and said: "I'm afraid we're too late to climb the Coma Pedrosa this time. Most of us are just a bit too flaked. Anyway, there's still some way to go before we reach Arinsal."

"Guess you're probably right," he replied, shrugging his shoulders. "Pity though. It looks a good peak."

"Sorry, David, but we had best be going. Lead us down to Arinsal."

"Arinsal here we come!" shouted Julian gleefully. "Just wait till we hit that bar."

A deep snow bowl enclosed by high ridges fell away to the east and beyond the V of the Coma Valley, a bank of ballooning cumulus golden tinted by the late afternoon sun welled up above another distant range of mountains. Careless now, we skied down past a frozen lake and then more cautiously set a steeper spiralling course towards the valley bottom. Three hours later we were sitting awkwardly in the Bar Asterix at Arinsal eyed curiously by a vulgar mélange of beer-gutted Brits and an aggressive Antipodean ski bum called Barry.

Arinsal was about to close down for the season and the flotsam was making up with lager what the resort lacked for snow. For days we had been thinking of this moment but the company and atmosphere were alien so we took our glasses outside and sat until our teeth chattered with cold. We had come down to earth too quickly. Alone in the solitude of the mountains, journeying through the remotest Pyrenees, our tight world of shared adventure and cameraderie had been too fragile to withstand so sudden a re-entry to reality.

Next day, the taxi which took us from Andorra La Vella to Salardu covered in four hours the same distance that had taken us seven days. It only occurred to me later that on this tour we had been up to the Laporte average of ten hours a day and had achieved precisely what I had originally set out to do.

9

THE MAGIC MOUNTAIN
El Serrat to Fillols

Count Henri Russell, most quotable of *Pyrénéistes*, once observed that east of Andorra the Pyrenees assumed an oriental grace and languor. Less rhapsodically, David Williams was told by a rustic Catalan that the mountains of these parts were nothing but "cow hills". David's misgivings were echoed in his letter to me that "getting good conditions will be more chancy than usual I fear".

We had been corresponding about my plans for what I hoped would be the last phase of the Pyrenean High Route. Starting from El Serrat in Andorra near where we had finished last year we would close with a flourish by climbing Canigou, the magic mountain of Catalonia and the last great summit of the Pyrenees. So much for the theory. I had assumed that after last year's epic traverse from Salardu to Arinsal we would have an easy run in but, when I got down to planning the itinerary with guidebook and maps, I realised that whether we would be crossing cow hills or bull horns, this last 130 kilometre stretch would be no push-over. In the first place, the distance to be covered represented almost a quarter of the entire traverse. Secondly, Ollivier – always economical with his guidebook times – reckoned that the last two stages could each take up to 12 hours. However, the one factor that I reckoned would at last run in our favour was the weather. Conventional weather wisdom has it that once beyond Andorra, Mediterranean influences predominate. I banked on this and, time pressed as always, cut the length of the tour to an overall ten days.

I had written to Alan Wedgwood hoping to tempt him to join up for this last leg but that was not to be and the final team shook down as David Williams, now engaged to be married to the heroic Anna, Rupert Hoare, David Seddon, Roger Childs and myself. With Williams, Hoare and Seddon representing eager youth, Childs and I, concerned as ever about our fitness, took the precaution of taking a long weekend in the Sierra de Gredos a month before departure day but had our best intentions confounded by a three-day blizzard.

In a desperate effort to get up to speed, I slipped in an Eagle Ski Club Scottish ski touring weekend with the effervescent Rupert a week before leaving. We made a good hand of traversing Ben Lawyers but on the following day I almost came unstuck while attempting the traverse of Stob Ghabar and the Black Mount near Glencoe. The guidebook had recommended crampons as indispensable for this "magnificent mountaineering expedition" but for some unmemorable reason I had left mine behind. So it was that on an discomfortingly steep and icy ridge I was reduced to the humiliatiing expedient of asking Rupert if I could borrow one of his before breaking my neck.

There are arguments for and against taking crampons on long ski traverses.

Walter Good was always against them on grounds of their extra weight and for much of the Pyrenean traverse we had managed without them. But Walter was reared in the classic Swiss tradition and the forgotten art of step cutting whereas the modernist Rupert considered this a complete waste of time when you could move so much faster in crampons. He never let me forget my omission and when we discussed the equipment list, Rupert insisted that everyone should bring crampons. This posed a curious dilemma for Childs who was never a man to resist the equipment challenge yet had never owned a pair of his own. To save time and talk I offered to lend him a spare pair of mine – an unexceptional gesture which was to have unforeseen repercussions.

Following the precedent set ten years before, we drove to the Pyrenees by car in March as we had on that first unguided trip with the Wedgwood brothers and Richard Morgan. In that intervening decade, a whole chapter of my life had passed by and on this tenth anniversary I was determined that we would finish what I had started whatever came our way. Things began badly. Our departure was delayed by a P&O/NSU dispute and from the moment we arrived in France a mixture of rain, sleet and snow followed us all the way south. Then, at an unscheduled over-night stop at Neuvy Le Roi, I discovered that I had left my ski boots behind in London.

"First crampons, now ski boots," Rupert crowed. "Whatever next, John?"

The omission was remedied by an expensive and time-wasting shopping foray in Toulouse which gave Roger the excuse to buy a new set of bindings but not crampons. On reaching the foothills of the Pyrenees on the evening of the second day, I was bothered that we had already lost a precious day but relieved to find that the snow level was lower than I could remember. Disconcertingly low in fact. As we climbed out of the Ariège Valley towards the 1,920 metre Col de Puymorens, with the snow piled up high along the roadside and my old Volvo sliding all over the place, I realised that even with chains we were not going to reach El Serrat that night across the 2,408 metre Port d'Envalira. Barely managing to breast the top of the col, we scrapped the original plan and drove straight through to Font Romeu in the French Cerdagne.

Pondering on this unexpected turn of events that evening in the fusty Edwardian comfort of Font Romeu's Bellevue-Beausite hotel while helping Roger to adjust my spare crampons to the unusual configuration of his boots – trophies he had persuaded Steven Venables to part with at a knock-down price – I noted gloomily that we had already managed to reach the half way point along our intended ski route.

"Why don't we start from here and have done with it?" suggested Roger.

"You know perfectly well why," I replied testily. "We'll have to leave the car here and tomorrow morning back-track 80 kilometres to El Serrat by taxi to start from where we intended."

"I had better order a taxi then," he groaned, flipping through the hotel's brochure. "There's a character here called Monsieur Jean-Pierre Rolland who operates 'day and night over all distances in comfort'."

Monsieur Rolland was in the best tradition of Pyrenean taxi drivers and fetched up at 6.30 am precisely next morning. To simplify instructions and to secure his services, we had told him over the telephone that we wanted to be dropped just a little to the west of the popular ski resort of Soldeu, assuming that he might never have heard of the hamlet of El Serrat. This was a silly mistake for when we came clean about our ultimate destination on the way to the Col Puymorens he shook his head.

"This way no good," he frowned. "This way we cross two high passes. Col de Puymorens is high. Port d'Envalira is higher. The port is bad pass. Too much snow. Maybe not open today."

"But we crossed the Puymorens only last night," I insisted. "It can't be that much worse today."

"Okay, Messieurs," he said with a Gallic shrug. "But I tell you the *météo* is bad. There is a much faster way to El Serrat through Spain."

The drive up and over the two passes came and went without incident even though the snow ploughs had had to cut a three metre deep trench through the drift near the top of the Port d'Envalira. But we had lost more precious time and took little pleasure driving through Andorra's canyon-like valleys along a trunk road lined with duty-free superstores and tourist hotels all the way to its garish capital, Andorra La Vella.

"Bloody awful weather this," grumbled Roger. "In two hours I haven't seen a damned thing except tacky shops. Why don't we nip down into sunny Spain for a couple of days and wait for this lot to clear?"

"Do belt up, Roger," growled David.

None of us were feeling too jokey that morning but once we reached El Serrat itself, tucked away between the confluence of the heavily wooded Tristiana, Rialb and Sorteny valleys, the mood lifted. With its solid stone tiled houses and rustic calm, El Serrat was an ideal start point for our journey.

Mountaineers are privileged to enjoy a range of aesthetic and natural wonders whether they choose to do so or not. Flowers, forests, birds and wild animals, great scenery and the freedom of the hills are a part of it and, when all else is forgotten, may survive that other mountaineering essence sometimes expressed as the duel between mountain and man. Yet for me, the quintessence of ski mountaineering is the concept of quest. In this respect, the Pyrenees seem to have a quality which exceeds both aesthetics and romanticism. The journeys of its most famous travellers from Ramond de Carbonnieres, Von Parrot, Russell, Packe, Belloc and Fedden became voyages akin to pilgrimage. Belloc, who was both a sailor and walker, wrote in *Hills and the Sea* that "pilgrimage is the fulfilling of an instinct in us, the realisation of imagined horizons, the reaching of a goal".

Fedden, too, revealed his underlying motivation in the sub-title to *The Enchanted Mountains,* which he described as *A Quest in the Pyrenees.* In the silent, undisturbed streets of El Serrat, it came to me that my own ski mountaineering pilgrimage might soon be coming to an end.

The itinerary for this last leg of my Pyrenean High Route was to kick off with three easy days staying at *hostals* in Soldeu, Porte Puymorens and Font Romeu. This would be followed up with four tough days when we would have to carry all our own food, cooking and bivouac equipment and stay at unguarded huts. Co-incidentally, Font Romeu, where we had been forced to leave the car, was the natural break point for these two phases.

Already, I was regretting that I had cut the programme so tight. Although I had allowed a couple of days in hand for contingencies, we had already used up one of them but I was still banking on the geographical convention that once beyond the Porte de Puymorens it was bound to improve.

The first day of the tour was no different from any others – unloading, discarding, fixing skins, adjusting sacs and saddling up ready for the off. But this time I had a perverse feeling that if we didn't make it to the end, I might not be able to try again.

"All set?" I said to the others, pointing my skis up the valley. "It's nine o'clock already and we have a long day ahead."

"But why are we going that way?" asked Roger. "Why don't we carry on up this road and contour round?"

"Because we'll have to gain and then lose height, Roger," broke in David tersely. "The road's much the longer way round and it's a lousy route anyway."

Oh dear, I thought to myself, here we go again. This early exchange set me wondering whether navigational quibbles en route would again ripple tranquil waters.

"I'm sure that this route straight up the valley is right, Roger," I interjected. "It's a long way to Soldeu with a 1,200 metre climb to the Col de la Mine ahead of us. Let's not waste time arguing this particular toss."

"Okay, maestro," he shot back with a grin. "Just wanted to rid us of navigational ballast."

It took us five hours short of 20 minutes to reach the Col de la Mine, with scarcely a glimpse of the sun throughout but with everyone going well. Looking over the leeward eastern side of the col, I stopped short. The thigh-deep accumulations of fresh snow leading down steeply to a bank of wind-slabbed slopes looked dangerous. David Williams and Rupert skied this tricky section while Roger, David Seddon and I copped out by climbing down the slope kicking steps facing inwards.

Scudding mist and driving snow slowed progress down the steep sided upper Ransol Valley. The snow changed capriciously from perfect powder to treacherous, crusted stuff which caused Roger's new bindings to break on the turn. For all except Williams, the answer was to make do with sweeping long traverses and kick turns. Half way down the valley, we ran into two bearded climbers without skis staggering upwards in knee-deep snow under back breaking loads.

"Where are you going?" I asked.

"We go to make snow caves beneath the col," one of them replied with an inane grin.

"The snow is very dangerous on the col," I said.

"No matter," he replied. "We *montañeros*."

Lower down the valley we met a large party of pisteurs accompanied by a fat man driving a Snomobile.

"Where are you going?" I asked.

"Up the valley," they replied. "We prepare a ski mountaineering race from Ransol to El Serrat across the Collada dels Meners."

"We've just come that way," I said. "That col is very dangerous with much new snow."

"No problem," they replied. "Perhaps you like to enter as British team?"

"Let's get out of here," growled David. "I know these Andorrans. They're just crazy."

The race across the Col de la Mine never took place. That same evening, just as Roger finished a masterly piece of negotiation to secure the one studio apartment still vacant in El Tatar for our exclusive occupation, the storm that had been long impending broke at last. As we sank *mucho cerveza* and tested Good Doctor David on medical matters outside his geriatric speciality, I wondered how our friends in their snow hole might be faring.

Next morning, the successive sheets of snow that raced past the panoramic windows of our studio apartment confirmed the start of a seriously bad day. The wild swings of barometric pressure so confused my altimeter that it recorded dramatic pressure rises as the weather simply got worse and worse.

"What's your Sportplan now?" asked Roger, as we stared out gloomily into the white maelstrom outside.

"I had hoped we might follow Charles Laporte's original route to Porta across the Portella de Joan Antoni," I replied, "but in these conditions we'll have to settle for something easier."

"We could try the Grau Roig route or possibly this other one across the Port Dret to get us to the Col de Puymorens," suggested David Williams, studying the map.

"Before we make a plan, why don't we get an up-dated weather forecast and take it from there?" suggested David Seddon.

We trudged down through calf-deep snow to the ski lift only to find that the place was deserted save for a listless crowd of middle-aged German ski tourers with their mournful looking guide hanging around the lift office.

"Lift *kaputt*," said one.

No member of the staff was visible but Roger's manic gesticulations through the kiosk window eventually engaged the attentions of a pretty girl inside.

"Sorry," she said looking anything but, "today we have no weather reports here but there is definitely no skiing. See for yourself. That is why we have closed the lifts."

"But where can we get a weather report?" Roger persisted. "Can we telephone from here please?"

"No, you cannot but here is a number." She slipped a piece of paper with a number scribbled on it in ballpoint under the glass grille.

Back at the *hostal*, an automatically recorded telephone weather message warned of high winds, extreme avalanche risk and a continuation of the bad weather for the foreseeable future.

"What are we going to do now, John?" asked Roger. "This weather looks set in for days. I can't see much point in hanging around here. We could easily nip down into Spain and find some fun places while it clears."

This time, I could see that he meant it.

"The tour's barely begun, Roger," I replied. "We've got no spare days in hand and we're not going to cop out here."

"But we can't begin to move in this weather," he persisted.

"Maybe it will improve," I replied unconvincingly. "Anyway, we've already wasted a couple of hours hanging around so let's at least get ourselves to Soldeu. Maybe from there we can catch a bus or hire a taxi to give us a start up the road."

What would normally have been a stroll up the hill to Soldeu took half an hour's skinning through a horizontal blizzard. The streets were thronged with vacant looking skiers from Barcelona adulterated by a rabble of foul-mouthed Brits who were wandering around aimlessly in the expectation of better weather. The information office was shut so we took refuge in the bar of the Hotel de la

Poste placed directly opposite the bus station and taxi rank.

"I can't stand this bloody place," confessed David. "I once spent an entire season here as a Ski Club of Great Britain rep."

He had kept this dark secret to himself but I saw what he meant. Two hours on, after we had each eaten two expensive omelettes and drunk several rounds of beer, the barmaid proprietoress was as unhelpful and bolshie as she had been when we first arrived. The promised bus to Grau Roig never fetched up and even Roger had failed to raise a local taxi. As morning turned to afternoon with no let-up in the weather I came to a decision.

"It's too late now to try any of those fancy routes but somehow we've got to get to the Col de Puymorens tonight or abandon the traverse."

It was Roger's sweep through the pages of the Andorra La Vella telephone directory that eventually broke the impasse. At 1.15 pm a small, wizened man appeared at the door of the bar looking around for *"Engleez"*.

"My taxi is outside," he said in Spanish, "but I can only take three of you to the Col d'Envalira at a time. I will then come back for the other two."

Roger and I did the first shift. In that weather it was difficult to envisage the Tour de France coming this way in summer. The roadside was invisible, several cars had been abandoned in the snow and the snow plough, which passed on its way down the hill like a leviathan, left barely an impression of its tyres in the snow. When the driver suddenly stopped at a building that looked like a deserted Siberian petrol station, I had lost all sense of time or direction.

"I stop here," he announced.

"Where are we?" asked Roger.

"This is the Porte," he replied. "You can't stay here but you can stay at an hotel at Pas de la Casa down the road. I will now return to Soldeu to fetch your friends."

A sudden gust of wind blew us across the tarmac to the other side of the road like dried leaves. We pushed through a doorway which said *"Bar"*. The place was completely deserted save for its bartender. We bought ourselves two large *cafés con leche* after which Roger put in a quick kip. At 3 pm the five of us were edging our way down the hillside through the blizzard, past foresaken pistes until we reached an abandoned lift complex and the rash of tower chalets which make up the resort of Pas de la Casa. From here the way to the Col de Puymorens lay straight on down the road.

The road by which we had come only the day before was now impassable to vehicles but still made a serviceable skiing piste as it sliced through head-high banks of snow. But as we were gliding past the Andorran customs post, two gendarmes with revolvers emerged from hiding and gesticulated to us to stop.

"Where are you going?" bellowed the Sergeant at a range of two metres.

"To the Col du Puymorens," I replied.

"You cannot go to the Col du Puymorens," the man retorted. "There is nothing there – nowhere for you to stay. You must go back."

"We are *ski randonneurs*," I replied, pointing meaningfully at my skis. "We can stay at Porte Puymorens or Porta."

"You can go nowhere. You can stay nowhere," he bawled out. "This road is closed. It is dangerous to ski." And as an afterthought, "You can only ski on mountains."

We went over the same ground a second time with the red faced Sergeant's minion enacting a mime that if we continued we would lose fingers, noses and other vital parts from frostbite. The decibel level dropped a fraction when Roger explained that we were only seeking the Sergeant's advice about the road but it was clear that at this Andorran outpost *ils ne passeront pas*.

"We had better make a strategic retreat," I muttered to Roger.

"Merci, merci Monsieur. Vous êtes très gentil," we mumbled as we started back up the road. Some way on, after checking that the *douane* had returned to their post, we climbed off the road up the hillside. With visibility less than a hundred metres, it was simple enough to traverse parallel to the line of the road higher up the hill and then re-join it a few hundred metres further out of sight of the customs post. The road made for easy skiing and within an hour we had reached a junction marked by a signpost which pointed to Aix les Thermes in one direction and the Col de Puymorens in the other.

The storm that had dogged us all day reserved its paroxysms for the evening. It was already dark when we reached the Col de Puymorens where an icy wind did its best to shred the skin off our faces. This "Khyber of the Cerdagne" always had a bad reputation but I couldn't believe it to be the same place that we had limped across only three days before. The wind was gusting down simultaneously from Pic Carlitte and the Andorran mountains to create an inferno of whirling snow with us in the middle.

"Where's that parador you promised us?" Roger shouted in my ear.

The map marked a *petite hostellerie de montagne* and when we had groped our way off the pass bent double by the wind, a building's outline not far below gave me a surge of relief but when we tried the door it wouldn't budge an inch. The place was deserted.

"Bloody hell," I growled to David. "Perhaps that bolshie gendarme was right after all. We'll have to carry on down the road to Porte de Puymorens."

Suddenly, I felt cold and tired. The prospect of having to flog on down the valley through this blinding snow-storm appalled me. I cursed myself for

Sastrugi. The Porteille de Mantet

carrying on through this storm when the sensible thing would have been to stop off at Pas de la Casa – by now we would be propping up the bar about to have a slap-up supper. In trying to stick to the schedule, I had lost perspective.

"Look, John, I can see a light," shouted Rupert. "There's a building up there with a light on."

Again we started to climb up towards the col and once again the outline of a building emerged through the murk. Rupert was already at the top of a flight of icy wooden steps banging on the door with the end of his ski stick. Soon enough, the iron latch was drawn back and framed in the doorway by a yellow backcloth of light were two silhouettes.

"What d'you want?" The heavily built man with a drooping George Brassens moustache seemed none too pleased to see us.

"We want to stay here the night," replied Roger.

"This isn't a hotel," said the man but he now looked quickly across to his companion.

"What are you doing here," asked the other man who was now standing alone at the threshold.

"We're *ski randonneurs*," I broke in. "We've come from the Col d'Envalira, We want somewhere to stay the night."

"Ah," he said, "*ski randonneurs*. You'd better come inside."

We trooped in one by one, shaking the snow off our clothing like dogs.

"Welcome. My name is Bernard. This is a youth hostel but you are lucky to have found it open. I'm the guardian here. The young people who were staying here have had to go home because of the weather so you can stay here tonight. Please have supper and a shower too if you wish. My staff will serve you." Bernard was fair haired, with clear direct eyes.

Over our supper I explained our plans. "We're trying to complete the last stage of a Pyrenean ski traverse," I told him. "Tomorrow, we want to traverse Pic Carlitte by the East Couloir and then stay the night at Font Romeu."

He raised his eyebrows slightly and made a non-committal grunt.

"But this weather looks very bad," I continued. "Can you give us tomorrow's forecast and tell us something about the route?"

"The weather's been like this for the past five days," he grimaced. "The Col de Puymorens really catches it. It won't have cleared by tomorrow. To traverse Carlitte would be '*un fol espoir*'. That mountain is avalanche prone and particularly dangerous just now. So are any routes up the Garcie Valley or the HRP Cortal Roussou route."

"Can you suggest an alternative? We must reach Font Romeu. What about the route north of Carlitte over the Porteille de Grave and then down the Grave Valley?"

"That would be a very long day in these conditions and I don't recommend it," he replied. "However, you might be able to get up the east side of the Lanous Valley tomorrow and spend the night at the Baraque des Ingénieurs just below the Lanous lake. If the weather really improves, you could try the Grave Valley route to Font Romeu but you'd probably have to make an intermediate stop at the Lac des Bouillouses CAF Hut."

"What is this Baraque des Ingénieurs?" I asked.

"It's an unguarded old building at the top of the Lanous Valley mainly used by summer walkers. It will certainly be open but you'll probably have to dig it out."

Things were not working out the way I had planned. A diversion of more than two days would make it impossible to complete the traverse but Carlitte was a prize I had long coveted.

The bad weather continued over night and at 7 am next morning a vicious blizzard was whipping across the col. No question of leaving while this lasted so we filled in time helping a distraught French couple dig out the car they had had to abandon just below the col and then got warm push-starting them down the hill towards Porta. I felt us grinding to a halt.

"We can't just sit here," I argued over coffee. "We've got to keep moving despite the weather."

"I agree," said Rupert. "But where to?"

"We should follow Bernard's advice and get up to the Baraque des Ingénieurs," I replied. "From there we can ski on to Font Romeu if the weather clears. If not, we can come back here."

"We'll telephone you the moment we get to Font Romeu," I promised Bernard as we emerged from the youth hostel to face the storm for the second time that morning.

"It should only take you four hours to get to the Baraque," were his last words.

Skiing off the Col de Puymorens to the valley bottom through the blinding eddies that came with the vicious *Tramontana* wind, we narrowly missed demolition by a monster snow-plough powering up the road and taking all before it.

The Lanous Valley was like an oasis of calm after all the noise and bluster up above. The snow never let up and it was never possible to see across the valley but at least we gave ourselves the impression of going somewhere with an objective. Bernard had assured us that the route would be straightforward but I soon realised that it wasn't going to be like that. Early on Rupert almost fell into the river when forcing his way through a willow thicket and soon after that we must have missed the line of the path, if it ever existed. With the lie of the land almost invisible, the business of working our way up an enclosed valley through dense forest was claustrophobic and confusing. Pursuing a strictly logical line of march that followed its natural contours took us through an obstacle course of inclines, dips and hollows and included an awkward traverse across a dodgy snow slope where a slip would have involved an icy plunge. Eventually, I knew that we were bound to come out at the top of the Lanous Valley but in the process we were all becoming progressively wet, cold and weary without seeming to get anywhere.

"I suppose we're doing the right thing trying to reach this wretched hut," said Rupert to me in an aside. "We're not moving fast enough for my liking and the weather's not getting any better."

"Let's just keep going and see how things pan out," I replied. But David Williams was next in line.

"Frankly, John, I don't feel too happy about this. I'm sure that we'll make the hut okay tonight but the weather's getting progressively worse. If it goes on like this, we could find ourselves stuck up at the hut unable to retreat for days because of the avalanche risk. Maybe we should call it a day and get down to Porta while we still can."

I would never take either Rupert or David's views lightly but I had got it fixed in my own mind that retreat at this stage would be tantamount to abandoning the traverse.

"We're well past the point of no return," I replied thickly. "I don't want to turn back now. The hut can't be that far away."

As we were speaking, David had pulled out the map.

"I don't think we're as far on as you think," he said shaking his head. "On my reckoning, there's still a good way to go. I'm also worried about Roger. He's looking very tired."

Roger might have looked tired and was certainly moving slowly but that didn't over-concern me. I knew his mettle.

"You're probably right about the Baraque," I replied, "but don't worry about Roger. He'll keep going for as long as the rest of us. I don't like this weather either but I'm not prepared to retreat down this bloody valley with all this new snow." He had touched a raw nerve. I was determined to carry on.

Six hours after leaving the Col de Puymorens, we reached the Baraque des Ingeniéurs tucked away in a forest clearing. We had taken two hours longer to get here than Bernard had estimated. David's progress assessment had also been correct. I couldn't understand why we had been so slow. On that first day when we had crossed most of Andorra, we had covered twice the distance and climbed twice this height in only seven hours. Most of the party were looking played out.

As Bernard had predicted, the entrance to the Baraque was completely blocked with snow. When we eventually dug our way through the drift and forced open the door, we stepped back in time. This wasn't so much a hut as a proper house built in 1910 for a Monsieur Lafon, the engineer who had constructed the Lanous dam. Above the mantlepiece over the chasmic fireplace were faded period photographs. Below it the snow had filled the place to table-top height. This once familiar sight came as a shock. So often in the French Pyrenees we had arrived at huts which had been totally engulfed but in recent years had become used to better ordered Catalan ways.

"Are you sure this is the right place?" queried David. "There's another building over there. Let's take a look at it."

It was now after 5 pm with the blizzard unabated. While the others set about shifting snow from the Baraque's inside, he and I plodded 50 metres to a newer building.

"This must be the modern hut," pronounced David as we dug our way through yet another snow-drift to get to the door.

"Unfortunately, the bloody things locked."

In the Baraque's refrigerator-cum-living-room it was back to the Epp routine of sawing logs with Swiss Army knives and splitting the pieces with ice axes to feed Doctor David's fires. David Williams manufactured some "mattresses" from a heap of plastic fillings he had discovered in the rat-infested wood shed; I managed to light the stove in a bedroom and Roger cooked supper.

Spindrift blew in through cracks and crannies with every gust of wind spinning fine snow traceries across the floor. Despite the fire, the air temperature remained such that our frozen anoraks, over-trousers, socks and gloves suspended on nails from wooden beams in the ceiling wouldn't drip, let alone dry. Yet for all the cold and discomfort life was sweet. We had made safe haven and, as I glanced round at the semi-circle of woollen hatted, bearded faces glowing red in the reflection of the leaping flames eating Roger's macaroni and *chorizo* houch, I felt lucky to be with such friends.

We had shared many adventures together and well knew each others' strengths and weaknesses. Our conversation could survive comfortably on silly jokes and facetious comment. David Williams was *le Moniteur,* David Seddon *the Good Doctor* aka *Avicenna*, Roger *le Vieux Sage,* myself *le savant* while Rupert had a number of sobriquets including *Pyrénéiste Aspirant* and *Hermann Hoare*. We were a happy ship.

Yet, as I snuggled down into the sleeping bag around which I had wrapped my bivouac tent to keep warm, a darker mood descended. With the wind still shrieking outside, our fate was once again being determined by the weather. Where was the "oriental grace and langour" that Henri Russell had wittered on about? Barometric pressure was still falling so there was only the faintest hope that it would clear by tomorrow. Almost half the time I had allotted for this trip had already been used up. With only five scheduled days left, I cursed myself for allowing pressures of work to cut the tour from its original fourteen days to ten – even more for prejudicing what little time was left by persisting with my obsession to climb Carlitte, the mountain of Charlemagne, especially when Bernard had made it quite clear that it would be crazy to attempt it and difficult to reach Font Romeu from here within two days. So much effort, energy and more had been spent getting this far. The Pyrenees weren't going to go away but at this critical moment I had swung off course and there was no guarantee that next year anyone else would want to go another round.

When nature's call forced me out of the Baraque before dawn next morning and spindrift had filled my trousers before mission accomplished I knew that we would have to retreat forthwith.

"Forget about Carlitte or reaching Font Romeu across the Porteille de la Grave in this weather," I told the others over breakfast. "Avalanches apart, we would be fighting this blizzard all the way."

"What's your plan then?" asked Rupert.

"If there's the faintest hope of completing the traverse we've got to reverse the Lanous Valley to Porte du Puymorens and find a taxi from there to Font Romeu."

"That's if they're still running," said Roger.

We gave the weather a couple of hours to clear but when it didn't we quit the Baraque at 10.15 am. If anything, the driving snow and visibility were worse than yesterday but at least it was downhill all the way. David Williams let rip through the fresh powder snow and it should have been a fun descent but the thought that we had almost certainly blown the traverse made my legs feel leaden and, when turning on a rock, I tore a great chunk out of my ski bottom. We set a more direct course down the valley but it still took four hours to reach the crêperie at Porte de Puymorens where the egg and ham crepes were as delectable as the *glutea majora* of the waitress who served them.

It was still snowing as our taxi followed in the footsteps of Charlemagne down the gloomy Carole Valley – a place of ghosts which reflected my sombre mood. But when we emerged onto the Cerdagne plain, it stopped snowing for the first time since we had landed in France six days earlier. Unlike the run of Pyrenean valleys, which are characterised by deep-cut gorges and turbulent rivers, the Cerdagne is a smiling upland plain with the highest sunshine levels in the Pyrenees. Although geographically part of

Spain and basically Catalan in character, it has been French, save for the tiny Spanish enclave of Livia, ever since the 1659 Treaty of the Pyrenees.

By the time we had re-occupied our old rooms at Font Romeu's Bellevue-Beausite hotel and relaxed in a hot bath there was a new lightness in the air. When I got back to the hotel after supper with my newly repaired skis and looked out from our bedroom balcony, the clouds were lifting and directly across the plain the summit snows of a huge black mountain shone faintly in the sun's afterglow.

"That must be Puigmal," I whistled softly to Roger. "That's the mountain we must cross tomorrow to get to Spain."

I leapt out of bed next morning, padded across the room barefoot, flung back the curtains and walked out onto the balcony. The sky was clean washed and pale blue save for a flush of tiny clouds suspended high above the hills that encircled the Cerdagne, whose scattered ochre-coloured villages were stirring into life under the first rays of the sun. Away to the south-west, bounding the plain like an interminable wall receding imperceptibly into a blue dimness, rose the 1,500 metre high scarp of the snow-capped Sierra del Cadi. Their name, the *Mountains of the Judge*, still commemorates the memory of the Moorish high tide that engulfed this land over a thousand years ago.

We had all been sleeping in the same room and I burst in on them excitedly: "Take a look at this amazing view. The sun's shining and it's a wonderful day."

At breakfast there was a new air of expectancy with every minute precious.

"Okay, John, what's the new Sportplan?" asked Roger.

"On with the traverse. We've cut things a bit fine but we've still got four days in hand."

"How far to Canigou?"

"Just over 70 kilometres."

"That's over 17 kilometres a day," said the Doctor thoughtfully.

"That's the average," I replied, "but it doesn't work quite like that. The first two days are short but we finish up with two marathons."

"Like what?" asked Roger.

"Like twelve hours a day."

"Grief," he gasped. "We had better get weaving immediately."

Jean-Pierre Rolland, the same taxi man who had taken us to El Serrat, now agreed to drive us to the mid-way telesiege station at the Chalet Aris half way up the Err Valley to save us time. Throughout the drive, he was harrassed incessantly on the telephone by his wife who kept telling him to ditch us at Err to pick up a better fare. Jean-Pierre resolutely kept his bargain and, after dropping us at the lift, our luck still held when two mountain gendarmes, well disposed when we had told them our plans, persuaded a less pliant *pisteur* to let us on without tickets.

At the top of the lift, Rupert and David Williams shot off like rockets towards La Tosse, a peaklet that marks the start of the frontier ridge that leads the Cerdagne's highest peak, the 2,910 metre Puigmal. After six days of continuous bad weather, I was worried that the build-up of snow would create dangerous cornices and avalanche prone slopes but when we reached La Tosse, the bumpy ridge that rolled away towards the massive hump of Puigmal was broad shouldered and almost bare of snow. The ferocious winds of the last week had blown most of it and what remained had turned to ice. Danger took the form of a bitter wind blowing across from the north which scarified our faces.

"I'm putting on my *harscheisen*," announced Rupert decisively. "With all this ice, we could easily be blown off the ridge."

I followed his example but after trying to climb a short incline, which undig-nifyingly landed me on my backside, switched to crampons. As I fiddled with the straps, Rupert sidled up.

"Putting on crampons already, John? That Scottish experience must have taught you something."

"Just mountaincraft and anticipation, Rupert," I replied, still struggling with the frozen straps.

"Good heavens," he blurted out, "I can't believe you're still using strap-ons. I thought they had gone out with the ark. Those look like ten pointers. They must be pre-war."

"Rupert, these lightweight crampons were made for me by Grivel of Cour-mayeur just about the time you were born. Those were the days of the great forge-masters."

"Anvil bashers you mean," sniggered Rupert. "Mine are Grivels too but you've got museum pieces there and technology has moved on a bit."

He was really beginning to enjoy himself but when I diverted his attention to a solo French ski mountaineer who had just overtaken us with a flanking move-ment, his competitive instincts took over.

"Damned Frenchman's managed to get ahead of us," he snorted. "We shouldn't be hanging around nattering. I'll keep going if you don't mind."

By now Roger had closed the gap and seeing that I had put on crampons decided to follow suit.

"Hope these things you've lent me are a proper modern set," he grunted as he grappled with their metre long straps.

"Rupert's always strong on equipment."

"They're not step-ins," I replied, "but they're my newest and they're even big enough to fit your boots."

By now, everyone except Rupert who had vanished over a hump in pursuit of the Frenchman, had decided to climb this part of the ridge in crampons but Roger was comparatively new to the game.

"We really must keep moving Roger," I said impatiently.

"Bloody things won't fasten properly," he grunted.

"Why don't you two carry on," suggested David Williams. "They look as if they need some adjustment." He had already whipped out his repair kit and was now squatting in the snow with a minute spanner.

"Okay then," I replied. "We'll push on slowly."

Actually, my immediate objective was to try to pip Rupert to the top of Puigmal. Although he had got a good start, he would be hard pushed to move as fast on skis over this rough ground as I could with crampons. As we approached the summit, I was closing fast when he rumbled the challenge.

"Close run thing that, Rupert," I said, making a supreme effort to appear nonchalant as my chest was near bursting.

"Oh, the Frenchman you mean," he replied slyly. "I reckon I saw him off."

When I had recovered myself sufficiently, we both looked back down the ridge we had just pounded up. David Williams was coming up very fast, with David Seddon not far behind. Much further down in a little hollow a more distant figure had come to a halt.

"What on earth's happened to Roger?" I asked Rupert. "He's miles behind. What's he doing down there."

When David Williams joined us on the summit I asked him, "Is anything the matter with Roger?"

"Nothing that I could see," he replied. "I fixed his crampons but he keeps fiddling around with them. I can't understand why he's being so slow. This is our first good weather and we must make the most of it."

When Roger rolled in another thirty-five minutes later grinning sheepishly, we didn't think it that funny.

"We really must move faster than this Roger," I remonstrated peevishly. "We'll never get through the big days at this pace."

"What's the problem?" he replied, taken aback. "Surely, we're not that far from Nuria. It's a beautiful day and, anyway, I've had every sort of problem with those bloody crampons of yours."

"Maybe," I retorted, "but we still can't afford to dawdle." With that, both David and Rupert had a go at him.

Roger said nothing but as he turned away, I could see that the criticism had stung.

We skied off the summit and then straight down the valley through excellent snow to reach Nuria in 45 minutes. It was only 2 pm. There had been no need to hurry and still less to chide Roger whose real problem had been a pair of crampons designed to fit no known make of boot.

Even in Spain, where the extraordinary is commonplace, Nuria's combination of ski resort, abbey church, tourist centre and place of pilgrimage tucked away in the heart of the mountains is miraculous. It occupies the site of a sixth century monastery founded by the first king of the Visigoths to be converted to Catholicism but was re-built in the eleventh century after its destruction by the Moors to commemorate the shepherd who saw the Virgin Mary.

Having completed the course within guidebook time and enjoyed our first day of good weather, this should have been the ideal place to enjoy a celebratory alfresco lunch along with all the other bronzed, shirt-sleeved skiers. But feathers had been ruffled and after a subdued drink, Roger announced that he would be taking the 4 pm train down the Nuria Gorge to Ribas for a change of scene. I wasn't going to see the party fragment so we all trooped after him into a carriage filled with noisy Catalan schoolchildren. The cog railway that descends this tremendous gorge defies both engineering and economics to link Nuria with the outside world but another wonder was Roger's gift for communication with the young. Long before we had disembarked, he had picked up a gaggle of new friends. But all was not yet well within our own party. Words spoken in haste on the top of Puigmal had upset equilibrium. Supper was a stilted affair with none of the nonsense that usually passed for conversation. What should have marked a happy climax had ended on a strained note. Before we went to bed I told Roger that we would all be lost without him. His reply was monosyllabic. That night a fox barked throughout my waking hours. Nuria had not been our sanctuary.

"What's the weather like today then?" Roger's voice was muffled by the blanket he had draped over his head.

"It's another great day, Roger," I replied, gazing out of our bedroom window towards the ring of sunlit snow peaks above Nuria. "Let's have some breakfast."

The sleepy Señora whom we had had to rouse to make coffee explained that yesterday evening the *hostal*'s helpful manager had fallen on the ice and dislocated his shoulder. This misfortune generated some black jokes and by the end of the meal relations were back to normal.

"What's the programme for today?" opened the Good Doctor with what had become the conventional conversational gambit.

"If the good weather holds, we should be in for another easy day," I replied breezily.

"Remind me what's involved," said Roger.

"Guidebook time to the Refuge Ull de Terr is between five to seven hours," I replied. "We just follow the Mulleras Valley as far as the Col de Neuf Croix and from the frontier ridge we'll climb the Pic de la Vache. We'll be climbing about 1,000 metres, descending 800 metres and covering ten kilometres overall."

"Those bloody cow peaks at last," exclaimed David Williams. But for once this wasn't to be David Williams's day nor were the cow peaks that placid.

On leaving Nuria we made a steeply angled traverse above the Mulleras Valley which gave an icy ride over awkward, bumpy ground when the better ski route would have been straight up the valley bed. The 800 metre climb to the Col de Neuf Croix, so named after the nine climbers killed here by freak lightning, culminated in a steep headwall where Rupert dropped his prescription sunglasses. Rupert's extra 100 metres of descent and ascent might have explained why I managed to pip him to the top of the 2,826 metre Pic de la Vache.

"Must be another British ski mountaineering first, Rupert," I called across to him while we took a short breather on the summit. "Bad luck about your specs. That extra climb must have taken it out of you."

"Cow peaks aren't worthy of record," he retorted.

"Come, come, Rupert," I chided. "This is today's high point and the views are magnificent."

And so they were. From here, the Cerdagne looked like a field of gold. Directly ahead of us, the elegant Pic de l'Enfer belied its lowly altitude and to the south an intricate pattern of wooded ranges dwindled away into dim mystery.

Only then did I notice that David Williams was leaning on his sticks breathing heavily. The fitness and performance gap between the two of us had been widening with every passing year but, until that moment, I hadn't taken on board the significance of my holding the lead for most of today.

"What's the matter David? You don't look too well."

"I don't know what's wrong with me," he replied quietly.

"My stomach's upset and my legs feel like jelly."

I had never known David ill on any trip. I had taken it for granted that he was as impervious to sickness as he was to other mortal failings in the mountains, but then I remembered his attack of meninghitis only two years back and my stomach tightened.

"Let's stop here and have a rest," I suggested. "We're making good time. No point in rushing things. The weather's fine and the Ull de Terr Hut's supposed to be guarded."

"Thanks John but I would prefer to push on while I can and get to the hut as soon as possible," he replied.

He might have been feeling dreadful but his skiing never showed it. He was still the man to follow as we swept down the steep *nevees* of the Col de Tiraptz into the deep bowl that holds the headwaters of the Freser River. It was very hot now and the sun burned through the backs of our shirts as we climbed through soft, heavy snow towards the Col de la Marenna.

Now for the first time in my life I saw the great mountain that I knew could only be Canigou. It rose far away in the east, massive in form yet floating ethereally above the horizon, more a concept rather than reality. This last blue mountain had for so long been the object of my quest that I felt a sudden urge to take a group photograph. But Roger was now in playful mood and when he insisted on striking silly poses the moment passed.

Despite the hitches en route, we reached the superbly sited Refuge Ull de Terr, a handsome modern hut built of mellow granite, well within guidebook time but when I tried the door it was bolted.

"I thought you said this hut was guarded," said Rupert reproachfully.

"That's what the guidebook said," I retorted. "I'm afraid that we're out of luck but let's make David comfortable as soon as we can."

A shy Spanish climber mysteriously appeared from nowhere and pointed the way to the hut's winter quarters. These were inconveniently located under the hut's wide verandah, which in summer would have been a sun trap but which now provided a roof for the snowdrift which blocked both door and windows. Once we had dug our way inside, the place resembled an under-pavement coal cellar.

"Cold, damp and badly ventilated," muttered Doctor David. "Just perfect for a sickbay."

As David Williams slipped unobtrusively into his sleeping bag, I said to the Doctor, "He's still shivering."

"Just keep him quiet and I'll get a fire going," he replied, busying himself to the task.

Galen, Avicenna or just plain consultant geriatrician? David Seddon was all and everything that represented medicine to us. Though we teased him about his degrees from both Oxford and Cambridge and the string of letters after his name, he was ever the most stalwart companion who had become and was to remain an automatic choice for my ski mountaineering tours. The geriatrics' criticism of David was his reluctance to dispense prophylactics and placebos on call but, without him, neither intelligent nor intelligible conversation would have been possible. Mercifully, the range of acceptable conversational topics was proscribed. Women – save for Child's maudlin reminiscences of Carmen Valdosera – were never discussed and when Rupert's inexhaustible thesaurus of matters mountaineering paled, the one topic of abiding mutal interest was medicine.

Instructive hours were spent in storm-bound huts discussing and debating with the Good Doctor a host of medical issues ranging from the common problems of the urinary tract to the more esoteric aspects of cranial osteopathy, anopheles induced Aids and the side effects of radon gas. Although willing to put us right on the philosophy of medicine, he was also prepared to discuss Babylonian trepanning techniques, Assyrian suppositories and ant mandible sutures. However, alternative medicine, palmistry, physiography, aromatherapy or herbalism tended to presage eye rolling and apoplexy.

The Good Doctor had also made petrol or paraffin stoves something of a speciality yet I was never as confident about his fire management as his medicine for, in this department, he manifested symptoms which another specialist might have diagnosed as Pyrophiliac Rage. A classic case study was the conflagration that he now created in the winter quarters of the Refuge Ull de Terr. This may have been a delayed reaction to the unlightable log syndrome or a case of pine log/ice axe split denial. Surrounded as we were by heaps of ready cut wood with none of the usual restraints, Galen became Vulcan and let his fires rip. As he piled log upon log, the sick bay filled with dense smoke, Roger, Rupert and I quietly evacuated the place. We were wary of interfering with the prescribed treatment yet wondered how the patient could survive it. Mercifully, David had chosen a bunk just above floor level so escaped the worst of the waist high smog. Another useful side to this essay into incendiarism was to clear the hut of the three Catalans who had booked in before us but who now opted to sleep on the open verandah.

For the first time on this tour, we were back to basic touring rations of soup, salami, cheese, ships' biscuits, dried fruit and custard. David's illness had drawn us even closer together, though like the Doctor's fires, it hung over us like a black cloud. On this of all nights Roger, Rupert and the Doctor, their vocal chords irritated by the smoke, snored both solo and in unison. As each woke the others up, they played the game of Snoring Scapegoat to gales of silly laughter. David slept throughout.

The wind never stopped gusting throughout the night. With only two scheduled touring days left, I spent most of it pondering on life's slings and arrows and cups being dashed but more particularly on how we were going to get David safely off this mountain, let alone manage the next 25 kilometres stage to the Refuge de Marialles with a sick man when the guidebook's estimated time was twelve hours.

Of all those who had accompanied me on the Pyrenean High Route, David most closely shared my own mountaineering philosophy. It was ridiculous that I should be much the same age as his father, Bansall, yet I had never felt a generation gap between us. That David, our spearhead, the complete ski mountaineer, should have fallen at this last fence was a cruel cut but unless he had made a miraculous recovery by tomorrow morning, we would have to scrap what remained of the tour.

At 6 am Rupert's digital watch buzzed reveille to be followed by his Butlinesque "Wake up everybody." I slid out of my bunk and padded across to the window. The wind was still blowing strongly but the dawn was pink and the skies were clear. I walked gingerly across to David's bunk. He was already awake and preparing myself for the worst I whispered to him: "How are you feeling this morning, David?"

"Don't worry, John," he replied, as if he were reading my thoughts, "I think I'm going to be okay."

"Are you sure?" I said. "This is one helluva long stage but we don't have to go all the way to the Marialles Hut. We can always stay at the Refuge Pla Guillem. Anyway, it's a cold but lovely day."

He knew exactly what was involved for he and I had often pored over the maps and guidebook together. "Let's just see how we go," he grinned back.

With David back in the frame, the atmosphere at breakfast crackled with expectancy but we were all too hyped up to talk much about the day which lay ahead. We left the hut at 7.15 am with the wind still blowing hard from the north-west as it had done for days. The skies were clear and as we climbed out of the valley towards the Porteille de Mantet, we might have been in Antartica for the freezing wind had transformed the slopes into alternate layers of *neve*, ice and *sastrugi*. *Sastrugi* – formations of frozen snow waves – are a common phenomenon in Polar regions but to encounter them in the Pyrenees was a novelty. On the northern slopes of the frontier ridge overlooking the Pla da Coma Armada, we crossed a sea of *sastrugi* but blown along by the wind, we sped along the ice fields which interspersed its successive lips and troughs like ships in full sail.

Three hours on we had reached the kilometre long passage beneath the Pic Colom which the map signifies with the dotted lines of a *passage délicat*. We were about to leave Spain forever for, despite being named Esquerdes de Rotja, the long ridge that now flighted north-eastwards like an arrow towards Canigou lay wholly in France. This rocky passage involved some scrambling, with everyone except David Williams swopping crampons for ski. Again, I kept wondering how different our progress might have been had we been attempting this section in bad weather.

Back again on easier ground, we swopped back to skis and skimmed along this sweeping ridge like a flight of choughs for 12 kilometres at an almost constant altitude of 2,300 metres. Densely white cumulus clouds billowed up from a haze that marked the distant plains of Roussillon and unknown snow peaks peeped up coyly from beyond the valley of the Tet. We were now on a roll and moved as if in a dream. The wind had dropped to a whisper and, with the sun behind us, we cruised along the crest of the last great snow ridge of the Pyrenees uplifted high above a maze of deep shadowed valleys and blue green ranges that fell away on either side of us. Always before us rose the great mass of Canigou.

We had been concentrating so intently on the way ahead that I had almost forgotten about the hut at Pla Guilhem which I had earlier set as our objective for that night. Throughout the day David Williams had been moving so effortlessly, with us in his slipstream, that it now seemed incredible that only yesterday he had been a sick man. When David Seddon and I closed up, he and Rupert were waiting by some sort of obelisk.

"Well done everybody!" I burst out. "A fantastic run and a great lead David. You've been moving like a train. But where's the Pla Guilhem Hut? It should be just around here."

"You're at the hut," replied David, pointing behind me. "You're almost standing on it."

I swung round on our tracks and saw that we had just missed skiing over its eaves. The rest was buried under a mass of snow which had filled the inside to ceiling height.

"Bloody Hell!" I ejaculated. "We'll never be able to shift this lot."

Suddenly, I felt tired and uncertain what to do next. We had not stopped all day and the prospect of digging out this hut appalled me. For once, I had forgotten about time but now its immediacy came back. It must be getting late. I glanced at my watch. Only 2.30 pm? That couldn't be right. I distinctly remembered that we had left the Ull de Terr Hut at 7.15 am. On that analysis, we had only been going for just over seven hours. This must be the wrong place.

"What do you make the time, David?" I asked wearily. "My watch seems to have stopped."

"Just after 2.30," he replied with a grin. "We've demolished the guidebook time and I've got a suggestion. Why don't we carry on over the Puig Roja and stay tonight at the Refuge Arago. That way we'll lose no height and be perfectly positioned to climb Canigou tomorrow. It would also make a classic finish to a great day."

I looked at him warily. I had heard this kind of talk somewhere before. To have almost completed this stage in just over seven hours and cut the guidebook time by over four made this the fastest time we had ever recorded. But to push it still further?

"Let's have another look at the map," I said guardedly.

"As you can see, my route over the Pic des Sept Hommes and the Puig Roja is just a variant of the *Haute Randonnee Pyrénéenne*," David enthused.

I stared to where his finger was pointing. A ski touring route was clearly marked but it would involve traversing another big mountain block to the south-west of Canigou.

"But David, we've already had one helluva day," I began slowly. "This would add on at least another eight kilometres and a 450 metres climb. Obviously, we can't stay here but we can easily get ourselves down to the Marialles Hut."

"But that way we would be losing over 500 metres in height," he insisted. "We would also be risking two dicey dotted line sections through enclosed valleys – one this afternoon and the other tomorrow morning. We can cut all that out completely if we take my route to the Refuge Arago."

Theoretically, he was right on both counts but for once I couldn't agree with him. Despite yesterday's relapse I didn't doubt that he could go the full distance but the rest of us weren't necessarily up to it. At that very moment Roger came clattering in feigning complete exhaustion with his usual puffing and panting pantomime.

"What's all this then 'ere," he gasped.

"You've just arrived at Pla Guillem, Roger," said Rupert portentously. "The hut's buried and we're debating how best to dig it out."

"You must be bloody joking, Rupert," snapped Roger, "I've already done all the digging I'm going to on this tour."

"David's got an alternative plan," I added quickly and then went through it. "However, after all we've done today, I believe it's trying to do too much and could bust us for another big day tomorrow. The snow's completely settled so we can ski down to the Marialles Hut this afternoon perfectly safely. If the weather does break tomorrow we'll probably have to forget about Canigou anyway but I don't think it will."

I had stopped making predictions about Pyrenean weather long ago but, as I looked up to the purple sky framing the snowy mass of Canigou, I felt confident that I was right.

"Well, I'm definitely *not* in favour of having to flog up another mountain today," said Roger. "I agree with John. We should get down to the Marialles Hut."

Most of us were too tired to appreciate that last ski run of the day through the pine trees but it only needed half an hour to get to the hut and gave the added satisfaction of completing the Ull de Ter to Marialles leg in under eight hours.

One feature of the Marialles which I hadn't mentioned when we had been debating the options at Pla Guillem was the guidebook's assessment of it – filthy, with nothing inside but six dilapidated iron bedsteads. So, as we approached the clearing in the forest, I anticipated recrimination and an uncomfortable night but as with everything else that happened that day, our luck held. Only four months before, the old forester's lodge had been converted to a hut for *randonneurs* and we were amongst its first winter visitors.

Set in a forest clearing which only opened to the east, the eye was led inexorably across the Cady Gorge and then upwards to Canigou whose snows shone like pale gold in the fading evening sun. The place engendered a feeling of peace and tranquility as if it had been expecting us.

Canigou, *Lo Canigou*, the sacred mountain of Catalonia and inspiration of Jacinto Verdaguer's epic poem, was at last within our grasp. For the past two days its unmistakable shape had been our landmark. Vignemale, Posets and Aneto had each in their turn repulsed us but Canigou, a world unto itself, had seemed to beckon us. In history and art no mountain in the Pyrenees matches it. Kipling's Magician among Mountains springs from the sea like Etna, Vesuvius or the Thessalian Olympus and aspires to heaven. In the reign of the Sun King, Louis XIV, French geographers used it as their benchmark to determine the meridian of Paris. Until the early nineteenth century, it was thought to be the apex of the Pyrenees and when the blue skies of the Mediterranean were unpolluted, it could be seen from Marseilles 180 miles away. Although its mean height is only 2,784 metres, it gives the impression of prodigious size as it rises straight from the plain of Roussillon. Canigou dominates everything around, inspiring the lives of all who live within sight of it, as it has fired the imaginations of generations of writers and artists.

Centuries before the recorded ascent of any other major Pyrenean peak, Canigou was climbed in 1285 by King Pedro III of Aragón to slay the dragon that infested the mountain's upper reaches thus inspiring a contemporary friar chronicler to compare the feat with any exploit of Alexander the Great. Since then, the mountain has been subjected to every kind of stunt and indignity including ascents by bicycle, horseback and, even, in 1903, by a Gladiator 10 hp motorcar. On this evidence, I had assumed that our ski ascent would present no problems but after studying the guidebook and map, wondered whether our last day might still spring a nasty surprise.

"Remind me what's happening tomorrow, John," asked Roger over supper.

"We're going to climb Canigou, silly," I replied, "and after that we're going to go home."

Rupert on the south face of Canigou

"Yes, I know all that," he retorted, "but what about the nitty gritty – crampons and all that? I want to prepare myself for the worst."

"We've certainly got another long, hard day ahead so let's hope that the weather holds. We won't be bowling along a ridge as we did yesterday and there's a good 1,000 metres to go from here to the top of Canigou, with some steep passages in between."

"What then?"

"To get off the mountain we've got to traverse a longish ridge and then descend over 2,000 metres to our roadhead at Fillols. It's a 27 kilometre day which is further than yesterday and the guidebook reckons it will take at least eleven hours."

"Phew," groaned Roger, "I had better get to bed immediately."

"But what happens if the weather does break?" demanded Rupert. "We should have a fall back plan for that eventuality."

"Precisely," I continued. "If the weather turns really bad we'll have to forego the Canigou traverse. In that case, we could leave our sacs here in the hut, climb the mountain lightweight and then ski out to Vernet."

"That's a bit drastic isn't it," snorted Rupert. "From what I've seen of it, this doesn't look a particularly serious mountain."

"Maybe," I replied, "but according to the map, the south to north traverse of Canigou involves four kilometres of *'passage délicat'* and the descent ridge might be corniced."

"Hah!" exclaimed Rupert triumphantly. "Jolly glad I've brought my crampons."

"What *is* tomorrow's forecast," asked Doctor David.

"No idea," I replied, "but my altimeter's been pretty constant."

"According to the long term forecast," interrupted Rupert, "we could be in for a spell of unsettled weather with the possibility of snow."

I didn't ask him how he had gleaned this information but before going to bed took a short walk outside. It was a lovely, clear evening and above the canopy of pine trees a myriad of twinkling stars promised fair for the morrow.

I slept little that night partly due to excitement but also on account of another snoring cacophony punctuated by imbecile giggles of "Doctor, Doctor please do something about Roger". The noise forced Williams to abandon the upstairs bunk-room for the kitchen downstairs where he slept on the table. This atmosphere of an end-of-term dorm rag put things into perspective. With journey's end imminent, I felt curiously detached and impatient to close the final chapter.

We left the hut at 7 am when it was barely light. At first, the summer path up the Cady Valley was easy enough to follow but Williams seemed to have scored a point about the advantages of the Refuge Arago when we started to cross the *passage délicat* below the Couloir des Septs Hommes. The guidebook had described this as *"le prototype parfait du couloir d'avalanches"* and, in traversing its frozen *neve,* we had to stamp our ski edges into the steeply inclined slope with full body weight and use our poles as daggers to avoid a disastrous slip.

As we had passed the Refuge Arago, Roger had made his Roger Award for *Best Decision of the Tour.* Like the Pla Guillem Refuge, the Arago had been overwhelmed by the snow and was now quite uninhabitable. Once we had broken out of the forest, the upper reaches of the Cady Valley were bathed in sunshine and we marched on into the great south-facing cwm of Canigou as if to a drumbeat.

Here we took off our anoraks for the first time during the entire trip. The sun was warm but it never broiled us as it had on that final day's passage into Andorra. The snow was so hard that we successively switched to *harscheisen* and then crampons to climb the narrowing 200 metre backwall of the Cady Cwm. Re-grouping on the wild and wind-swept Porteille de Velmanya, the inner secrets of Canigou were at last revealed.

From here, we were no longer looking at the monumental snow mass but rather a finely sculpted mountain of sweeping ridges and sheer rock faces culminating in a shapely summit pyramid. This now rose before us across a stretch of broken ground which led to a snow couloir splitting Canigou's south face which culminated in a dark chimney that led directly to the summit.

"Not such a pushover," I muttered as Rupert and David Williams marched off together towards the snow couloir, matching stride for stride. They looked so purposeful with Rupert so clearly fired up that for, an absurd moment, I had a vision of Mallory and Irvine. They stopped short at the foot of the rock chimney and waited while the rest of us closed up. In summer, you wouldn't have given this chimney more than a passing thought but now I found myself wondering how we were going to tackle its steep, broken rocks choked with snow and coated with black ice with skis and heavy sacs.

As I pondered on the wisdom of Walter Good's dictum that crampons were unnecessary on ski tours, Roger said, "I think John should lead this last pitch. He should be first up this mountain."

Until that moment, I had assumed that as our strongest climber David would lead the chimney. I blessed Roger for his thought. It meant a great deal to me.

"Absolutely right," said David. "Go on John, take us up it."

"Okay," I replied, "but someone please give me a good belay."

At exactly 12.30 pm I scrambled out of the chimney and, within a few strides, stood on the sunlit summit of Canigou with the rope trailing in the snow behind me. It was a brilliant day with the sky washed clear. The hills were shining all about. I had climbed my Magic Mountain.

As I hauled in the rope hand over hand for David Williams to race up behind me, I tried to recall the adventures and incidents I had had along the way to reach this last mountain but my mind wouldn't focus. I could only take in what I saw around me. At my feet lay the hidden heart of Canigou, a deeply incised north-facing cirque contained on one side by the 350 metre high Barbet Face and on the other by the long north ridge down which we would have to make our descent. To the east, beyond the snow crested lip of the Barbet's precipice, the last blue hills of the Pyrenees dipped and faded into the deeper blue of the Mediterranean. To the north-east, almost 3,000 metres below me, the plain of Roussillon was laid out like a brown carpet with its edges creased by scattered ridges. Away to the west was the way we had come – the whole wondrous range of the Pyrenees stretched out as an infinity of peaks jostling the sky like a sea of white-topped rollers.

I tried to pick out the routes that we had followed and the peaks and passes we had climbed but from here they all looked the same. They had shrunk into a uniform mountainscape and now that the journey was behind me, the detail no longer seemed to matter. My quest to reach Canigou had taken in sixty-eight stages, twenty peaks and a hundred passes. Once upon a time, such things had seemed important but at journey's end they had become mere statistics. I could never repeat this journey but even when the springs of adventure ran dry, I knew that the memory of my companions would survive.

David quickly joined me and then Rupert, who belayed himself to bring up the others. Almost an hour drifted by in a dreamtime before we were ready to begin the long descent to the plain. The broken rocks of the kilometre-long ridge that drops 400 metres from the summit to the Pic Joffre were plastered in snow and ice and needed care all the way. Rupert was in his element.

"Jolly glad we brought our crampons," he kept reminding me.

From the Fenêtre de la Pedrix David Williams let rip with an exhibition of *wedelning* through deep snow. The rest of us did it our own way but the mood was contagious and we became over-confident. David's uncompromising line through the pine forest took us into some terrible snow and when he plunged down the fall line to short cut the track, I thought we might be heading for trouble. Roger took a purler on the track's lip but managed to save himself from going over the edge of the steep bank. Worse was to come.

When climbing on skins, you may choose either Naismith's formula to measure progress or adopt the less scientific method that Childs favours. But when descending on skis over difficult ground, the golden rule is never to follow

David Seddon below Canigou

Williams in hot pursuit. I had long ago discovered this truth for myself but Rupert was more ingenuous.

It was about this time that the exploits of the British Olympic ski jumper, Eddy Edwards began to encourage a rash of imitators. Rupert was always the competitive type and had already strayed into dangerous territory earlier in the tour when he had tried to wrest the medical initiative from the Doctor by offering him his own prescription for a headache. Not only do medicine and ski mountaineering have little in common, there are also fundamental differences between the skills required of a ski jumper and those of a ski mountaineer. In the former, a pre-requisite is to jump straight while in the latter you must make your turns exactly when the occasion demands. To confuse the one discipline with the other invites cataclysmic consequences.

In terms of general mountaineering experience and fitness there was little to chose between David Williams and Rupert Hoare but none matched David as a skier. We were flying down a steep section of the track with David in the lead closely followed by Rupert, with myself, Roger and Doctor David at the rear.

Who knows what was coursing through Rupert's mind during this furious descent? It may simply have been the stimulus of an exciting run home – just a matter of "fly Rupert, fly". Alternatively, it might have been an altogether more complex crisis of identity, involving cult heroes such as the dare-devil Austrian climber, Hermann Buhl, the human cannonball, Evel Kneivel, Icarus or even Major Tom. Whatever the root cause, what had begun as the last joyful run of the tour precipitated its only serious crisis.

I was still in relatively close contact with the two leaders when I saw David suddenly change direction with a dramatic 45 degree "jet" turn to his left. He took this course of action because, at this particular juncture, the path, now running along the top of a very steep embankment, suddenly swung round sharply to follow the lie of the land. To have carried straight on would have involved a flight into the forest at roughly canopy height. Seeing the danger ahead, I yelled over my shoulder to Roger, "Brake Roger, brake!" as I slewed my skis round into a grinding halt.

Only then did I realise that instead of following David's tracks, Rupert was still schussing straight ahead. He appeared to make no attempt to check himself, suddenly left the ground like a Harrier jet and began flying through the air at tree-top level before vanishing from sight.

Christ, I said to myself, he's killed himself.

David Williams had somehow climbed back up the path in a frenzied burst of herring-boning by the time the rest of us had gathered at the top of the embankment to peer over its lip. Some ten metres below us, at the bottom of a steep

David Williams at the summit of Canigou

bank of boulders, lay a tangle of skis, sac, poles and the inert form of Rupert. To complete this gruesome tableau, a heap of newly severed branches, several dangerously perched logs and boulders and a fine layer of sawdust were strewn around him. Was this, I thought to myself, the ultimate disaster: a ghastly accident on our last day to mark this whole venture with a curse?

Doctor David had already kicked his skis off, thrown his sac onto the ground and was now chucking all his clothing out of it to get at the first aid kit.

"You'd better get down there fast David," I blurted out. "It looks as if he's broken his back. For God's sake look out for those loose stones, you could start an avalanche."

"I can see all that for myself," he retorted. "You'd better come down with me. I'll need some help."

Yet, even as we started to scramble down the boulder-strewn slope dislodging rocks in the process, Rupert began to move like an up-turned beetle trying to right itself. We gently helped him to his feet and I was amazed when he stood upright.

A fall as serious as this would have maimed or even killed a lesser man but apart from shock and a mass of bruises, Rupert had had a miraculous escape. After the Good Doctor administered something more than the usual placebos, we each took one of Rupert's arms to help him back up the slope. At the top we shared out his equipment and started to ski very circumspectly down the track.

At 4 pm we took off skis for the very last time and proceeded on foot down the GR10 track for Fillols. The sun beat down and, although it was only early March, its heat stirred the dense *maquis* which lined our route. With the extra weight on top, it felt as if I was walking on hot cinders but by 6 pm we had reached Fillols – eleven hours after leaving the Marialles Hut. It was the longest day of the tour and one of the most memorable in my life.

At the village square, we rolled into a bar called Le Loup Sauvage whose signpost depicted a snarling creature. Its malevolence was mirrored in *le patron's* manner for when Roger asked if he would kindly order us a taxi to Font Romeu, he simply chucked the telephone directory at him. We decamped to the friendlier atmosphere of the cafe next door to the church where a charming young lady confirmed that "taxi no problem".

I had saved the final photograph of my film for a last shot of Canigou at sunset. When we had first reached Fillols, the whole mountain had been glowing like a beacon but by the time we left only the weakest afterglow lingered on its summit. I had missed my chance. As we drove away in our taxi, I kept looking back at Canigou to try to keep it in sight but the road suddenly plunged down into a gorge and the Magic Mountain disappeared into the night.

Route, Huts and Participants in Chronological Order

T here is no one way to traverse the Pyrenees on ski but the most direct west-east traverse from Mendive to Fillols in 34 stages is described in the Ollivier-Peres CAF guide *La Haute Route d'Hiver des Pyrenees* (Pau, 1978). This guide includes some variants. For general touring information I used the Federation Française de la Montagne's four volume *Pyrenées Itinéraires Skieurs* (Pau, 1973) edited by Ollivier. In retrospect, an east-west traverse would probably have given better snow and this was both Laporte's and Serra's direction of travel.

The ideal would be a continuous traverse but, fitness and logistics apart, few amateurs would have sufficient time for such a project. My compromise was to do it by stages over a period of ten years, from 1978 to 1988, if I exclude the first Eagles tour in 1975. This involved 68 separate stages which, in part, reflected route variations, some repeats and bad weather retreats. Part of the 1978 tour repeated 1975; the 1979 tour was abortive and four others in 1980, 1981, 1985 and 1987 involved significant diversions through the Three Cirques, Néouvielle and Aigues Tortes. Otherwise, the Ollivier-Peres line was generally followed.

The nine stages of the Pyrenean High Route with intermediate huts or other accommodation used en route together with the names of participants as follows:

1975 (March 9 to 16). Chapter 2.
Pau: Laberouat: Urdos: Ayous: Pombie: Gabas: Cauterets.
Party – *Michael de Pret Roose, Martin Epp, Hamish Brown, Robin Day, David Dorrell, Patrick Fagan, Charles Knowles, Mike Williamson.*

1978 (March 17 to April 1). Chapter 3.
Pau: Larry: Ayous: Pombie: Gabas: Arremoulit: Penalara: Wallon: Oulettes: Cauterets.
Party – *Alan and Nick Wedgwood, Richard Morgan.*

1979 (April 8 to 13). Chapter 1.
Cauterets: Baysallence: Oulettes: Cauterets.
Party – *Susan Baldock, Alain Bevan-John, Jean-Pierre Leire, Richard Reynolds.*

1980 (April 26 to May 6). Chapter 4.
Cauterets: Wallon: Gavarnie: Sarradets: Gaulis: Estaube: Des Aires: Gèdre.
Party – *Walter Good, Jean-Pierre Leire, Alan Wedgwood.* Also *Martine and Véronique Leire and Serge.*

1981 (March 27 to April 8). Chapter 5.
Barèges: Glère: Orédon: St Lary: Bastanet: Aigues Cluses: Lienz: Barèges.
Party – *Alan and Janet Wedgwood, Jean-Pierre Leire, Colin Chapman. Also Jacques and Jean-Claude.*

1983 (March 6 to 18). Chapter 6.
Gèdre: Le Sausset: St Lary: Campana de Cloutou: Rioumajou: Viados: Estos: Benasque: Portillon: Luchon.
Party – *Alan and Nick Wedgwood, David Williams, Julian Lush, John Wilkinson.*

1985 (March 7 to 19). Chapter 7.
Luchon: Poulane: Renclusa: Bénasque: Arties: Restanca: Ventosa: Boi.
Party – *Patrick Bailey, Roger Childs, Rupert Hoare, Julian Lush, David Seddon.*

1987 (March 18 to 29). Chapter 8.
Salardu: Colomers: Amitges: Espot: Isil o Gil: Pujol: Certescan: Val Ferrara: Arinsal.
Party – *David Williams, Anna Lindberg, Roger Childs, Julian Lush.*

1988 (March 3 to 13). Chapter 9.
Font-Romeu: El Tartar: Col de Puymorens: Baraque des Ingénieurs: Font-Romeu: Nuria: Ull de Terr: Marialles: Fillols.
Party – *David Williams, Rupert Hoare, David Seddon, Roger Childs.*

A year after we had stood on the summit of Canigou, Roger Childs, Rupert Hoare, David Seddon, Simon Kirk and I returned to complete the unfinished business of climbing both Aneto and Posets on ski, using Bénasque as our base. I have often returned to the Pyrenees since but never again to ski.

GLOSSARY

Abri	A crude shelter
Abseil	Descending difficult ground by fixed rope
Aigue	Water
Aiguille	A sharp, pointed peak
Alp	Upland pasturage
Arete	A ridge
Autophon	Trade name of Swiss-made avalanche search device
Balling up	Accumulated snow sticking to skins or crampons
Barranco	A ravine
Belay	Method of safeguarding a climber
Bluff	A cliff
Breche	A gap in a ridge
Cabane	A rough shelter (often made of concrete)
Chimney	A rock fissure
Cirque	A mountain hollow gouged out by glacial action
Col	A pass
Cornice	An overhanging snow lip leeward of a ridge
Couloir	A gully
Coume	A narrow valley or cirque
Crampons	Steel claws which attach to boots to climb ice
Crust	Hard crusted snow which is soft underneath
Cwm	A cirque
Estang	A mountain lake
Gave	A water course or river
Garganta	An enclosed gorge
Harscheisen	A form of crampon which fit under the ski
Hourquette	A high col
Karabiner	A snap link with spring hinged gate
Oulette	A basin
Port/Portillon	A high col
Powder snow	Powdery, unthawed snow
Soum	A secondary summit
Tramontane	A violent north wind
Wind slab	Snow crust formed by wind

The English were the pioneer eighteenth and early nineteenth century travellers in the Pyrenees and extensive bibliographies recording their journeys are contained in Charles de Gorsse's *Les Anglais aux Pyrenees* [Pau, 1956], Spender's *Through the High Pyrenees* [Innes, 1898] and the Alpine Club Library's *Catalogue.*

A useful selected bibliography which includes many articles published in British mountaineering journals (in particular the Alpine Club's *Alpine Journal*) will be found in Kev Reynolds' *Mountains of the Pyrenees* [Cicerone Press, 1982]. Heavyweight French tomes on the Pyrenees have been written by Taine, Soubiron and Beraldi amongst others. An extensive French and Spanish Pyrenean bibliography is contained in *Montagnes Pyrenees* by Jean-Louis Peres and Jean Ubiergo [Arthaud, 1973].

Books in English on the Pyrenees and allied subjects which have given me particular pleasure include:

> *The Pyrenees* by Henry Blackburn [Sampson Low, 1867;
>   with illustrations by Gustave Dore]
> *Through the High Pyrenees* by Harold Spender [Innes, 1898]
> *Hills and the Sea* by Hilaire Belloc [Methuen, 1906]
> *The Pyrenees* by Hilaire Belloc [Methuen, 1909]
> *Pyrenean* by J. B. Morton [Longmans, 1938]
> *Les Anglais aux Pyrenees* by Pierre de Gorsse [Pau, 1956]
> *The Enchanted Mountains* by Robin Fedden [Murray, 1962]
> *The Spanish Pyrenees* by Henry Myhill [Faber, 1966]
> *L'Aneto et les Hommes* by Jean Escudier [Pau, 1977]
> *Walkers* by Miles Jebb [Constable, 1986]
> *Hilaire Belloc* by A. N. Wilson [Hamish Hamilton, 1984]
> *Landscape and Memory* by Simon Scharma [Harper Collins,1995]

Guidebooks consulted include Ollivier's four volume *Pyrenées, Itinéraires Skieurs* [Ollivier, Pau]; his Pyrenean climbing guides and, particularly, his *La Haute Route d'Hiver des Pyrenées* [Pau, 1978]. Charles Laporte's account of his pioneer traverse will be found in *La Montagne 1968* and Robin Fedden's article on his Pyrenean ski traverse, *A Pyrenean High Route,* appeared in the winter 1974 edition of *Ski Survey.*